Cybersecurity: Key Legal Considerations for the Aviation and Space Sectors

Aerospace Law and Policy Series

VOLUME 18

Editors

Pablo Mendes de Leon, Professor of Air and Space Law, and Tanja Masson-Zwaan, Assistant Professor of Space Law, Leiden University, The Netherlands.

Introduction

The *Aerospace Law and Policy Series* critically examines the fundamental changes that international aviation and space activities have undergone since the last century, growing up as mature industries while freeing themselves from traditional regulatory constraints and displaying a variety of innovative applications that call for creative legal solutions.

Objective

The objective of the Series is to make a contribution to legal thinking on public international air and space law and policy, and their implementation at the regional and national levels, responsibility and liability of public bodies and service providers, competition law, insurance law, company law, and the complex relationship between EU law and public international law.

Readership

Aviation and space lawyers, academics, representatives of governments, international organizations, and companies involved in aviation and space activities.

The titles published in this series are listed at the end of this volume.

Cybersecurity: Key Legal Considerations for the Aviation and Space Sectors

Federico Bergamasco

Roberto Cassar

Rada Popova

Benjamyn I. Scott

Wolters Kluwer

Published by:
Kluwer Law International B.V.
PO Box 316
2400 AH Alphen aan den Rijn
The Netherlands
E-mail: international-sales@wolterskluwer.com
Website: lrus.wolterskluwer.com

Sold and distributed in North, Central and South America by:
Wolters Kluwer Legal & Regulatory U.S.
7201 McKinney Circle
Frederick, MD 21704
United States of America
Email: customer.service@wolterskluwer.com

Sold and distributed in all other countries by:
Air Business Subscriptions
Rockwood House
Haywards Heath
West Sussex
RH16 3DH
United Kingdom
Email: international-customerservice@wolterskluwer.com

ISBN 978-94-035-0110-9

e-Book: ISBN 978-94-035-0111-6
web-PDF: ISBN 978-94-035-0112-3

About the Authors

Federico Bergamasco is currently a PhD candidate at the University of Luxembourg. The topic of his thesis is the interaction of the International Civil Aviation Organization and the International Telecommunication Union in the regulation of aeronautical services and related frequency spectrum. He publishes and lectures on a regular basis on topics related to space and aviation law, with special focus on legal aspects of air navigation. Before that, he studied law at the University of Studies of Padua (Italy) and subsequently specialised in air and space law at Leiden University (the Netherlands), and has worked for international organisations such as the European Space Agency (ESA) and Eurocontrol.

Roberto Cassar is an associate at Camilleri Cassar Advocates (Valletta, Malta) where he practices across all of the main areas of work of the firm, with particular focus on litigation and defence, aviation, space, and telecommunications law. Roberto read law at the University of Malta before proceeding to Leiden University where he obtained a Master of Laws degree in Air and Space Law. Roberto has contributed to leading books and journals relating to air and space law and is Managing Editor of *Air & Space Law* (Wolters Kluwer).

Rada Popova is a graduate of the Law Faculty of the University of Vienna (mag. iur.) and currently works as a senior research fellow and lecturer and as a legal adviser at the University of Cologne. There she teaches international law, European Union law and constitutional law, and carries out analytical research in various fields of law, in particular space law, environmental law, cyber law and on the cross-section between technology and legal regulation. As a lawyer, Rada has provided expertise, among other fields of law, in aerospace-related projects with the ESA, the German Aerospace Center and the aerospace industry in Germany and France. Previously, she carried out work for the United Nation (UN) Office for Outer Space Affairs and the National Assembly of the Republic of Bulgaria, as well as for law firms in Austria and Bulgaria.

Benjamyn I. Scott studied Law at the University of Kent and the University of Amsterdam. Further, he obtained an LL.M. in International Commercial Law from the University of Kent and then an LLM (Adv) in Air and Space Law from the International Institute for Air and Space Law at Leiden University. Finally, he holds a PhD from the University of Cologne, where his thesis focused on the regulation of aviation cybersecurity. Benjamyn has a strong background in developing aviation technologies, having worked for several years in this area, and having written numerous journal articles and book chapters on cybersecurity, unmanned aircraft, suborbital transportation and roadable aircraft, as well as teaching at different universities. He is also a member of the Board of Editors of *Air & Space Law* (Wolters Kluwer).

Table of Contents

Foreword

Since its inception a little more than a hundred years ago, international air law has developed in a myriad of directions. Whereas it initially focused on safety, security and market access on the public law side, and airline liability on the private law side, international air law increasingly interacted with other fields of law over time. In the 1970s, we witnessed the emergence of aviation security conventions, followed by movements pertaining to regulating the market behaviour of airlines in the context of deregulation and liberalisation processes. In the 1990s and onwards, environmental measures, that is, the formulation of noise standards and, subsequently, norms of controlling aircraft emissions, as well as passenger protection regulations were drawn up by regulatory authorities around the world.

Space law has evolved in a similar manner. Starting with the 'Space Race', a conquest for military supremacy in outer space among the two superpowers (the Soviet Union and the United States), the 1960s began to see a realisation of the potential benefits of using space for applications like telecommunications or earth observation. Since space was mainly a State-driven domain in those days, the main legal instruments consisted of UN treaties, principles and resolutions. In more recent years, the concept of 'NewSpace' came up to illustrate the growing trend of commercialisation and privatisation in the sector. This led to an increase in national space legislation in recent years. In addition, many emerging space States have joined the sector. This exponential growth in stakeholders and activities led to new topics that had to be addressed by law. The growing congestion of some orbits in outer space necessitates guidelines on long-term sustainability, space traffic management and debris removal. New activities such as the use of space resources or suborbital flights require global regulation, while military tests and the threat of weaponisation have led to increased global political tension and the need for confidence-building measures.

A new 'kid on the block' concerns the use of digital technologies in aviation and space-related activities. Such technologies provide tremendous means for communication and management of instruments. At the same time, they can be abused for criminal purposes. While aviation and space activities are subject to different legal regimes, they have in common that they are carried out in very vulnerable circumstances, that is, mid-air, outer space, or ground stations, with invisible lines of communication between them. Moreover, whenever such activities are attacked from the outside, the implications are or at least can be, dramatic.

It is appropriate that this new and critical subject of cybersecurity in the aerospace sector is addressed by the young and bright minds of a new generation of aviation and space lawyers. They are able to understand, analyse and explain the challenging and complex topics across disciplines in a clear and transparent manner. Four young, ambitious and promising lawyers have picked up this challenge and have not only conducted an in-depth study of cybersecurity, but have also joined forces to write a book on this fascinating subject. They have chosen a multidisciplinary approach covering all aspects affecting cybersecurity in aviation and space activities. These include, but are not limited to, the 'umbrella' themes such as responsibility for the safe management of infrastructure and the concerned vehicles, namely aircraft, rockets and satellites. They also pay attention to liability in case of damage caused by cyberattacks. These themes are topped by an even higher and broader level of discussion on international law as applied to the use of force and armed attacks.

These principal legal themes are completed with a very useful explanation of terms and the use of technologies in a multilevel legal jurisdictional context pursuant to which international law, European Union law and national regimes are analysed. We are also impressed by the structured and transparent approach which the authors have adopted. Moreover, we wish to record the completeness of this work which includes useful sources of research, lists of acronyms and definitions, and other tools for understanding statements, events and terms.

We wish to pay tribute to the four authors for marking international air and space law with an in-depth and sophisticated study that promises to be, and, in our view ought to be, the standard work on this topical subject.

Obviously, we are extremely proud that three of the four authors are distinguished alumni of the International Institute of Air and Space Law at Leiden University. We sincerely congratulate all authors with this remarkable achievement which will guide professionals, academics and students in a complex and increasingly relevant field of law.

Pablo Mendes de Leon & Tanja Masson-Zwaan
International Institute of Air and Space Law
Leiden University

List of Abbreviations

Art. / Arts	Article(s)
ASA	Air Service Agreement
ASAT	Anti-satellite Weapons
ATM	Air Traffic Management
AV-CERT	Aviation Computer Emergency Response Team
AVSEC	Aviation Security
CCDCOE	Cooperative Cyber Defence Centre of Excellence
CEPOL	European Union Agency for Law Enforcement Training
CERT	Computer Emergency Response Team
CERT-EU	Computer Emergency Response Team-European Union
CIL	Customary International Law
CJEU	Court of Justice of the European Union
CS	Certification Specifications
CSDP	Common Security and Defence Policy
CSIRT	Computer Security Incident Response Team
CSRS	Computer Security Resource Center
DNS	Domain Name System
EACCC	European Aviation Crisis Coordination Cell
EASA	European Union Aviation Safety Agency
EATM-CERT	European Air Traffic Management Computer Emergency Response Team
EC3	European Cybercrime Centre
ECAC	European Civil Aviation Conference
ECCSA	European Centre for Cyber Security in Aviation
ECI	European Critical Infrastructures
ECSCG	European Cyber Security for Aviation Standards Coordination Group

ECSO	European Cyber Security Organisation
EDA	European Defence Agency
EEAS	European External Action Service
EEC	European Economic Community
EGNOS	European Geostationary Navigation Overlay Service
ENISA	European Union Agency for Network and Information Security
ESA	European Space Agency
ESCP	European Strategic Coordination Platform
EU	European Union
EU-LISA	European Agency for the Operational Management of Large-Scale IT Systems in the Area of Freedom, Security and Justice
EUROCAE	European Organisation for Civil Aviation Equipment
European GNSS Agency	European Global Navigation Satellite Systems Agency
Europol	European Union Agency for Law Enforcement Cooperation
FBI	Federal Bureau of Investigation
FP9	Research Framework Programme Nine
GASeP	Global Aviation Security Plan
GDPR	General Data Protection Regulation
GA	General Assembly
GLONASS	Globalnaya Navigazionnaya Sputnikovaya Sistema
GNSS	Global Navigation Satellite System
GPS	Global Positioning System
HLCAS	High-Level Conference on Aviation Security
IANA	Internet Assigned Numbers Authority
IBM	International Business Machines Corporation
ICANN	Internet Corporation for Assigned Names and Numbers
ICAO	International Civil Aviation Organization
ICASS	ICAO Comprehensive Aviation Security Strategy
ICCAIA	International Coordinating Council of Aerospace Industries Associations
ICJ	International Court of Justice
ICRC	International Committee of the Red Cross
ICT	Information and Communications Technology
IEC	International Electrotechnical Commission
IETF	Internet Engineering Task Force
IFALPA	International Federation of Air Line Pilots' Associations
IHLG	Industry High Level Group
IOCTA	Internet Organised Crime Threat Assessment
IoT	Internet of Things

IP	Internet Protocol
ISMS	Information Security Management System
ISO	International Organization for Standardization
ISS	International Space Station
IT	Information Technology
ITU	International Telecommunication Union
MIFR	Master International Frequency Register
MoC	Memorandum of Cooperation
MSL	Mean Sea Level
NASA	National Aeronautics and Space Administration
NATO	North Atlantic Treaty Organization
NIS	Network and Information Systems
NIST	(US) National Institute of Standard and Technology
OECD	Organisation for Economic Co-operation and Development
OST	Outer Space Treaty
PNR	Passenger Name Record
PNT	Positioning, Navigation and Timing
PSC	Peace and Security Council
RB	Radiocommunication Bureau
RBB	Radio Regulations Board
RES	Research
RMT	Rulemaking Task
SAGAS	Stakeholder Advisory Group for Aviation Security
SARPs	Standards and Recommended Practices
SDR	Special Drawing Rights
SESAR	Single European Sky ATM Research Joint Undertaking
SIS	Schengen Information System
SPT	Safety Promotion Task
SSGC	Secretariat Study Group on Cybersecurity
STM	Space Traffic Management
TEU	Treaty on European Union
TFEU	Treaty on the Functioning of the European Union
TFSG	Trust Framework Study Group
TT&C	Telemetry, Tracking and Command
TV	Television
UK	United Kingdom
UN	United Nations
UNCITRAL	United Nations Commission on International Trade Law
UNOOSA	United Nations Office for Outer Space Affairs

(UN)COPUOS	(United Nations) Committee on the Peaceful Uses of Outer Space
US	United States
USAP-CMA	Universal Security Audit Programme Continuous Monitoring Approach
USB	Universal Serial Bus
USOAP	Universal Safety Oversight Audit Programme
VIS	Visa Information System
W3C	World Wide Web Consortium
WAAS	Wide Area Augmentation System
WP	Working Paper
WRC	World Radio Conference

Acknowledgements

The authors would like to express their deep gratitude to each and every person who has dedicated his or her free time, patiently dealt with our requests and provided fascinating information. In particular, we would like to pay special thanks to John Balfour, PJ Blount, Ivo Emanuilov, Stefano Fantin, Petri Freundlich, Peter Haanappel, Stephan Hobe, Mahulena Hofmann, Angeliki Karakoliou, Attila Matas, Lisa Schöttmer, Dimiter Shalvardjiev, and Andrea Trimarchi. All of these people provided careful reviews of the sections of this book, and for that, the authors wholeheartedly thank them.

CHAPTER 1
Introduction: Overview

§1.01 GENERAL INTRODUCTION

The rise of digital technologies since the end of the Second World War has, without doubt, changed the societal landscape of the world. Possibly, the most significant digital technology which has caused the global society to mutate in an unprecedented manner is the Internet and the cyberspace that it has created. The Internet and cyberspace have changed the manner in which society communicates, trades and works, to name a few examples. Accordingly, the Internet and cyberspace have led society to adapt its conduct accordingly. Social conduct, however, is not always positive.

As the use of cyberspace grows, it is only natural that its misuse also grows. This misuse, which comes in different forms, generally revolves around the digital – at times even physical – safety and security of people and their property.

Examples of such misuse can be traced back nearly forty years ago. At the height of the Cold War in June 1982, a malfunction in the computer-control system of a gas pipeline in Siberia (in what was then the Union of Soviet Socialist Republics) caused the pipeline to explode.[1] This was not an accident; allegedly, the United States (US) allowed Soviet spies to steal pipeline control software from a Canadian company which, unbeknownst to the Soviets, was programmed to wreak havoc.[2]

This pipeline control software, which was designed to run the pumps, turbines, and valves of the pipeline, included malicious code known as a Trojan Horse.[3] Eventually, this malicious code ran during a pressure test on the pipeline and massively increased the usual pressure far beyond that acceptable to the pipeline joints and

1. The Economist, 'Cyberwar: War in the Fifth Domain', 1 July 2010, https://www.economist.com/briefing/2010/07/01/war-in-the-fifth-domain.
2. Thomas C. Reed, *At the Abyss: An Insider's History of the Cold War* (Presidio, 2005), at 269.
3. Eric J. Byres, 'Cyber Security and the Pipeline Control System', 236(2) *Pipeline and Gas Journal* 58 (2009).

welds,[4] thereby causing the pipeline to explode and creating an explosion of extensive proportions.[5]

Fast-tracking to June 2010, over a thousand centrifuges at the Natanz uranium enrichment facility in Iran were damaged.[6] Once again, this was not an accident; rather, a worm termed 'Stuxnet', which first infected computers belonging to contractors who then inadvertently transmitted it to the Iranian enrichment control system via Universal Serial Bus (USB) flash drives,[7] exploited flaws in Microsoft Windows and disrupted plant processes that were controlled by Siemens-manufactured systems.[8]

Stuxnet – allegedly developed by the US and Israel – carried out this disruption by indefinitely causing centrifuge rotors[9] to first speed up to 1,410 Hz for fifteen minutes, then return to the normal speed of 1,064 Hz for twenty-seven days, slow down to 2 Hz for fifty minutes, and return back to 1,064 Hz for another twenty-seven days.[10] At the time, Stuxnet clearly was "the most technologically sophisticated malicious program developed for a targeted attack."[11]

Still further, in May 2017, more than a third of England's 236 National Health System trusts had their computer devices locked, causing an estimated 19,000 appointments to be cancelled.[12] This outbreak was due to ransomware called 'WannaCry', which has been attributed to North Korea by some experts,[13] and which is a type of malicious software that takes a computer hostage and holds it for ransom – in this case, for at least USD 300 in Bitcoin for each computer affected.[14]

4. Clay Wilson (CRS Report for Congress), 'Computer Attack and Cyberterrorism: Vulnerabilities and Policy Issues for Congress', CRS Report for Congress, 1 April 2005, http://www.dtic.mil/dtic/tr/fulltext/u2/a444799.pdf, at 29.
5. Byres, *supra* no. 3; Reed, *supra* no. 2.
6. Julia Edwards and Dustin Volz, 'Retired U.S. General Charged with Lying to FBI in "Stuxnet" Leak Case', Reuters, 17 October 2016, https://www.reuters.com/article/usa-iran-cyber-idUSL1N1CN12C.
7. James M. Acton, 'Cyber Weapons and Precision Guided Munition', *in* George Perkovich and Ariel E. Levite (eds), *Understanding Cyber Conflict: Fourteen Analogies* (Georgetown University Press, 2017), at 45-47.
8. Scott J. Shackelford, *Managing Cyber Attacks in International Law, Business, and Relations* (Cambridge University Press, 2014), at xv.
9. The rotors can mechanically withstand a maximum speed of about 1,400 Hz.
10. Jon R. Lindsay, 'Stuxnet and the Limits of Cyber Warfare', 22(3) *Security Studies* 365 (2013), at 383-384.
11. Aleksandr Matrosov, et al., 'Stuxnet under the Microscope', ESET, 20 January 2011, https://www.esetnod32.ru/company/viruslab/analytics/doc/Stuxnet_Under_the_Microscope.pdf.
12. Report by the Comptroller and Auditor General (National Audit Office), 'Investigation: WannaCry Cyber Attack and the NHS', National Audit Office, 25 April 2018, https://www.nao.org.uk/wp-content/uploads/2017/10/Investigation-WannaCry-cyber-attack-and-the-NHS.pdf, at 11-14.
13. BBC, 'Cyber-attack: US and UK blame North Korea for WannaCry', BBC, 19 December 2017, https://www.bbc.com/news/world-us-canada-42407488.
14. Brian Fung, 'How to Protect Yourself from the Global Ransomware Attack', The Washington Post, 15 May 2017, https://www.washingtonpost.com/news/the-switch/wp/2017/05/15/how-to-protect-yourself-from-the-global-ransomware-attack/?noredirect=on&utm_term=.ef067b0551b1.

A separate attack known as 'NotPetya', which took place in June 2017 and which was attributed by some experts to Russia,[15] similarly put computers out of operation across some sixty States worldwide,[16] causing billions of USD in damage across the continents of Europe, Asia, and the Americas.[17]

Evidently, the misuse of the Internet and cyberspace has existed nearly since their birth, and in all likelihood, such misuse is going to continue. This is all the more probable when one considers that, as of January 2020, on a worldwide scale, almost 4.54 billion people were active Internet users.[18]

Within the European Union (EU) alone, seven in ten people use the Internet every day, and billions of new devices are connected to the Internet each year. However, it is not only individuals that are increasingly using such digital technologies. Businesses are also becoming more dependent on them, and, as a matter of fact, such technologies have become the backbone of the economy.

Due to the fundamental importance of digital technologies, it is sensible to conclude that they can be expected to be targeted and exploited by misusers. Incidents in cyberspace are indeed increasing at an alarming pace, and they can have a criminal, political, terrorist, or State-sponsored nature.

During the most recent global crisis – the COVID-19 pandemic that, by March 2020, had spread to all parts of the globe – working online and remotely became a *conditio sine qua non* for almost all industries, governments and international organisations. The vast dependence on cyberspace in times of crisis consequently raises concerns for cybersecurity and data protection, especially as the integrity and stability of (normally closed) official networks have been challenged by the necessity to access them remotely.[19]

The misuse of the Internet and cyberspace thus threatens the fundamental sectors of society, and three industries which are intertwined with the smooth functioning of such fundamental sectors are the aviation, space and telecommunications industries.

[A] Cybersecurity in Aviation

Cyberattacks within the context of aviation are not a new phenomenon. For example, the first recorded cyberattack against an aviation stakeholder happened on 10 March 1997 when a teenager disabled numerous safety and security services at Worcester,

15. Deutsche Welle, 'UK, US Blame Russia for "NotPetya" Cyber Attack', Deutsche Welle, 15 February 2018, https://www.dw.com/en/uk-us-blame-russia-for-notpetya-cyberattack/a-42598806.
16. *Ibid.*
17. The White House, 'Foreign Policy: Statement from the Press Secretary', The White House, 15 February 2018, https://www.whitehouse.gov/briefings-statements/statement-press-secretary-25/.
18. Statista, 'Global Digital Population as of 2020', https://www.statista.com/statistics/617136/digital-population-worldwide/.
19. Stefan Grobe and Alasdair Sandford, 'COVID-19: EU Cybersecurity "At Risk from Hackers"', 24 March 2020, https://www.euronews.com/2020/03/24/covid-19-eu-cybersecurity-at-risk-from-hackers.

Massachusetts airport in the US. While the attack did not have an impact on safety, it did cause major disruption, which resulted in flight delays.

Cyberattacks against aviation stakeholders have continued and evolved since the first reported case in 1997. A notable case took place on 21 June 2016 at Warsaw Chopin Airport, Poland. Approximately 1,400 passengers of the Polish airline LOT were affected due to a cyberattack against its ground computers used to issue flight plans. While the airport itself was not affected and there was no reported risk to safety, it resulted in numerous flights being delayed or cancelled.

In addition to delays and cancellations, as well as financial damage (direct loss or reputation damage), there may also be safety concerns. A prominent case took place in 2015. A cybersecurity consultant in the US allegedly hacked into the in-flight entertainment systems on board around fifteen-twenty aircraft from 2011 to 2014 and controlled aircraft while in flight. While no injuries were reported, the claims were taken seriously and thoroughly investigated. If this type of intrusion is easily executable, then there is a real and immediate risk to safety.

There are more examples of cyberattacks against aviation stakeholders, but the effects of the reported cybersecurity threats in aviation have been fairly minimal to safety. This does not mean there is no problem; there are likely to be new, unthought-of cyber threats which may become manifest in the future. This is because aviation stakeholders are:

> increasingly relying on computers in all aspects. These computers are increasingly being connected to the Internet and other networks, as well as becoming more automated. Therefore, the aviation sector is producing more vulnerabilities that can be exploited by an attacker. In addition, the aviation sector is an appealing target. As a result, there are many reasons why aviation is being subjected to a growing number of cyberattacks. None of the reasons highlighted [... are] unlikely to fade away.[20]

Regulators – at a national, regional and international level – are reacting in order to promote cybersecurity by creating law and policy documents. Further, other stakeholders are reacting to fill the gaps that laws cannot cover or to satisfy the obligations prescribed in cyber-based law. Therefore, in aviation, there is a proliferation of regulations, industry standards, information sharing and reporting, risk assessments, training, commitment of resources, and awareness promotion. In essence, "cybersecurity in aviation is [...] a serious issue that all aviation stakeholders must consider in order to protect passengers, third parties and themselves."[21]

[B] Cybersecurity in Outer Space

The importance of establishing standards and risk management mechanisms for cybersecurity protection through legal regulation has become relevant also in the

20. Benjamyn I. Scott, *Aviation Cybersecurity: Regulatory Approach in the European Union* (Eleven, 2019), at 15-16.
21. *Ibid.*, at 3.

global space industry. While outer space has been subject to human use and exploration for more than sixty years, it is only recently that the vulnerability of space assets for cyber intrusions has gained practical importance, not least due to the vital importance of space systems and space applications for almost all spheres of modern life and for critical infrastructure.

The complexity of all issues resulting in the general vulnerability of space systems to malicious cyber activities is characterised by numerous factors. These include the growing accessibility to space technology and the growing number of space objects which, in the last few years, has mostly been discussed in relation to large constellations. Small satellites in general, and large constellations such as the ones developed by OneWeb, SpaceX and Facebook, have raised concerns about the abilities and the instruments needed, both on a technological, as well as on a policy and regulatory level.[22]

In 2019, the relevance of cybercrime in outer space and specifically on board the only currently inhabited space object on a long-term basis – the International Space Station (ISS) – gained much media coverage as a National Aeronautics and Space Administration (NASA) astronaut was accused of having gained improper access to another person's bank account while on board the ISS. While this act had no direct relevance to 'hacking' in or from outer space[23] as the password seemed to have been voluntarily shared with the astronaut and not acquired illegally, it does illustrate that the use of cyberspace easily crosses boundaries and spaces, and may have further implications, both on Earth and in outer space.

The integration and linking of space objects and space applications in the global cyber network is a process that will inevitably develop at a quicker pace in the upcoming years. This puts an emphasis on the need to elaborate adequate legal rules for ensuring that the multiple inlets for cyber intrusions do not open up an uncontrollable Pandora's Box for malicious cyber activities as such activities may have effects on a global scale. So far, such regulatory incentives have not led to the adoption of a dedicated international agreement or strategy. Nevertheless, the technological expertise provided by certain governmental entities and some international organisations could serve as a starting point for elaborating specific rules internationally.

22. Debra Werner, 'Government, Industry Officials Share Small Satellite Cybersecurity Concerns', 5 February 2020, https://www.spacenews.com/smallsat-cybersecurity-2020/; William Akoto, 'To Secure Satellites, Bolster Cybersecurity Standards in Space', 25 February 2020, https://www.undark.org/2020/02/25/satellite-cybersecurity-standards/.

23. *See*, for example, Mike Baker, 'NASA Astronaut Anne McClain Accused by Spouse of Crime in Space', New York Times, 23 August 2019, https://www.nytimes.com/2019/08/23/us/nasa-astronaut-anne-mcclain.html; Davey Winder, 'NASA Astronaut Accused of Hacking Bank Account From Space', Forbes, 25 August 2019, https://www.forbes.com/sites/daveywinder/2019/08/25/nasa-astronaut-accused-of-hacking-bank-account-from-space/#b4ec4f754e96. *See*, for an account of the applicable US law, David P. Fidler 'Cyber Crime in Outer Space: Houston, Do We Have a Problem?', Council on Foreign Relations, 29 August 2019, https://www.cfr.org/blog/cyber-crime-outer-space-houston-do-we-have-problem.

[C] Cybersecurity in Satellite Services

Satellite services are the backbone of modern society and economy and provide crucial services to applications such as banking, agriculture, transport, search-and-rescue, and many others. Their dependence on free and unrestricted access to the radio spectrum, however, constitutes a vulnerability that has become increasingly critical in the past years, and will probably continue to grow in the foreseeable future.

Looking into the transmission of data through telecommunications, the harmful use of radio frequencies by malicious entities – which takes place mainly for political reasons or in the context of military operations – holds great potential to affect the regular functioning of satellite-based services, and cause interruption of services for users as well as serious losses in terms of revenues and reputation for service providers. The interference techniques employed are several. The most common ones, for instance jamming and spoofing, disturb the legitimate signal or replace it with a false one, thus blocking the reception of the transmission or, in the latter case, feeding the receiver with false information.

In 2007, for instance, Libya jammed two satellites belonging to the Abu Dhabi-based operator Thuraya Satellite Communications in an attempt to block a small commercial radio station from broadcasting on human rights and freedom of speech, causing severe loss of service as well as serious diplomatic consequences at the international level.

An even more severe threat is constituted by interference against satellite navigation services, which, as a side consequence, may heavily affect civil aviation operations, especially in geographical proximity to geopolitically sensitive areas. This results in a direct threat against human life, as exemplified by the fact that, between 2011 and 2012, in South Korea, several hundreds of flights were affected by electromagnetic interference, causing at least four missed approaches.

A robust reaction by national and, even more importantly, international regulators is needed in order to counter this phenomenon. The lack of strong enforcement mechanisms in the international legal order, however, reflects also upon the telecommunications field, thus leaving a question mark on how and by whom this threat should be dealt with.

§1.02 AIM OF THE BOOK

The consequences of the reported cybersecurity threats to aviation and outer space stakeholders have been relatively minimal thus far; however, the types of cybersecurity threats and the motives behind the attacks are varied and unpredictable. All these fields are heavily reliant on technology, and as they are becoming more reliant on cyber technology, they are becoming more exposed to potential attacks.

Cyberattacks are indeed becoming more common, while protection and prevention remain some steps behind. Thus, cybersecurity is becoming a more serious issue and a growing one that all the stakeholders must consider. This book will highlight any current laws relevant to aviation and space cybersecurity and analyse them from a critical perspective.

Additionally, there are several discussions taking place regarding the future regulation of aviation and space cybersecurity which this book will explore. Therefore, this book will come at a crucial time in the regulation of aviation and space cybersecurity and will serve as a tool for stakeholders to understand specific associated risks, interpret existing rules, and develop new rules.

§1.03 CHAPTER BREAK DOWN

[A] Chapter 2: Definitions and Terminology

After having set the scene in this chapter (Chapter 1) by providing an overview of the growing relevance of cybersecurity in general and in the more specific contexts of aviation and outer space, Chapter 2 is dedicated to a terminological overview. It attempts to clarify the most relevant terms and provide definitions – either already existing or, where suitable and necessary, proposed by the authors for the purposes of this book – for cybersecurity in aviation, telecommunications and outer space. The aim of such a definitional chapter is to provide a better understanding of the terminology underlying the legal analysis that follows in Chapters 3–9 as the cyber discourse often builds upon language at the intersection of technology and law.

First, the lack of established and universally accepted cybersecurity terminology, both in academic writings and in the emerging regulatory attempts, is addressed before the general cyber-related terminology is provided. Terms in this first section of Chapter 2 include, for example, 'cyberspace', 'cybersecurity' in aviation and outer space, 'cyberattack' and 'cybercrime'. The overview does not only refer to existing definitions from national cybersecurity policy documents and international documents, but provides information on, and analyses the context, development and use of these terms.

Next, the second section treats the relevant legal and technical aviation terminology by referring to the relevant legal sources, including treaty texts, and the work of international organisations involved in the regulation of cybersecurity such as the International Civil Aviation Organization (ICAO).

The chapter then moves on to provide the relevant terms and definitions for cybersecurity in telecommunications and outer space that have been elaborated on at the national and international level. In this regard, treaty-based definitions, as well as broadly used complex terms that have not yet been defined are included, such as 'space activities', 'space infrastructure' and 'space assets', as are technical terms of relevance like 'electromagnetic interference', 'jamming' and 'spoofing'.

In the last section, the use of terms of a general character that are relevant for aviation and outer space is clarified before the book proceeds with analysing the perspective of international law to cybersecurity.

[B] Chapter 3: Cyberattacks from an International Law Perspective

Chapter 3 seeks to provide the foundations of the book by looking at attacks and threats in cyberspace from an international law point of view. In order to fulfil its purpose, this chapter commences with a brief overview of international law, focusing on its sources.

The discourse then proceeds with a concise analysis of the two regimes of international law that relate to conflict: the regime which determines when resort to armed force is permissible, and the regime of law which governs the conduct of hostilities during an armed conflict. These two regimes are respectively termed the *jus ad bellum* and the *jus in bello*.

Once the relevant tenets of international law are set out, Chapter 3 seeks to identify whether international law instruments that address the eventuality of conflict in cyberspace exists. Apart from this attempt at identifying legal instruments which address conflict in cyberspace, this chapter also attempts to understand how, if at all, the general rules on conflict apply in cyberspace.

To this end, Chapter 3 attempts to determine particularly whether the rules of *jus ad bellum* apply in cyberspace. The primary reason for this specific treatment of *jus ad bellum* lies in the fact that, from the examples of cyberattacks listed in this chapter (Chapter 1), it seems that the cyberattacks documented to date are not cyberattacks employed in conflicts.

In carrying out the analysis of the applicability of the *jus ad bellum* vis-à-vis cyberattacks, Chapter 3 focuses on whether and when a cyberattack can amount to the use or threat of use of force. Moreover, Chapter 3 looks into the question of whether and when a cyberattack can amount to an armed attack, thereby allowing States to respond to any such attack.

Following this analysis, Chapter 3 treats the notion of State responsibility in the context of cyberattacks. Finally, this chapter provides a succinct synopsis of various initiatives undertaken by international and regional organisations towards the regulation of cyberattacks in an international context.

[C] Chapter 4: Promotion of Cybersecurity and Combating Cybercrime in the EU

In order to support the previous chapter, Chapter 4 will look at the EU and how it promotes cybersecurity and protects against cyberattacks.

The chapter addresses three core areas: policy, regulation and stakeholders' activities. First, the chapter will show that cybersecurity and cyberattacks are not new topics for the EU, and that giant steps have been taken, starting in 2013, for forming an EU-wide policy. This resulted in the creation of the Cybersecurity Strategy in that same year, which clarifies the guiding principles that EU cybersecurity policy and law should adopt. It was revised in 2017 to focus it on 'resilience', 'deterrence' and 'defence'. Separate, but connected to the Cybersecurity Strategy due to its cyber-based deliverables, is the 2015 Digital Single Market Strategy for Europe, which was also updated in

2017. The focused review on policy concludes with the endorsement of the two strategies during the Tallinn Digital Summit that took place in September 2017.

Second, Chapter 4 will look at cyber-related primary and secondary sources of EU law. The cited primary law will be on the Solidarity Clause found in Article 222 of the Treaty on the Functioning of the European Union (TFEU). The part on secondary sources will look at the Network and Information Systems (NIS) Directive, which covers several aviation stakeholders as operators of essential services; the Directive on Attacks Against Information Systems; the Recommendation on Coordinated Response to Large-Scale Cybersecurity Incidents and Crises; the Cybersecurity Act, including certification and industry standards; Data Protection, including the General Data Protection Regulation (GDPR), Cookies Directive and access to documents for information sharing; and sanctions.

Finally, Chapter 4 will look at relevant institutions, bodies and entities. This will involve, *inter alia*, an analysis of the European Union Agency for Network and Information Security (ENISA), Computer Emergency Response Team-European Union (CERT-EU), European Union Agency for Law Enforcement Cooperation (Europol) and European Agency for the Operational Management of Large-Scale IT Systems in the Area of Freedom, Security and Justice (EU-LISA).

[D] Chapter 5: Space (Law) and Cybersecurity

Chapter 5 will commence by providing an outlook on the constantly increasing importance of the space domain and by illustrating this trend with statistical data on the growth of the space economy. The role of cyberspace in the space sector becomes visible when the combination of factors such as accessibility and constant progress of technology, competition and global interconnectivity are considered as the trigger for exposing strategic and costly space assets to cyber-related intrusions.

The analysis of the applicable law to cyber activities in outer space starts with outlining the question about the extent to which general international law and, in particular, space law governs human activities in outer space before looking at the most relevant, fundamental legal principles on the exploration and use of outer space.

Next, the chapter will investigate various challenges for the cybersecurity of space assets from a factual perspective. This is done by looking specifically at satellite systems as systems of multiple units consisting of a 'ground' and a 'space' segment which depend on the secure deployment of hardware and software, and which communicate via electromagnetic transmission and in an increasingly digital – rather than merely analogous – form. Most of these single elements can be used as inlets for cyber intrusions that may target valuable data and signals, but also the physical control over the satellite. The picture is further complicated by the remoteness of space objects as this does not allow for hardware to be upgraded in order to ensure timely and maximum possible protection from cyber threats vis-à-vis advanced hacking abilities available on Earth.

This chapter continues with an exemplary list of known cyber-related events concerning satellites and satellite-transmitted data before providing a comprehensive classification of cybersecurity challenges for space objects and satellite systems, possible threats, and potential outcomes. A section of the chapter is dedicated to the steadily emerging phenomenon of large constellations which, due to a large number of small, low-cost satellites, will significantly add to the overall picture of cybersecurity challenges and to the stability of the orbital population in the upcoming years.

The chapter then goes into more detail on the legal challenges at the intersection between outer space and cyberspace. While having certain common features, such as a global character and lack of geographical boundaries, the two domains are each characterised by their specific problems. For example, the applicability of space law to cyber activities in outer space is a largely disputed question to which answers are sought.

Furthermore, the issue on how jurisdiction and attribution can be established reliably and in how far the international law of state responsibility can play a role in cyberspace is examined before in the chapter, an overview of existing regulatory initiatives on the international regulatory level is given. In conclusion, based on the previous sections, some findings on the way forward for future regulation are presented.

[E] Chapter 6: Critical Infrastructure for Aviation and Space Activities: Satellite Communication and Navigation

Chapter 6 is dedicated to satellite communication and navigation services, to the electromagnetic-based threats against them, and to the regulatory responses in place at international level. In the first part, it will investigate the role of communication and navigation satellite services in the global society and economy. Their relationship with the notion of critical infrastructure in Europe and in the US will be examined, putting a particular focus on key features such as interdependency, cross-border nature, mixed public-private ownership, and dual civil-military uses.

The analysis will continue by illustrating the main radio spectrum-related threats to such services, namely jamming and spoofing, and will look at the reasons why they constitute such a dangerous issue. These malicious techniques are increasingly used against satellite operators, thereby leading to financial losses and reputational harm, and causing the interruption of services for millions of users. In the worst case, they can even threaten human life, as exemplified by interference against satellite navigation used in civil aviation.

The chapter will then move to the response provided by the international community against such threats. The United Nations (UN) agency responsible for telecommunications and Information and Communications Technology (ICT) at a global level is the International Telecommunication Union (ITU), the structure and role of which will be explained accordingly. Particular attention will be dedicated to the legal framework for radio communications, constituted by the Radio Regulations, and their suitability to counter the phenomenon of intentional harmful interference. Despite not possessing strong enforcement powers, the ITU relies on the wilful cooperation between the Member States and it employs alternative techniques such as naming-and-shaming and an intensive monitoring programme. These can prove effective, to a certain extent, against politically motivated interference.

Lastly, a consideration about the difference between the concepts of 'harmful interference' and 'cyberattack' will be offered, both in the perspective of existing legal instruments and of possible future ones.

[F] Chapter 7: Public International Civil Aviation Law

Chapter 7 will be used to examine public international air law and how it promotes cybersecurity and helps to combat cyberattacks. At the centre of this chapter will be the Convention on International Civil Aviation of 1944 (the 'Chicago Convention 1944').

This chapter will not offer a full analysis of the Chicago Convention but will provide context hereto by providing a brief background and highlighting the circumstances in which it is applicable, both generally and specifically vis-à-vis cybersecurity. It will then go into more detail, for example, by analysing Article 3 *bis* which forbids the use of weapons against civil aircraft in flight with passengers on board to assess if the term 'weapon' can include a cyberattack. Further, the chapter will look at Articles 5 and 6 of the Chicago Convention to determine if bilateral and multilateral air services agreements, as secondary sources of law to the Convention, have relevance for cybersecurity.

Keeping with international treaties, Chapter 7 will look at international criminal aviation law, notably the treaties that ICAO has facilitated, to determine if they are relevant to aviation cybersecurity. Therefore, it will assess the Tokyo Convention 1963, the Hague Convention 1970, the Montreal Convention 1971, the Montreal Protocol 1988, the Beijing Convention 2010, the Beijing Protocol 2010 and the Montreal Protocol 2014 to access if they have direct or indirect relevance to aviation cybersecurity.

The Chicago Convention is supported by its Annexes. Therefore, the Annexes to the Chicago Convention will also be examined. While focus will be given to Annex 17, which addresses security, as it contains text on cybersecurity, other Annexes will also be considered to see their relevance to the topic.

ICAO, which was created by the Chicago Convention and is tasked with the development of the Annexes, is also active in cybersecurity in other areas. Not only will these activities be documented, such as relevant General Assembly Resolutions and the Declaration on Cybersecurity in Civil Aviation, but it will also highlight the split in competencies that ICAO is facing between 'safety' and 'security', and how cybersecurity does not fit comfortably in either heading.

ICAO does not act independently; rather, it extensively relies on and cooperates with different stakeholders. As a result, Chapter 7 will discuss some of the core activities of aviation stakeholders, such as the Industry High Level Group (IHLG) and the different groups within ICAO where stakeholders are active, notably the Secretariat Study Group on Cybersecurity (SSGC), Trust Framework Study Group (TFSG) and Aviation Security (AVSEC) Panel.

Due to the increased competencies that the EU aviation safety regime has for cybersecurity, Chapter 7 will, furthermore, introduce the legal fundamentals of EU aviation safety, specifically the work of the European Union Aviation Safety Agency (EASA), under Regulation 2018/1139, as well at the European Commission's aviation security work, focusing on Regulation 300/2008. It will also look at key policy documents, such as the Bucharest Declaration 2016 and Krakow Declaration of 2017, which set out key EU policy points on cybersecurity. Further, it will comment on other EU activities, such as information sharing and incident response, thus providing a more practical overview. Therefore, this chapter will map the key European aviation cybersecurity legal and policy landscape.

[G] Chapter 8: Aviation Liability in Cases of Cyberattacks

Complementary to the previous chapter, Chapter 8 will be used to examine private international air law and how it applies in cases of cyberattacks. This chapter, therefore, starts by focusing on the international law regime of liability in the case of air carrier passengers, namely the Warsaw System and the Convention for the Unification of Certain Rules for International Carriage by Air of 1999 (the 'Montreal Convention').

By focusing on the international law regime of liability for air carrier passengers, Chapter 8 seeks to determine whether a cyberattack may be classified as an 'accident' in terms of that regime, and whether, accordingly, passengers may claim remuneration for any damages resulting therefrom.

This chapter also seeks to determine whether a cyberattack that leads to a flight delay may allow passengers to claim compensation. In this context, Chapter 8 shifts its focus onto the EU, particularly on Regulation 261/2004. By focusing on this Regulation, Chapter 8 analyses the possibility of a cyberattack being classified as an extraordinary circumstance since, in terms of the Regulation in question, air carriers are exonerated from compensating passengers if they can prove such an extraordinary circumstance.

Chapter 8 proceeds by analysing the applicability of the international law regime of liability in the case of damage to third parties caused by cyberattacks. In doing so, it analyses the Convention on Damage Caused by Foreign Aircraft to Third Parties on the Surface of 1952, and the Convention on Compensation for Damage to Third Parties, Resulting from Acts of Unlawful Interference Involving Aircraft.

This chapter concludes by examining the Convention on the Suppression of Unlawful Acts Relating to International Civil Aviation of 2010 which, in an aviation-treaty first, makes specific reference to the eventuality of a cyberattack.

Ultimately, Chapter 8 draws to a close by analysing whether air carriers may face novel barriers, imposed by insurers and underwriters, in obtaining insurance coverage against cyber risks.

[H] Chapter 9: Lessons Learned

Chapter 9 will navigate through the main cybersecurity principles and strategies on the basis of international standards and industry practice and will draw conclusions based on the findings of the preceding chapters, thereby providing a bird's-eye overview of the relevant key elements for cybersecurity in aviation and outer space.

Although space activities and air transport have their own peculiarities and may require additional tailored measures, the defence strategies described in this chapter are transversal across sectors and need to be applied by all the stakeholders relying on cyberspace, independently of the specific field of activity.

At first, the main elements of a cyberattack will be analysed specifically from a technical point of view, providing an overview of the different types of malicious actors and operations, as well as of the typical lifecycle of a cyberattack.

Subsequently, the chapter will move to cybersecurity measures, going through legal and regulatory initiatives, industry standards and best practices aimed at countering a cyber threat, both in a preventive and responsive perspective.

Lastly, a special focus will be dedicated to the contractual practice of the industry aimed at securing an adequate level of security via contract clauses.

CHAPTER 2

Definitions and Terminology

§2.01 INTRODUCTION

Before going into specific considerations about the law applicable to cybersecurity in aviation and outer space in the subsequent chapters, this chapter will provide an overview of the meaning of the most relevant terms relating to cyberspace in this context in alphabetical order. Where necessary and suitable, this chapter will also formulate definitions relevant for the purposes of the book. The reasoning for inserting a chapter dedicated entirely to terminology and definitions lies in the fact that many terms which are being widely used in the cyber context such as 'cyberspace' and 'cyber operation' among others are, in fact, primarily rooted in technology and have not been defined in law. Even if some attempts to clarify the relevant terms have been undertaken by some States on a national level, as well as by some organisations, as will be shown below, in many cases, no definitions or no complete definitions have been established internationally.

In fact, the lack of established definitions has not been an obstacle for analytic publications to emerge during the past few years. These include, among others, the two volumes of the *Tallinn Manual* on the international law applicable to cyber operations during war and in peacetime[1] and the 2013 book edited by Katharina Tsiolkovsky *Peacetime Regime for State Activities in Cyberspace* under the facilitation of the North Atlantic Treaty Organization (NATO) Cooperative Cyber Defence Centre of Excellence (CCDCOE).[2]

1. Michael N. Schmitt (ed.), *Tallinn Manual on International Law Applicable to Cyber Warfare* (Cambridge University Press, 2013); Michael N. Schmitt (ed.), *Tallinn Manual 2.0 on International Law Applicable to Cyber Operations* (Cambridge University Press, 2017).
2. Katharina Tsiolkovsky (ed.), *Peacetime Regime for State Activities in Cyberspace* (NATO Cooperative Cyber Defence Centre of Excellence, 2013).

Nevertheless, any research work in the emerging field of cybersecurity regulation is inevitably challenged by the uncertainty in terminology and the blurred lines that originate from the diverging uses of relevant cyber-related notions.

That is why, before embarking on the substantial legal analysis of cybersecurity aspects of aviation, outer space and telecommunication activities, the most relevant notions and terms must be clarified. The methodology that has been used to this end includes:

- an identification of the terms that are relevant for the scope of the book; and
- a determination of whether and how these terms have already been defined by States or organisations.

For the sake of conciseness, the list of relevant terms and definitions in Chapter 2 is not exhaustive of all existing definitional attempts in the literature. Further, for the most critical terms and for terms that are not purely technical, a compact legal appraisal has been provided accordingly.

§2.02 RELEVANT CYBER TERMINOLOGY

[A] Cyberspace: Etymology, History and Main Characteristics

The main aim of the regulation of activities in cyberspace is the establishment of legal mechanisms for the prevention of and reaction against malicious activities taking place in or through cyberspace. Cyberspace emerged in the 1960s with the establishment of the first experimental computer communications networks, such as the Advanced Research Projects Agency Network that was developed in the US as a research project of the Pentagon with the aim to link computers over telephone lines. Over the next decades, further networks were developed to share data and storage, and in 1986, the National Science Foundation of the US provided American researchers with access to supercomputers, which led to the emergence of the Internet. Since 1989, the Internet became open for public commercial uses, and in 1995, it was fully commercialised in the US. In the mid-1990s, when the Internet had become globally accessible, the US started to regulate online interaction through the Communications Decency Act of 1996.[3]

The main characteristic of cyberspace as an environment used for various types of electronic communication is its virtual, transnational character.[4] Cyberspace is not a natural environment that is being governed partially or wholly through natural predispositions. It is a man-made global environment used only for human activities through the interaction of persons through the use of hardware, software and world-wide technological services. It is a 'network of networks' based on a technological

3. Protection for Private Blocking and Screening of Offensive Material, 47 US Code § 230.
4. *See*, on the global validity of IP addresses, domain names, and Internet standards, Ralf Bendrath, et al., 'Governing the Internet: The Quest for Legitimacy and Effective Rules', *in* Achim Hurrelmann, et al. (eds), *Transforming the Golden-Age Nation State* (Palgrave Macmilian, 2007), at 130 and 146.

infrastructure in which the 'language' of protocols is used to transfer various forms of information and data.[5]

Cyberspace is a medium without a solid territorial origin. Nevertheless, it functions on the basis of exchange of signals and data between information-emitting sources which are usually rooted in State territory or at least related to an element of sovereignty based on the personality or territoriality principle. Therefore, States having sovereignty over the geographical location of cyber infrastructure may exercise jurisdiction over the users of cyberspace and their cyber activities.[6]

This means that regulation in cyberspace through single States can take place only on the basis of sovereignty. Sovereignty finds expression in the jurisdiction through the exercise of legal prescriptive and law enforcement powers. Jurisdiction is thus the sovereign power of States to lawfully enact and enforce laws in their territory, and upon persons and objects therein, and to control the conduct of their national natural and legal persons and to other persons in their territory.[7] Especially relevant for the regulation in cyberspace is the so-called protective principle (the principle of international criminal jurisdiction),[8] which allows States to confer their legal power extraterritorial effect.

The application of these principles is challenged through the transnational nature of cyberspace. The main reason is that the geographic basis of allocation does not meet the challenges posed by the transnational and global nature of cyberspace. Thus, the application of jurisdiction, as the lawful power of States to prescribe, adjudicate and enforce legal rules in their national territory and on their national persons, is challenged by the lack of physical boundaries in this global space and currently does not offer a satisfactory basis to effectively extend jurisdiction over all activities in cyberspace.

The etymology of the term 'cyber' originates from Greek where the verb ***κυβερνώ*** means 'to steer' or 'to lead'. It was used by Plato for the first time as a metaphor in his work to depict governing systems[9] and later became the origin of the words 'governance' and 'government'.

Today, the notion 'cyber' can be defined and is mostly used as an adjective "[r]elating to or characteristic of the culture of computers, information technology, and

5. Stephan Hobe and Rada Popova, 'Law in Cyberspace?', 67(2) *German Journal for Air and Space Law* 254-278 (2018), at 254 and 256.
6. *See* Chapter 5, section §5.04[C].
7. *See*, for an extensive account on the basis for state jurisdiction, for example, Bernhard H. Oxman, 'Jurisdiction of States', *in* Max Planck Encyclopedia of Public International Law, November 2007, https://www.opil.ouplaw.com/view/10.1093/law:epil/9780199231690/law-9780199231690-e1436. *See also*, Hobe and Popova, *supra* no. 5, at 254 and 263.
8. UN, International Law Commission, *Historical Survey of the Question of International Criminal Jurisdiction – Memorandum Submitted by the Secretary-General*, Document A/CN.4/7/Rev.1 (New York, 1949); Philippa Webb and Morten Bergsmo, 'International Criminal Courts and Tribunals, Complementarity and Jurisdiction', *in* Max Planck Encyclopedia of Public International Law, November 2010, https://opil.ouplaw.com/view/10.1093/law:epil/9780199231690/law-9780199231690-e1381.
9. Plato, *The Republic: Book VII*, 380 BC.

virtual reality"[10] and is widely used in the modern language, mostly with a connotation to computers, Internet and information technology (IT) in general.

Currently, no universal definition of the term 'cyberspace' exists. According to the Oxford English Dictionary, it means:

> the space of virtual reality; the notional environment within which electronic communication (esp. via the Internet) occurs.[11]

More than twenty proposals have been formulated at the international level, including the definition used by the International Organization for Standardization (ISO) and the International Electrotechnical Commission (IEC) in the 2012/2018 Guidelines for Cybersecurity:

> The complex environment resulting from the interaction of people, software and services on the Internet by means of technology devices and networks connected to it, which does not exist in any physical form.[12]

Moreover, some States have provided a definition of the term 'cyberspace' for the purposes of their national cybersecurity strategies. Canada's Cyber Security Strategy of 2010[13] defines cyberspace as "the electronic world created by interconnected networks of information technology and the information on those networks." In the German Cyber Security Strategy of 2011,[14] it is stated that "Cyberspace includes all information infrastructures accessible via the Internet beyond all territorial boundaries"[15] and the definition reads:

> Cyberspace is the virtual space of all IT systems linked at data level on a global scale. The basis for cyberspace is the Internet as a universal and publicly accessible connection and transport network which can be complemented and further expanded by any number of additional data networks. IT systems in an isolated virtual space are not part of cyberspace.

The US Department of Defense is using the following definition:

10. Oxford Online Dictionary, 'Definition of Cyber', https://www.en.oxforddictionaries.com/definition/cyber.
11. Oxford Online Dictionary, 'Definition of Cyberspace', https://www.lexico.com/en/definition/cyberspace.
12. International Electrotechnical Commission, 'ISO/IEC 27032:2012, Information Technology – Security techniques – Guidelines for Cybersecurity', https://www.iso.org/standard/44375.html.
13. Government of Canada, 'Cyber Security Strategy', 2010, https://www.publicsafety.gc.ca/cnt/rsrcs/pblctns/ntnl-cbr-scrt-strtg/ntnl-cbr-scrt-strtg-en.pdf.
14. German Federal Ministry of the Interior, Building and Community, 'Cyber-Sicherheitsstrategie für Deutschland', https://www.bmi.bund.de/cybersicherheitsstrategie/BMI_CyberSicherheitsStrategie.pdf.
15. *Ibid.* English translation available at, https://www.enisa.europa.eu/topics/national-cyber-security-strategies/ncss-map/strategies/cyber-security-strategy-for-germany/@@download_version/bca1e34aca9b411eb3d382b5d220482a/file_en.

> A global domain within the information environment consisting of the interdependent networks of information technology infrastructures and resident data, including the Internet, telecommunications networks, computer systems, and embedded processors and controllers.[16]

From the definitions mentioned above, a few common elements of cyberspace stand out:

- its technological, man-made origin;
- its lack of boundaries;
- its global, far-reaching character;
- its reliance and dependence on physical infrastructure; and
- the fact that its physical elements have a link to territoriality and therefore to jurisdiction.

Based on these observations, for the purposes of this book, the following definition of the term 'cyberspace' is proposed:

> Cyberspace is a realm using the protocol-based global electronic network. It is an artificial man-made medium, based on physical infrastructure such as computers and communication servers located in the sovereign territory, or falling under the jurisdiction of States.

[B] Cybersecurity

There is no universal or legally binding definition of the term 'cybersecurity' either. It relates both to safety as well as to security aspects of various types of activities, including those relating to aviation, telecommunications and outer space.

According to the definition of the Computer Security Resource Center (CSRS) at the US Department of Commerce, 'cybersecurity' can be defined as:

> Prevention of damage to, protection of, and restoration of computers, electronic communications systems, electronic communications services, wire communication, and electronic communication, including information contained therein, to ensure its availability, integrity, authentication, confidentiality, and nonrepudiation.[17]

Again, according to the CSRS at the US Department of Commerce, the term refers to "[t]he process of protecting information by preventing, detecting, and responding to attacks."[18] Therefore, the term 'cybersecurity' is mostly used as an overarching title

16. US Department of Defense, 'DOD Dictionary of Military and Associated Terms', https://www.jcs.mil/Portals/36/Documents/Doctrine/pubs/dictionary.pdf, at 55.
17. US Department of Commerce, NIST, Computer Security Resource Center, 'Glossary', https://www.csrc.nist.gov/glossary/term/cybersecurity.
18. US Department of Commerce, NIST, Computer Security Resource Center, 'Framework for Improving Critical Infrastructure Cybersecurity, Version 1.0', https://www.nist.gov/sites/default/files/documents/itl/draft_framework_glossary.pdf.

regarding, in the first place, cyber activities with harmful potential, cyber-related vulnerabilities, and the measures undertaken to prevent or combat these.

[C] Cybersecurity in Aviation

With regard to cybersecurity in aviation, there are no explicit references to the term 'cybersecurity' (or even 'cyberattack' or any other related terms) within the text of the Chicago Convention, the criminal law conventions or the liability conventions drafted under the auspices of ICAO. The Chicago Convention does not provide an indication on whether cybersecurity falls under aviation safety or aviation security, or whether it falls under a completely separate topic. ICAO has made comments linking cybersecurity to both the safety and security domain. ICAO has been active in the area of cybersecurity insofar as the topic of security has been designated to the Air Transport Bureau.[19] At the same time, safety is the responsibility of the Air Navigation Bureau without cybersecurity fitting clearly in the overall ICAO system.[20] It would, thus, seem that cybersecurity is a concern for both safety and security, with security being prioritised.[21]

Within the context of the EU, the classification is clearer. The first reference to 'cybersecurity' is made in Recital 12 of Regulation 2018/1139 of the European Parliament and of the Council of 4 July 2018 on common rules in the field of civil aviation and establishing EASA. Measures taken in accordance with the Regulation shall take into account the relationship between safety and cybersecurity. Recital 12 makes it explicitly clear that the two are distinct areas; cybersecurity is not *stricto sensu* a part of safety. This is repeated in Recital 59, which takes the classification of 'cybersecurity' further as it places 'cybersecurity' under the scope of aviation security.

[D] Cybersecurity in Outer Space

As far as cybersecurity in outer space is concerned, this term does not appear in any of the international instruments regulating space activities.[22] For the purposes of this

19. Benjamyn I. Scott, *Aviation Cybersecurity: Regulatory Approach in the European Union* (Eleven, 2019), at 131-214.
20. *Ibid.*
21. *Ibid.*
22. These instruments include five international agreements, namely the Treaty on Principles Governing the Activities of States in the Exploration and Use of Outer Space, including the Moon and Other Celestial Bodies, 610 UNTS 205, adopted on 27 January 1967, entered into force 10 October 1967 (Outer Space Treaty); the Agreement on the Rescue of Astronauts, the Return of Astronauts and the Return of Objects Launched into Outer Space, 672 UNTS 119, adopted on 22 April 1968, entered into force 3 December 1968 (Rescue Agreement); the Convention on International Liability for Damage Caused by Space Objects, 961 UNTS 187, adopted on 29 March 1972, entered into force 1 September 1972 (Liability Convention); Convention on Registration of Objects Launched into Outer Space, 1023 UNTS 15, adopted on 14 January 1975, entered into force 15 September 1976 (Registration Convention); and the Agreement Governing the Activities of States on the Moon and Other Celestial Bodies, 1363 UNTS 3, adopted on 18 December 1979, entered into force 11 July 1984 (Moon Agreement) as well as the following non-binding Resolutions by the UN General Assembly: UN GA Res. 37/92, Principles Governing the Use by States of Artificial Earth Satellites for International Direct Television Broadcasting, 10

book, it is used as an overarching term including technological, policy and legal aspects of cybersecurity for a wide scope of measures aimed at protecting the space infrastructure, space operations as well as the data transmitted from and to outer space from malicious cyber activities.[23]

[E] Cyber Activities and Cyber Operations

The terms 'cyber activities' and 'cyber operations' are general notions that encompass various types of activities relating to or making use of cyberspace. For the purposes of this book, the two terms may, where suitable, be used interchangeably. However, depending on the context, 'cyber operations' may also be understood as an accumulation of single activities.

In literature, 'cyber operations' have been defined as "the employment of cyber capabilities with the primary purpose of achieving objectives in or by the use of cyberspace."[24]

The definition formulated by the US Department of Defense refers to:

> The employment of cyberspace capabilities where the primary purpose is to achieve objectives in or through cyberspace.[25]

The International Committee of the Red Cross (ICRC) has defined 'cyber operations' as:

> operations against or via a computer system through a data stream [that] can aim to do different things, for instance to infiltrate a system and collect, export, destroy, change or encrypt data or to trigger, alter or otherwise manipulate processes controlled by the infiltrated computer system.[26]

The ICRC further stated that:

> cyber operations could be used to manipulate civilian infrastructure or services, leading to malfunctions or disruptions not necessarily causing immediate death or

December 1982; UN GA Res. 41/65, Principles Relating to Remote Sensing of the Earth from Outer Space, 3 December 1986; UN GA Resolution 47/68, Principles Relevant to the Use of Nuclear Power Sources in Outer Space, 14 December 1992; UN GA Res. 51/122, Declaration on International Cooperation in the Exploration and Use of Outer Space for the Benefit in the Interest of All States, Taking into Particular Account the Needs of Developing Countries, 13 December 1996; UN GA Res. 59/115, Application of the Concept of the 'launching State', 10 December 2004; UN GA Res. 68/74; UNGA Res. 62/217, Space Debris Mitigation Guidelines of the Committee on the Peaceful Uses of Outer Space, 22 December 2007; UN GA Res. 62/101, Recommendations on Enhancing the Practice of States and International Intergovernmental Organizations in Registering Space Objects, 17 December 2008, UN GA Res. 68/74, Recommendations on National Legislation Relevant to the Peaceful Exploration and Use of Outer Space, 11 December 2013.

23. *See* Chapter 2, section §2.04[G] below.
24. Schmitt (ed.), *supra* no. 1, at 564.
25. US Department of Defense, 'DOD Dictionary of Military and Associated Terms', *supra* no. 16, at 56.
26. ICRC, *International Humanitarian Law and the Challenges of Contemporary Armed Conflicts*, Report 32IC/15/11 (Geneva, October 2015), at 39.

> injury. The effects of such 'bloodless' attacks could obviously be severe – for instance, if power or water supplies were to be interrupted or if a banking system were to be taken down.[27]

As can be seen, depending on the specific context, definitions of the term 'cyber operation' may be closely related to the content of an act constituting a cyberattack. Both on the definitional level, as well as in terms of legal consequences, it is thus crucial to define criteria for establishing the threshold between cyber operations and cyberattacks.[28] The ICRC considers operations that are intended to disable an object – including a computer or a computer network – to constitute an attack under the rules on the conduct of hostilities, regardless of the fact whether the object has been disabled through kinetic or cyber means.[29] Under international humanitarian law,[30] cyber operations amounting to an attack[31] and directed at essential civilian infrastructure in an armed conflict already constitute violations of international humanitarian law, unless such infrastructure is simultaneously used for military purposes in a way that turns it into a military objective.[32]

In aviation, cyber activities directed to access flight control systems and payloads are possible through the following gateways:

- radio communication links (electromagnetic signals);
- air-gapping (as a method of separating systems) of computer networks at ground stations; and
- over the Internet.[33]

In the context of space activities, cyber operations may be directed at space infrastructure, including the ground segment and space objects, as well as the data transmitted through space infrastructure. Both cyber activities and cyber operations must be differentiated from uses of the electromagnetic spectrum which do not necessarily employ cyberspace, such as jamming and spoofing.[34]

For the purposes of this book, the terms 'cyber activities' and 'cyber operations' are various types of activities that make use of cyberspace with the purpose to create effects in the information flows taking place in the cyber realm.

---

27. *Ibid.*, at 39.
28. *See* Chapter 2, section §2.02[G].
29. ICRC, *supra* no. 26, at 37:

> The definition of military objectives is not dependent on the method of warfare used and must be applied to both kinetic and non-kinetic means; the fact that a cyber operation does not lead to the destruction of an attacked object is also irrelevant.

30. Protocol Additional to the Geneva Conventions of 12 August 1949 and Relating to the Protection of Victims of International Armed Conflicts (Protocol I), 8 June 1977, Art. 49(1):

> Definition of attacks and scope of application': 'Attacks' means acts of violence against the adversary, whether in offence or in defence.

31. *See* Chapter 3, section §3.03[B].
32. ICRC, *supra* no. 26, at 40.
33. *See* Chapter 7, section §7.05.
34. *See* the relevant definitions below as well as Chapter 6, section §6.03[B].

[F] Cyber Threat

The term 'cyber threat' is used to depict cyber activities that do not necessarily cross the threshold of a cyberattack but nevertheless have the potential to adversely impact operations or functions or have the potential to cause harm to a system through the use of an information system via unauthorised access, destruction, disclosure, modification of information, and/or denial of service.[35] According to the ISO/IEC definition, a threat is a "potential cause of an unwanted incident, which may result in harm to a system or organization."[36]

[G] Cyberattack

In the context of cybersecurity and the risks posed by malicious cyber activities, the term 'cyberattack' has been widely used to depict cyber activities that may produce negative effects, and which may even involve or rise to the level of use of force.[37]

The general meaning of an attack in an ordinary context can be defined as an "attempt to destroy, expose, alter, disable, steal or gain unauthorized access to or make unauthorized use of an asset."[38] In the cyber discussion, multiple definitions have been used for the term 'cyberattack'.

A definition by the International Business Machines Corporation (IBM) reads: "A cyber attack is deliberate exploitation of computer systems and networks using malicious software (malware) to compromise data or disable operations."[39]

The US Department of Commerce defines the term as:

> An attack, via cyberspace, targeting an enterprise's use of cyberspace for the purpose of disrupting, disabling, destroying, or maliciously controlling a computing environment/infrastructure; or destroying the integrity of the data or stealing controlled information.[40]

In the military context, 'cyberspace attacks' have been defined by the US Department of Defense as:

> Actions taken in cyberspace that create noticeable denial effects (e.g. degradation, disruption, or destruction) in cyberspace or manipulation that leads to denial that appears in a physical domain, and is considered a form of fires.[41]

---

35. *See*, for example, the definition provided by the US Department of Commerce, National Institute of Standards and Technology, Computer Security Resource Center, 'Cyber Threat', https://www.csrc.nist.gov/glossary/term/Cyber-Threat.
36. ISO, International Standard ISO/IEC 27000:2018 'Information Technology – Security Techniques – Information Security – Management Systems – Overview and Vocabulary'.
37. *See*, for a detailed analysis, Chapter 3, section §3.03.
38. ISO, *supra* no. 36.
39. IBM Services, 'Learn about Cyber Attacks and How to Defend Against Them', 2 October 2018, https://www.ibm.com/services/business-continuity/cyber-attack.
40. US Department of Commerce, National Institute of Standards and Technology, 'NIST Special Publication 800-53 Security and Privacy Controls for Federal Information Systems and Organizations' (Rev. 4, April 2013), Appendix B, a. B-6.
41. US Department of Defense, 'DOD Dictionary of Military and Associated Terms', *supra* no. 16.

A distinction can be made between an active and a passive cyberattack based on whether the cyberattack has produced disruption or alteration to a service or an activity.[42] Thereby, an attack resulting in, for example, slowing down or disabling use, denial of service, modification, removal or deletion of data or restricting access, is considered an active attack. Due to the element of disruption, the victim usually becomes aware of the attack.

Passive attacks, in contrast, while making use of information, do not lead to disruption of systems. Examples of passive attacks include information and data gathering, and traffic analysis, resulting in the victim sometimes being unaware.

Examples of cyberattacks include, among others, the following cases. A major cyberattack involved the targeting of Estonian institutions in 2007 and led to collapses of websites of multiple ministries in Estonia. In 2008, in the US, a breach in the US military system was actualised through an infected USB flash drive. In 2009, incidents were recorded in South Korea and the US when thousands of computers were 'hijacked' in order to cause data traffic congestion. The 'Stuxnet' case of 2010 against Iran is one of the most prominent cyberattacks when a cyberweapon addressed at Iran's Nuclear program accessed parts of the control and data systems and caused damage to nuclear centrifuges. The computer network of the Natanz facility had been intruded through the 'Stuxnet' attack causing loss of control over centrifuges of the power plant and causing relevant damage to the facility.[43] In 2013 and 2018, in Singapore, several attacks occurred with the aim to protest against censorship and steal personal data, among others. More recently, it has been reported that a cyberattack might have influenced the outcome of the 2017 presidential elections in the US[44] and the German foreign ministry and the German government, in general, had suffered a continuing, ongoing 'powerful cyberattack' against their computer systems.[45]

For the purposes of this book, based on the existing definitions and examples listed above, the term 'cyberattack' is used to depict cyber operations which may result in death and/or injury of a person/s, and/or in damage to property, be it physical or virtual.

[H] Cybercrime

There is no universally accepted definition of 'cybercrime.' The term is commonly used to depict either crimes enabled by cyberspace (for example, computer fraud) or crimes

42. *See*, On the difference between active and passive cyberattacks, UpGuard 'What Is a Cyber Attack?', https://www.upguard.com/blog/cyber-attacks.
43. BBC News, 'Stuxnet "Hot" Iran Nuclear Plans', 22 November 2010, http://www.bbc.com/news/technology-11809827. *See*, for more on the Stuxnet attack, Chapter 1, section §1.01 and Chapter 3, section §3.03[B].
44. Patricia Zengerle and Doina Chiacu, 'U.S. 2018 Elections "Under Attack" by Russia: U.S. Intelligence Chief', 13 February 2018, https://www.reuters.com/article/us-usa-security-russia-elections/u-s-2018-elections-under-attack-by-russia-u-s-intelligence-chief-idUSKCN1FX1Z8.
45. Thorsten Severin and Andrea Shalal, 'German Government under Cyber Attack, Shores up Defences', 1 March 2018, https://www.reuters.com/article/us-germany-cyber/german-government-under-cyber-attack-shores-up-defenses-idUSKCN1GD4C8.

that take place in cyberspace (for example, malware spread).[46] Interpol uses the term 'pure cybercrime' as:

> crimes against computers and information systems, where the aim is to gain unauthorized access to a device or deny access to a legitimate user.[47]

There is, however, one multilateral treaty which addresses crime in cyberspace: the Convention on Cybercrime of the Council of Europe.[48] Known as the 'Budapest Convention', it is, in fact, the first binding international instrument to regulate 'cybercrime' and States' behaviour in the context of cybersecurity (*lex specialis*), and it obliges State Parties to criminalise certain cyber activities by individuals.

Although the term 'cybercrime' is not explicitly defined in the Budapest Convention, from a reading of the Preamble, it may be broadly understood as "the committal of criminal offences through the use of computer networks and/or electronic information," or even more specifically, as any "action directed against the confidentiality, integrity and availability of computer systems, networks and computer data as well as the misuse of such systems, networks and data."

[I] Weapon and Cyberweapon

As far as the general term 'weapon' is concerned, there is currently no definition thereof in international law. Rather, the extensive body of international law related to weapons opts to create different categories of weapons.[49] However, some guidance has been offered within the scope of international aviation:

> The term 'weapons' has not been defined but its interpretation in practice should not cause any difficulties when the ordinary meaning of the word is considered; it would include guns, machine guns, cannons, missiles or targeted drones or any other object or substance that can damage or destroy an aircraft in flight.[50]

In the emerging legal discussion and regulatory attempts on cybersecurity, the notion 'cyberweapon' has become relevant in the context of cyber warfare. While currently no legal definition of 'cyberweapon' has been provided, the Tallinn Manual, which is an academic resource analysing the international law applicable to cyber operations and cyber warfare,[51] addresses the question as to what constitutes a cyberweapon as follows:

> cyber weapons are 'cyber means of warfare' that are by design, use, or intended use capable of causing either (i) injury to, or death of, persons; or (ii) damage to,

---

46. INTERPOL, 'Cybercrime', https://www.interpol.int/Crime-areas/Cybercrime/Cybercrime; Ian Walden, *Computer Crimes and Digital Investigations*, Second Edition (Oxford University Press, 2016), at 19-26.
47. *Ibid.*
48. Convention on Cybercrime (opened for signature 23 November 2001, entered into force 1 July 2004) ETS 185. *See* Chapter 3, section §3.02[B].
49. *See*, for related information, Chapter 3, section §3.03 and Chapter 7, section §7.02.
50. Michael Milde, *International Air Law and ICAO*, Third Edition (Eleven, 2016), at 61.
51. *See* Chapter 3, section §3.02[C].

> or destruction of, objects, that is, causing the consequences required for qualification of a cyber operation as an attack.[52]

This definition includes any cyber operation that causes injury, death, damage or destruction.

Whether malicious cyber activities constitute a weapon depends on the actual outcome, and they cannot be classified without looking at the specific circumstances of each case. This means that cases in which a cyberattack causes injury, death, damage or destruction should not be equalled to a cyber activity which replaces a signal, e.g., through spoofing, but does not cause substantial injury.

At the same time, however, it should not be precluded that any cyberattack may be classified as a cyberweapon. In any event, this classification would require a cyber operation to fulfil certain conditions, such as having the capability to damage or destroy.

§2.03 RELEVANT AVIATION TERMINOLOGY

[A] Aircraft

In 1967, ICAO provided a revised definition of the term 'aircraft' in Annex 7 to the Convention on International Civil Aviation (Chicago Convention) as:

> Any machine that can derive support in the atmosphere from the reactions of the air other than the reactions of the air against the earth's surface.[53]

Thus, if the vehicle uses a source of power and achieves lift from its fixed wings, then it shall be classified as an 'aircraft' for the purpose of the Chicago Convention. Furthermore, a vehicle is to be considered as an aircraft if it is capable of deriving support, rather than if it constantly derives support from the air at all times.[54]

[B] Airspace

The airspace comprises the area above the land and territorial waters of a State,[55] including the high seas.[56] Article 1 is a recognition of the customary international law (CIL) principle of state sovereignty over the adjacent airspace:

---

52. Schmitt (ed.), *supra* no. 1, at 452.
53. Other Annexes to the Chicago Convention define aircraft identically. *See*, Convention on International Civil Aviation, 61 Stat. 1180, 15 U.N.T.S. 295, Chicago, US, 7 December 1944, Annex 2, 6, and 8.
54. ICAO/UNOOSA Working Group, *Report on the Legal Regime Applicable to Suborbital Flights* (29 September 2019). Definition provided by Benjamyn I. Scott as a member of the Working Group.
55. Convention on International Civil Aviation, 61 Stat. 1180, 15 U.N.T.S. 295, Chicago, US, 7 December 1944, Art. 2. *See* Chapter 7, section §7.01. *See also*, for more information on the high seas, Convention on the Law of the Sea (entered into force 16 November 1994), 1833 UNTS 397, 21 ILM 1261 (1982).
56. Chicago Convention, Art. 12 and Annex 2 on Rules of the Air. *See*, Military and Paramilitary Activities in and Against Nicaragua (Nicaragua v. U.S.), I.C.J. Rep. 14, 111 (1986).

> The contracting States recognise that every State has complete and exclusive sovereignty over the airspace above its territory.

The airspace is divided into different classifications, as defined in Annex 11, with defined dimensions specified in national law. Class A airspace is the highest airspace which, for example, in the US extends from 18,000 feet (ca. 5,500 m) mean sea level (MSL) to FL600 which is ca. 60,000 feet (ca, 18,000 m) MSL. As a result, while no vertical limit has been established in international law,[57] airspace can be interpreted as going at least to the highest point of controlled airspace.[58]

[C] Aviation Safety Versus Aviation Security

The Chicago Convention has had a strong focus on safety. However, safety has not been the sole focus of aviation regulation at an international level as ICAO, as established by Part II of the Chicago Convention, has five strategic objectives:

- Aviation Safety.
- Air Navigation Capacity and Efficiency.
- Security and Facilitation.
- Economic Development.
- Environmental Protection.

As noted in section §2.02[C] above, security is also a competency of ICAO. There is, therefore, a distinction between aviation safety and aviation security. If there is a classification of cybersecurity as a branch of security, this could result in the other strategic objectives being overlooked. This is especially important for safety which often exists in its own regulatory silo separate from security. However, as cyberattacks become more prevalent, as more and new vulnerabilities manifest and as regulations develop, this distinction may no longer be suitable. While Chapter 7 will look at the regulatory consequences and potential solutions, this subchapter will look at the definitional issue.

Linguistically, 'security' and 'safety', although not always distinguished (such as in French, where 'securité' is used for both 'safety' and 'security'), mean different things in practice.

This is evident from the definitions provided in the Annexes to the Chicago Convention. Annex 17 defines 'security' as:

> Safeguarding civil aviation against acts of unlawful interference. This objective is achieved by a combination of measures and human and material resources.[59]

57. Similarly, there is no legally set 'boundary' or definition of outer space. *See* Chapter 2, section §2.04[H].
58. ICAO/UNOOSA Working Group, *supra* no. 54. Definition provided by Benjamyn I. Scott as a member of the Working Group.
59. Annex 17 to the Chicago Convention, Security: Safeguarding International Civil Aviation Against Acts of Unlawful Interference, Tenth Edition, April 2017.

This highlights that 'security' based measures should attempt to combat unlawful interference.

Alternatively, Annex 19 defines 'safety' as:

> The State in which risks associated with aviation activities, related to, or in direct support of the operation of aircraft, are reduced and controlled to an acceptable level.[60]

Instead of focusing on combating unlawful interference, safety is concerned with producing measures that reduce 'risks' to an acceptable level. The 'risks' are those connected to the operation of the aircraft, rather than external factors like unlawful interference.

Safety and security mean different things and are consequently dealt with under different regulatory instrument:

(1) Safety:
 - The remaining Annexes.
 - Chicago Convention Part I.
 - Regulation 2018/1139.

(2) Security:
 - Parts of Annex 9 on Facilitation.[61]
 - Annex 17 on Security: Safeguarding International Civil Aviation Against Acts of Unlawful Interference.[62]
 - Criminal Law Treaties.
 - Regulation 300/2008.

By observing the usage of the terms in air law, it becomes clear that they are used to denote different systems of rights and obligations. As a result, a cybersecurity measure will be regulated and implemented differently depending on whether it is perceived as a safety or security matter.

[D] Standards and Recommended Practices

The Standards and Recommended Practices (SARPs) have been adopted by the ICAO Council under the provisions of the Chicago Convention and are defined in Annex 2 of the Chicago Convention. 'Standards' have been defined as follows:

> Any specification for physical characteristics, configuration, matériel, performance, personnel or procedure, the uniform application of which is recognized as necessary for the safety or regularity of international air navigation and to which Contracting States will conform in accordance with the Convention; in the event of

60. Annex 19 to the Chicago Convention, Safety Management, Second Edition, July 2016.
61. Annex 9 to the Chicago Convention, Facilitation, Fourteenth Edition, October 2015.
62. Annex 17 to the Chicago Convention, *supra* no. 59.

impossibility of compliance, notification to the Council is compulsory under Article 38.[63]

'Recommended Practices' are:

> Any specification for physical characteristics, configuration, matériel, performance, personnel or procedure, the uniform application of which is recognized as desirable in the interests of safety, regularity or efficiency of international air navigation, and to which Contracting States will endeavour to conform in accordance with the Convention.[64]

The legal status of SARPs must be kept in mind when applying them. They do not form part of the Chicago Convention but only stem from it.[65] As a consequence, they do not have treaty status, but rather constitute secondary/quasi-legislative acts of an international organisation.

[E] Interference in Aviation

In the context of aviation, the term 'unlawful interference' is prominently used in Annex 17 on Security[66] as:

> acts or attempted acts such as to jeopardize the safety of civil aviation, including but not limited to:
>
> - unlawful seizure of aircraft,
> - destruction of an aircraft in service,
> - hostage-taking on board aircraft or on aerodromes,
> - forcible intrusion on board an aircraft, at an airport or on the premises of an aeronautical facility,
> - introduction on board an aircraft or at an airport of a weapon or hazardous device or material intended for criminal purposes,
> - use of an aircraft in service for the purpose of causing death, serious bodily injury, or serious damage to property or the environment,
> - communication of false information such as to jeopardize the safety of an aircraft in flight or on the ground, of passengers, crew, ground personnel or the general public, at an airport or on the premises of a civil aviation facility.

The term 'interference' is not only contained in Annex 17 but also in the safety Annexes. For example, part IIIB of Annex 8 on Airworthiness of Aircraft utilises the term 'electromagnetic interference', which is to be understood as lawful but unwanted interference of an electromagnetic nature.[67] In other words, it refers to accidental interference of an electromagnetic nature and not a cyberattack.

63. Annex 2 to the Chicago Convention, Rules of the Air, Tenth Edition, November 2016.
64. *Ibid.*
65. *See*, for example, Pablo Mendes de Leon, *Introduction to Air Law*, Tenth Edition (Kluwer, 2017), at 24.
66. Annex 17 to the Chicago Convention, *supra* no. 59.
67. Annex 8 to the Chicago Convention, Airworthiness of Aircraft, Eleventh Edition, July 2010.

§2.04 RELEVANT OUTER SPACE AND SATELLITE SERVICES TERMINOLOGY

[A] Electromagnetic Attack

An electromagnetic attack can be defined as "the use of electromagnetic energy for offensive purposes, including the use of weapons that primarily use electromagnetic or directed energy for destruction (lasers, radio frequency weapons, and particle beams)."[68]

The most common forms are jamming and spoofing, which take place in the radio spectrum, which is the part of the electromagnetic spectrum used by radio communications. Unlike kinetic ones, electromagnetic attacks may be reversible. They do not necessarily entail the physical destruction or harm of the target, but only the temporary disruption, denial or deception of radio signals.

[B] Electromagnetic Interference

The ITU legal framework defines interference as:

> the effect of unwanted energy [...] upon reception in a radiocommunication system, manifested by any performance degradation, misinterpretation, or loss of information [...].[69]

According to the US Department of Defense, electromagnetic interference is:

> Any electromagnetic disturbance, induced intentionally or unintentionally, that interrupts, obstructs, or otherwise degrades or limits the effective performance of electronics and electrical equipment.[70]

Electromagnetic interferences, however, are not necessarily harmful. They can also be permissible, namely when they are contained in certain quantitative and sharing criteria defined in the Radio Regulations or ITU-R Recommendations,[71] and accepted, namely when they surpass such thresholds but have been agreed upon between two or more administrations.[72]

Interference becomes harmful - and thus, in principle, prohibited - when it "seriously degrades, obstructs, or repeatedly interrupts a radiocommunication service operating in accordance with the Radio Regulations."[73]

68. NATO, NATO Term, Record 19644 'Electronic Attack'.
69. ITU Radio Regulations Articles, Edition of 2016, https://www.itu.int/pub/R-REG-RR, Art. 1.166.
70. US Department of Defense, 'DOD Dictionary of Military and Associated Terms', *supra* no. 16, at 70.
71. ITU Radio Regulations, *supra* no. 69, Art. 1.167.
72. *Ibid.*, Art. 1.168.
73. Constitution and Convention of the International Telecommunication Union adopted by the 2014 Plenipotentiary Conference, Annex 1003; ITU Radio Regulations, *supra* no. 69, Art. 1.169. *See* Chapter 2, section §2.04[D] below.

[C] Electromagnetic Spectrum

A definition has been provided by the ITU as follows:

> The range of frequencies of electromagnetic radiation from zero to infinity that is divided into 26 alphabetically designated bands.[74]

While this is a purely technical definition, it does have relevance for understanding the applicable law within the context of electromagnetic interference issues.

[D] Harmful Interference

In the ITU Radio Regulations, harmful interference is defined as:

> interference which endangers the functioning of a radio navigation service or of other safety services or seriously degrades, obstructs, or repeatedly interrupts a radiocommunication service operating in accordance with Radio Regulations.[75]

In the regulation of the allocation of frequencies, Article 45 of the ITU Constitution[76] prohibits only harmful electromagnetic interference, but not unauthorised cyber activities. According to Article I(2) of the ITU Constitution, the ITU shall:

> coordinate efforts to eliminate harmful interference between radio stations of different countries and to improve the use made of the radio-frequency spectrum for radio-communication services.

Harmful interference provisions do not address operators directly, but rather bind Member States to the duty of ensuring compliance by operators.[77] In particular, Article 45 of the ITU Constitution obliges the Member States to require the agencies they authorised to "operate in such a manner as not to cause harmful interference."[78] Rather than a strict prohibition, thus, it is rather formulated as a duty of prevention.

In some respects, however, such activities can be compared to acts covered by the prohibition of intervention as contained in Article 2(1) of the UN Charter which interdicts any non-forceful interference into the domestic affairs of the State.[79]

[E] Jamming

Jamming is a type of electromagnetic interference that consists in disrupting the communication with a satellite by overpowering the signals being sent to or from it

74. US Department of Defense, 'DOD Dictionary of Military and Associated Terms', *supra* no. 16.
75. ITU Radio Regulations, *supra* no. 69, Art. 1.169.
76. ITU Constitution and Convention, *supra* no. 73.
77. *Ibid.*, Art. 6.
78. *Ibid.*, Art. 45.
79. *See* Chapter 3.

with the use of a signal at the same frequency and at higher power. The receiver, therefore, is no longer able to accurately recover the legitimate signal.[80]

[F] Launching State

The term 'launching State' is a key term in space law as it provides the connection for imposing liability[81] to a certain State for damage caused by a space object and therefore establishes legal consequences for space activities. It is defined in the Liability Convention[82] and the Registration Convention[83] as "a State that launches or procures the launching of a space object, or from whose territory or facility a space object is launched."[84] The practices for establishing the liable State are complex as, for one particular launch, there can be multiple launching States. In these cases, the launching States are jointly and severally liable for any damage caused[85] and must agree on the (one) State that registers the space object.[86]

Not only States fulfil the requirements of Article I(c) Liability Convention and Article I(a) Registration Convention as also intergovernmental organisations (e.g., European Space Agency (ESA)) can also be considered as 'launching States'.

[G] Malicious Cyber Activities Against Space Infrastructure

Malicious cyber activities are unauthorised infringements targeting computer systems without the consent of the owner or the operator. They can include various intrusions, such as jamming, spoofing and hacking of communication networks; targeting control systems or mission packages; and attacks on the ground infrastructure such as satellite control centres. Possible cyber threats against space infrastructure may be addressed against segments on Earth as well as in outer space and can be both unintentional (e.g., electromagnetic interference) or intentional (e.g., jamming, cyberattacks and anti-satellite weapons (ASAT)).[87]

The following possible harmful cyber operations can be addressed at space infrastructure:

- Prohibited retrieval of data/information.
- Manipulation of data.
- Interference with transmission flow.
- Partial or complete software and hardware destruction.
- Manipulation of satellite controls, possibly causing third-party damage.

---

80. *See*, on the different types of jamming, Chapter 6, section §6.03[B].
81. Outer Space Treaty, *supra* no. 22, Art. VII and Liability Convention, *supra* no. 22, Arts II and III.
82. Liability Convention, *supra* no. 22.
83. Registration Convention, *supra* no. 22.
84. Liability Convention, *supra* no. 22, Art. I(c) and Registration Convention, *supra* no. 22, Art. I(a).
85. Liability Convention, *supra* no. 22, Art. V(1).
86. Registration Convention, *supra* no. 22, Art. II(2).
87. US Department of Defense, US Joint Chiefs of Staff, 'Joint Publication 3-14, Information Operations', https://www.jcs.mil/Portals/36/Documents/Doctrine/pubs/jp3_14.pdf, at viii.

- Unauthorised seizure of the flight control of a space object.
- Unauthorised seizure of the payload control of a space object.

Actors may include "well-resourced organized criminal elements seeking financial gain; terrorist groups wishing to promote their causes, even up to the catastrophic level of cascading satellite collisions; and individual hackers who want to fanfare their skills."[88]

[H] Outer Space

While there is no legally binding definition of outer space, it is commonly recognised as starting at an altitude of about 100-118 km above MSL.[89] Theoretically, it could be perceived as the (physical) space beyond the Earth's atmosphere, meaning that outer space encompasses the whole universe. However, following a more practical approach to not overstretch the applicability of human-made normative rules to domains in outer space which are not (yet) accessible for human activities, it can be perceived as those parts of the Solar System which are used for human space activities.

Three States, respectively Australia, Kazakhstan, and Denmark, have referred in their national space laws to a precise geographical delimitation between airspace and outer space, that is at 100 km above sea level. Accordingly, their relevant domestic legislation applies to space activities that take place from an altitude of 100 km upwards.[90]

[I] Space Activities

The body of international space law does not contain a definition of the term 'space activities'. Typically, such activities include the launch and operation of satellites, probes, platforms and space stations as well as scientific experiments and data transmission from and to space objects.[91] Article I of the Outer Space Treaty (OST) introduces three types of space activities and uses the terms 'use', 'exploration' and 'scientific investigation'.

Generally, space activities can be understood as all human activities that take place in or are aimed at outer space. They include the use, the exploration and the scientific investigation in outer space and celestial bodies for civil or military purposes. Moreover, not only activities taking place entirely in space but also activities taking

88. David Livingstone and Patricia Lewis, *Space, the Final Frontier for Cybersecurity?*, Project: International Security Department, https://www.chathamhouse.org/publication/space-final-frontier-cybersecurity, at 2.
89. Stephan Hobe, *Space Law* (Nomos, 2019), at 13-15.
90. ICAO/UNOOSA Working Group, *supra* no. 54. Definition provided by Rada Popova as a member of the Working Group.
91. Michael Gerhard, 'Article VI OST', *in* Hobe/Schmidt-Tedd/Schrogl (eds), *Cologne Commentary on Space Law Volume I* (Heymanns, 2009), at 109 et seq.

place on the Earth, e.g., at a ground station, if predominantly addressed and intended for outer space, can be considered to be space activities.[92]

Cyber operations could arguably be regarded as 'use' of outer space as the OST grants governments (Article I) and private persons (Article VI) the freedom to exercise economic and non-economic activities in outer space and on celestial bodies, including the exploitation of space resources.[93] Specific uses are only excluded if they are explicitly prohibited in the space legislation – such is the case, for example, with regard to the limitations posed by Article III and IV of the OST.

[J] Space Infrastructure

Generally, infrastructure is understood as a complex encompassing term:

> The basic physical and organizational structures and facilities (e.g. buildings, roads, power supplies) needed for the operation of a society or enterprise.[94]

With regard to space activities, infrastructure includes a myriad of facilities, e.g., launchpad, ground stations, launching and servicing facilities and related equipment devices and parts, including the space objects (satellite-based components) together with the ground and user segment as well.[95]

Space-based systems are an essential component of the worldwide economy and everyday life[96] as nowadays they enable a wide scope of applications, ranging from broadband Internet and television (TV) broadcasting to financial transactions, transport systems and emergency services.[97]

Despite not having the rank of autonomous critical infrastructure in most national security policies, they constitute the backbone for the functioning of several other infrastructures and are a key element of modern society. It is thus common to refer to space-based systems as 'space infrastructure'. The components of such systems

92. Bin Cheng, 'Revisited: International Responsibility, National Activities and the Appropriate State', 27 *Journal of Space Law* 7-32 (1998), at 19; Frans von der Dunk, *Private Enterprise and Public Interest in the European Spacescape* (Leiden, 1998), at 13; Henry A. Wassenbergh, 'An International Institutional Framework for Private Space Activities', XXIII *Annals of Air and Space Law* (1997), at 529, 533; Henry A. Wassenbergh, 'The Law Governing International Private Commercial Activities', 12 *Journal of Space Law* 97 (1983), at 108.
93. Stephan Hobe, 'Article I OST', *in* Stephan Hobe, Bernhard Schmidt-Tedd and Kai-Uwe Schrogl (eds), *Cologne Commentary on Space Law Volume 1* (Heymanns, 2009), at 35.
94. Oxford Online Dictionary, Definition of 'Infrastructure', https://www.lexico.com/en/definition/infrastructure.
95. *See also*, for the definition of 'aeronautical and space vehicles', 'Definitions', US Code, 51 U.S. Code §20103.
96. *See*, generally, US General Accounting Office, 'Critical Infrastructure Protection: Commercial Satellite Security Should be More Fully Addressed', https://www.gao.gov/new.items/d02781.pdf.
97. *See*, for a survey of satellite applications in modern society, Olaf Acker, Florian Potscher and Thierry Lefort, 'Why Satellites Matter: The Relevance of Commercial Satellites in the 21st Century – A Perspective 2012-2020', https://www.esoa.net/Resources/Why-Satellites-Matter-Full-Report.pdf.

can be grouped into the following categories: communication satellites; location, navigation and timing satellites; remote sensing satellites; and weather forecast satellites.[98]

[K] Space Objects and Space Assets

The definition of the term 'space object' is provided in Article I(d) of the Liability Convention and Article I(b) of the Registration Convention and reads:

> The term 'space object' includes component parts of a space object as well as its launch vehicle and parts thereof.

Thus, under international space law, a 'space object' is not only a man-made object, launched or attempted to be launched into orbit but also its component parts (active or non-active) and its launch vehicle. This definition is, in fact, a circular one,[99] as it defines a space object by the space object itself. The late Bin Cheng provided a definition reading as follows:

> any object which humans launch, attempt to launch or have launched into outer space. It embraces satellites, spacecraft, space vehicles, equipment, facilities, stations, installations and other constructions, including their components, as well as their launch vehicles and parts thereof.[100]

An attempt has, moreover, been made to provide more clarity through a definition of a term strongly related to and used synonymously for space objects: 'space assets'. This notion has been defined in the Space Assets Protocol[101] to the Cape Town Convention[102] as follows:

> any man-made uniquely identifiable asset in space or designed to be launched into space, and comprising
>
> (i) a spacecraft, such as a satellite, space station, space module, space capsule, space vehicle or reusable launch vehicle, whether or not including a space asset falling within (ii) or (iii) below;
> (ii) a payload (whether telecommunications, navigation, observation, scientific or otherwise) in respect of which a separate registration may be effected in accordance with the regulations; or
> (iii) a part of a spacecraft or payload such as a transponder, in respect of which a separate registration may be effected in accordance with the regulations,

98. Linda L. Haller and Melvin S. Sakazaki, 'Commercial Space and United States National Security', prepared for the Commission to Assess US National Security Space Management and Organization, https://www.fas.org/spp/eprint/article06.html. *See* Chapter 6, section §6.02[B].
99. *See*, for example, Frans von der Dunk, 'Defining Subject Matter under Space Law: Near Earth Objects Versus Space Objects Versus Space Objects', Proceedings of the 51st Colloquium on the Law of Outer Space (2008), at 293.
100. Bin Cheng, *Studies in International Space Law* (Clarendon Press, 1997), at 464.
101. Protocol to the Convention on International Interests in Mobile Equipment on Matters Specific to Space Assets, adopted on 9 March 2012 (Space Assets Protocol).
102. Cape Town Convention on International Interests in Mobile Equipment, 2307 UNTS 285, adopted on 16 November 2001, entered into force 1 March 2006.

together with all installed, incorporated or attached accessories, parts and equipment and all data, manuals and records relating thereto.[103]

The definition of 'space assets' builds upon and extends the definition of 'space object' to enumerate specific types of spacecraft and payload, including parts thereof that are man-made and designed to be or already launched in outer space.

Moreover, the term 'space object' has been referred to and/or defined in a number of national space laws:

- Australia: "'space object' means a thing consisting of:
  (a) a launch vehicle; and
  (b) a payload (if any) that the launch vehicle is to carry into or back from an area beyond the distance of 100 km above mean sea level; or any part of such a thing, even if:
  (c) the part is to go only some of the way towards or back from an area beyond the distance of 100 km above mean sea level; or
  (d) the part results from the separation of a payload or payloads from a launch vehicle after launch."
- Austria: "an object launched or intended to be launched into outer space, including its components."
- Belgium: "any object launched or intended to be launched into outer space, including the material elements composing that object."
- France: The French Space Operations Act does not provide a definition of a 'space object'. However, the Technical Regulation to which it is referred for delivering authorisation under the French Space Operations Act states that 'space object' means "any man made object, functional or not, during launch time, its time spent in extra-atmospheric space or return, including the elements of a launcher placed into orbit."
- The US national legislation differentiates between:
  - 'space vehicles', defined as "satellites, and other space vehicles, manned and unmanned, together with related equipment, devices, components, and parts." and
  - 'launch vehicles', defined as "a vehicle built to operate in, or place a payload or human beings in, outer space; and (B) a suborbital rocket."[104]

Despite the lack of a comprehensive legal definition, the notion of 'space object' is of fundamental importance within international space law. A State may face liability claims for damage caused by a 'space object' to persons or property in outer space or in airspace and on the surface of the Earth if it qualifies as a 'launching State' of that object. Furthermore, pursuant to Article VIII of the OST, registered space objects are the 'link' for exercising jurisdiction in the sovereignty-free domain of outer space.

Space objects are subject to the jurisdiction and control of the State on whose registry an object launched into outer space is carried.[105] The concept of jurisdiction and control provides that the State of registry has full authority over the space object which is on its registry. It has prescriptive and enforcement jurisdiction over such

103. Space Assets Protocol, Art. I(2)(k).
104. ICAO/UNOOSA Working Group, *supra* no. 54. Definition provided by Rada Popova as a member of the Working Group.
105. Outer Space Treaty, *supra* no. 22, Art. VIII.

space objects to which it applies its law while it is in outer space. There may be, however, multiple jurisdictions, e.g., on board the ISS, where in addition to the provisions of the State of registry principles of the personal jurisdiction of the astronauts on board the station may also be applicable.

[L] Spoofing

Spoofing is a type of electromagnetic interference which is in many aspects similar to jamming. Spoofing also uses the radio spectrum and is aimed at interfering with the satellite's regular transmissions whereby the wanted, true signal, is not corrupted, but mimicked with a false one, with the purpose of introducing false or corrupted information into the communication system.[106]

§2.05 GENERAL TERMS

[A] Critical Infrastructure

There is no internationally agreed definition of the term 'critical infrastructure'. It emerged in the late 1990s in the US, when the Marsh Report and the subsequent executive order EO-13010 provided the first definition of infrastructure as "a network of independent, mostly privately-owned, man-made systems that function collaboratively and synergistically to produce and distribute a continuous flow of essential goods and services."[107]

The current US description of critical infrastructure includes:

> systems and assets, whether physical or virtual, so vital to the United States that the incapacity or destruction of those systems and assets would have a debilitating impact on security, national economic security, national public health or safety, or any combination of those matters.[108]

It has also been defined as "[e]ssential services and related assets that underpin American society and serve as the backbone of the nation's economy, security, and health."[109]

Despite its domestic origin, such definition can be considered as sufficiently paradigmatic for general considerations. Examples of critical infrastructure sectors – relevant to most modern States – include but are not limited to key commercial facilities, power grids, chemical industries, dams, emergency services, telecommunications, government facilities, transportation systems, banking and finance, and

106. *See*, for a detailed account, Chapter 6, section §6.03[C].
107. Executive Order EO-13010 (1996), Critical Infrastructure Protection, as Amended by Executive Order 13077 (1998); Further Amendment to Executive Order 13010, Critical Infrastructure Protection; *see also*, Robert T. Marsch, 'Report of the President's Commission on Critical Infrastructure Protection', https://www.fas.org/sgp/library/pccip.pdf.
108. US Patriot Act of 2001, 42 US Code 5195c(e), section 1016(e).
109. National Institute of Standards and Technology, 'Internal Report 8183', September 2017, https://nvlpubs.nist.gov/nistpubs/ir/2017/NIST.IR.8183.pdf.

defence industrial bases.[110] Critical infrastructure sectors are characterised by cross-sector interdependence, mixed public-private ownership and cross-border synergies.

In other words, they are the totality of assets and networks essential to the functioning of the economy and society.

[B] Denial of Service

Denial of service refers to an action or series of actions that prevents any part of a system from functioning in accordance with its intended purpose. This includes any action that causes unauthorised destruction, modification, or delay of service.[111]

[C] Internet of Things

According to the Cisco Internet Business Solutions Group, Internet of Things (IoT) is "simply the point in time when more 'things or objects' were connected to the Internet than people."[112] The Cambridge Dictionary defines it as: "objects with computing devices in them that are able to connect to each other and exchange data using the internet."[113] According to Techopedia, IoT is:

> a computing concept that describes the idea of everyday physical objects being connected to the internet and being able to identify themselves to other devices. The term is closely identified with RFID as the method of communication, although it also may include other sensor technologies, wireless technologies or QR codes.[114]

The IoT is significant because an object that can represent itself digitally becomes something greater than the object itself. No longer does the object relate just to its user, but it is now connected to surrounding objects and database data. When many objects act in unison, they are known as having 'ambient intelligence'.

110. *See*, on the Internet as autonomous critical infrastructure, Georg Kerschischnig, *Cyberthreats and International Law* (Eleven, 2012), at 48-50.
111. The Consultative Committee for Space Data Systems, 'Security Guide for Mission Planners', Informational Report CCSDS 350.7-G-1, October 2011, at 2-1.
112. Dave Evans, 'The Internet of Things, How the Next Evolution of the Internet Is Changing Everything', April 2011, https://www.cisco.com/c/dam/en_us/about/ac79/docs/innov/IoT_IBSG_0411FINAL.pdf, at 2.
113. Cambridge Dictionary, 'The Internet of Things', https://www.dictionary.cambridge.org/dictionary/english/internet-of-things.
114. Techopedia, 'What Does Internet of Things (IoT) Mean?', https://www.techopedia.com/definition/28247/internet-of-things-iot.

[D] Liability

The notion of 'liability' can be succinctly defined as the duty to indemnify a person, with whom there is a relationship based on the law of contract or of tort, who has suffered damage in one form or another.[115]

In aviation, liability stems from both a relationship based on the law of obligations and a relationship based on the law of tort. Whereas with regard to air carrier passengers, liability stems from the law of obligations, with regard to third parties, it stems from the law of tort. In both cases, passengers and third parties have a right to be indemnified for the damage caused to them.[116]

In space law, liability is borne by the launching State whose object the damage stems from. The Liability Convention regulates two types of liability:

- absolute liability for damage caused "to persons or property on the surface of the Earth or to aircraft in flight";[117] and
- fault-based liability for damage caused by the space object of a launching State "elsewhere than on the surface of the Earth to a space object of one launching State or to persons or property on board such a space object."[118]

In the context of cybersecurity of space objects, liability can be invoked when through a malicious cyber operation, a space object is used to cause damage to persons or property in outer space, on Earth or to aircraft in flight.[119]

[E] Malware

For the purposes of this book, the notion 'malware' is to be understood as:

> Software or firmware intended to perform an unauthorized process that will have adverse impact on the confidentiality, integrity, or availability of an information system. A virus, worm, Trojan horse, or other code-based entity that infects a host. Spyware and some forms of adware are also examples of malicious code.[120]

[F] Resilience of Information Systems

The US Department of Commerce has defined resilience as:

> The ability of an information system to continue to: (i) operate under adverse conditions or stress, even if in a degraded or debilitated state, while maintaining

115. *See*, for an analysis of the concept of 'liability', Martin Hogg, *Obligations: Law and Language* (Cambridge University Press, 2017), at 12-72.
116. *See*, on aviation liability in cases of cyberattacks, Chapter 8.
117. Liability Convention, *supra* no. 22, Art. II.
118. *Ibid.*, Art. III.
119. *See* Chapter 5, section §5.04[B].
120. US Department of Commerce, *supra* no. 40, Appendix B, at B-13.

> essential operational capabilities; and (ii) recover to an effective operational posture in a time frame consistent with mission needs.[121]

The term 'resilience' in cybersecurity is mostly used to describe the ability of an information system to support the functions necessary for successful operation even in cases of periods of reduced capability and across a wider range of scenarios, conditions, and threats, in spite of hostile action or adverse conditions.

[G] Vulnerability

Vulnerability of the electromagnetic spectrum has been defined as:

> The characteristics of a system that cause it to suffer a definite degradation (incapability to perform the designated mission) as a result of having been subjected to a certain level of electromagnetic environmental effects.[122]

According to the ISO/IEC definition, vulnerability is the "weakness of an asset or control that can be exploited by one or more threats."[123] Vulnerability in the context of cybersecurity is the weakness in an information system, or cryptographic system, or components (e.g., system security procedures, hardware design, internal controls) that could be exploited to violate the system security policy.

121. *Ibid.*, at B-11; US Department of Defense, US Joint Chiefs of Staff, 'Joint Publication 3-14, Information Operations', 10 April 2018, https://www.jcs.mil/Portals/36/Documents/Doctrine/pubs/jp3_14.pdf, at I-8 et seq.
122. US Department of Defense, 'DOD Dictionary of Military and Associated Terms', *supra* no. 16, at 70.
123. International Organisation for Standardisation, International Standard ISO/IEC 27000:2018 'Information Technology – Security Techniques – Information Security – Management Systems Overview and Vocabulary'.

CHAPTER 3
Cyberattacks from an International Law Perspective

From a brief history of the various cyberattacks detailed in Chapter 1, two observations can be drawn. First, cyberattacks are very much a reality and have been so for several decades. Second, many a time cyberattacks seem to carry an international dimension with them. From the examples listed in the above-mentioned chapter, it emanates that cyberattacks appear to be directly or indirectly designed, or effected, or designed and effected by one or several States on others.

While this should not be taken to mean that cyberattacks are never designed, effected, or designed and effected by individuals on the basis of a private agenda, it should be nonetheless taken to mean that, at present, cyberattacks seem to be predominantly used as a new method of warfare which States are resorting to.

In this light, it is apt to undertake an analysis of how cyberattacks are treated, if at all, under the law which operates outside and between States – international law.[1] Further, since cyberattacks are seemingly a new method of warfare, this analysis shall focus on the branch of international law which regulates conflict.

The branch of international law which regulates conflict is bifurcated into the law which determines when resort to armed force is permissible, that is, the *jus ad bellum*, and the law which governs the conduct of hostilities during armed conflict, that is, the *jus in bello*.[2]

Although this chapter commences by providing a general overview of both these sets of law and of the legislative landscape which relates to cyberattacks, it shall proceed by focusing only on the treatment of cyberattacks under the *jus ad bellum*.

The primary reason for this is that, from the analysis of cyberattacks, it transpires that the cyberattacks documented to date have not been employed in conflicts.

1. Malcolm N. Shaw, *International Law*, Seventh Edition (Cambridge University Press, 2014), at 1.
2. *See* Chapter 3, section §3.02.

Certainly, this does not mean or imply that cyberattacks cannot or will never be employed therein.

A secondary reason for treating cyberattacks under the *jus ad bellum* only relates to the fact that, as shall be seen below, a major question requiring particular attention is that of whether and when a cyberattack amounts to use, or threat of use, of force in breach of the Charter of the UN (UN Charter).

This chapter shall then proceed to deal with the corollary question of whether and when a cyberattack may be considered to amount to an 'armed attack'. This question is corollary to the one before it because a cyberattack which amounts to use, or threat of use, of force does not automatically allow a State to respond to it; a State can do so only when a cyberattack amounts to an 'armed attack'.

Following these two questions, this chapter shall analyse a third question that asks whether and when States may be held responsible and liable for cyberattacks. This chapter shall then draw to a close by analysing legal initiatives and policies undertaken by international and regional organisations with regard to the regulation of cyberattacks.

The intention of this chapter is to set the scene for an analysis of how cyberattacks are treated specifically under international air, space, and telecommunications law, which shall be conducted in detail in the next chapters.

§3.01 SOURCES OF PUBLIC INTERNATIONAL LAW

Public international law is primarily concerned with the legal regulation of the international interaction of States which are both 'sovereign', in that they are not subject to any superior authority, and 'equal', in that, from the smallest to the largest, they are all symmetrically sovereign.[3]

In this respect, one cannot ignore the fact that, upon entering the realm of cyberspace, the principle of sovereignty, expressed in and by the supreme authority within a territory,[4] experiences a dilution of sorts.

The principle of sovereignty experiences a dilution of sorts because, while it is intimately linked with territory, 'cyberspace' is a transnational, man-made, global environment without a solid territorial origin.[5] The legal consequence of such a lack of territory in cyberspace is that, effectively, States can only exercise their sovereignty over the relevant cyberspace components in the physical world.

States can only exercise their sovereignty over the territory wherein cyber infrastructure is located. This, in turn, means that States can only exercise sovereignty over the users and the infrastructure of cyberspace located in their respective territory.

3. Peter Malanczuk, *Akehurst's Modern Introduction to International Law*, Seventh Edition (Routledge, 1997), at 3; Antonio Cassese, 'States: Rise and Decline of the Primary Subjects of the International Community', *in* Bardo Fassbender and Anne Peters (eds), *The Oxford Handbook of the History of International Law* (Oxford University Press, 2012), at 50-51.
4. Samantha Besson, 'Sovereignty', Oxford Public International Law, https://opil.ouplaw.com/view/10.1093/law:epil/9780199231690/law-9780199231690-e1472.
5. *See*, for more on the nature of cyberspace, Chapter 2, section §2.02[A].

Having laid out this difficulty with the applicability of the fundamental principle of sovereignty in cyberspace, it is possible to proceed by examining the rules of public international law and determining whether their applicability in cyberspace experiences any similar mutation.

In public international law, rules may be extracted from 'sources', and in public international law, the 'sources' are 'formal' and 'material'.[6] A 'formal' source is one from which a rule derives its legal validity: it is the legal element which gives the rule its quality as law.[7] A 'material' source is one which denotes the provenance of the substantive content of the rule: it is the place where the rule can be found.[8]

The recognised formal sources are reflected in Article 38(1) of the Statute of the International Court of Justice (ICJ Statute),[9] which is considered the epicentre of the whole system of sources under public international law.[10]

Article 38(1) of the ICJ Statute provides that:

> The [ICJ], whose function is to decide in accordance with international law such disputes as are submitted to it, shall apply:
>
> a. international conventions, whether general or particular, establishing rules expressly recognized by the contesting states;
> b. international custom, as evidence of a general practice accepted as law;
> c. the general principles of law recognized by civilized nations;
> d. subject to the provisions of Article 59, judicial decisions and the teachings of the most highly qualified publicists of the various nations, as subsidiary means for the determination of rules of law.[11]

Although Article 38(1) of the ICJ Statute reflects the recognised 'formal sources', the sources listed therein may be categorised into two: 'formal' sources, namely international treaties, international custom, and general principles of law, and 'material' sources, namely judicial decisions and juristic teachings.[12] According to Thirlway, judicial decisions and juristic teachings are categorised as 'material' sources because the judge or author will pronounce a rule of international law not as his or her own rule, but as one which derives from a treaty, international custom or the general principles of law.[13]

---

6. Shaw, *supra* no. 1, at 70-71.
7. Hugh Thirlway, *The Sources of International Law*, Second Edition (Oxford University Press, 2019), at 6; *see*, R. Jennings and J. Watts (eds), *Oppenheim's International Law*, Ninth Edition (Oxford University Press, 1992), at 23 §8; James Crawford, *Brownlie's Principles of Public International Law*, Eight Edition (Oxford University Press, 2012), at 20.
8. *Ibid.*
9. Thirlway, *supra* no. 7, at 20.
10. "*L'art. 38 dello Statute della Corte Internazionale* [...] *è considerato la chiave di lettura del sistema delle fonti del diritto internazionale*"; Mara Stella Messina, *Compendio di Diritto Internazionale Pubblico* (Primiceri Editore, 2016), at 86.
11. Charter of the United Nations (adopted 26 June 1945, entered into force 24 October 1945), 1 UNTS XVI Annex, Art. 38(1).
12. Thirlway, *supra* no. 7, at 8.
13. *Ibid.*, at 131; Rebecca Wallace and Olga Martin-Ortega, *International Law*, Sixth Edition (Sweet & Maxwell, 2009), at 8.

Notwithstanding the traditional sources of public international law enshrined in Article 38(1) of the ICJ Statute, a different category of instruments which does not emanate therefrom also exists: 'soft law'.[14]

'Soft law' has a range of possible meanings,[15] yet for the purposes of this book, it can be said to denote "non-legally binding instruments used in contemporary international relations"[16] which express obligations that, although not binding in the same way as those imposed by international law proper, are expected to be complied with nonetheless.[17]

Similar to the sources of public international law encapsulated in Article 38(1) of the ICJ Statute, soft law can also be categorised into two: primary soft law, which consists of instruments addressed to the entire international community, and secondary soft law, which includes, *inter alia*, instruments of international supervisory organs and decisions of special rapporteurs and other ad hoc bodies.[18]

The soft law instruments employed in these two categories can be of different forms. They can range from treaties, which – although by definition are hard law[19] – can be soft if they only provide for general goals rather than specific rights or obligations,[20] to non-binding or voluntary resolutions formulated and accepted by international and regional organisations.[21]

In terms of air law, examples of instruments which are regarded as soft law include the SARPs annexed to the Chicago Convention of 1944[22] and the Acceptable Means of Compliance and Guidance Material.[23] In terms of space law, notable examples of soft law include the Space Debris Mitigation Guidelines[24] of 2007.[25]

Regardless of the fact that the very nature of soft law instruments implies that they are not themselves binding, this is not as much of a troublesome characteristic as

14. Steven Freeland, 'The Role of "Soft Law" in Public International Law', *in* Irmgard Marboe (ed.), *Soft Law in Outer Space: The Function of Non-binding Norms in International Space Law* (Böhalu, 2012), at 19.
15. Alan Boyle, 'The Choice of a Treaty: Hard Law Versus Soft Law', *in* Simon Chesterman, David M Malone and Santiago Villalpando (eds), *The Oxford Handbook of United Nations Treaties* (Oxford University Press, 2019), at 104.
16. Alan Boyle and Christine M. Chinkin, *The Making of International Law* (Oxford University Press, 2007), at 212.
17. Thirlway, *supra* no. 7, at 189.
18. Dinah L. Shelton, 'Soft Law', *in* David Armstrong (ed.), *Routledge Handbook of International Law* (Routledge, 2009), at 70.
19. Boyle and Chinkin, *supra* no. 16, at 213.
20. Christine M. Chinkin, 'The Challenge of Soft Law: Development and Change in International Law', 38 *International and Comparative Law Quarterly* 850 (1989), at 851.
21. *Ibid.*
22. Pablo Mendes de Leon, *Introduction to Air Law*, Tenth Edition (Kluwer, 2017), at 25.
23. Christopher M. Petras and Mathieu Vaugeois, 'Safety Regulation and Oversight', *in* Paul Stephen Dempsey and Ram S. Jakhu (eds), *Routledge Handbook of Public Aviation Law* (Routledge, 2017), at 79. In this work, the authors do not explicitly classify the Acceptable Means of Compliance as soft law, but classify them as non-binding standards.
24. COPUOS Legal Subcommittee, 'Report of the Scientific and Technical Subcommittee on its Forty-Fourth Session' (6-15 June 2007) A/AC.105/890, at para. 99; These Guidelines were endorsed by the UN General Assembly on the 22 December 2007, A/Res/62/217, at para. 26.
25. Peter Jankowitsch, 'The Background and History of Space Law', *in* Frans von der Dunk and Fabio Tronchetti (eds), *Handbook of Space Law* (Edward Elgar, 2015), at 27.

it might prima facie seem; quite to the contrary, this lack of binding nature often facilitates consensus between States which is much harder to achieve on hard law instruments.[26]

In conclusion, public international law is constituted by various sources, some of which are termed 'formal', in that they are the rules themselves, and others of which are termed 'material', in that they embody or indicate what the rules are. These sources can also be said to include 'soft law', which refers to non-binding rules which still require adherence to in some form or another.

§3.02 PUBLIC INTERNATIONAL LAW AND CONFLICT: *JUS AD BELLUM* AND *JUS IN BELLO*

Within the body of public international law, conflict is regulated by *jus ad bellum* and *jus in bello*.[27] The *jus ad bellum* is the regime of law which determines when resort to armed force is permissible,[28] and the *jus in bello* is the regime of law which governs the conduct of hostilities during an international armed conflict,[29] and which always applies irrespective of the lawfulness of the original resort to armed force.[30]

Starting with the *jus ad bellum*, the backbone thereof is comprised by both the prohibition against the use of force amongst States,[31] set out under Article 2(4) of the UN Charter,[32] and the exceptions to it, namely the right of self-defence[33] and the authorisation by the UN Security Council for the use of force.[34]

A further possible exception to the prohibition against the use of force enshrined in Article 2(4) of the UN Charter is that of the use of force to avert an overwhelming humanitarian catastrophe.[35] This exception, termed the 'responsibility to protect',[36] seeks to ensure that States protect their citizens from mass atrocities and assist one

26. Malanczuk, *supra* no. 3, at 54.
27. Robert D. Sloane, 'The Cost of Conflation: Preserving the Dualism of Jus ad Bellum and Jus in Bello in the Contemporary Law of War', 34(1) *Yale Journal of International Law* 56 (2009), at 47.
28. Mary E. O'Connell, 'Historical Development and Legal Basis', *in* Dieter Fleck (ed.), *The Handbook of International Humanitarian Law*, Third Edition (Oxford University Press, 2013), at 1.
29. Yoram Dinstein, *War, Aggression and Self-Defence*, Fifth Edition (Cambridge University Press, 2011), at 10. Nowadays, a considerable amount of *jus in bello*, particularly customary international law, governs non-international armed conflict too; *see*, ICRC, 'Study on Customary International Humanitarian', *in* ICRC, *Customary International Humanitarian Law* (ICRC), https://www.casebook.icrc.org/case-study/icrc-customary-international-humanitarian-law#toc-2-customary-rules-of-international-humanitarian-law.
30. Hilaire McCoubrey, *International Humanitarian Law: The Regulation of Armed Conflicts* (Dartmouth Publishing, 1990), at 1.
31. ICRC, *International Humanitarian Law: Answers to Your Questions* (ICRC, 2015), at 8.
32. Charter of the United Nations, *supra* no. 11, Art. 2(4).
33. *Ibid.*, Art. 51.
34. *Ibid.*, Art. 42.
35. *See*, for the first documentation of the exception, Christopher Greenwood, 'Humanitarian Intervention: The Case of Kosovo', *in* Jarna Petman and Martti Koskenniemi (eds), *Finnish Yearbook of International Law, Volume 10 (1999)* (Brill, 2002), at 141.
36. The responsibility to protect was enshrined in the World Summit Outcome of 2005 which, in turn, was adopted by the UNGA in a resolution on the 16 September 2005, A/Res/60/1, at paras 138-139.

another in doing so.[37] This exception, however, is not found in the UN Charter, and it has been suggested chiefly by United Kingdom (UK) Governments from time to time.[38] Therefore, in order for this exception to be considered binding, it must find anchorage in a source of international law such as CIL.[39]

Although it is, therefore, clear that exceptions exist to the prohibition against the use of force, the ICJ has confirmed that this prohibition forms part of *jus cogens*,[40] that is, the body of peremptory norms of general international law which are accepted and recognised by the international community of States and which cannot be derogated from.[41]

Turning to the *jus in bello*, the foundation thereof is comprised by the four Geneva Conventions of 1949,[42] as supplemented by two additional Protocols of 1977,[43] whose collective aim is to protect victims of war.[44] Along with these instruments, the

37. ICRC, 'IHL and the "Responsibility to Protect"', https://www.icrc.org/en/document/what-are-jus-ad-bellum-and-jus-bello-0.
38. *See*, for the most recent example of the position of the UK Government on the matter, UK Policy Paper (Prime Minister's Office), *Syria Action – UK Government Legal Position*, https://www.gov.uk/government/publications/syria-action-uk-government-legal-position/syria-action-uk-government-legal-position?utm_source=POLITICO.EU&utm_campaign=6409ed57d4-EMAIL_CAMPAIGN_2018_04_15&utm_medium=email&utm_term=0_10959edeb5-6409ed57d4-189002913.
39. Michael Wood, 'International Law and the Use of Force: What Happens in Practice', 53 *Indian Journal of International Law* 345 (2013), at 352. *See*, for more on the responsibility to protect, Michael Byers, 'International Law and the Responsibility to Protect', *in* Christine Chinkin and Freya Baetens (eds), *Sovereignty, Statehood and State Responsibility: Essays in Honour of James Crawford* (Cambridge University Press, 2015).
40. *Case Concerning Military and Paramilitary Activities in and against Nicaragua* (Nicaragua v. US) (Merits), [1986] ICJ Rep 14, at 100-101, at para. 190; Alexander Orakhelashvili, *Peremptory Norms in International Law* (Oxford University Press, 2006), at 50. Academic acceptance of this view that the prohibition against the use of force forms part of *jus cogens* is extremely widespread; *see*, James A. Green, 'Questioning the Peremptory Status of the Prohibition on the Use of Force', 32(2) *Michigan Journal of International Law* 215 (2011), at 216 fn 4.
41. Thomas Weatherall, *Jus Cogens: International Law and Social Contract* (Cambridge University Press, 2015), at xxxvii-xxxviii; Vienna Convention on the Law of Treaties (with Annexe) (adopted 23 May 1969, entered into force 27 January 1980), 1155 UNTS 331, Art. 53.
42. Geneva Convention (I) for the Amelioration of the Condition of the Wounded and Sick in Armed Forces in the Field (adopted 12 August 1949, entered into force 21 October 1950), 75 UNTS 31; Geneva Convention (II) for the Amelioration of the Condition of Wounded, Sick and Shipwrecked Members of Armed Forces at Sea (adopted 12 August 1949, entered into force 21 October 1950), 75 UNTS 85; Geneva Convention (III) Relative to the Treatment of Prisoners of War (adopted 12 August 1949, entered into force 21 October 1950), 75 UNTS 135; Geneva Convention (IV) Relative to the Protection of Civilian Persons in Time of War (adopted 12 August 1949, entered into force 21 October 1950), 75 UNTS 287.
43. Protocol (I) Additional to the Geneva Conventions of 12 August 1949, and Relating to the Protection of Victims of International Armed Conflicts (adopted 8 June 1977, entered into force 7 December 1978), 1125 UNTS 3; Protocol (II) Additional to the Geneva Conventions of 12 August 1949, and Relating to the Protection of Victims of Non-International Armed Conflicts (adopted 8 June 1977, entered into force 7 December 1978), 1125 UNTS 609.
44. Jean Pictet (ed.), *The Geneva Conventions of 12 August 1949: Commentary* (ICRC, 1952), at 11.

foundation of the *jus in bello* is further comprised by The Hague Conventions of 1899 and 1907[45] which mainly address means and methods of warfare,[46] and by CIL.[47]

In the *Legality of the Threat or Use of Nuclear Weapons*, the ICJ held that the great majority of the provisions of the Geneva Conventions are considered to be part of CIL.[48] Similarly, numerous provisions of Additional Protocols I[49] and II[50] are also considered to be part of CIL,[51] as are the rules of land warfare expressed in The Hague Convention of 1907.[52]

Having laid out the bases of the *jus ad bellum* and the *jus in bello*, it is now possible to determine whether these two branches of international law contain any specific instruments which specifically address the eventuality of conflict in cyberspace.

[A] A Potential Digital Geneva Convention

While it is accepted both that the *jus in bello* does provide rules relating to the conduct of hostilities during an armed conflict, and that a variety of these rules are considered to be part of CIL, it is however clear that this regime does not address the specific eventuality of conflict in cyberspace.

To this end, on the 14 February 2017 at the RSA Conference in San Francisco, the President and Chief Legal Officer of Microsoft, Brad Smith, put forth the case for a

45. Hague Convention (II) on the Law and Customs of War on Land and its Annex (Regulations concerning the Laws and Customs of War on Land) (adopted 29 July 1899, entered into force 4 August 1900); Hague Convention (IV) Concerning the Laws and Customs of War on Land and its Annex (Regulations Concerning the Laws and Customs of War on Land) (adopted 18 October 1907, entered into force 26 January 1910), 187 CTS 227.
46. Marco Roscini, *Cyber Operations and the Use of Force in International Law* (Oxford University Press, 2014), at 118.
47. *See*, ICRC, *supra* no. 29.
48. *Legality of the Threat or Use of Nuclear Weapons (Advisory Opinion)* [1996] ICJ Rep 226, at para. 79.
49. Such as Rules 1, 7, 11-32, 34, 36, 37, 46-48, 53, 54, 57-65, 87-105, 117, 134-137, Protocol (I) Additional to the Geneva Conventions of 12 August 1949, and Relating to the Protection of Victims of International Armed Conflicts (adopted 8 June 1977, entered into force 7 December 1978), 1125 UNTS 3.
50. Such as Rules 1, 25-30, 53, 54, 87-105, 109-113, 118, 119, 121, 125, 129, 134-137, Protocol (II) Additional to the Geneva Conventions of 12 August 1949, and Relating to the Protection of Victims of Non-International Armed Conflicts (adopted 8 June 1977, entered into force 7 December 1978), 1125 UNTS 609.
51. Jean-Marie Henckaerts, 'Study on Customary International Humanitarian Law: A Contribution to the Understanding and Respect for the Rule of Law in Armed Conflict', 87(857) *International Review of the Red Cross* 175 (2005), at 187-188.
52. *See*, The Judgment of the International Military Tribunal at Nüremberg, 'The Law Relating to War Crimes and Crimes Against Humanity', *in* Yale Law School Avalon Project, *Judgment of the International Military Tribunal*, http://www.avalon.law.yale.edu/subject_menus/judcont.asp; Betsy Baker, *Hague Peace Conferences (1899 and 1907)* (Max Planck Encyclopedia of Public International Law, November, 2009), at para. 18, http://www.opil.ouplaw.com/view/10.1093/law:epil/9780199231690/law-9780199231690-e305?rskey=TgeE9m&result=1&prd=OPIL.

'Digital Geneva Convention' which would provide civilians with specific protection from cyberattacks.[53]

The argument for such a Digital Geneva Convention is rooted in the uniqueness of cyberspace: because it is a specific kind of domain which is owned and operated by the private sector, be it by submarine cables, servers, laptops, or smartphones, when it comes to cyberattacks, the first responders to them are civilians, not States.[54]

Accordingly, the rationale for a treaty such as the Digital Geneva Convention would be to ensure that States would not engage in cyberattacks against the private sector and that they would not target civilian infrastructure.[55] As idealistic as this proposal may be, two realities of particular weight seem to dent the indispensability of such an international agreement.

First, the ICJ has held that the great majority of the provisions of the existing Geneva Conventions are considered to be part of CIL.[56] Therefore, it can be sensibly argued that these provisions of the Geneva Conventions are to apply to each and every State[57] regardless of whether a particular State is a State party to them or not, and regardless of whether the provisions of those treaties are enshrined in a specific treaty addressing conflict in cyberspace.

Second, the production of treaties has been on the decline in recent years. While the number of new multilateral treaties deposited with the UN Secretary General in each decade from the year 1950 to the year 2000 was never below thirty-four, in the ten years between 2000 and 2010, this number dropped to twenty, and in the years 2011, 2012, and 2013 it stood at nil.[58]

Although it is hard to put a finger on one sole factor behind this decline in treaty adoption,[59] it is nonetheless possible to determine that this downward trend over the past decade undoubtedly stems from the success that States have had beforehand in negotiating a large number of hard law instruments and which, in turn, has led to treaty congestion.[60]

53. Joseph Guay and Lisa Rudnick, 'What the Digital Geneva Convention Means for the Future of Humanitarian Action', UN High Commissioner for Refugees, 25 June 2017, https://www.unhcr.org/innovation/digital-geneva-convention-mean-future-humanitarian-action/.
54. Brad Smith, 'The Need for a Digital Geneva Convention', Transcript of Keynote Address at the RSA Conference, 14 February 2017, San Francisco, California, at 3-4, https://www.1gew6o3qn6vx9kp3s42ge0y1-wpengine.netdna-ssl.com/wp-content/uploads/2017/03/Transcript-of-Brad-Smiths-Keynote-Address-at-the-RSA-Conference-2017.pdf.
55. *Ibid.*
56. *Legality of the Threat or Use of Nuclear Weapons (Advisory Opinion)*, *supra* no. 48, at para. 79.
57. The application of rules of CIL to each and every State is however subject to the 'persistent objector' rule. This rule holds that "if a state persistently and consistently objects to a newly emerging norm of [CIL] during the period of the 'formation' of that norm (i.e. prior to its crystallization as a binding rule of [CIL]), then the objecting state is exempt from the customary norm in question once it has crystallized and for so long as the objection is maintained." James A. Green, *The Persistent Objector Rule in International Law* (Oxford University Press, 2016), at 1. *See*, for more on the 'persistent objector' rule, *Ibid.*
58. Joost Pauwelyn, Ramses A. Wessel and Jan Wouters, 'When Structures Become Shackles: Stagnation and Dynamics in International Lawmaking', 25 *European Journal of International Law* 733 (2004), at 734-735. This is the most recent statistic available.
59. *Ibid.*, at 734-735.
60. Edith Brown Weiss, 'International Environmental Law: Contemporary Issues and the Emergence of a New World Order', 81 *Georgetown Law Journal* 675 (1993), at 697. The essence of

In view of the fact that treaty congestion has led to a decline in the production of treaties over the last few years, the potential of States agreeing upon a new Digital Geneva Convention does not seem, as a result, particularly strong. This improbability, however, should not be much of a hindrance to the applicability of the *jus in bello* to attacks carried out in cyberspace since, as stated above, the vast part of this regime is deemed to be CIL.

[B] Convention on Cybercrime of the Council of Europe

Notwithstanding that currently there is no specific treaty addressing conflict in cyberspace, there exists a treaty which addresses crime in cyberspace: the Convention on Cybercrime[61] of the Council of Europe (Budapest Convention), which is the first multilateral, binding instrument to regulate 'cybercrime',[62] and which is the first instrument to impose certain obligations on States (rather than individuals) in this respect.

Although the term 'cybercrime' is not explicitly defined in the Budapest Convention, from a reading of the Preamble this term may be broadly understood as "the committal of criminal offences through the use of computer networks and/or electronic information."[63] More specifically, it may be understood as any "action directed against the confidentiality, integrity and availability of computer systems, networks and computer data as well as the misuse of such systems, networks and data."[64]

Setting aside the meaning of the term 'cybercrime', the Budapest Convention effectively provides for four broad categories of substantive offence:

- offences against the confidentiality, integrity, and availability of computer data and systems;
- computer-related offences (computer-related fraud and forgery);
- content-related offences (child pornography); and
- criminal copyright infringement.[65]

treaty congestion lies in the appearance of too much law, too fast; Donald K. Anton, '"Treaty Congestion" in Contemporary International Environmental Law', *in* Shawkat Alam, et al. (eds), *Routledge Handbook of International Environmental Law*, Third Edition (Routledge, 2015), at 652. Although E.B. Weiss originally coined the concept of 'treaty congestion' in terms of international environmental law, this concept can be equally applied to public international law in general; Pauwelyn, Wessel and Wouters, *supra* no. 58, at 739.

61. Convention on Cybercrime (opened for signature 23 November 2001, entered into force 1 July 2004), ETS 185. The Budapest Convention has an Additional Protocol Concerning the Criminalisation of Acts of a Racist and Xenophobic Nature Committed through Computer Systems. Further note that discussions are being had on a Second Protocol to the Budapest Convention; *see*, 'Cybercrime Convention Committee (T-CY) Preparation of the 2nd Additional Protocol to the Budapest Convention on Cybercrime State of play: Note by the Chair for the attention of the 21st Plenary of the T-CY (8 July 2019)', https://www.rm.coe.int/t-cy-2019-19-protocol-tor-extension-chair-note-v3/16809577ff.
62. Johnathan Clough, 'A World of Difference: The Budapest Convention on Cybercrime and the Challenges of Harmonisation', 40(3) *Monash University Law Review* 698 (2014), at 699-670.
63. Convention on Cybercrime 2001, *supra* no. 61, Recital 5.
64. *Ibid.*, Recital 8.
65. Clough, *supra* no. 62, at 702.

With particular reference to offences against the confidentiality, integrity, and availability of computer data and systems, the Budapest Convention stipulates that the intentional damaging, deletion, deterioration, alteration, or suppression of computer data without right shall be a criminal offence.[66] The Budapest Convention further stipulates that this is also the case with the intentional and serious hindering without right of the functioning of a computer system by inputting, transmitting, damaging, deleting, deteriorating, altering, or suppressing computer data.[67]

The Budapest Convention adds, among other things, that the intentional production, sale, procurement for use, import, distribution or otherwise making available of a device, including a computer program, designed or adapted primarily for the purpose of committing any of the offences established in accordance with its Articles 2 through 5 shall be a criminal offence.[68]

The Budapest Convention also provides that each State Party shall adopt such legislative measures as may be necessary to establish jurisdiction over any offence established in accordance with its Articles 2 to 11 when the offence is committed, *inter alia*, on board an aircraft registered under the laws of that Party.[69]

Although this particular provision is true to the present reality that the offences incorporated in the Budapest Convention are such that can be committed by a person on board an aircraft rather than a space object, it may soon face the possibility of becoming outdated.

Recently, in fact, NASA astronaut Anne McClain was accused of having illegally accessed – while on board the ISS – the bank account of her former spouse.[70] Although this specific example does not purport to fall within the remit of the Budapest Convention, it nevertheless demonstrates that, soon enough, a person may carry out a crime listed in the Budapest Convention, such as the intentional damaging, deletion, deterioration, altering, or suppression of computer data without right, while on board a space object.

Reverting to the above-mentioned offences of the Budapest Convention, it may be determined that, although said offences are quite encapsulating, the Convention does not cover the complete spectrum of cybercrimes, with cyberterrorism being a notable omission.[71]

In this respect, some clarity ought to be given to the term 'cyberterrorism'. Indeed, a distinction must be drawn between 'cyberterrorism' which qualifies as a 'cyberattack',[72] and 'cyberterrorism' which does not so qualify and which, to the contrary, would fall under the remit of the Budapest Convention.

---

66. Convention on Cybercrime 2001, *supra* no. 61, Art. 4.
67. *Ibid.*, Art. 5.
68. *Ibid.*, Art. 6.
69. *Ibid.*, Art. 22(1)(c).
70. Mike Baker, 'NASA Astronaut Anne McClain Accused by Spouse of Crime in Space', The New York Times, 23 August 2019, https://www.nytimes.com/2019/08/23/us/nasa-astronaut-anne-mcclain.html.
71. Clough, *supra* no. 62, at 702.
72. *See* Chapter 2, section §2.02[G].

If a 'cyberterrorism' operation constitutes 'computer network exploitation' the main purpose of which is reconnaissance, surveillance, and the exfiltration of data and information,[73] then it is highly likely that such an operation would not qualify as a cyberattack. Rather, it would seemingly qualify as an offence against the confidentiality, integrity, and availability of computer data and systems under the Budapest Convention.

If, however, a 'cyberterrorism' operation constitutes 'computer network exploitation' which seeks to generate harmful effects on or against a targeted system or device, and which could have effects even on human beings,[74] then it is highly likely that such an operation would qualify as a cyberattack as defined in this book and thus require legal treatment under public international law.

It is sensible to therefore conclude that, in cases of cyberattacks or 'cyberterrorism' operations which qualify as cyberattacks,[75] one would not be able to resort to the Budapest Convention due to its defined framework. In such cases, however, one would still be able to resort to the *jus ad bellum* and the *jus in bello*.

[C] Tallinn Manual on International Law Applicable to Cyber Operations

An endeavour which seeks to address the applicability of international law to cyberattacks is the Tallinn Manual, which was drafted by Michael N. Schmitt and a group of international legal experts gathered by the Cooperative Cyber Defense Center of Excellence of NATO.[76]

Although the Tallinn Manual, which was published in 2013 and updated in 2017,[77] is neither an official document nor a representation of the views of NATO or any State,[78] it is meant to be a reflection of the law as it existed at the point of adoption of the Manual.[79] In other words, the Tallinn Manual is intended as an objective restatement of the *lex lata* (the law as it is) and avoids the inclusion of statements reflecting *lex ferenda* (the law as it should be).[80]

The Tallinn Manual contains 154 rules which were unanimously agreed upon by the groups of experts. Among these rules, the Tallinn Manual contains three rules

73. ICRC, *The Potential Human Cost of Cyber Operations* (ICRC Expert Meeting, 14-16 November 2018), at 12.
74. *Ibid.*
75. *See* Chapter 2, section §2.02[G].
76. David Wallace and Mark Visger, 'Responding to the Call for a Digital Geneva Convention: An Open Letter to Brad Smith and the Technology Community', 6(2) *Journal of Law and Cyber Warfare* 3 (2018), at 18.
77. Michael N. Schmitt (ed.), *Tallinn Manual on International Law Applicable to Cyber Warfare* (Cambridge University Press, 2013); Michael N. Schmitt (ed.), *Tallinn Manual 2.0 on International Law Applicable to Cyber Operations* (Cambridge University Press, 2017).
78. *Ibid.*
79. *Ibid.*, at 2-3.
80. *Ibid.*; Wallace and Visger, *supra* no. 76, at 19.

which pertain to 'Air law',[81] three rules which pertain to 'Space law',[82] and four rules which pertain to 'International Telecommunication law'.[83]

The rules of the Tallinn Manual demonstrate that, although cyber-specific international law is lacking, cyber operations do not exist in a normative void.[84] To the contrary, these rules indicate that the existing international law does apply to cyber operations, and this assessment, the Tallinn Manual holds, is now shared by most States.[85]

A possible downside of the Tallinn Manual is the fact that, as it makes amply clear, it is not an official document, meaning that attempts could be made to diminish its weight. Nevertheless, since the Tallinn Manual is intended as an objective restatement of the *lex lata* (the law as it is), it can be held that the Tallinn Manual is an indicator of existing State practice.

§3.03 APPLICABILITY OF THE *JUS AD BELLUM* TO CYBERATTACKS

Considering that there is no specific international law instrument on the applicability of the *jus ad bellum* to cyberattacks, it is thus essential to determine how, if at all, this body of laws applies to attacks carried out in cyberspace.

Article 2(4) of the UN Charter states:

> All Members shall refrain in their international relations from the threat or use of force against the territorial integrity or political independence of any state, or in any other manner inconsistent with the purposes of the United Nations.[86]

At the outset, reference must be made to the *Legality of the Threat or Use of Nuclear Weapons* wherein the ICJ observed that Article 2(4) and the exceptions thereto under Article 51 (right of self-defence) and Article 42 (Security Council authorisation for the use of force) of the UN Charter "do not refer to specific weapons."[87]

The ICJ held that these exceptions "apply to any use of force, regardless of the weapons employed. The Charter neither expressly prohibits, nor permits, the use of any specific weapon."[88] From this observation of the ICJ, it follows that Article 2(4) of the UN Charter applies even when a cyberweapon is employed.

On this note, it must be heeded that there is no definition of 'weapon' in international law.[89] In terms of the meaning of the notion 'cyberweapon', the Tallinn Manual provides guidance by stating that:

81. *Ibid.*, Michael N. Schmitt (ed.), *Tallinn Manual 2.0 on International Law Applicable to Cyber Operations* (Cambridge University Press, 2017) Rules 55-57.
82. *Ibid.*, Rules 58-60.
83. *Ibid.*, Rules 61-64.
84. *Ibid.*
85. *Ibid*, 3.
86. Charter of the United Nations, *supra* no. 11, Art. 2(4).
87. *Legality of the Threat or Use of Nuclear Weapons* (*Advisory Opinion*), *supra* no. 48, at para. 39.
88. *Ibid.*, at para. 39.
89. *See* Chapter 2, section §2.02[I].

> cyber weapons are 'cyber means of warfare' that are by design, use, or intended use capable of causing either (i) injury to, or death of, persons; or (ii) damage to, or destruction of, objects, that is, causing the consequences required for qualification of a cyber operation as an attack.[90]

Therefore, it may be concluded that, if a 'cyberweapon' (as described in the Tallinn Manual) is used in a 'cyberattack' which constitutes the use or threat of use of 'force', Article 2(4) of the UN Charter applies since the UN Charter does not refer to specific weapons.

The Tallinn Manual substantiates this conclusion as it provides that "a cyber operation that constitutes a threat or use of force against the territorial integrity or political independence of any State, or that is in any other manner inconsistent with the purposes of the United Nations, is unlawful."[91]

Although this statement confirms that Article 2(4) of the UN Charter does apply to cyberattacks which employ cyberweapons, it still leaves unanswered the question as to when a cyberattack amounts to use or threat of use of force, and thus also the question on when – rather than if – Article 2(4) applies to such attacks in cyberspace.

[A] Use or Threat of Use of 'Cyber' Force

Although the ICJ has explained that the use of force applies to any use of force, the ICJ has not explained what type of 'force' it is that Article 2(4) of the UN Charter enfolds within it. Similarly, the UN Charter does not provide any guidance on the meaning of 'force' contemplated in its Article 2(4).

Setting aside this lack of interpretative certainty, the 'prevailing'[92] view is that 'force', under Article 2(4), covers only 'armed force'.[93] In this respect, the ICJ provides further guidance since, in the case of *Military and Paramilitary Activities in and against Nicaragua*, it held that the laying of mines in Nicaraguan harbours by US actors constituted a prohibited use of force, and the various attacks on Nicaraguan oil industry facilities and military bases amounted to the same.[94]

---

90. Schmitt (ed.), *supra* no. 77, at 452. *See*, for more on 'cyberweapon', Chapter 2, section §2.02[I].
91. *Ibid.*, Rule 68.
92. Albrecht Randelzhofer and Oliver Dörr, 'Article 2(4)', *in* Bruno Simma, et al. (eds), *The Charter of the United Nations: A Commentary Volume I*, Third Edition (Oxford University Press, 2012), at 200 and 208; Crawford, *supra* no. 7, at 747. Ian Brownlie, *International Law and the Use of Force by States* (Oxford University Press, 1963), at 362 and 376; Brownlie contends that Art. 2(4) also covers physical force which includes, for example, the diversion of a river by an up-stream State, or the release of large quantities of water down a valley.
93. Randelzhofer and Dörr, *supra* no. 92, at 200 and 208; Alina Kaczorowska-Ireland, *Public International Law*, Fifth Edition (Routledge, 2015), at 689.
94. *Case Concerning Military and Paramilitary Activities in and against Nicaragua* (Nicaragua v. US) (Merits), *supra* no. 40, at 118, para. 227; Douglas J. Pivnichny, 'The International Court of Justice and the Use of Force', *in* Leila N. Sadat (ed.), *Seeking Accountability for the Unlawful Use of Force* (Cambridge University Press, 2018), at 194 and 202-203.

In that case, the ICJ additionally held that, whereas the arming and training of rebels by the US certainly did involve the threat or use of force against Nicaragua, the mere supply of funds by the US to the rebels did not in itself amount to a use of force.[95]

With regard to this consideration of the ICJ that the supply of funds did not amount to a use of force, reference may be made to the proceedings leading to the adoption of the Declaration on Principles of International Law Concerning Friendly Relations and Co-operation Among States in Accordance with the Charter of the UN[96] (Declaration Concerning Friendly Relations) by the General Assembly, during which 'forms of pressure' of 'a political or economic character' were in fact excluded from the ambit of use of force.[97]

It can be consequently held that 'force' in Article 2(4) of the UN Charter does not cover political or economic coercion,[98] but covers only armed force, that is, 'force' which denotes violence. Thus, 'force' in Article 2(4) of the UN Charter requires violence to occur.[99]

Turning to cyberattacks, possibly the most straightforward criterion to qualify them as use, or threat of use, of force is if they cause, or are reasonably likely to cause, the damaging consequences normally produced by kinetic weapons.[100] The Tallinn Manual, however, provides for a more nuanced qualification of cyberattacks as use, or threat of use, of force.

The Tallinn Manual lays down that "a cyber operation constitutes a use of force when its scale and effects are comparable to non-cyber operations rising to the level of a use of force,"[101] and that "a cyber operation, or threatened cyber operation, constitutes an unlawful threat of force when the threatened action, if carried out, would be an unlawful use of force."[102]

The Tallinn Manual, it must be recalled, is intended as an objective restatement of the *lex lata*. The relevant *lex lata*, in this context, states that a cyber operation constitutes use of force when its scale and effects are comparable to non-cyber operations rising to the level of use of force.

As determined above, non-cyber operations rise to the level of use of force when they involve armed force, that is, force which denotes violence. On this basis, it can be concluded that a cyberattack qualifies as 'use of force' in terms of Article 2(4) if it denotes violence.

95. *Ibid.*, at para. 228; Pivnichny, *supra* no. 94, at 194 and 203.
96. UN General Assembly, Declaration on Principles of International Law concerning Friendly Relations and Cooperation among States in accordance with the Charter of the United Nations, 24 October 1970, A/RES/2625.
97. UN General Assembly Special Committee on Friendly Relations, A/AC.125/SR.110 to 114 (1970). *See*, Report of the Special Committee on Friendly Relations and Cooperation Among States, 1969, UN GAOR, 24th Sess, Supp No 19, 12, A/7619 (1969); Michael N Schmitt, 'The Use of Cyber Force and International Law', *in* Marc Weller (ed.), *The Oxford Handbook of the Use of Force in International Law* (Oxford University Press, 2015), at 1113.
98. Crawford, *supra* no. 7, at 747; Shaw, *supra* no. 1, at 1125.
99. Dinstein, *supra* no. 29, at 88.
100. Roscini, *supra* no. 46, at 47.
101. Schmitt (ed.), *supra* no. 77, Rule 69.
102. *Ibid.*, Rule 70.

From this conclusion, it may be further reasoned that, if, for instance, a State were to provide individuals with malware and training to conduct a cyberattack (similar to what the US did when it armed and trained rebels in the case of *Military and Paramilitary Activities in and against Nicaragua*), it would also have used force in breach of Article 2(4) of the UN Charter.[103]

Although in such cases it may be said that a cyberattack would constitute a breach of Article 2(4) of the UN Charter, this does not necessarily mean that such a cyberattack would automatically allow the attacked State to respond thereto.

[B] From 'Use of Cyber Force' to 'Armed Cyber Attack'

In order for an attacked State to be able to respond to a cyberattack, it is not sufficient that the attack qualifies merely as a 'use of force', but the attack must further qualify as an 'armed attack'.

As the ICJ held in the case of *Military and Paramilitary Activities in and against Nicaragua*, an 'armed attack' must constitute the "most grave forms of the use of force."[104] Thus, an 'armed attack' may be said to "only [exist] when force is used on a relatively large scale, is of a sufficient gravity, and has a substantial effect."[105]

A case illustrating the unsettled nature of the 'armed attack' threshold is that of the 2010 Stuxnet operation. In light of the damage which the operation caused to the Iranian centrifuges, some members of the international group of experts of the Tallinn Manual were of the view that this operation effectively reached the threshold of an 'armed attack'. Although other experts took the contrary view, all members agreed that Stuxnet amounted to prohibited 'use of force'.[106]

While it is 'almost impossible to fix the threshold of force employed to define the notion of armed attack,'[107] an 'armed attack' can nonetheless be said to imply:

> an act or the beginning of a series of acts of armed force of considerable magnitude and intensity [...] which have as their consequence [...] the infliction of substantial destruction upon important elements of the target State namely, upon its people, economic and security infrastructure, destruction of aspects of its governmental authority, i.e. its political independence, as well as damage to or deprivation of its physical element namely, its territory.[108]

Succinctly put, and applied to attacks in cyberspace, in order for a cyberattack to reach the threshold of an 'armed attack', it must produce substantial and immediate destructive effects.[109] In this light, it can be plausibly postulated that a cyberattack

103. *Ibid.*, at 331-332, para. 4.
104. *Case Concerning Military and Paramilitary Activities in and against Nicaragua* (Nicaragua v. US) (Merits), *supra* no. 40, at 101.
105. Randelzhofer and Dörr, *supra* no. 92, at 1397 and 1409.
106. Schmitt (ed.), *supra* no. 77, at 342, para. 10.
107. Natalino Ronzitti, 'The Expanding Law of Self-Defence', 11(3) *Journal of Conflict and Security Law* 343 (2006), at 351.
108. Avra Constantinou, *The Right of Self-Defence under Customary International Law and Article 51 of the UN Charter* (Sakkoulas/Bruylant, 2000), at 63-64.
109. Randelzhofer and Dörr, *supra* no. 92, at 1397 and 1419.

fulfils the conditions of an 'armed attack' if and when it results in a considerable loss of life and/or extensive destruction of property.[110]

Should such results ensue from a cyberattack, an affected State would thus be able to respond by using armed force without itself being in violation of Article 2(4) of the UN Charter since, in such a case, the exceptions to such prohibition on the use of force would be prompted, these being:

- the right of self-defence laid down under Article 51 of the UN Charter; and
- SC authorisation to maintain or restore international peace and security laid down under Chapter VII of the UN Charter.

Having established that a cyberattack tantamount to an 'armed attack' would prompt the two exceptions to the prohibition of the use of force, an analysis of these two exceptions shall be undertaken - in the following sections - in the context of cyberattacks.

[1] Responding to an Armed Cyber Attack: Self-Defence

The right of States to act in self-defence is an important exception to the prohibition on the use of force laid down by the UN Charter.[111] As the ICJ declared in the *Oil Platforms* case, measures of self-defence are necessary to protect the essential security interests of a State.[112]

The Tallinn Manual addresses the right of self-defence in response to hostile cyber operations by stating that:

> A State that is the target of a cyber operation that rises to the level of an armed attack may exercise its inherent right of self-defence. Whether a cyber operation constitutes an armed attack depends on its scale and effects.[113]

While it is only if and when the prohibited use of force rises to an armed attack that a State can unilaterally resort to forcible measures for its defence, in such instances, the State acting in self-defence is limited in two ways:

- it must observe the principles of necessity and proportionality;[114] and

110. Karl Zemanek, *Armed Attack* (Max Planck Encyclopedia of Public International Law, 2013), at para. 21.
111. Anthony Aust, *Handbook of International Law*, Second Edition (Cambridge University Press, 2010), at 208-209.
112. *Oil Platforms* (Islamic Republic of Iran v. US), [2003] ICJ Rep 161, at 196.
113. Schmitt (ed.), *supra* no. 77, Rule 71.
114. *Case Concerning Military and Paramilitary Activities in and against Nicaragua* (Nicaragua v. US) (Merits), *supra* no. 40, at 103. On the one hand, the principle of necessity provides that a use of force in self-defence is only permissible when a response not rising to the level of a use of force is unlikely to prove sufficiently effective to counter an armed attack, and on the other, the principle of proportionality requires that the use of force is no more extensive than necessary to effectively defend against the armed attack. Schmitt (ed.), *supra* no. 97, at 1124-1125.

- it has to report immediately to the SC the measures taken, as well as discontinue them when the latter takes the measures necessary for the maintenance of international peace.[115]

Further, the possibility of 'cyberattacks' amounting to 'armed attacks' and triggering the right of self-defence does not mean that the possibility of exercising this right can be easily established.

This is because, in cases of cyberattacks, it is difficult to identify the attacker swiftly and attribute the attack to a particular actor within the necessary time frame,[116] and even if this requirement of attribution is satisfied, it is difficult to identify the source of the attack.[117] Still further, even if the source of the cyberattack is located, additional conditions must be fulfilled before the right of self-defence can be actually exercised, particularly the condition that the attack be still ongoing.[118]

Ultimately, even if all the above-mentioned conditions are fulfilled, the principle of proportionality may be interpreted as allowing States to exercise the right of self-defence (in certain cases) solely by cyber means and not by way of kinetic or other weapons that produce direct physical effects.[119]

While this interpretation of the principle of proportionality may come across as a natural implication of the 'proportionality' referred to in its name, another interpretation of this principle argues that lawful self-defence is restricted to what is necessary for repelling an armed attack,[120] meaning, therefore, that the weapons used in self-defence need not necessarily be comparable to those used for the attack.[121]

In light of this latter view, it can be determined that, in the case of a cyberattack amounting to an 'armed attack', States exercising the right of self-defence need not necessarily be confined to self-defence solely by cyber means or operations.[122]

Whether a State may or may not respond to a cyberattack amounting to an 'armed attack' by using operations which are not necessarily cyber is, however, an unanswered question which, more likely than not, may be clarified only by the law - be it hard or soft - or by an adjudicating body.

---

115. Randelzhofer and Dörr, *supra* no. 92, at 1397 and 1401-1402.
116. *Ibid.*, at 1420.
117. *Ibid.*
118. *Ibid.* In such a case, the burden of establishing the fact that the attack is still ongoing would lie on the State purporting to exercise its right of self-defence; *Oil Platforms* (Islamic Republic of Iran v. US), *supra* no. 112, at 189. *See*, for more on the potential difficulties outlined in this paragraph, Chapter 6, section §6.03[A].
119. *Ibid. See*, for the burden of demonstrating the proportionality of the response would lie on the State purporting to exercise its right of self-defence; *Oil Platforms* (Islamic Republic of Iran v. US), *supra* no. 112, at 198.
120. *Ibid.*, at 1426. In this context, the term 'repelling' means ending the attack so that the specific impulse from which the attack emerged is no longer present.
121. Schmitt (ed.), *supra* no. 77, at 349, para. 5.
122. *Ibid.*

[2] *Responding to an Armed Cyber Attack: Security Council Authorisation*

Another exception to the prohibition on the use of force laid down by the UN Charter is that of SC authorisation per Chapter VII of the UN Charter. This exception allows the SC to counteract threats to peace, breaches of peace, and acts of aggression[123] via recommendations, or measures taken in accordance with Articles 41 and 42 of the UN Charter, so as to maintain or restore international peace and security.[124]

Article 41 of the UN Charter provides that:

> The [SC] may decide what measures not involving the use of armed force are to be employed to give effect to its decisions, and it may call upon the Members of the United Nations to apply such measures [which] may include complete or partial interruption of [...] telegraphic, radio, and other means of communication [...].[125]

A careful consideration of this Article sheds light on the fact that, first, the range of measures available under Article 41 – which is broad and not exhaustive in nature[126] – explicitly excludes action involving the use of armed force.[127] Second, the range of measures available under Article 41 mentions the "interruption of [...] means of communication" as an available measure to be employed by the Security Council.

Article 41 thus suggests, albeit in an indirect manner, that the interruption of means of communication is, at face value, not an action involving the use of armed force. This supposition of the UN Charter is, however, refutable at this day and age, not least because the interruption of means of communication may lead to disastrous consequences, especially if such means of communication relate to critical infrastructure.[128]

Setting aside the possible qualification of "interruption of [...] means of communication" as use of armed force, Article 41 is particularly important in the context of cyberattacks. This is because it confirms that the SC, by virtue of its wide margin of discretion and via the term "other means of communication," may in fact decide upon a complete or partial interruption of cyber communications.[129]

The crux of Article 41 of the UN Charter is also spelt out as *lex lata* in Rule 76 of the Tallinn Manual which not only states that "[s]hould the UN Security Council determine that an act constitutes a threat to the peace, breach of the peace, or act of

---

123. Anna M. Vradenburgh, 'The Chapter VII Powers of the United Nations Charter: Do They Trump Human Rights Law', 1(11) *Loyola of Los Angeles International and Comparative Law Review* 175 (1991), at 178.
124. Charter of the United Nations, *supra* no. 11, Art. 39.
125. *Ibid.*, Art. 41.
126. Nico Krisch, 'Article 41', *in* Bruno Simma, et al. (eds), *The Charter of the UN: A Commentary Volume II*, Third Edition (Oxford University Press, 2012), at 1311.
127. *Ibid.*
128. *See*, for more on critical infrastructure, Chapter 6, section §6.02[A].
129. Schmitt (ed.), *supra* no. 77, at 358, para. 4.

aggression, it may authorize non-forceful measures"[130] but also that such measures may "[include] cyber operations."[131]

Thus, a combined reading of Article 41 of the UN Charter and the above-cited Rule 76 of the Tallinn Manual allows the argument to be made that certain cyber operations may be authorised by the SC to interrupt means of communication, including cyber communication, in response to an armed attack, provided that they do not involve the use of armed force.

Further, should the SC consider that the measures provided for in Article 41 of the UN Charter would be inadequate,[132] the SC may, by virtue of Article 42, take "such action by air, sea, or land forces as may be necessary to maintain or restore international peace and security. Such action may include demonstrations, blockade, and other operations by air, sea, or land forces of Members of the United Nations."[133]

Once again, the crux of this provision is reproduced as *lex lata* in the Tallinn Manual which holds that "[i]f the Security Council considers such measures to be inadequate, it may decide upon forceful measures, including cyber measures."[134] Consequently, action by the SC under Article 42 of the UN Charter may be legally implemented by means of, or against cyber operations which reach the level of an 'armed attack'.

§3.04 STATE RESPONSIBILITY UNDER INTERNATIONAL LAW

In view of the fact that cyberattacks appear to be directly or indirectly designed, or effected, or designed and effected by one or several States on others, reference shall here be made to the notion of responsibility of States for their international conduct.

James Crawford explains that:

> In international relations [...], the invasion of the legal interest of one subject of the law by another creates responsibility in a form and to an extent determined by the applicable legal system. [...] It is a general principle of international law that a breach of an international obligation entails the responsibility of the state concerned.[135]

In discussing State responsibility, particular reference can be made to the Articles on Responsibility of States for Internationally Wrongful Acts of 2001 (Articles on State Responsibility)[136] as they provide the practical and conceptual structure within which issues of State responsibility can be considered.[137]

130. *Ibid.*, Rule 76.
131. *Ibid.*
132. Charter of the United Nations, *supra* no. 11, Art. 42.
133. *Ibid.*, Art. 42.
134. Schmitt (ed.), *supra* no. 77, Rule 76.
135. James R. Crawford, *State Responsibility* (Max Planck Encyclopedia of Public International Law, 2006), at para. 5.
136. Adopted by the ILC at its fifty-third session in 2001 (Final Outcome), UN Doc A/56/10, 43, UN Doc A/RES/56/83, Annex, UN Doc A/CN.4/L.602/Rev.1, GAOR 56th Session Supp 10, 43.
137. Crawford, *supra* no. 7, at 539-540.

Prior to analysing the Articles on State Responsibility, it must be clarified that, while they 'formally pertain to soft law',[138] tribunals and commentators alike consider them to accurately reflect CIL on State responsibility.[139]

Article 2 of the Articles on State Responsibility is the primary point of reference in this regard as it holds that there is an internationally wrongful act of a State when conduct consisting of an action or omission is attributable to the State under international law, and additionally, constitutes a breach of an international obligation of the State.

The requirement that the conduct consisting of an action or omission is 'attributable' to the State primarily revolves around the notion that a State cannot act in and of itself[140] as "States can act only by and through their agents and representatives."[141] The question, therefore, is which persons should be considered as acting on behalf of the State?[142]

Chapter II of the Articles of State Responsibility seeks to answer precisely this question as it lays down eight provisions[143] treating the notion of attribution of conduct to a State. In speaking of attribution to the State, what is meant in this context is the State as a subject of international law; the State is treated as a unity, consistent with its recognition as a single legal person in international law.[144]

Chapter II of the Articles on State Responsibility contain several provisions on attribution, including:

- Article 4, which refers to the conduct of State organs;
- Article 5, which refers to the conduct of persons or entities exercising elements of governmental authority;
- Article 8, which refers to the conduct directed or controlled by a State; and
- Article 11, which refers to the conduct acknowledged and adopted by a State as its own.

In the case of a cyberattack, therefore, if such were to qualify as an internationally wrongful act attributable to the State, and unless a State were able to preclude wrongfulness on the ground of consent, self-defence, countermeasures, force majeure, distress, necessity, or compliance with peremptory norms,[145] the result would be the obligation of the responsible State to render full reparation for the injury caused.

---

138. Pierre Bodeau-Livinec, 'Responsibility of States and International Organizations', *in* Simon Chesterman, et al. (eds), *The Oxford Handbook of United Nations Treaties* (Oxford University Press, 2019), at 599-600.
139. Michael Feit, 'Responsibility of the State under International Law for the Breach of Contract Committed by a State-Owned Entity', 28(1) *Berkeley Journal of International Law* 143 (2010), at 146.
140. ILC, 'Draft Articles on Responsibility of States for Internationally Wrongful Acts, with Commentaries' (UN, 2008), at 35.
141. *German Settlers in Poland*, Advisory Opinion, 1923, P.C.I.J., Series B, No. 6, at 22.
142. ILC, *supra* no. 140, at 35.
143. ILC, 'Articles on the Responsibility of States for Internationally Wrongful Acts', Arts 4-11.
144. ILC, *supra* no. 140, at 35.
145. ILC, *supra* no. 143, Arts 20-26.

Needless to say, in order for a State to be compensated by the responsible State for the injury caused, the States concerned would have to either settle the matter amicably or resort to adjudication by the ICJ.

§3.05 INTERNATIONAL REGULATION

At present, States have not come to an agreement on an international framework for the regulation of cyber activities.

While there exist international efforts such as the Tallinn Manual, the Organisation for Economic Co-operation and Development (OECD) Guidelines on the Protection of Privacy and Transborder Flow of Personal Data[146] and the United Nations Commission on International Trade Law (UNCITRAL) Model Law on Electronic Commerce,[147] the only binding international instrument of a 'cyber' aspect, to date, is the Budapest Convention.[148]

Nevertheless, various international initiatives aimed at addressing the growing risks of cyberattacks exist. One such initiative is the UN Digital Blue Helmets programme, the aim of which is to support the substantive partners of the UN in delivering on their missions in cyberspace, protect the UN from cyber threats, and promote cybersecurity worldwide.

The UN Digital Blue Helmets thus seek to:

- help prevent and combat cyberwarfare;
- counter cyber threats to human and economic development;
- prevent and stop human trafficking and online exploitation of people;
- facilitate dialogue to ensure a peaceful, open, secure, and cooperative cyberspace; and
- protect critical infrastructure - including food chains, supply networks, and commodities markets - from cyberattacks (not necessarily 'cyberattacks' as defined in this book).[149]

---

146. OECD Guidelines on the Protection of Privacy and Transborder Flows of Personal Data (OECD, Paris, 1981), adopted as a Recommendation of the Council of the OECD, 23 September 1980, revised in 2013. The Guidelines were one of the earliest formulations of a comprehensive set of information privacy principles and they are proposed as minimum standards for the protection of privacy and individual liberties. They are in the form of a Recommendation by the Council of the OECD, thus they are not legally binding on Member States; Graham Greenleaf, 'It's Nearly 2020, So What Fate Awaits the 1980 OECD Privacy Guidelines?', University of New South Wales Research Series, Paper No. 19-42, https://papers.ssrn.com/sol3/papers.cfm?abstract_id=3405156.
147. United Nations Commission on International Trade Law, UNCITRAL Model Law on Electronic Commerce with Guide to Enactment 1996 with Additional Article 5 *bis* as adopted in 1998 (United Nations 1999). CETS No. 185. This Model Law sets out basic rules on the validity, attribution, and effect of computer-based and other forms of electronic messaging in commerce; Harold S. Burman, 'United Nations: UNCITRAL Model Law on Electronic Commerce', 36(1) *International Legal Materials* 197-209 (1997), at 197.
148. Convention on Cybercrime 2001, *supra* no. 61.
149. UN, 'Digital Blue Helmets', https://www.unite.un.org/digitalbluehelmets/sites/unite.un.org.digitalbluehelmets/files/docs/digitalbluehelmets_brochure_final.pdf.

A further initiative of NATO was brought to life in 2016 at a summit in Warsaw. At that summit, NATO recognised that it faces a range of security challenges and threats that originate, *inter alia*, from State and non-State actors, and from terrorist, cyber, or hybrid attacks.[150] Accordingly, the NATO Allies recognised cyberspace as a domain of operations in which NATO must defend itself as effectively as it does in the air, on land, and at sea.[151]

In a Cyber Defence Pledge of July 2016,[152] the NATO Allies consequently resolved on the way forward with regard to the growing threat of cyber warfare, and among other things, the NATO Allies:

- pledged to keep pace with the fast-evolving cyber threat landscape, and to ensure that each of their nations will be capable of defending themselves in cyberspace as in the air, on land as at sea;[153]
- reaffirmed the applicability of international law to cyberspace;[154] and
- pledged to strengthen and enhance the cyber defences of their national networks and infrastructures, as a matter of priority.[155]

Moreover, a NATO Guide was endorsed in February 2019 to set out tools for further strengthening the response ability of the Alliance to significant malicious cyber activities,[156] and a NATO Cyberspace Operations Centre – which will be fully operational in 2023 – has been set up so as to support military commanders with situational awareness to inform NATO operations and missions, strengthen the cyber defences of NATO, and coordinate operational activity of NATO in cyberspace.[157]

Ultimately, NATO has declared that "the private sector is a key player in cyberspace,"[158] and on that basis, the NATO Industry Cyber Partnership was founded. This Partnership seeks to allow for cooperation with the private industry as the expertise of the latter is crucial to NATO achieving the objectives of the Enhanced Cyber Defence Policy, and as information sharing on threats and vulnerabilities therewith can help NATO prevent, respond to, and recover from cyberattacks.[159]

The EU and NATO are also cooperating in the framework of the Technical Arrangement on cyber defence that has been signed in 2016.[160] In 2018, the Secretary

150. NATO, 'Warsaw Summit Communique', https://www.nato.int/cps/en/natohq/official_texts_133169.htm, at para. 5.
151. *See*, NATO, 'Cyber Defence', Factsheet, https://www.nato.int/nato_static_fl2014/assets/pdf/pdf_2019_02/20190208_1902-factsheet-cyber-defence-en.pdf; NATO, 'Cyber Defence', https://www.nato.int/cps/en/natohq/topics_78170.htm.
152. NATO Official Texts, 'Cyber Defence Pledge', 8 July 2016, Press Release 124, 2016, https://www.nato.int/cps/en/natohq/official_texts_133177.htm.
153. *Ibid.*, at para. 1.
154. *Ibid.*, at para. 3.
155. *Ibid.*, at para. 5.
156. NATO, *supra* no. 151.
157. *Ibid.*
158. NATO, 'Industry Cyber Partnership', https://www.ncia.nato.int/Industry/Pages/NATO-Industry-Cyber-Partnership.aspx.
159. *Ibid.*
160. EU External Action, 'EEAS Update', https://www.eeas.europa.eu/delegations/un-paris/3667/eu-and-nato-cyber-defence-cooperation_en.

General of NATO came together with the Presidents of the European Council and European Commission to issue a Joint Declaration on NATO-EU Cooperation.[161]

Under the auspices of this declaration, as well as a technical arrangement concluded between the incident response teams of NATO and the EU, the two organisations have increased their collaboration, notably in the areas of information exchange, training and research.

In the framework of the Joint Declaration on NATO-EU Cooperation, the two organisations have committed to ensuring the security of citizens in Europe and in the NATO Member States,[162] among other measures (maritime cooperation, defence and security capacities), also through the ability to:

- respond to hybrid threats;
- exchange information on cyberattacks;
- confront disinformation; and
- and build resilience.[163]

In conclusion, it can be seen how, on the international plateau, although specific international instruments addressing cyberattacks do not yet exist, various initiatives and policies intended at curbing the proliferation of such attacks have been and are being undertaken.

§3.06 CONCLUSION

In this chapter, it may be seen how conflict in cyberspace does not go unregulated, even though no specific treaty exists thereon. In particular, the *jus ad bellum* applies both due to it – or parts of it – being given the status of CIL and due to the fact that it applies regardless of the weapon employed.

Notwithstanding the general applicability of this law to cyberattacks, questions still remain on the particular requirements that have to be fulfilled in order for it to apply. In other words, questions still remain on when cyberattacks amount to use or threat of use of force in violation of Article 2(4) of the UN Charter. Similarly, questions remain on when cyberattacks amount to armed attacks, allowing, as a result, States to respond through self-defence or SC authorisation under Chapter VII of the UN Charter. These questions, it must be said, are long-standing and generic, and they do not stem from the novelty of cyberattacks.

State responsibility, in a discussion on international law and breaches thereof, also plays an important role. If a cyberattack is attributable to a State in terms of the Articles on State Responsibility, then that State is to compensate the injured State(s). Problems related to attributability shall, however, be touched upon further in the subsequent chapters.

161. NATO, Official Texts, Joint Declaration on EU-NATO Cooperation, Press Release (2018) 095, 10 July 2018, https://www.nato.int/cps/en/natohq/official_texts_156626.htm.
162. *Ibid.*, at para. 4.
163. *Ibid.*, at para. 5.

Ultimately, this chapter has demonstrated that initiatives for the regulation of cyberattacks are being undertaken on an international and regional basis. In this respect, it is not surprising that most initiatives have an underlying military tone, and it is indeed diligent that States and international organisations are seeking to ensure that cyberspace does not become an incubator for cyber means of warfare.

On this note, prior to delving into the specifics of international aviation and outer space law vis-à-vis cybersecurity, an analysis of the relative legal landscape of the EU shall be undertaken.

CHAPTER 4
Promotion of Cybersecurity and Combating Cybercrime in the EU

§4.01 INTRODUCTION: EU AND CYBERSECURITY POLICY

[A] Early Regulatory and Policy Steps by the EU

In understanding the importance of technology in EU citizens' private life, for commercial actors, critical infrastructure and public entities, the EU has taken steps to create a cybersecurity strategy. The European Commission and the High Representative of the Union for Foreign Affairs and Security Policy published on 7 February 2013 the Cybersecurity Strategy of the EU: An Open, Safe and Secure Cyberspace (Cybersecurity Strategy). The Cybersecurity Strategy outlined:

> the EU's vision, clarified the roles and responsibilities for different stakeholders, and set out the actions required to make the online environment within the EU the safest in the world with a focus on a strong and effective protection and promotion of citizens' rights to make the EU's online environment the safest in the world.[1]

It is sometimes forgotten or overlooked that the Cybersecurity Strategy was not the first step taken by the EU to promote cybersecurity and combat cybercrime.[2] The EU published several policy documents, prior to the publication of the Cybersecurity Strategy in 2013, which have varying degrees of relevance for cybersecurity and cybercrime. These policy documents include:

---

1. Cybersecurity Strategy of the European Union: An Open, Safe and Secure Cyberspace, 7 February 2013, JOIN (2013) 1 Final, at 3.
2. The early regulatory and policy efforts of the EU have been diligently compiled by the NATO CCDCOE. *See*, CCDCOE, 'Organisations: European Union', https://www.ccdcoe.org/eu-0.html.

(1) Commission Communication: Network and Information Security: Proposal for A European Policy Approach.[3]
(2) Report on the Existence of a Global System for the Interception of Private and Commercial Communications.[4]
(3) European Parliament Resolution on the Existence of a Global System for the Interception of Private and Commercial Communications.[5]
(4) Council Resolution on a Common Approach and Specific Actions in the Area of Network and Information Security.[6]
(5) Council Resolution on a European Approach Towards a Culture of Network and Information Security;[7]
(6) Council Resolution on a Strategy for a Secure Information Society in Europe.[8]
(7) Commission Communication: Protecting Europe from Large-Scale Cyberattacks and Disruptions: Enhancing Preparedness, Security and Resilience.[9]
(8) Commission Communication: A Digital Agenda for Europe.[10]
(9) Commission Communication: Achievements and Next Steps: Towards Global Cybersecurity.[11]
(10) Commission Communication: Safeguarding Privacy in a Connected World A European Data Protection Framework for the 21st Century.[12]

3. Communication from the Commission to the Council, the European Parliament, the European Economic and Social Committee and the Committee of the Regions Network and Information Security: Proposal for a European Policy Approach, 6 July 2001, COM (2001) 298 Final.
4. Report on the Existence of a Global System for the Interception of Private and Commercial Communications (Echelon Interception System) (2001/2098(INI)), 11 July 2001, Session Document Final A5-0264/2001 PAR1.
5. European Parliament Resolution on the Existence of a Global System for the Interception of Private and Commercial Communications (Echelon Interception System) (2001/2098(INI)), 5 September 2001, A5-0264/2001, C 72 E/221-229.
6. European Council Resolution of 28 January 2002 on a Common Approach and Specific Actions in the Area of Network and Information Security (2002/C 43/02).
7. European Council Resolution of 18 February 2003 on a European Approach towards a Culture of Network and Information Security (2003/C 48/01).
8. European Council, Resolution of 22 March 2007 on a Strategy for a Secure Information Society in Europe (2007/C 68/01).
9. Communication from the Commission to the European Parliament, the Council, the European Economic and Social Committee and the Committee of the Regions on Critical Information Infrastructure Protection, 'Protecting Europe from Large Scale Cyber-Attacks and Disruptions: Enhancing Preparedness, Security and Resilience', 30 March 2009, COM (2009) 149 Final.
10. Communication from the Commission to the European Parliament, the Council, the European Economic and Social Committee and the Committee of the Regions a Digital Agenda for Europe, 19 May 2010, COM (2010) 245 Final.
11. Communication from the Commission to the European Parliament, the Council, the European Economic and Social Committee and the Committee of the Regions on Critical Information Infrastructure Protection 'Achievements and Next Steps: Towards Global Cyber-Security', 31 March 2011, COM (2011) 163 Final.
12. Communication from the Commission to the European Parliament, the Council, the European Economic and Social Committee and the Committee of the Regions Safeguarding Privacy in a Connected World a European Data Protection Framework for the 21st Century, 25 January 2012, COM (2012) 9 Final.

(11) Commission Communication: Tackling Crime in Our Digital Age: Establishing a European Cybercrime Centre (EC3).[13]
(12) European Parliament Resolution on Critical Information Infrastructure Protection - Achievements and Next Steps: Towards Global Cybersecurity.[14]
(13) Commission Communication: Unleashing the Potential of Cloud Computing in Europe.[15]
(14) Directive of the European Parliament and of the Council Concerning Measures to Ensure a High Common Level of Network and Information Security Across the Union (Proposal).[16]

These early policy efforts, as listed above, highlight where the EU wanted to, *inter alia*, develop the law, protect citizens, and create economic and investment opportunities. As a result, they are important documents and should not be overlooked as they have greatly influenced the EU's approach to regulating cybersecurity and cybercrime. There have also been pre-2013 regulatory efforts with a link to cybersecurity, including:

(1) Directive 95/46/EC on the Protection of Individuals with Regard to the processing of Personal Data and on the Free Movement of Such Data.[17]
(2) Directive 2002/21/EC on a Common Regulatory Framework for Electronic Communications Networks and Services.[18]

13. Communication from the Commission to the Council and the European Parliament Tackling Crime in our Digital Age: Establishing a European Cybercrime Centre, 28 March 2012, COM (2012) 140 Final.
14. Critical Information Infrastructure Protection: Towards Global Cyber-Security European Parliament Resolution of 12 June 2012 on Critical Information Infrastructure Protection - Achievements and Next Steps: Towards Global Cyber-Security (2011/2284(INI)), P7_TA (2012) 0237.
15. Communication from the Commission to the European Parliament, the Council, the European Economic and Social Committee and the Committee of the Regions Unleashing the Potential of Cloud Computing in Europe, 27 September 2012, COM (2012) 529 Final.
16. Proposal for a Directive of the European Parliament and of the Council Concerning Measures to Ensure a High Common Level of Network and Information Security Across the Union, 7 February 2013, COM (2013) 48 Final, 2013/0027 (COD).
17. Directive 95/46/EC of the European Parliament and of the Council of 24 October 1995 on the Protection of Individuals with Regard to the Processing of Personal Data and on the Free Movement of Such Data, OJ L 281, 23 November 1995, pp. 31-50 (Not in Force).
18. Directive 2002/21/EC of the European Parliament and of the Council of 7 March 2002 on a Common Regulatory Framework for Electronic Communications Networks and Services (Framework Directive), OJ L 108, 24 April 2002, pp. 33-50.

(3) Directives 2002/19/EC,[19] 2002/20/EC,[20] 2002/21/EC,[21] 2002/22/EC[22] on Electronic Communications Networks and Associated Facilities.[23]
(4) Directive 2002/58/EC Concerning the Processing of Personal Data and the Protection of Privacy in the Electronic Communications Sector,[24]
(5) Council Framework Decision 2004/68/JHA of 22 December 2003 on Combating the Sexual Exploitation of Children and Child Pornography.[25]
(6) Council Framework Decision 2005/222/JHA of 24 February 2005 on Attacks Against Information Systems.[26]
(7) Directive 2006/24/EC on the Retention of Data Generated or Processed in Connection with the Provision of Publicly Available Electronic Communications Services or of Public Communications Networks.[27]
(8) Council Directive 2008/114/EC of 8 December 2008 on the Identification and Designation of European Critical Infrastructures (ECI) and the Assessment of the Need to Improve their Protection.[28]
(9) Directive 2011/93/EU of the European Parliament and of the Council of 13 December 2011 on combating the sexual abuse and sexual exploitation of children and child pornography, and replacing Council Framework Decision 2004/68/JHA. [29]

19. Directive 2002/19/EC of the European Parliament and of the Council of 7 March 2002 on Access to, and Interconnection of, Electronic Communications Networks and Associated Facilities (Access Directive), OJ L 108, 24 April 2002, pp. 7-20.
20. Directive 2002/20/EC of the European Parliament and of the Council of 7 March 2002 on the Authorisation of Electronic Communications Networks and Services (Authorisation Directive), OJ L 108, 24 April 2002, pp. 21-32.
21. *Ibid.*
22. Directive 2002/22/EC of the European Parliament and of the Council of 7 March 2002 on Universal Service and Users' Rights Relating to Electronic Communications Networks and Services (Universal Service Directive), OJ L 108, 24 April 2002, pp. 51-77.
23. The Directives on Electronic Communications Networks and Associated Facilities were repleaded by Directive (EU) 2018/1972 of the European Parliament and of the Council of 11 December 2018 Establishing the European Electronic Communications, OJ L 321, 17 December 2018, pp. 36-214. Linked is also Article 5 of Decision 243/2012/EU of the European Parliament and of the Council of 14 March 2012 Establishing a Multiannual Radio Spectrum Policy Programme, OJ L 81, 21 March 2012, pp. 7-17.
24. Directive 2002/58/EC of the European Parliament and of the Council of 12 July 2002 Concerning the Processing of Personal Data and the Protection of Privacy in the Electronic Communications Sector (Directive on Privacy and Electronic Communications), OJ L 201, 31 July 2002, pp. 37-47.
25. Council framework Decision 2004/68/JHA of 22 December 2003 on Combating the Sexual Exploitation of Children and Child Pornography, OJ L 13, 20 January 2004, pp. 44-48.
26. Council Framework Decision 2005/222/JHA of 24 February 2005 on Attacks Against Information Systems, OJ L 69, 16 March 2005, pp. 67-71.
27. Directive 2006/24/EC of the European Parliament and of the Council of 15 March 2006 on the Retention of Data Generated or Processed in Connection with the Provision of Publicly Available Electronic Communications Services or of Public Communications Networks and Amending Directive 2002/58/EC, OJ L 105, 13 April 2006, pp. 54-63 (Not in Force).
28. Council Directive 2008/114/EC of 8 December 2008 on the Identification and Designation of European Critical Infrastructures and the Assessment of the Need to Improve their Protection, OJ L 345, 23 December 2008, pp. 75-82.
29. Directive 2011/93/EU of the European Parliament and of the Council of 13 December 2011 on Combating the Sexual Abuse and Sexual Exploitation of Children and Child Pornography, and Replacing Council Framework Decision 2004/68/JHA, OJ L 335, 17 December 2011, pp. 1-14.

(10) Regulation (EU) No 526/2013 of the European Parliament and of the Council of 21 May 2013 Concerning ENISA and Repealing Regulation (EC) 460/2004.[30]

While the above lists are not exhaustive and have different relevance for cybersecurity, they clearly highlight that the EU was not inactive in the area of cybersecurity and cybercrime prior to the publication of its EU-wide Cybersecurity Strategy.

[B] Cybersecurity Strategy of the EU

[1] Cybersecurity Strategy of the EU: An Open, Safe and Secure Cyberspace

The Cybersecurity Strategy clarified the guiding principles that EU cybersecurity policy and law should adopt.[31] It highlighted the following five principles that are directly related to fundamental values and rights:

(1) EU's core values apply as much in the digital world as in the physical world: cybersecurity should be a part of the EU system, not something additional. Therefore, general laws equally apply to the digital world.
(2) Protection of fundamental rights, freedom of expression, personal data and privacy: cybersecurity should be based on the fundamental rights and freedoms. Therefore, the Cybersecurity Strategy makes a link to the Charter of Fundamental Rights of the EU,[32] as well as to the EU's core values.[33]
(3) Access for all: all EU citizens should have access to the Internet and the unhindered flow of information and data.

30. Regulation (EU) 526/2013 of the European Parliament and of the Council of 21 May 2013 Concerning the European Union Agency for Network and Information Security (ENISA) and Repealing Regulation (EC) 460/2004, OJ L 165, 18 June 2013, pp. 41-58.
31. *See*, European Parliament Resolution of 12 September 2013 on a Cybersecurity Strategy of the European Union: An Open, Safe and Secure Cyberspace (2013/2606(RSP)); and Commission Scientific Advice Mechanism, 'Scoping Paper: Cybersecurity', 29 January 2016 (Revised).
32. Charter of Fundamental Rights of the European Union, 26 October 2012, 2012/C 326/02 (2012).
33. Consolidated Version of the Treaty on the Functioning of the European Union, 13 December 2007, 2008/C 115/01, Art. 2:

> The Union is founded on the values of respect for human dignity, freedom, democracy, equality, the rule of law and respect for human rights, including the rights of persons belonging to minorities. These values are common to the Member States in a society in which pluralism, non-discrimination, tolerance, justice, solidarity and equality between women and men prevail.

(4) Democratic and efficient multi-stakeholder governance: there is no single stakeholder in control of the Internet; thus, all stakeholders are important for proper Internet governance.[34]
(5) A shared responsibility to ensure security: all stakeholders, whether public authorities, private entities or individual citizens have a responsibility towards cybersecurity.[35]

The EU aims to actualise its EU Cybersecurity Strategy through five strategic priorities involving policy, legislative and operational measures.[36]

These five strategic points are:

(1) Achieve cyber resilience primarily through ENISA and the NIS Directive, which also includes raising awareness.
(2) Drastically reduce cybercrime by having strong and effective legislation (e.g., the NIS Directive and encouraging the Member States to ratify the Budapest Convention[37]); enhancing operational capability to combat cybercrime such as cooperating with EC3; and improving coordination at an EU level, which again involves EC3 and European Union Agency for Law Enforcement Training (CEPOL).
(3) Develop cyber defence policy and capabilities related to the Common Security and Defence Policy (CSDP).[38]
(4) Develop the industrial and technological resources for cybersecurity by promoting a single market for cybersecurity products through the NIS Directive, ENISA support and industry standards; and foster research and development investments and innovation, such as through Horizon 2020.[39]

---

34. *See*, Communication from the Commission to the European Parliament and the Council Internet Governance: The Next Steps, 18 June 2009, COM (2009) 277 Final.
35. Commission, *supra* no. 1. *See*, Commission, 'The European Agenda on Security', Communication from the Commission to the European Parliament, the Council, the European Economic and Social Committee and the Committee of the Regions, COM (2015) 185 Final, 28 April 2015.
36. *See*, for more information on hybrid threats involving cybersecurity, Joint Communication to the European Parliament and the Council, Joint Framework on Countering Hybrid Threats a European Union Response, 6 May 2016, JOIN (2016) 18 Final.
37. Convention on Cybercrime (opened for signature 23 November 2001, entered into force 1 July 2004), ETS 185. *See* Chapter 3, section §3.02[B].
38. *See*, European Parliament, 'Cybersecurity in the EU Common Security and Defence Policy (CSDP) Challenges and risks for the EU', May 2017, EPRS/STOA/SER/16/214N, PE 603.175; and European Parliament, Report on Cyber Defence, 25 June 2018, A8-0189/2018 (2018/2004(INI). *See also*, Council of the European Union, 'EU Cyber Defence Policy Framework (2018 Update)', 14413/18, 19 November 2018.
39. The 8th EU Framework Programme for Research and Innovation (Horizon 2020) runs until the end of 2020. It is the largest ever EU Research and Innovation programme with circa EUR 80 billion of funding available between 2014 and 2020. It has taken numerous theoretical ideas, such as within the scope of the transport and cybersecurity sectors, and delivered them to market. It will be superseded by the Framework Programme FP9. *See*, Commission, 'Horizon 2020', https://www.ec.europa.eu/programmes/horizon2020/. EU funding is also an important element in cybersecurity. "During the period 2014-2016, the EU has so far invested EUR 160 million under the Horizon 2020 Research and Innovation Framework Programme (H2020) in cybersecurity research and innovation projects. The EU will also invest up to EUR 450 million of

(5) Establish a coherent international cyberspace policy for the EU and promote core EU values. For this, the Council seeks to cooperate with entities like the OECD, UN, Organization for Security and Co-operation in Europe, NATO, Association of Southeast Asian Nations and *Organisation Armée Secrète*.[40]

The implementation of these five above points will be looked at throughout this chapter via the various secondary sources of EU law[41] and relevant entities.[42]

It must be stressed that the Cybersecurity Strategy is not limited to just one stakeholder. It covers the 'roles and responsibilities'[43] of numerous actors as it "can only be realised through a true partnership, between many actors, to take responsibility and meet the challenges ahead."[44] The cited stakeholders include:

(1) International: as indicated above, the Council will pursue coordination with various international stakeholders.
(2) EU: a number of EU institutions and bodies have been highlighted, such as ENISA, Europol/EC3, European Defence Agency (EDA) and CERT-EU.
(3) Member States: these, for example, "should set out in their national cybersecurity strategies the roles and responsibilities of their various national entities."[45]
(4) Private sector: These are relevant as they play a leading role in the construction and day-to-day management of the Internet.[46]

Apart from these stakeholders, there exist additional ones that are relevant. The relevance of such additional stakeholders is exemplified via the reference to the UN in

---

H2020 funding to pursue cybersecurity research and innovation under the contractual public-private partnership on cybersecurity for the period 2017-2020." Commission, 'EU cybersecurity initiatives working towards a more secure online environment', Fact Sheet, http://www.ec.europa.eu/information_society/newsroom/image/document/2017-3/factsheet_cybersecurity_update_january_2017_41543.pdf.

40. *See*, for more information on international elements, Chapter 3.
41. *See*, for an introduction on secondary sources of EU law in the transport sector (Regulations, Directives, Decisions, Recommendations and Opinions), Benjamyn I. Scott and Andrea Trimarchi, *Fundamentals of International Aviation Law and Policy* (Routledge, 2019), Chapter 1.
42. *See*, for a summary of the five strategic priorities, IT Governance, 'Cyber Security Strategy', https://www.itgovernance.eu/de-de/eu-cybersecurity-strategy-de.
43. *Ibid.*
44. Commission, *supra* no. 1, at 19.
45. *Ibid.*, at 17.
46. *Ibid.*, at 3. For example:

> As part of the EU cybersecurity strategy, the European Commission and the European Cyber Security Organisation (ECSO) signed a cPPP on 5 July 2016. The aim of the partnership is to foster cooperation between public and private actors at early stages of the research and innovation process in order to allow people in Europe to access innovative and trustworthy European solutions (ICT products, services and software). These solutions take into consideration fundamental rights, such as the right for privacy.

ECSO is a fully self-financed non-for-profit organisation under the Belgian law, established in June 2016. European Cyber Security Organisation, 'About the cPPP', https://www.ecs-org.eu/cppp.

the fifth strategic priority, whereby this could include ICAO, the ITU and United Nations Office for Outer Space Affairs (UNOOSA),[47] as well as EASA at the EU level.

[2] Revisiting the Cybersecurity Strategy of the EU

In September 2017, the Commission revisited its Cybersecurity Strategy and updated it, focusing on 'resilience',[48] 'deterrence' and 'defence'.[49] In addition to updating the 2013 Cybersecurity Strategy, the revision "can also be understood as a stepping stone in the Commission's goal to create a so-called digital single market."[50] The document thus focuses on the following areas:

(1) Building-up EU resilience to cyberattacks and step-up the EU's cybersecurity capacity through:
    (a) strengthening ENISA;
    (b) moving towards a single cybersecurity market;
    (c) implementing the NIS Directive;
    (d) having resilience through rapid emergency response;
    (e) creating a cybersecurity competence network with a European Cybersecurity Research and Competence Centre;
    (f) building a strong EU cyber skills base; and
    (g) promoting cyber hygiene and awareness.
(2) Creating an effective criminal law response through:
    (a) identifying malicious actors;
    (b) stepping-up law enforcement responses;
    (c) having public-private cooperation against cybercrime;
    (d) stepping-up political responses; and
    (e) building cybersecurity deterrence through Member State defence capabilities.
(3) Strengthening global stability through international cooperation through:
    (a) cybersecurity external relations;
    (b) cybersecurity capacity building; and
    (c) EU-NATO cooperation.

In order to address the above areas, the Commission and the High Representative proposed to reinforce the EU's resilience, deterrence and response to cyberattacks by:

47. *See*, for more information on space law, Chapter 5.
48. *See*, Communication from the Commission to the European Parliament, the Council, the European Economic and Social Committee and the Committee of the Regions, Strengthening Europe's Cyber Resilience System and Fostering a Competitive and Innovative Cybersecurity Industry, 5 July 2016, COM (2016) 410 Final.
49. Commission, Joint Communication to the European Parliament and the Council, Resilience, Deterrence and Defence: Building Strong Cybersecurity for the EU, 13 September 2017, JOIN (2017) 450 Final.
50. Global Risk Insights, 'New EU Cyber Strategy Leaves Key Security Gaps', https://www.globalriskinsights.com/2017/10/new-eu-cyber-strategy-leaves-key-security-gaps/.

(1) establishing a permanent EU Cybersecurity Agency, the core function of such an Agency would be to assist the Member States in strengthening cybersecurity, reducing cyber vulnerabilities and assisting victims of cyberattacks;
(2) creating an EU cybersecurity certification scheme that attests to a product's cyber resilience;
(3) producing a *Blueprint* covering large-scale cyberattacks;
(4) creating a network of competence centres and a European Cybersecurity Research and Competence Centre to facilitate cybersecurity;
(5) publishing a Directive on the combatting of fraud and counterfeiting of non-cash means of payment to harmonise and improve national criminal law responses;
(6) realising a Framework for a Joint EU Diplomatic Response to Malicious Cyber Activities;
(7) producing measures to strengthen international cooperation on cybersecurity, including deepening of the cooperation between the EU and NATO; and
(8) assisting, where possible, with cyber training and education.[51]

The focus and proposed methods of the revisited Cybersecurity Strategy demonstrate that the EU, notably the Commission, regard cybersecurity as critical.[52]

[C] Digital Single Market

[1] Digital Single Market Strategy

Separate, but connected to the Cybersecurity Strategy due to its cyber-based deliverable, is the Digital Single Market Strategy for Europe. The Commission has defined 'digital single market' as a market:

> in which the free movement of goods, persons, services and capital is ensured and where individuals and businesses can seamlessly access and exercise online activities under conditions of fair competition, and a high level of consumer and personal data protection, irrespective of their nationality or place of residence.[53]

The EU noted that legal fragmentation and trade barriers that do not exist in the physical single market exist in the digital market, and these are hindering trade and investment. The EU has predicted that removing these barriers within Europe could contribute an additional EUR 415 billion to the combined EU Member States' Gross Domestic Product.[54] This is because the "digital economy can expand markets and

51. *See*, for the list's source, Commission, 'Cybersecurity', Fact Sheet, 2017.
52. European Council - Council of the European Union, 'Reform of Cyber Security in Europe', http://www.consilium.europa.eu/en/policies/cyber-security/.
53. Communication from the Commission to the European Parliament, the Council, the European Economic and Social Committee and the Committee of the Regions: A Digital Single Market Strategy for Europe, 6 May 2015, COM (2015) 192 Final, at 3.
54. *Ibid.*

foster better services at better prices, offer more choice and create new sources of employment."[55]

In order to achieve a digital single market within the EU, the Commission published on 6 May 2015 its Digital Single Market Strategy, which is built upon three pillars, respectively:

(1) Provide better access to online goods and services for consumers and businesses.
(2) Create the right conditions for digital networks and services to flourish.
(3) Maximise the growth potential of the European digital economy.[56]

The Digital Single Market Strategy sets out sixteen key actions under the three pillars, which the Commission planned to deliver by the end of 2016.[57] These may generally affect relevant air and space stakeholders, such as through a review of the Regulation on consumer protection cooperation.[58] However, they may also be targeted, for example, through a review of the Satellite and Cable Directive[59] and the overhaul of EU telecoms rules.[60] Notable deliverables so far are the:

(1) end of roaming charges;[61]
(2) modernisation of data protection;[62]
(3) cross-border portability of online content,[63] and
(4) agreement to unlock e-commerce by stopping unjustified geo-blocking.[64]

---

55. *Ibid.*
56. *Ibid.*, at 4.
57. Commission Press Release, 'A Digital Single Market for Europe: Commission Sets out 16 Initiatives to Make It Happen', 6 May 2015, http://www.europa.eu/rapid/press-release_IP-15-4919_en.htm.
58. Regulation (EU) 2017/2394 of the European Parliament and of the Council of 12 December 2017 on Cooperation Between National Authorities Responsible for the Enforcement of Consumer Protection Laws and Repealing Regulation (EC) 2006/2004, OJ L 345, 27 December.2017, pp. 1-26.
59. Council Directive 93/83/EEC of 27 September 1993 on the Coordination of Certain Rules Concerning Copyright and Rights Related to Copyright Applicable to Satellite Broadcasting and Cable Retransmission, OJ L 248, 6 October 1993, pp. 15-21.
60. Commission Press Release, *supra* no. 57. *See*, Directive (EU) 2018/1972. *See*, for more information on telecommunications, Chapter 6.
61. Regulation (EU) 2017/920 of the European Parliament and of the Council of 17 May 2017 Amending Regulation (EU) 531/2012 as Regards Rules for Wholesale Roaming Markets, OJ L 147, 9 July 2017, pp. 1-8.
62. Regulation (EU) 2016/679 of the European Parliament and of the Council of 27 April 2016 on the Protection of Natural Persons with Regard to the Processing of Personal Data and on the Free Movement of Such Data, and Repealing Directive 95/46/EC (General Data Protection Regulation), OJ L 119, 4 May 2016, pp. 1-88.
63. Regulation (EU) 2017/1128 of the European Parliament and of the Council of 14 June 2017 on Cross-Border Portability of Online Content Services in the Internal Market, OJ L 168, 30 June 2017, pp. 1-11.
64. Regulation (EU) 2018/302 of the European Parliament and of the Council of 28 February 2018 on Addressing Unjustified Geo-Blocking and Other Forms of Discrimination Based on Customers'

There are also other related legislative steps, such as on Internet access,[65] including the implementation of 5G Internet,[66] which may also be relevant for air and space stakeholders.[67] In the Joint Declaration on the EU's legislative priorities for 2018-2019, as signed by the then European Commission President, Jean-Claude Juncker, the commitment to implement a connected Digital Single Market was present. This, then, shows continued support for this strategy.

[2] Digital Single Market Review

On 10 May 2017, the Commission published a mid-term review of the strategy. It presents and evaluates the progress in implementing the Digital Single Market Strategy since 2015 and highlights where further action is required.[68] It is also:

> accompanied by the European Digital Progress Report, which gives an in-depth assessment of how the EU and Member States are progressing in their digital development and identifies potential steps to help improve national performance in digital.[69]

The review focuses on three key areas:

(1) Timely delivery by the EU and its effective implementation by the Member States of secondary legislation, such as the numerous proposed and in force Directives.
(2) Providing a fair, open and secure digital environment to manage current and emerging technologies.
(3) Managing the digital transformation of society and economy so individuals and businesses can benefit from digitisation.

Nationality, Place of Residence or Place of Establishment Within the Internal Market and Amending Regulations (EC) 2006/2004 and (EU) 2017/2394 and Directive 2009/22/EC, OJ L 60I, 2 March 2018, pp. 1-15.

65. Regulation (EU) 2015/2120 of the European Parliament and of the Council of 25 November 2015 Laying Down Measures Concerning Open Internet Access and Amending Directive 2002/22/EC on Universal Service and Users' Rights Relating to Electronic Communications Networks and Services and Regulation (EU) 531/2012 on Roaming on Public Mobile Communications Networks Within the Union, OJ L 310, 26 November 2015, pp. 1-18.
66. *See*, Commission, 'Towards 5G', https://www.ec.europa.eu/digital-single-market/en/towards-5g.
67. *See*, Commission, 'Digital Agenda for Europe', November 2014, http://www.eige.europa.eu/resources/digital_agenda_en.pdf.
68. Commission, 'Shaping the Digital Single Market', https://www.ec.europa.eu/digital-single-market/en/policies/shaping-digital-single-market. *See*, Commission, 'A Digital Single Market for Europe', https://www.ec.europa.eu/commission/sites/beta-political/files/2-years-on-dsm_en_0.pdf.
69. Commission, 'Digital Single Market Mid-Term Review: Commission Calls for Swift Adoption of Key Proposals and Maps out Challenges Ahead', 10 May 2017, https://www.ec.europa.eu/digital-single-market/en/news/digital-single-market-mid-term-review. *See*, for the 2017 Report, Commission Staff Working Document Europe's Digital Progress Report 2017, 10 May 2017, SWD (2017), 160 Final.

The review identified three main areas where further action is required, namely developing the European data economy to its full potential, protecting Europe's assets by tackling cybersecurity challenges and promoting online platforms as responsible players of a fair Internet ecosystem.[70] Therefore, the work is not complete as, for example, the review explores several areas that require focus in the future, which include; digital skills; digitising industry and services (e.g., connected cars[71]); high performance computing; artificial intelligence;[72] modernising public services and e-government; and health and care.[73] As a result, the work is not complete and further developments should be expected in the future.

[D] Tallinn Digital Summit

Endorsement for the Cybersecurity Strategy and Digital Single Market Strategy is well recognised. The Estonian Presidency of the Council of the EU, in cooperation with the President of the European Council and the European Commission, organised the Tallinn Digital Summit that took place on 29 September 2017. It brought together the heads of EU Member States to discuss "further plans for digital innovation with the aim of keeping Europe ahead of the technological curve while becoming a digital leader, globally, in the years to come."[74] Key conclusions included:[75]

(1) Create a Digital Single Market.
(2) Fair taxation of the digital economy.
(3) Build strong cybersecurity through resilience, deterrence and defence.
(4) Digital Skills in Europe.
(5) Complete the Digital Single Market State of Play.[76]

Therefore, the Summit also provided a good indication of the opinions of key political and legal players in the EU system, as well as where new laws and policies are going to be created.

70. Commission Press Release, 'Digital Single Market: Commission Calls for Swift Adoption of Key Proposals and Maps out Challenges Ahead', 10 May 2017, http://www.europa.eu/rapid/press-release_IP-17-1232_en.htm.
71. *See*, Communication from the Commission to the European Parliament, the Council, the European Economic and Social Committee, the Committee of the Regions on the Road to Automated Mobility: An EU Strategy for Mobility of the Future, 17 May 2018, COM (2018) 283 Final; and European Parliament, 'A Common EU Approach to Liability Rules and Insurance for Connected and Autonomous Vehicles', PE 615.635 1, February 2018.
72. *See*, Commission, 'Factsheet: Artificial Intelligence for Europe', https://www.ec.europa.eu/digital-single-market/en/news/factsheet-artificial-intelligence-europe.
73. *See*, for a timeline of events, European Council – Council of the European Union, 'Digital single market for Europe', http://www.consilium.europa.eu/en/policies/digital-single-market/.
74. Estonian Presidency of the Council of the European Union, 'Tallinn Digital Summit', https://www.eu2017.ee/political-meetings/tallinn-digital-summit.
75. *See*, for full text of the conclusions of the Summit, Estonian Presidency of the Council of the European Union, 'Conclusions of the Prime Minister of Estonia Jüri Ratas after the Tallinn Digital Summit', https://www.eu2017.ee/news/insights/conclusions-after-tallinn-digital-summit.
76. Commission, 'Tallinn Digital Summit – Files', https://www.ec.europa.eu/commission/publications/tallinn-digital-summit-factsheets_en.

§4.02 PRIMARY AND SECONDARY EU LEGISLATION[77]

There are two main sources of EU law:

(1) Primary law: this is the supreme source of law, comprised of treaties that are ratified by each EU Member State, which lay down the legal framework of the EU.
(2) Secondary law: this comprises the legal instruments based on these treaties (i.e., Regulations, Directives and Decisions).

Both primary and secondary sources which have a link to cybersecurity and cybercrime will be assessed below.

[A] Article 222 TFEU

The Cybersecurity Strategy makes it clear that cooperation between the Member States is an important factor in fighting cyberattacks. In light of this, the Cybersecurity Strategy notes that "a particularly serious cyber incident or attack could constitute sufficient ground for a Member State to invoke the EU Solidarity Clause."[78] The Solidarity Clause is in Article 222 of the TFEU:

> 1. The Union and its Member States shall act jointly in a spirit of solidarity if a Member State is the object of a terrorist attack or the victim of a natural or man-made disaster. The Union shall mobilise all the instruments at its disposal, including the military resources made available by the Member States, to:
>
> (a)
> - prevent the terrorist threat in the territory of the Member States;
> - protect democratic institutions and the civilian population from any terrorist attack;
> - assist a Member State in its territory, at the request of its political authorities, in the event of a terrorist attack;
>
> (b) assist a Member State in its territory, at the request of its political authorities, in the event of a natural or man-made disaster.

Therefore, the EU and its Member States shall cooperate when a Member State is the object of a terrorist attack or the victim of a natural or man-made disaster.

---

77. It is not the purpose of this subchapter to list every EU primary legislation clause relevant for cybersecurity. For example, Art. 114 of the TFEU deals with the approximation of laws of the Member States to achieve the objectives set out in Art. 26 TFEU (i.e., the proper functioning of the internal market). These Articles are relevant and are often quoted, but they are of general application and do not refer specifically to cybersecurity. Article 222 was chosen as a case study as it is often cited in EU cybersecurity literature as being directly relevant for cybersecurity.
78. Commission, *supra* no. 1, at 19.

In order to provide the Member States with more details, in June 2014, the Council adopted Decision 2014/415/EU[79] on the rules and procedures for the implementation of the solidarity clause. Accordingly, 'disaster' in the context of Article 222 "means any situation, which has or may have a severe impact on people, the environment or property, including cultural heritage."[80] This then provides a broad definition of the term 'disaster', which may include a cyberattack:

> It is noteworthy that the 'severe impact' requirement does not seem to be necessarily tied to physical or financial damage. Hence, according to the proposed definition, a sophisticated and long-lasting Distributed Denial of Service attack against the private and public networks of a country that is heavily dependent on e-services in its everyday life, which results in severe impact on people, such as blocking their access to public information, denying access to the e-services provided by the State or affected private entities, hindering overall communication and in other ways interfering with the lives of the whole population, could be considered as having a 'severe impact', and thus being a cyber 'disaster'. Unless clarified further in EU documents, the currently vaguely-defined threshold of the cyber 'disaster' would become more precise only by interpretations reflected in state practice in invoking the solidarity clause and by EU precedents in assisting a requesting State.[81]

This conclusion is supported by the inclusion of Article 222 in the Commission's Cybersecurity Strategy documents.[82]

[B] Cybersecurity Legislation

[1] NIS Directive

Directive 2016/1148,[83] more commonly referred to as the NIS Directive, is the first piece of EU-wide legislation on cybersecurity and it "provides legal measures to boost

---

79. Council Decision of 24 June 2014 on the Arrangements for the Implementation by the Union of the Solidarity Clause (2014/415/EU), OJ L 192, 1 July 2014, pp. 53-58.
80. *Ibid.*, Art. 3(a).
81. CCDCOE, 'EU Solidarity Clause and 'Cyber Disaster'', https://www.ccdcoe.org/EU%20Solidarity%20Clause%20and%20Cyber%20Disaster.html.
82. The Solidarity Clause should not be confused with the mutual defence clause found in Art. 42(7) of the Treaty on European Union (TEU). This mandates Member States to aid and assist another Member State that has been the victim of armed aggression on its territory. *See*, for an overview of future EU internal and external security, The Bratislava Declaration and Bratislava Roadmap, Bratislava, Slovakia, 16 September 2016. This is not the only relevant primary EU law as, for example, the Charter of Fundamental Rights of the European Union is relevant. Most notably, Art. 7 on the Respect for Private and Family Life and Art. 8 on the Protection of Personal Data. These are addressed within the dedicated sections on data protection.
83. Directive (EU) 2016/1148 of the European Parliament and of the Council of 6 July 2016 Concerning Measures for A High Common Level of Security of Network and Information Systems Across the Union, OJ L 194, 19 July 2016, pp. 1-30. *See*, for more information, Commission Staff Working Document Impact Assessment, Accompanying the Document Proposal for a Directive of the European Parliament and of the Council Concerning Measures to Ensure a High Level of Network and Information Security Across the Union, 7 February 2013, SWD/2013/032 Final.

the overall level of cybersecurity in the EU."[84] The NIS Directive was adopted by the European Parliament on 6 July 2016 and entered into force in August 2016. The Member States then had twenty-one months to transpose the Directive into national laws and an additional six months to identify 'Operators of Essential Services', which was until 9 May 2018.[85] While the date has expired, not every Member State has fully transposed the NIS Directive into its national law; therefore, the NIS Directive's cybersecurity measures are not in place uniformly across the EU.[86]

Article 1(1) of the NIS Directive sets out its subject and scope:

> This Directive lays down measures with a view to achieving a high common level of security of network and information systems within the Union so as to improve the functioning of the internal market.

It then provides legal measures to boost the overall level of cybersecurity in the EU, as contained in Article 1(2):

> To that end, this Directive:
>
> (a) lays down obligations for all Member States to adopt a national strategy on the security of network and information systems;
> (b) creates a Cooperation Group in order to support and facilitate strategic cooperation and the exchange of information among Member States and to develop trust and confidence amongst them;
> (c) creates a computer security incident response teams network (CSIRTs network) in order to contribute to the development of trust and confidence between Member States and to promote swift and effective operational cooperation;
> (d) establishes security and notification requirements for operators of essential services and for Digital ServiceProviders;
> (e) lays down obligations for Member States to designate national competent authorities, single points of contact and CSIRTs with tasks related to the security of network and information systems.

The Directive applies to two separate subjects, these being 'Operators of Essential Services' that are established in the EU and 'Digital Service Providers' that offer services to persons within the EU.

84. Commission, 'The Directive on Security of Network and Information Systems (NIS Directive)', https://www.ec.europa.eu/digital-single-market/en/network-and-information-security-nis-directive.
85. *See*, for implementation by the Member States, Communication from the Commission to the European Parliament and the Council, Making the most of NIS – Towards the Effective Implementation of Directive (EU) 2016/1148 Concerning Measures for a High Common Level of Security of Network and Information Systems Across the Union, 4 October 2017, COM (2017) 476 Final/2, at 42-43; and Commission, 'State-of-Play of the Transposition of the NIS Directive', https://www.ec.europa.eu/digital-single-market/en/state-play-transposition-nis-directive. *See*, for failure of Member States to implement the NIS Directive, Commission, July Infringements Package: Key Decisions, http://www.europa.eu/rapid/press-release_MEMO-18-4486_en.htm.
86. *See*, to track the transposition of the NIS Directive, Digital Europe, 'NIS Implementation Tracker', https://www.digitaleurope.org/resources/nis-implementation-tracker/.

Pursuant to Article 4(4), an 'Operator of Essential Services' means "a public or private entity of a type referred to in Annex II, which meets the criteria laid down in Article 5(2)."

(a) an entity provides a service which is essential for the maintenance of critical societal and/or economic activities;
(b) the provision of that service depends on network and information systems; and
(c) an incident would have significant disruptive effects on the provision of that service.

This covers any sector and subsector referred to in Annex II of the Directive, including transport. The Member States may choose to include other sectors at their discretion as specified in Article 3. For transport, this translates into:

(1) Air carriers as defined in Article 3(4) of Regulation 300/2008.[87]
(2) Airport managing bodies as defined in Article 2(2) of Directive 2009/12/EC.[88]
(3) Airports as defined in Article 2(1) of Directive 2009/12/EC, including the core airports listed in section 2 of Annex II to Regulation (EU) No 1315/2013 of the European Parliament and of the Council,[89] and entities operating ancillary installations contained within airports.
(4) Traffic management control operators providing air traffic control services as defined in Article 2(1) of Regulation (EC) No 549/2004.[90]

These aviation stakeholders, therefore, have certain rights and obligations under the Directive. Annex II does not list space transportation as a sector falling under the NIS directive as an Operator of Essential Services.

Pursuant to Article 4(6), the term 'digital service provider' "means any legal person that provides a digital service." Pursuant to Annex III, this means any legal person providing and operating search engines, cloud computing services and online marketplaces. This may not automatically seem relevant for any aviation or space stakeholders, as these activities are outside of their core businesses, but companies may provide cloud services to, for example, airlines. Blockchain may, under certain definitions, include cloud computing, of which many transportation stakeholders are deploying, researching or considering.[91]

---

87. Regulation (EC) 300/2008 of the European Parliament and of the Council of 11 March 2008 on Common Rules in the Field of Civil Aviation Security and Repealing Regulation (EC) 2320/2002, OJ L 97, 9 April 2008, p. 72.
88. Directive 2009/12/EC of the European Parliament and of the Council of 11 March 2009 on Airport Charges, OJ L 70, 14 March 2009, p. 11.
89. Regulation (EU) 1315/2013 of the European Parliament and of the Council of 11 December 2013 on Union Guidelines for the Development of the Trans-European Transport Network and Repealing Decision 661/2010/EU, OJ L 348, 20 December 2013, p. 1.
90. Regulation (EC) 549/2004 of the European Parliament and of the Council of 10 March 2004 Laying Down the Framework for the Creation of the Single European, OJ L 96, 31 March 2004, p. 1.
91. *See*, IN2DREAMS, 'D4.1 – The Data Transaction Model in Railways Ecosystem', IN2DR-T4.1-D-CFR-013-02, 14 March 2018:

[2] Directive on Attacks Against Information Systems

In 2010, the European Commission published a Proposal for a Directive of the European Parliament and the Council on 'attacks against information systems'.[92] The proposal was adopted and published in the Official Journal on 14 August 2013 as Directive 2013/40/EU on Attacks Against Information Systems and replaced Council Framework Decision 2005/222/JHA.[93] The Directive, which the Member States had until 4 September 2015 to transpose into national law, imposes new obligations, tasks and expectations on certain key stakeholders, including:

(1) Computer Emergency Response Teams (CERTs);
(2) security specialists; and
(3) telecommunication services providers.[94]

Some space stakeholders include telecommunication providers, and CERTs exist within the aviation context, so this has relevance for transportation stakeholders.

Directive 2013/40/EU, pursuant to Article 1, "establishes minimum rules concerning the definition of criminal offences and sanctions in the area of attacks against information systems. It also aims to facilitate the prevention of such offences and to improve cooperation between judicial and other competent authorities." The scope of criminal offences is specified in Articles 3-8:

Article 3: Illegal Access to Information Systems.
Article 4: Illegal System Interference
Article 5: Illegal Data Interference.
Article 6: Illegal Interception.

Blockchain-based systems may under certain circumstances qualify as a 'digital service' within the meaning of the NIS directive and, more precisely, as a "cloud computing service." The legal definition of a cloud computing service refers to 'a digital service that enables access to a scalable and elastic pool of shareable computing resources'. From a functional perspective, the public distributed infrastructure in this way very similar to traditional cloud computing services. It could be considered as a kind of cloud computing service where the computing resource is constituted by the network-powered platform (Platform as a Service) and the computing resources are provided and allocated according to the governance rules applicable to the platform. Pending further authoritative guidance, to the extent a blockchain service may be considered a cloud computing service, the obligations under the NIS Directive need to be taken into account.

92. Proposal for a Directive of the European Parliament and of the Council on Attacks against Information Systems and Repealing Council Framework Decision 2005/222/JHA. COM (2010) 517.
93. Council Framework Decision 2005/222/JHA. *See*, Commission, Report from the Commission to the European Parliament and the Council Assessing the Extent to which the Member States Have Taken the Necessary Measures in Order to Comply with Directive 2013/40/EU on Attacks Against Information Systems and Replacing Council Framework Decision 2005/222/JHA, 13 September 2017, COM (2017) 474 Final.
94. EU Cyber Direct, 'Directive on Attacks Against Information Systems', https://eucyberdirect.eu/content_knowledge_hu/directive-on-attacks-against-information-systems/.

Article 7: Tools Used for Committing Offences.
Article 8: Incitement, Aiding and Abetting and Attempt.[95]

The Directive contains parts of Directive 2013/40/EU and, therefore, does result in significant changes. For example, the types of crimes remain the same with the possibility of higher penalties as per Article 9, as well as the rules concerning liability of legal persons as per Article 10 and jurisdiction in Article 12. There are, however, new elements:

> The Directive introduces new aggravating circumstances, including the committing of crimes where 'a significant number of information systems have been affected through the use of a tools' (i.e. botnet attacks), and crimes 'committed by misusing the personal data of another person, with the aim of gaining the trust of a third party, thereby causing prejudice to the rightful identity owner' (i.e. identity theft). Furthermore, Member States will in the future need to be able to respond to urgent information requests with a response time of no more than 8 hours, and they will be required to collect statistical data and report on cybercrime prevalence and criminal convictions within their borders.[96]

As a result, it contains new rights and obligations that the Member States and stakeholders must be aware of to ensure the accepted level of security.

[3] Blueprint for Large-Scale Cybersecurity Incidents and Crises

The Council invited, in its conclusions on Critical Information Infrastructure Protection of 27 May 2011,[97] the EU Member States to:

> strengthen collaboration among Member States and contribute, on the basis of national crisis management experiences and results and in cooperation with ENISA to the development of European cyber incident cooperation mechanisms to be tested in the framework of the next Cyber Europe exercise in 2012.[98]

95. EU efforts in the area cybercrime has also focused in two main areas. First, are the rules to criminalise non-cash payments in fraud. The Commission published a Directive on combating fraud and counterfeiting of non-cash means of payment to replace Council Framework Decision 2001/413/JHA. Directive (EU) 2019/713 of the European Parliament and of the Council of 17 April 2019 on Combating Fraud and Counterfeiting of Non-Cash Means of Payment and Replacing Council Framework Decision 2001/413/JHA, OJ L 123, 10 May 2019, pp. 18-29. Second, on 13 December 2011 a Directive on combating the sexual abuse and sexual exploitation of children and child pornography, stepping up the fight against child sexual abuse was published. Directive 2011/92/EU of the European Parliament and of the Council of 13 December 2011 on Combating the Sexual Abuse and Sexual Exploitation of Children and Child Pornography, and Replacing Council Framework Decision 2004/68/JHA, OJ L 335, 17 December 2011, pp. 1-14. The Directive is a comprehensive legal framework, which covers investigation and prosecution of crimes, assistance to and protection of victims, and prevention.
96. Time Lex, 'New Directive on Attacks against Information Systems', http://www.timelex.eu/en/blog/detail/new-directive-on-attacks-against-information-systems.
97. Council Conclusions on Critical Information Infrastructure Protection 'Achievements and Next Steps: Towards Global Cyber Security', 27 May 2011, Document 10299/11, at 9.
98. *Ibid.*

The NIS Directive does not provide for an EU cooperation framework for 'large-scale' cybersecurity incidents and crises, so the EU Member States subsequently asked the Commission to prepare a 'Blueprint' for consideration by the bodies and other relevant stakeholders.

The Blueprint is an Annex to Commission Recommendation 2017/1584 on Coordinated Response to Large-Scale Cybersecurity Incidents and Crises.[99] This Recommendation states that "Member States and EU institutions should establish an EU Cybersecurity Crisis Response Framework integrating the objectives and modalities of cooperation presented in the Blueprint following the guiding principles described therein."[100] This should be limited to:

> cybersecurity incidents which cause disruption too extensive for a concerned Member State to handle on its own or which affect two or more Member States or EU institutions with such a wide-ranging and significant impact of technical or political significance that they require timely policy coordination and response at Union political level. Such large-scale cybersecurity incidents are considered a cybersecurity 'crisis'.[101]

This should be guided by four general principles: proportionality, subsidiarity, complementarity and confidentiality of information. The core objectives of cooperation under the Blueprint shall consider political, operational and technical and are to enable an effective response, share situational awareness and agree on key public communication messages. These are then explained in detail throughout the Annex and Appendix.[102]

[C] Cybersecurity Certification

[1] Cybersecurity Act

On 13 September 2017, the Commission issued a proposal for a Regulation on ENISA[103] and on cybersecurity certification.[104] The Cybersecurity Act[105] was published on 7 June

99. Commission Recommendation (EU) 2017/1584 of 13 September 2017 on Coordinated Response to Large-Scale Cybersecurity Incidents and Crises, C/2017/6100, OJ L 239, 19 September 2017, pp. 36-58.
100. *Ibid.*, at Recommendation 1. *See*, for more information, Annex to the Commission Recommendation on Coordinated Response to Large-Scale Cybersecurity Incidents and Crises, 13 September 2017, C (2017) 6100 Final Annex 1; and Opinion of the European Economic and Social Committee on the Communication from the Commission to the European Parliament, the Council, the European Economic and Social Committee and the Committee of the Regions on Critical Information Infrastructure Protection "Protecting Europe from Large Scale Cyber-Attacks and Disruptions: Enhancing Preparedness, Security and Resilience," 22 September 2010, COM (2009) 149 Final, OJ C 255, pp. 98-102.
101. Commission Recommendation (EU) 2017/1584, *supra* no. 99, at Annex – Introduction.
102. *See*, for more information, Commission Recommendation (EU) 2017/1584, *supra* no. 99, at Appendix – Reference Documents.
103. *See* Chapter 4, section §4.03[A].
104. Proposal for a Regulation of the European Parliament and of the Council on ENISA, The 'EU Cybersecurity Agency', and Repealing Regulation (EU) 526/2013, and on Information and

2019 and entered into force twenty days later. The Regulation, as noted in Article 1(b), lays:

> a framework for the establishment of European cybersecurity certification schemes for the purpose of ensuring an adequate level of cybersecurity for ICT products, ICT services and ICT processes in the Union, as well as for the purpose of avoiding the fragmentation of the internal market with regard to cybersecurity certification schemes in the Union.

Pursuant to Article 2(9), the European cybersecurity certification scheme will be:

> a comprehensive set of rules, technical requirements, standards and procedures that are established at Union level and that apply to the certification or conformity assessment of specific ICT products, ICT services or ICT processes.

Certification is important as it establishes and preserves trust, which is crucial in transportation where manufacturers sell parts to operators which do not necessarily have the technological capabilities to fully understand the product. Customers and users are "able to ascertain the level of security assurance of the products and services they procure or purchase."[106]

The Scheme shall be prepared by ENISA, through the help of expert advice and in close cooperation with the European Cybersecurity Certification Group. Once it is adopted:

> manufacturers of ICT products or providers of ICT services will be able to submit an application for certification of their products or services to a conformity assessment body of their choice. Conformity assessment bodies should be accredited by an accreditation body if they comply with certain specified requirements.[107]

Certification will be on a voluntary basis unless specified otherwise. Therefore, transport, communication and navigation manufacturers of ICT products will be able to apply for certification.[108] It is unclear whether these ICT products will be mandated

Communication Technology Cybersecurity Certification ('Cybersecurity Act'), 13 September 2017, COM/2017/0477 Final – 2017/0225 (COD).

105. Regulation (EU) 2019/881 of the European Parliament and of the Council of 17 April 2019 on ENISA (the European Union Agency for Cybersecurity) and on Information and Communications Technology Cybersecurity Certification and Repealing Regulation (EU) 526/2013 (Cybersecurity Act), OJ L 151, 7 June 2019, pp. 15-69.
106. Proposal for a Regulation of the European Parliament and of the Council on ENISA, *supra* no. 104, at 8.
107. *Ibid.*, at 11.
108. Article 2(11) of the Proposal states that '"ICT product and service" means any element or group of elements of network and information systems'. This is elaborated on in Art. 2(2) of the Proposal which states that '"network and information system" means a system within the meaning of point (1) of Article 4 of Directive (EU) 2016/1148'. Directive (EU) 2016/1148, *supra* no. 83, Art. 4(1):

    For the purposes of this Directive, the following definitions apply:
    (1) 'network and information system' means:
        (a) an electronic communications network within the meaning of point (a) of Article 2 of Directive 2002/21/EC;
        (b) any device or group of interconnected or related devices, one or more of which, pursuant to a program, perform automatic processing of digital data; or

in EU law to acquire a cybersecurity certificate. The Preamble provides guidance as it makes a link between the proposed regulation and aviation:

> (44) In order to ensure that it fully achieves its objectives, ENISA should liaise with the relevant Union supervisory authorities and with other competent authorities in the Union, Union institutions, bodies, offices and agencies, including CERT-EU, EC3, the European Defence Agency (EDA), the European Global Navigation Satellite Systems Agency (European GNSS Agency), the Body of European Regulators for Electronic Communications (BEREC), the European Agency for the Operational Management of Large-Scale IT Systems in the Area of Freedom, Security and Justice (eu-LISA), the European Central Bank (ECB), the European Banking Authority (EBA), the European Data Protection Board, the Agency for the Cooperation of Energy Regulators (ACER), the European Union Aviation Safety Agency (EASA) and any other Union agency involved in cybersecurity.

While it shows a link between the regulation and aviation, it does not go as far as to say aviation will be a part of the mandatory group for cybersecurity certification. Space is not mentioned; therefore, the link between the space sector and the Act is more obscure.

[2] Industry Standards

In addition to the steps taken by the EU, standardisation bodies are also helping with harmonisation while regulations are being developed. Standardisation bodies rely on industry to develop standards which meet the needs of those developing and using the technologies, which can also provide flexibility and can be amended more quickly than the law, so there is a level of adaptability in such process.[109]

The European Cyber Security for Aviation Standards Coordination Group (ECSCG), which is managed by European Organisation for Civil Aviation Equipment (EUROCAE), is an aviation example, whereby its work is explicitly referenced in the rulemaking activities of EASA. The ECSCG:

> is a joint coordination and advisory group established to coordinate the cyber security for aviation related standardisation activities. A specific focus will be on

---

> (c) digital data stored, processed, retrieved or transmitted by elements covered under points (a) and (b) for the purposes of their operation, use, protection and maintenance;

Finally, Directive 2002/21/EC, *supra* no. 18, Art. 2(a):

> 'electronic communications network' means transmission systems and, where applicable, switching or routing equipment and other resources which permit the conveyance of signals by wire, by radio, by optical or by other electromagnetic means, including satellite networks, fixed (circuit- and packet-switched, including Internet) and mobile terrestrial networks, electricity cable systems, to the extent that they are used for the purpose of transmitting signals, networks used for radio and television broadcasting, and cable television networks, irrespective of the type of information conveyed.

109. Benjamyn I. Scott, *Aviation Cybersecurity: Regulatory Approach in the European Union* (Eleven, 2019), at 81-82.

activities stemming from the [European Commission] and EASA regulations, this does not exclude other market-driven standards.[110]

The standards coming from EUROCAE, as well as other bodies, may be adapted by EASA to form the text of EU aviation 'soft law' (Acceptable Means of Compliance, Guidance Materials and Certification Specifications (CS)). Therefore, there is a link between standards and EASA's rulemaking.[111]

EUROCAE is not the only entity involved in standards in transport, for example, other important standard bodies, of which some are referenced by EASA in Notice of Proposed Amendment 2019-01, include ASD-STAN, which is an Associated Body to the European Committee for Standardization for Aerospace Standards, the Radio Technical Commission for Aeronautics, the National Institute of Standards and Technology and the ISO.

[D] Data Protection

[1] Overarching Rules

The protection of natural persons in relation to the processing of personal data is a fundamental right,[112] which the EU regulates the collection, use, retention, disclosure and disposal of personal information. There is a link between data protection and cybersecurity as, for example, it may also be the goal of a cyber attacker to access personal information to steal it and then sell. The EU is well aware of this link and has taken efforts to bridge the two.

According to Article 8(1) of the Charter of Fundamental Rights of the EU, everyone has the right to the protection of their personal data.[113] Further, Article 16(1) of the TFEU provides that everyone has the right to the protection of personal data concerning them. Both these provisions stipulate that every EU citizen has the right to protection of their personal data. Pursuant to Article 16(2) TFEU, the EU has been active in regulating data protection via secondary sources of law.[114] Data protection

110. EUROCAE, 'The European Cyber Security for Aviation Standards Coordination Group (EC-SCG)', https://www.eurocae.net/about-us/ecscg/.
111. *See*, for a detailed discussion on the technical standards and their position in law, Kai Purnhagen, 'Voluntary "New Approach" Technical Standards are Subject to Judicial Scrutiny by the CJEU!: The Remarkable CJEU Judgment "Elliott" On Private Standards', 8(3) *European Journal of Risk Regulation* 586-598 (2017).
112. *See*, The Human Rights, Big Data and Technology Project, 'The Universal Declaration of Human Rights At 70: Putting Human Rights at the Heart of the Design, Development, and Deployment of Artificial Intelligence', 20 December 2018.
113. Charter of Fundamental Rights of the European Union, *supra* no. 32.
114. Lisbon Treaty, *supra* no. 33, Art. 16(2):

> The European Parliament and the Council, acting in accordance with the ordinary legislative procedure, shall lay down the rules relating to the protection of individuals with regard to the processing of personal data by Union institutions, bodies, offices and agencies, and by the Member States when carrying out activities which fall within the scope of Union law, and the rules relating to the free movement of such data. Compliance with these rules shall be subject to the control of independent authorities.

was regulated by Directive 95/46/EC on the Protection of Individuals with Regard to the Processing of Personal Data and on the Free Movement of Such Data.[115] However, in order to make the EU's rules on data protection relevant to the 'digital age', the Commission put forward its EU Data Protection Reform in January 2012.[116]

[2] GDPR

In December 2015, the European Parliament, the Council, the Commission and the European Council reached an agreement on the new data protection rules. On 4 May 2016, the official text of Regulation 2016/679 and Directive 2016/680 was published.[117] The Regulation came into force on 24 May 2016 and applied as of 25 May 2018. The Directive entered into force on 5 May 2016, and the EU Member States had until 6 May 2018 to transpose it into their national law.

Regulation 2016/679,[118] more commonly known as the GDPR, pursuant to Article 1, regulates the processing by an individual, company or organisation of personal data relating to individuals. The material scope of the GDPR is set out in Article 2(1):

> This Regulation applies to the processing of personal data wholly or partly by automated means and to the processing other than by automated means of personal data which form part of a filing system or are intended to form part of a filing system.

'Personal data' is defined in Article 4(1) as:

> any information relating to an identified or identifiable natural person ('data subject'); an identifiable natural person is one who can be identified, directly or indirectly, in particular by reference to an identifier such as a name, an identification number, location data, an online identifier or to one or more factors specific to the physical, physiological, genetic, mental, economic, cultural or social identity of that natural person.

It, therefore, does not apply to the processing of personal data of deceased persons or of legal entities.[119] 'Processing' is defined in Article 4(2), and it includes:

115. Directive 95/46/EC, *supra* no. 17. This was supported by two other sources of secondary legislation: Directive 2002/58/EC; and Council Framework Decision 2008/977/JHA of 27 November 2008 on the Protection of Personal Data Processed in the Framework of Police and Judicial Cooperation in Criminal Matters, OJ L 350, 30 December 2008, pp. 60-71. (Not in Force).
116. Commission Press Release, Commission Proposes a Comprehensive Reform of Data Protection Rules to Increase Users' Control of their Data and to Cut Costs for Businesses, IP/12/46 (2012).
117. Regulation (EU) 2016/679, *supra* no. 62.
118. *See*, for more information, Communication from the Commission to the European Parliament and the Council, Stronger Protection, New Opportunities - Commission Guidance on the Direct Application of the General Data Protection Regulation as of 25 May 2018, 24 January 2018, COM (2018) 43 Final.
119. *See*, Joined Cases C-92/09 and C-93/09 Volker und Markus Schecke GbR and Hartmut Eifert v. Land Hessen where personal information of an individual is linked to a legal entity. In such a case, the personal data can be protected.

> a wide range of operations performed on personal data, including by manual or automated means. It includes the collection, recording, organisation, structuring, storage, adaptation or alteration, retrieval, consultation, use, disclosure by transmission, dissemination or otherwise making available, alignment or combination, restriction, erasure or destruction of personal data.[120]

This wide scope is, however, restricted by Article 2(2) as it deems that the Regulation does not apply to activities outside the scope of EU law; activities of Member States under Chapter 2 of Title V of the Treaty on European Union (TEU); data processed by an individual for purely personal reasons or for activities carried out in one's home, provided there is no connection to a professional or commercial activity; and "by competent authorities for the purposes of the prevention, investigation, detection or prosecution of criminal offences or the execution of criminal penalties."

The GDPR applies to 'controllers'[121] and 'processors':[122] the controller says 'how' and 'why' personal data is processed, and the processor acts on the controller's behalf. The Regulation then sets forth the rights and responsibilities of the controller and processor, as well as other relevant entities, such as independent supervisory authorities and data subjects.

The territorial scope is wider than the physical EU territory per Article 3(1), which declares that:

> [The] Regulation applies to the processing of personal data in the context of the activities of an establishment of a controller or a processor in the Union, regardless of whether the processing takes place in the Union or not.

Therefore, the GDPR applies irrespective of whether the actual data processing takes place in the EU. Further, Article 3(2):

> This Regulation applies to the processing of personal data of data subjects who are in the Union by a controller or processor not established in the Union, where the processing activities are related to:
>
> (a) the offering of goods or services, irrespective of whether a payment of the data subject is required, to such data subjects in the Union; or
> (b) the monitoring of their behaviour as far as their behaviour takes place within the Union.

---

120. Commission, 'What Constitutes Data Processing?', https://www.ec.europa.eu/info/law/law-topic/data-protection/reform/what-constitutes-data-processing_en.
121. Regulation (EU) 2016/679, *supra* no. 62, Art. 4(7):

> 'controller' means the natural or legal person, public authority, agency or other body which, alone or jointly with others, determines the purposes and means of the processing of personal data; where the purposes and means of such processing are determined by Union or Member State law, the controller or the specific criteria for its nomination may be provided for by Union or Member State law.

122. *Ibid.*, Art. 4(8):

> 'processor' means a natural or legal person, public authority, agency or other body which processes personal data on behalf of the controller.

Organisations, for example, which have EU sales offices, will likely be subject to the GDPR. This is because the processing of such personal data can be 'inextricably linked' to and thus carried out "in the context of the activities of those EU establishments."[123] Finally, as per Article 3(3), it applies "to the processing of personal data by a controller not established in the Union, but in a place where Member State law applies by virtue of public international law."[124]

As part of the privacy reform packages, the EU adopted the Passenger Name Record (PNR) Directive on 27 April 2016. The aim of the PNR framework is to harmonise and complement the different national laws among the Member States, thus filling "security information gaps and ensuring the highest data protection standards and full respect of fundamental rights."[125] Directive 2016/681[126] "limit[s] the use of PNR data for the purpose of prevention, detection, investigation and prosecution of serious crime and terrorism" as it requires the Member States "to set up a legal and technical framework for the transfer, processing and exchange of PNR data provided by airlines."[127] The Member States had until 25 May 2018 to incorporate the Directive into national law.

Directive 2016/680 on the Protection of Natural Persons with Regard to the Processing of Personal Data by Competent Authorities for the Purposes of the Prevention, Investigation, Detection or Prosecution of Criminal Offences or the Execution of Criminal Penalties, and on the Free Movement of Such Data is linked to the GDPR and PNR Directive.[128]

---

123. Google Spain SL, Google Inc. v. AEPD, Mario Costeja González (C-131/12). *See*, Bird & Bird, 'Material and Territorial Scope', https://www.twobirds.com/~/media/pdfs/gdpr-pdfs/11--guide-to-the-gdpr--material-and-territorial-scope.pdf?la=en.
124. The second piece of secondary legislation on data protection to come out of the EU's cyber initiatives is Directive 2016/680 on the Protection of Natural Persons Regarding Processing of Personal Data Connected with Criminal Offences or the Execution of Criminal Penalties, and on the free movement of such data. Article 1(1):

    > This Directive lays down the rules relating to the protection of natural persons with regard to the processing of personal data by competent authorities for the purposes of the prevention, investigation, detection or prosecution of criminal offences or the execution of criminal penalties, including the safeguarding against and the prevention of threats to public security.

    The intention of the EU was to ensure a high level of data protection while also ensuring that there is a free flow of data within the context of investigations and prosecutions of crime. Directive (EU) 2016/680 of the European Parliament and of the Council of 27 April 2016 on the Protection of Natural Persons with Regard to the Processing of Personal Data by Competent Authorities for the Purposes of the Prevention, Investigation, Detection or Prosecution of Criminal Offences or the Execution of Criminal Penalties, and on the Free Movement of Such Data, and Repealing Council Framework Decision 2008/977/JHA, OJ L 119, 4 May 2016, pp. 89-131.
125. Commission, 'Security Union: New Rules on EU Passenger Name Record Data', https://www.ec.europa.eu/commission/presscorner/detail/en/STATEMENT_18_3910.
126. Directive (EU) 2016/681 of the European Parliament and of the Council of 27 April 2016 on the Use of Passenger Name Record (PNR) Data for the Prevention, Detection, Investigation and Prosecution of Terrorist Offences and Serious Crime, OJ L 119, 4 May 2016, pp. 132-149.
127. Commission, *supra* no. 125.
128. Directive (EU) 2016/680, *supra* no. 124.

[3] Accessing Documents from the EU

Pursuant to Article 15(3) of the TFEU:

> Any citizen of the Union, and any natural or legal person residing or having its registered office in a Member State, shall have a right of access to documents of the Union institutions, bodies, offices and agencies, whatever their medium, subject to the principles and the conditions to be defined in accordance with this paragraph.

As a result, Regulation 1049/2001[129] "define[s] the principles, conditions and limits on grounds of public or private interest governing the right of access to European Parliament, Council and Commission [...] documents." It may, therefore, be used to request information on aviation, navigation and space from the relevant bodies, such as the Commission (including EASA).

Due to the number of information sharing initiatives proposed by different EU Institutions and Bodies, this could be relevant for cybersecurity. For example, if the information sharing system does not mandate information exchange, like the European Centre for Cyber Security in Aviation (ECCSA),[130] the EU may be mandated to provide documents under this Regulation. Therefore, there is a wider legal context that must be appreciated when hosting and sharing information and data.

[4] EU and Processing of Personal Data

The EU was governed by Regulation 45/2001 on the Protection of Individuals with Regard to the Processing of Personal Data by the Community Institutions and Bodies and on the Free Movement of Such Data.[131] On 10 January 2017, the Commission put forward a proposal to amend those rules to bring them in line with the GDPR,[132] which will involve the European Data Protection Supervisor as an independent EU body responsible for monitoring the application of data protection rules within European Institutions and for investigating complaints. The result was Regulation 2018/1725.

This Regulation dictates, under Article 1, that:

> 1. This Regulation lays down rules relating to the protection of natural persons with regard to the processing of personal data by the Union institutions and bodies and rules relating to the free movement of personal data between them or to other recipients established in the Union.

---

129. Regulation (EC) 1049/2001 of the European Parliament and of the Council of 30 May 2001 Regarding Public Access to European Parliament, Council and Commission Documents, OJ L 145, 31 May 2001, pp. 43-48.
130. *See* Chapter 7, section §7.07.
131. Regulation (EC) 45/2001 of the European Parliament and of the Council of 18 December 2000 on the Protection of Individuals with Regard to the Processing of Personal Data by the Community Institutions and Bodies and on the Free Movement of Such Data, OJ L 8, 12 January 2001, pp. 1-22.
132. Proposal for a Regulation of the European Parliament and of the Council on the Protection of Individuals with Regard to the Processing of Personal Data by the Union Institutions, Bodies, Offices and Agencies and on the Free Movement of Such Data, and Repealing Regulation (EC) 45/2001 and Decision 1247/2002/EC.

2. This Regulation protects fundamental rights and freedoms of natural persons and in particular their right to the protection of personal data.
3. The European Data Protection Supervisor shall monitor the application of the provisions of this Regulation to all processing operations carried out by a Union institution or body.

Thus, any personal data processed by EU Institutions and Bodies, such as the Commission, shall be managed under this Regulation.

[5] Cookie Directive

Directive 2002/58/EC on Privacy and Electronic Communications (ePrivacy Directive),[133] deals with data protection and privacy in the digital age. It was amended by Directive 2009/136, which came into force in May 2011 and covered the processing of personal data and the protection of privacy. The amendment is popularly known as the 'EU Cookie Directive' as it requires entities to obtain consent to place and access data, such as Internet cookies, on digital devices. The scope is, however, much broader as it covers provisions on:

(1) security of networks and services;
(2) confidentiality of communications;
(3) access to stored data;
(4) processing of traffic and location data;
(5) calling line identification;
(6) public subscriber directories; and
(7) unsolicited commercial communications – i.e., spam.[134]

The Digital Single Market Strategy also called for a review of the ePrivacy Directive with the aim of providing a higher level of privacy protection for those who are using electronic communications services and providing a level playing field for all market players. As a result, the Commission published a proposal on 10 January 2017 for a Regulation Concerning the Respect for Private Life and the Protection of Personal Data in Electronic Communications that would repeal the ePrivacy Directive.[135] The proposal:

> is *lex specialis* to the GDPR and will particularise and complement it as regards electronic communications data that qualify as personal data. All matters concerning the processing of personal data not specifically addressed by the proposal are

133. Directive 2002/58/EC, *supra* no. 24.
134. European Data Protection Supervisor, 'E-privacy Directive 2009/136/EC', https://www.edps.europa.eu/node/3100#e-privacy_directive2009-136-ec.
135. Proposal for a Regulation of the European Parliament and of the Council Concerning the Respect for Private Life and the Protection of Personal Data in Electronic Communications and Repealing Directive 2002/58/EC (Regulation on Privacy and Electronic Communications), 10 January 2017, COM (2017) 10 Final, 2017/0003 (COD).

covered by the GDPR. The alignment with the GDPR resulted in the repeal of some provisions, such as the security obligations of Article 4 of the ePrivacy Directive.[136]

As a result, its aim is to complement the GDPR and provide modernised, tailored rules on privacy for digital communications. Therefore, any transportation stakeholder must follow this Directive in its online presence.

[6] Cybersecurity Sanctions

On 17 May 2019, the EU Council adopted Council Regulation 2019/796[137] on Restrictive Measures Against Cyber-Attacks Threatening the Union or its Member States. The Regulation establishes a framework for the EU to impose sanctions in relation to cyberattacks which constitute an external threat to the EU or its Member States. The scope includes both actual and attempted cyberattacks that have a 'significant effect' which, pursuant to Article 1(2):

(a) originate, or are carried out, from outside the Union;
(b) use infrastructure outside the Union;
(c) are carried out by any natural or legal person, entity or body established or operating outside the Union; or
(d) are carried out with the support, at the direction or under the control of any natural or legal person, entity or body operating outside the Union.

The term 'significant effect' is determined on a case-by-case basis by assessing the different facts, as categorised in Article 2. The sanctions will apply to persons or entities, as listed in Article 3, which are either responsible for the cyberattack or attempted cyberattack; provide financial, technical or material support for the cyberattack; or are associated with the natural or legal person, or bodies involved. The sanctions can take two forms, which are travel bans and the freezing of assets. Annex 1 of the Regulation, which contains the list of natural and legal persons, entities and bodies referred to in Article 3, shall be amended by unanimous decision of the Council following a proposal by a Member State or the High Representative of the Union for Foreign Affairs and Security Policy to include legal persons, entities or bodies which are subject to sanctions. This currently has not been done.

136. Proposal for a Regulation of the European Parliament and of the Council Concerning the Respect for Private Life and the Protection of Personal Data in Electronic Communications and Repealing Directive 2002/58/EC, *supra* no. 135, at 1.2.
137. Council Regulation (EU) 2019/796 of 17 May 2019 Concerning Restrictive Measures Against Cyber-Attacks Threatening the Union or its Member States, OJ L 129I, 17 May 2019, pp. 1-12.

§4.03 RELEVANT INSTITUTIONS, BODIES AND ENTITIES[138]

[A] ENISA

ENISA is an Agency of the EU tasked to improve network and information security. It was established in 2004 by Regulation 460/2004[139] with a periodically renewed mandate, that was meant to expire in June 2020 as declared in Regulation 526/2013.[140] However, the Cybersecurity Act[141] was published on 7 June 2019 and entered into force twenty days later. The objectives of ENISA:

> is to enhance capability to prevent and respond to network and information security problems within the EU by building on national and Union efforts. The new EU Regulation strengthens the role of ENISA and provides it with a permanent mandate in order to give it a stronger and more central role. The Regulation clarifies ENISA's role as the EU Agency for cyber security and makes moderate revisions to the organisation and governance to give greater consideration to the needs of wider stakeholders.[142]

Its work includes enhancing the capabilities and preparedness of different stakeholders (e.g., the Member States and private entities), and improving cooperation, information sharing and coordination among the different Member States and EU institutions, bodies, offices and agencies. It is clear that ENISA has a mandate for transport, as private entities can include manufacturers and operators, and the EU entities include EASA. With its new mandate, its work and importance will grow, and the actual scope of its aviation and space activities are still to be seen.

[B] CERT-EU

The CERT-EU[143] was established on 11 September 2012 to act as the CERT for EU Institutions, bodies and agencies.[144] A CERT has a loose definition, but it can be understood as a team of experts, either public or private, who manage computer

138. The list of institutions, bodies and entities detailed below is not exhaustive. Other entities, such as Eurojust, European Public Prosecutor's Office, European Union Intellectual Property Office and European Anti-Fraud Office also have limited relevance.
139. Regulation (EC) 460/2004 of the European Parliament and of the Council of 10 March 2004 Establishing the European Network and Information Security Agency, OJ L 77, 13 March 2004, pp. 1-11.
140. Regulation (EU) 526/2013 of the European Parliament and of the Council of 21 May 2013 Concerning the European Union Agency for Network and Information Security (ENISA) and Repealing Regulation (EC) 460/2004, OJ L 165, 18 June 2013, pp. 41-58.
141. Regulation (EU) 2019/881.
142. UK Government, 'EU Regulation on ENISA and Cyber Security Certification: NOTICE', https://www.assets.publishing.service.gov.uk/government/uploads/system/uploads/attachment_data/file/807297/EU_regulation_on_ENISA_and_Cyber_Security_Certification_--NOTICE.pdf.
143. The term 'Computer Emergency Response Team' was first used by the CERT-CC at Carnegie Mellon University.
144. *See*, for more information on the EU's Internal Security Strategy, Commission, 'EU Internal Security Strategy', https://www.eur-lex.europa.eu/legal-content/EN/TXT/?uri=legissum:jl0050.

security incidents. The role of a CERT can vary, but it typically involves taking preventative measures, as well as corrective measures against a cyberattack. Members of CERT-EU comprise IT security experts from the main EU institutions and bodies, namely the European Commission, the General Secretariat of the Council, the European Parliament, the Committee of the Regions, and the Economic and Social Committee. The role of CERT-EU is to improve the EU's resilience against cyberattacks, which covers prevention, detection and corrective control modes. It also works in close cooperation with Member States' CERTs, as well as non-Member States and with computer security companies.

On 10 February 2017, EASA signed a Memorandum of Cooperation (MoC)[145] with CERT-EU. The MoC sets the foundations of cooperation between EASA and CERT-EU as they will work together to establish the ECCSA.[146] The mission of the ECCSA is:

> to provide information and assistance to European aviation manufacturers, airlines, maintenance organizations, air navigation service providers, etc. in order to protect the critical elements of the system such as aircraft, navigation and surveillance systems, datalinks, airports, etc. ECCSE will cover the full spectrum of aviation.[147]

EASA's role in this cooperation is important as it has specialised technical aviation knowledge and is a trusted member of the aviation community with well-established contacts across the industry. CERT-EU has specialised cybersecurity knowledge and will "make available cybersecurity tools and information for the development of ECCSA's specialized aviation cybersecurity components and services."[148] Therefore, EASA will benefit from the general cyber-based expertise provided by CERT-EU and CERT-EU will benefit from the specialised aviation knowledge provided by EASA that will allow the ECCSA to better cover the overall EU cyber-threat landscape.

On 13 March 2017, Eurocontrol and the CERT-EU signed a Service Level Agreement to improve cybersecurity. Under this Agreement:

> CERT-EU will provide services to Eurocontrol in order to support the setting up of the European Air Traffic Management Computer Emergency Response Team (EATM-CERT). CERT-EU will make available some information and cyber-security tools to EATM-CERT as well as sharing experience, expertise, advice and procedures on how to operate a CERT efficiently.[149]

145. A MoC is a non-binding document between two or more parties that outlines the key areas of that cooperation.
146. EASA, 'Implementation of a European Centre for Cyber Security in Aviation (ECCSA)', On Air, Issue 14: Cybersecurity in Aviation, 4 April 2017, https://www.easa.europa.eu/newsroom-and-events/news/implementation-european-centre-cyber-security-aviationeccsa.
147. EASA, 'EASA Cooperate with CERT-EU on Cybersecurity', https://www.easa.europa.eu/newsroom-and-events/press-releases/easa-cooperate-cert-eu-cybersecurity.
148. *Ibid.*
149. Eurocontrol, 'Agreement with the European Commission's CERT-EU on Cyber-Security', http://www.eurocontrol.int/press-releases/agreement-european-commission-cert-eu-cyber-security.

EATM-CERT will provide the following services to air navigation service providers and airport operators of Eurocontrol's forty-one Member States:

1. Proactive cyber-security services (e.g. penetration testing, vulnerability assessment, infrastructure/best practices review);
2. Collection, generation and distribution of ATM relevant cyber intelligence;
3. Coordination, with National CERTs as appropriate, of the pan-European ATM response to ATM relevant cyber-security alerts/incidents on a voluntary basis.[150]

This three-pronged approach to cybersecurity aims to strengthen defences with proactive measures; it will increase knowledge distribution so different stakeholders can benefit, and it will be reactive as it will coordinate with national CERTs.[151]

CERTs are a common tool in cybersecurity, and these have already been utilised within transportation. For example, EASA (Safety Promotion Task) SPT.072 – Aviation Computer Emergency Response Team introduced the desire to create an aviation computer emergency response team called 'AV-CERT'. The core goal of AV-CERT is "to provide information and assistance to European aviation stakeholders in implementing proactive measures to reduce the risks of computer security incidents as well as in responding to such incidents when they occur."[152] Further to this, AV-CERT will "offer support to European aviation stakeholders on the prevention of and response to information-related security incidents." To actualise this, it will:

(1) raise cybersecurity awareness through cybersecurity promotion initiatives;
(2) advise EASA and the Commission on aviation cybersecurity policy and regulatory matters; and
(3) advise the Commission, Member States and the European Aviation Crisis Coordination Cell (EACCC)[153] in cases of aviation cybersecurity.

Although the delivery date was set for 2016, as of March 2020 not a lot of information is available on the implementation of AV-CERT.

[C] Cyber and the EDA

The 2013 Cybersecurity Strategy emphasises that "[c]yber security efforts in the EU also involve the cyber defence dimension."[154] Consequently, the European Council

150. Eurocontrol, 'European Air Traffic Management Computer Emergency Response Team (EATM-CERT)', http://www.eurocontrol.int/eatm-cert.
151. Eurocontrol, 'Centralised Service 6-7: EATM-CERT and SOC, Centralised Service 6-6: PKI, Presentation World Aviation Congress (WAC)', 8 March 2017, https://www.eurocontrol.int/sites/default/files/events/presentation/cs-6-6-and-6-7-briefing-presentation-day-2-eurocontrol-wac-2017.pdf.
152. EASA, European Plan for Aviation Safety 2016-2020, Final, 25 January 2016.
153. *See*, Eurocontrol, 'The European Aviation Crisis Coordination Cell (EACCC)', http://www.eurocontrol.int/articles/european-aviation-crisis-coordination-cell-eaccc.
154. Commission, *supra* no. 1, at 11.

adopted a Cyber Defence Policy Framework in November 2014. The Framework contained five goals:

1. Supporting the development of Member States' cyber defence capabilities related to CSDP;
2. enhancing the protection of CSDP communication networks used by EU entities;
3. promotion of civil-military cooperation and synergies with wider EU cyber policies, relevant EU institutions and agencies as well as with the private sector;
4. improve training, education and exercises opportunities;
5. enhancing cooperation with relevant international partners.[155]

The CSDP, which is integral to the EU's approach towards crisis management, "enables the Union to take a leading role in peace-keeping operations, conflict prevention and in the strengthening of the international security."[156] In doing so, it draws on both civilian and military assets, which is important due to the dual nature of many assets of the key stakeholders in transport, communication and navigation.

The EDA is an EU Agency that was established on 12 July 2004 "to support the Member States and the Council in their effort to improve European defence capabilities in the field of crisis management and to sustain the European Security and Defence Policy as it stands now and develops in the future."[157] The EDA is active in the fields of cyber defence, research and technology, and works with the EU Military Staff to improve EU cyber defence capabilities.

In accordance with the 2014 Capability Development Plan Revision, the focus of EDA relies on supporting the Member States in building a skilled military cyber defence workforce and ensuring the availability of proactive and reactive cyber defence technology in the areas of:

(1) training and exercises;
(2) cyber situation awareness;
(3) advanced persistent threats detection;
(4) digital forensics for military use; and
(5) the Cyber Defence Strategic Research Agenda.[158]

Aware of the relevance of cybersecurity for transport, for example, the EDA organised, on 13 June 2018, an Aviation Cyber Security Seminar that brought together both the civil and military aviation and cyber defence communities. Its intention was

155. European Defence Agency, 'Cyber Defence', https://www.eda.europa.eu/what-we-do/activities/activities-search/cyber-defence.
156. European Union External Action, 'The Common Security and Defence Policy (CSDP)', https://www.eeas.europa.eu/topics/common-security-and-defence-policy-csdp/431/common-security-and-defence-policy-csdp_en.
157. European Defence Agency, 'Mission', https://www.eda.europa.eu/Aboutus/Missionandfunctions. Denmark has opted out of the Agency. *See*, the Mutual Defence Clause as found in Art. 42 of the Lisbon Treaty.
158. European Defence Agency, 'Cyber Defence', Fact Sheet, 22 May 2018, https://www.eda.europa.eu/docs/default-source/eda-factsheets/2018-05-22-factsheet_cyber-defence.

to develop a common understanding of the current and future cybersecurity challenges within the scope of aviation, with the focus being on military requirements.[159]

[D] Europol

Europol, which was previously the European Police Office and Europol Drugs Unit, was formed in 1998 and is an EU law enforcement agency, thus, relevant for law enforcement in the field of cybersecurity. Europol supports Member States' law enforcement authorities within its mandated areas, one of which is cybercrime.[160]

As a part of its work on cybercrime, the Commission announced its intention to establish EC3 in the EU Internal Security Strategy in Action,[161] which was adopted on 22 November 2010 by the Commission.[162] In 2013, Europol set up EC3 with the aim of strengthening law enforcements' responses in the EU to cybercrime, which should also have the knock-on effect of boosting protection to EU citizens, businesses and governments.

EC3 takes a three-pronged approach to the fight against cybercrime:

159. European Defence Agency, 'EDA Aviation Cyber Security Seminar to Focus on Priorities for Cooperation', https://www.eda.europa.eu/info-hub/press-centre/latest-news/2018/06/08/eda-aviation-cyber-security-seminar-to-focus-on-priorities-for-cooperation.

160. Lisbon Treaty, *supra* no. 33, Art. 88:

> 1. Europol's mission shall be to support and strengthen action by the Member States' police authorities and other law enforcement services and their mutual cooperation in preventing and combating serious crime affecting two or more Member States, terrorism and forms of crime which affect a common interest covered by a Union policy.
> 2. The European Parliament and the Council, by means of regulations adopted in accordance with the ordinary legislative procedure, shall determine Europol's structure, operation, field of action and tasks. These tasks may include:
>   (a) the collection, storage, processing, analysis and exchange of information, in particular that forwarded by the authorities of the Member States or third countries or bodies;
>   (b) the coordination, organisation and implementation of investigative and operational action carried out jointly with the Member States' competent authorities or in the context of joint investigative teams, where appropriate in liaison with Eurojust.
>
>   These regulations shall also lay down the procedures for scrutiny of Europol's activities by the European Parliament, together with national Parliaments.
> 3. Any operational action by Europol must be carried out in liaison and in agreement with the authorities of the Member State or States whose territory is concerned. The application of coercive measures shall be the exclusive responsibility of the competent national authorities.

See, Europol, 'Mandate', https://www.europol.europa.eu/about-europol.

161. Communication from the Commission to the European Parliament and the Council the EU Internal Security Strategy in Action: Five Steps Towards a More Secure Europe, 22 November 2010, COM/2010/0673 Final.

162. Commission, 'Commission Presents a New Set of EU Measures to Better Protect European Citizens', 22 November 2010, IP/10/1535; and The EU Internal Security Strategy in Action: Five Steps Towards A More Secure Europe', MEMO/10/598 2010.

(1) Forensics: EC3 has two forensics teams, digital forensics and document forensics, each of which focuses on operational support, and research and development.
(2) Strategy: EC3 has two strategy teams. The first focuses on outreach and support "establishes partnerships and coordinates prevention and awareness measures." The second works on strategy and development, which works on "strategic analysis, the formulation of policy and legislative measures, and the development of standardised training."[163]
(3) Operations: EC3 focuses on three types of cybercrimes: Cyber-dependent crime, online child sexual exploitation and payment fraud.

EC3 activities are supported by the Cyber Intelligence Team, which collects and processes cybercrime-related information from varies sources, as well as identifying emerging threats and patterns.

The Joint Cybercrime Action Taskforce was launched in September 2014 and is based at Europol and complements EC3. Its objective is "to drive intelligence-led, coordinated action against key cybercrime threats and targets by facilitating the joint identification, prioritisation, preparation and initiation of cross-border investigations and operations by its partners."[164]

Each year, EC3 publishes the Internet Organised Crime Threat Assessment (IOCTA),[165] which is a strategic report on key findings and emerging threats and developments in cybercrime. The IOCTA "provides key recommendations to law enforcement, policy makers and regulators to allow them to respond to cybercrime in an effective and concerted manner."[166] The report focuses on the crime areas that fall under EC3's mandate and is a useful tool to see the key threats and ways to combat them.

[E] CEPOL

CEPOL is an Agency of the EU that was established by Regulation 2015/2219.[167] Pursuant to Article 3(1), its objective is to:

163. Europol, 'European Cybercrime Centre: EC3', https://www.europol.europa.eu/about-europol/european-cybercrime-centre-ec3.
164. Europol, 'Joint Cybercrime Action Taskforce (J-CAT)', https://www.europol.europa.eu/activities-services/services-support/joint-cybercrime-action-taskforce.
165. *See*, for the 2017 report, Europol, 'Internet Organised Crime Threat Assessment (IOCTA) 2017', https://www.europol.europa.eu/activities-services/main-reports/internet-organised-crime-threat-assessment-iocta-2017.
166. Europol, 'Internet Organised Crime Threat Assessment (IOCTA)', https://www.europol.europa.eu/activities-services/main-reports/internet-organised-crime-threat-assessment.
167. Regulation (EU) 2015/2219 of the European Parliament and of the Council of 25 November 2015 on the European Union Agency for Law Enforcement Training (CEPOL) and Replacing and Repealing Council Decision 2005/681/JHA, OJ L 319, 4 December 2015, pp. 1-20. Denmark and the UK are not members of CEPOL in accordance with Protocols 21 and 22 of the Lisbon Treaty.

> support, develop, implement and coordinate training for law enforcement officials, while putting particular emphasis on the protection of human rights and fundamental freedoms in the context of law enforcement, in particular in the areas of prevention of and fight against serious crime affecting two or more Member States and terrorism, maintenance of public order, in particular international policing of major events, and planning and command of Union missions, which may also include training on law enforcement leadership and language skills.[168]

Within its assigned tasks and research relevant training, CEPOL has been active in cybersecurity. This has centred on the training through courses, including transport specific courses, such as airline fraud investigation procedure[169] and PNR information analysis.[170]

[F] European Cybersecurity Research and Competence Centre

The Commission, in its September 2017 Strategy update, "announced the intention to set up a network of cybersecurity centres of expertise with a European Research and Competence Centre at its heart with the aim to pool resources, overcome fragmentation of efforts across the EU and stimulate development and deployment of technology in cybersecurity."[171] This situation is driven by a number of underlying causes, which are closely linked to each other:

(1) Fragmentation of the effort and a lack of a dynamic EU-wide ecosystem.
(2) Size of the effort.
(3) Difficulty to get access to the latest cybersecurity capacities.
(4) Protecting the public sector as a major challenge but also an opportunity.
(5) Dual use is not developed enough.
(6) The cybersecurity skills challenge.

The aim is to set up a Network of Cybersecurity Competence Centres and a European Cybersecurity Research and Competence Centre. The network results from a Commission call for proposals on 1 February 2018 and will include such entities as university labs and research centres, and will aim to "bolster the existing cybersecurity

---

168. *See*, for more information on human rights and cybersecurity, Report on Human Rights and Technology: The Impact of Intrusion and Surveillance Systems on Human Rights in Third Countries, 3 June 2015, 2014-2019 Plenary Sitting, A8-0178/2015 (2014/2232(INI)).
169. CEPOL, 'Webinar 12/2016 Combatting Payment Card Fraud: Airline Fraud Investigation Procedure', 2 March 2016, https://www.cepol.europa.eu/education-training/what-we-teach/webinars/webinar-122016-combatting-payment-card-fraud-airline-fraud.
170. CEPOL, '36/2016 Passenger Name Record (PNR) Information Analysis: Train the Trainers', https://www.cepol.europa.eu/education-training/what-we-teach/residential-activities/362016-passenger-name-record-pnr-information. *See*, for more information on PNR, Elena Carpanelli and Nicole Lazzerini, 'PNR: Passenger Name Record, Problems Not Resolved? The EU PNR Conundrum after Opinion 1/15 of the CJEU', 42(4/5) *Air and Space Law* 377-402 (2017).
171. Commission, 'Inception Impact Assessment: Create a Cybersecurity Competence Network with a European Cybersecurity Research and Competence Centre', 22 March 2018, Ref. Ares (2018) 1598442, at 1.

research for the benefit of the Digital Single Market."[172] The locations and number of centres are not yet known; however, the Commission plans to further cooperate with other EU bodies, including ENISA and Europol.[173]

[G] Joint EU Diplomatic Response to Malicious Cyberattacks

The EU is concerned about the increasing willingness of States and non-State actors to pursue their objectives through cyberattacks, where such actions may constitute wrongful acts under international law and have effects on the EU.[174] At the Peace and Security Council (PSC) meeting of 14 March 2017, the EU External Action Service[175] (EU's diplomatic service) and the Commission services presented a paper on a joint EU diplomatic response to cyber operations. On 6 June 2017, the final text of the draft Council Conclusions was submitted to the PSC, with help from the Horizontal Working Party on Cyber Issues.[176] On 19 July 2017, the Council agreed on Council Conclusions on a Framework for a Joint Diplomatic Response to Malicious Cyber Activities, which

172. Roman Šulc, 'EU Launches Pilot Project to Build Cybersecurity Competence Centres', *European Security Journal*, 6 February 2018, https://www.esjnews.com/eu-cybersecurity-competence-centres.
173. Roman Šulc, 'EU to Build Cyber Centres for Research and Development', *European Security Journal*, 27 November 2017, https://www.esjnews.com/eu-cybercenters-research-development?page=2.
174. European Council - Council of the European Union, 'Cyber Attacks: EU Ready to Respond with a Range of Measures, Including Sanctions', http://www.consilium.europa.eu/en/press/press-releases/2017/06/19/cyber-diplomacy-toolbox/.
175. European External Action Service, 'About the European External Action Service (EEAS)', https://www.eeas.europa.eu/headquarters/headquarters-homepage/82/about-european-external-action-service-eeas_en:

    > The EEAS is the European Union's diplomatic service. It helps the EU's foreign affairs chief - the High Representative for Foreign Affairs and Security Policy - carry out the Union's Common Foreign and Security Policy.

176. European Council, 'Horizontal Working Party on Cyber Issue (HWP)', https://www.consilium.europa.eu/en/council-eu/preparatory-bodies/horizontal-working-party-on-cyber-issues/:

    > The Horizontal Working Party on Cyber Issues was established in 2016 and is responsible for coordination of Council's work on cyber issues mainly the cyber policy and legislative activities. The working party cooperates closely with other related working parties as well as with European Commission, EEAS, Europol, Eurojust, FRA, EDA and ENISA. The main objectives of the working party are:
    > 1. ensuring a horizontal working platform providing for harmonisation and unified approach on cyber policy issues;
    > 2. coherent progress in the cyber domain, while keeping up with cyber threats;
    > 3. identify and expand cooperation with Council preparatory bodies and other relevant actors;
    > 4. information sharing on cyber issues both among EU countries and national bodies;
    > 5. setting EU cyber priorities and strategic objectives as part of a comprehensive policy framework; and
    > 6. representation of the EU in accordance with the strategic EU cyber policy objectives.

has been called the 'Cyber Diplomacy Toolbox'.[177] This aims to allow the EU and its Member States to prevent and respond to malicious cyber activities. The EU and its Member States, through the Toolbox, seek to encourage cooperation, facilitate the mitigation of immediate and long-term threats, and influence the behaviour of potential aggressors in the long term.[178]

[H] EU-LISA

EU-LISA is an EU Agency that was established in 2011 by Regulation 1077/2011[179] and started its activities on 1 December 2012. It has its headquarters in Tallinn, Estonia, with other sites around Europe. EU-LISA provides "a long-term solution for the operational management of large-scale IT systems, which are essential instruments in the implementation of the asylum, border management and migration policies of the EU."[180] The Agency manages, for example, the Eurodac, the second-generation Schengen Information System (SIS) and the Visa Information System (VIS).

On 21 November 2018, Regulation 2018/1726 on EU-LISA was published and entered into force on 11 December 2018. It enhances EU-LISA's capacities to improve existing and develop new information systems for security, border management and migration. The Regulation builds upon its past work, aiming to reinforce it, as it will:

> Roll-out interoperability of EU information systems: once the Commission proposals are adopted, eu-LISA will be responsible for rolling out the technical components to make EU information systems interoperable;
>
> Develop Future Systems: With a proposed budget of €2 billion for the period 2019-2027, the Agency will develop and manage future large-scale EU information systems such as the Entry/Exit System (EES), the European Travel Information and Authorisation System (ETIAS) and the upgraded European Criminal Records Information System (ECRIS-TCN);
>
> Upgrade Existing Systems: The Agency will maintain and upgrade existing systems, such as the Schengen Information System (SIS), the Visa Information System (VIS) and Eurodac, for which it is already responsible;
>
> Support Member States: The Agency will be able to provide greater ad hoc technical and operational support to Member States.

These are positive steps, but time is needed for their full implementation, and it will be a test for this young Agency.

---

177. Council of the European Union, Draft Council Conclusions on a Framework for a Joint EU Diplomatic Response to Malicious Cyber Activities ('Cyber Diplomacy Toolbox'), 9916/17, 7 June 2017.
178. Commission, 'State of the Union 2017: The Commission Scales up Its Response to Cyberattacks', Fact Sheet, 19 September 2017, http://www.europa.eu/rapid/press-release_MEMO-17-3194_en.htm.
179. Regulation (EU) 1077/2011 of the European Parliament and of the Council of 25 October 2011 Establishing a European Agency for the Operational Management of Large-Scale IT Systems in the Area of Freedom, Security and Justice, OJ L 286, 1 November 2011, pp. 1-17.
180. EU-LISA, 'Who We Are', https://www.eulisa.europa.eu/AboutUs/WhoWeAre/Pages/default.aspx.

§4.04 CONCLUSION

Prior to 2013, the efforts of the European Commission in the promotion of cybersecurity and activities to mitigate the effects of cyberattacks were fragmented. In order to remedy this, the EU published its Cybersecurity Strategy, which was later complemented by the Digital Single Market Strategy, whereby both received a strong political endorsement on 29 September 2017 during the Tallinn Digital Summit. Since then, the EU has built upon the pre-2013 fragmented policy and regulatory landscape, to produce a comprehensive regime to promote cybersecurity and fight against cyberattacks and their consequences.

This chapter has documented these main activities and highlighted some of their strengths and weaknesses. As an overall observation, the EU needs to continue to fill the regulatory lacunas and amend the rules, where necessary, to strengthen cyber resilience and ensure the rules are adaptable to this fast-evolving environment. Further, the EU must continue to promote and support non-regulatory steps, such as information sharing, training and research, as law is only a part of the solution. Finally, a critical step is to ensure harmonisation between the rules outlined in this chapter and the *lex specialis* of air and space law. While aviation is sometimes linked to these activities, this is the exception. Further, space is mostly omitted from the general EU cybersecurity discussions. If they are not aligned, then it could create confusion, duplication of work, gaps and conflict (e.g., the competent authority could be the Commission, EASA or the Member States).

CHAPTER 5

Space (Law) and Cybersecurity

§5.01 GENERAL REMARKS

[A] Growth Tendencies in the Global Space Economy

Cybersecurity is becoming an increasingly relevant aspect of outer space activities. Although the space age started only six decades ago, the pace with which it became an indispensable enabler of numerous services on Earth for both civilian and military uses is considerable. In the recent three decades, space technology has experienced strong commercialisation which has transformed the originally state-owned and state-financed space activities domain to an increasingly privately-owned and – to a large extent – privately financed market.[1]

While the global space economy has been estimated to USD 360 million, the global satellite industry which consists of satellite services, satellite manufacturing, launch industry and ground equipment, created revenues of USD 277 million in 2018.[2] Thereby, the satellite industry currently forms up to 77% of the global space economy.[3] Constant growth has been registered especially in the manufacturing branch (with a growth factor of 26%) as well as in the launch segment (with a growth factor of 34%). Moreover, the ground equipment segment, which includes consumer, Global Navigation Satellite System (GNSS) and network equipment, makes up 28.7% of the overall revenues from the global space economy.[4] The annual growth of the satellite industry market, which has always been the largest commercial sector of space activities, is amounting to an average growth of 3%-4% *per annum*. The revenues from the

1. *See*, for an informative analysis of the trends, risks and challenges of the global space sector, Bank of America Meryll Lynch, 'To Infinity and Beyond: Global Space Primer', Report, 30 October 2017, https://www.api.guidants.com/db/a2/1e1ffc185c1d44bd.pdf.
2. Bryce Space and Technology, '2019 State of the Satellite Industry Report', May 2019, https://www.brycetech.com/download.php?f=downloads/SSIR-2019-2-pager.pdf.
3. Numbers in USD provided by the 2019 State of the Satellite Industry Report. *Ibid.*
4. *Ibid.*

consumer equipment for various terminals, including TV, radio, broadband and mobile satellite terminals are also increasing across all segments of the satellite industry.[5]

These statistics show that the global space economy is flourishing and constantly growing, becoming increasingly interwoven with services and infrastructure on Earth. This process is facilitated, in particular, by the fact that technology is becoming more affordable. Nowadays, satellite technology is economically and technologically accessible not only for States but also for private actors. This trend can be observed in particular throughout the past fifteen years, during which private companies such as SpaceX, Blue Origin, OneWeb, and Virgin Galactic have emerged and have been developing ambitious endeavours for the use and exploration of outer space. Space activities have been transformed substantially as the traditionally state-based space sector has been outpaced by the private industry, especially in terms of the development of launching and transportation capabilities.[6]

[B] Interconnectivity in the Space Sector: The Role of Cyberspace in Outer Space

Apart from technological progress, lower prices and strong competition, one other factor which is facilitating the growing accessibility of space technology for private actors is the process of introducing global (inter)connectivity on most levels of industry, services and communications.[7] As in any technological field, this process also affects the space domain that is getting increasingly digitised and interconnected. As has been correctly observed, satellites, despite forming an industry with its own specific characteristics, are not much different from any other type of devices on the IoT[8] in terms of their reliability on cyber technology as they are becoming increasingly connected to the Internet.[9]

As far as the users of cyberspace and the Internet are concerned, it is estimated that the number of users of the Internet as the main and most globally accessible part of cyberspace was 4.536 billion (as of June 2019), as compared to 4.157 billion in 2017.[10] This represents 58.8% of the world population and amounts to a growth in the number of end-users of the Internet of 1.157% in 19 years between 2000 and 2019, while Internet users are growing by an average of more than one million users every

5. *Ibid.*
6. *See*, for further analytical reports on the development of the launch market, NATO Economic and Security Committee, 'The Future of the Space Industry', General Report, 17 November 2017; Federal Aviation Administration, 'The Annual Compendium of Commercial Transportation: 2018', January 2018; Northern Sky Research, *Smallsat Launch Vehicle Markets*, Second Edition (June 2019).
7. *See*, for example, Huawei, 'The 2018 Global Connectivity Index', www.huawei.com/minisite/gci/en/index.html.
8. *See*, for a definition, Chapter 2, section §2.05[C].
9. P.J. Blount, 'Satellites Are Just Things on the Internet of Things', 42(3) *Journal of Air and Space Law* 273-294 (2017).
10. World Internet Users and 2019 Populations Stats, 'Internet Usage Statistics: The Internet Big Picture', https://www.internetworldstats.com/stats.htm.

day.[11] The geographical distribution of these users is as follows: most users live in Asia (2.3 billion users), followed by Europe (728 million users), Africa (523 million users), Latin America and the Caribbean (453.7 million users), North America (327.6 million users), the Middle East (175.5 million users) and Australia and Oceania (28.6 million users).[12]

According to an analytic comparison,[13] in 2003, the world population amounted to 6.3 billion people and 500 million devices were connected to the Internet. In 2010, the population had grown to 6.8 billion while there were 12.5 billion devices connected to the Internet. This means that, calculated per capita, in 2010, each person on the planet possessed 1.84 devices on average.[14] In 2018, the global number of connected devices was estimated at 17 billion[15] and was expected to reach 50 billion by 2020, excluding the existing cell phones, tablets, laptops, personal computers and related periphery, and to continue to grow exponentially.[16]

This prognosis visualises one clear tendency: humankind is living in an interconnected world in which the dependency on technology, in general, and on cyberspace, in particular, is steadily growing. The dependence on the use of space technology has also been growing on a global scale through the impact of outer space technology in various fields of life. The use of outer space is vital, in particular, not only for the establishment, employment and development of critical infrastructure, defence systems and transportation but also in everyday activities.[17]

Therefore, the interweaving of space technology and cyberspace is a highly relevant phenomenon which needs to be addressed from a legal, political and technical perspective.

§5.02 THE LEGAL FRAMEWORK GOVERNING HUMAN ACTIVITIES IN OUTER SPACE

In order to address issues of cybersecurity in space activities, first, a general picture of the legal framework applicable to space activities will be provided. Only then, questions on the relationship between cyberspace and outer space and the resulting consequences for the legal framework governing cybersecurity in outer space will be analysed.

11. We Are Social/Hootsuite, 'Global Digital Yearbook Report 2019', https://www.wearesocial.com/blog/2019/01/digital-2019-global-internet-use-accelerates.
12. World Internet Users and 2019 Populations Stats, *supra* no. 10.
13. *See*, for example, Dave Evans, 'The Internet of Things, How the Next Evolution of the Internet Is Changing Everything', April 2011, https://www.cisco.com/c/dam/en_us/about/ac79/docs/innov/IoT_IBSG_0411FINAL.pdf.
14. *Ibid.*
15. Knud Lasse Lueth, 'State of the IoT 2018', 8 August 2018, https://www.iot-analytics.com/state-of-the-iot-update-q1-q2-2018-number-of-iot-devices-now-7b/.
16. Evans, *supra* no. 13.
17. *See* Chapter 6.

[A] Applicability of General International Law and Space Law to Outer Space

Before an account can be given on the applicability of law on a natural environment such as outer space, it is worthwhile to outline its characteristics as such. Outer space is first and foremost governed by the laws of nature and physics, which presuppose that human activities therein can take place only in a certain way and subject to physics, for example to the Kepler's laws of planetary motion. The expansion of human activities in outer space also has to take into account the reach of human knowledge, which, as of today, has only allowed some areas of the Solar system to be explored.[18] Therefore, for the purposes of regulation, it can be stated that outer space, in the legal sense, comprises that part of the Universe that is accessible for human activities.[19]

Legally, outer space is a domain beyond national jurisdiction. Therefore, it is governed primarily by international law,[20] including space law as *lex specialis*.[21] According to Article VIII of the OST, national regulation can take place only insofar as the jurisdiction of States is extended to space objects and persons in outer space or on celestial bodies.[22]

Space law governs all human activities related to the use and exploration of outer space, including celestial bodies and asteroids.[23] Thereby, it relates to both commercial

18. For example, the farthest point to be reached by a manned mission, is the Moon, and the farthest that an unmanned space probe has gone is considered to be Voyager 1, on mission since 1978, that has left the Solar system in 2012.
19. Here, the authors refrain from the discussion on the delimitation between airspace and outer space. For a detailed account on this undecided issue, *see*, UN Committee on the Peaceful Uses of Outer Space, Historical Summary on the Consideration of the Question on the Definition and Delimitation of Outer Space, UN Doc. A/AC.105/769 (2002). *See also*, for different approaches to delimitation, Francis Lyall and Paul B. Larsen, *Space Law: A Treatise*, Second Edition (Routledge, 2018), at 143-151.
20. Treaty on Principles Governing the Activities of States in the Exploration and Use of Outer Space, including the Moon and Other Celestial Bodies, 610 UNTS 205, adopted on 27 January 1967, entered into force 10 October 1967 [Outer Space Treaty], Art. III:

    > States Parties to the Treaty shall carry on activities in the exploration and use of outer space, including the moon and other celestial bodies, in accordance with international law, including the Charter of the United Nations, in the interest of maintaining international peace and security and promoting international co-operation and understanding.

    See also, International Co-Operation in the Peaceful Uses of Outer Space, UN GA Res. 1721(XVI)A, UN Doc. A/RES/1721(XVI) (20 December 1961). As early as 1961, the General Assembly recognised that in the exploration and use of outer space "[i]nternational law, including the Charter of the United Nations, applied to outer space and celestial bodies."
21. Outer Space Treaty, *supra* no. 20, Art. III. Michael Akehurst, 'The Hierarchy of the Sources of International Law', 41(1) *British Yearbook of International Law* 273-285 (1976), at 273.
22. Outer Space Treaty, *supra* no. 20, Art. VIII:

    > A State Party to the Treaty on whose registry an object launched into outer space is carried shall retain jurisdiction and control over such object, and over any personnel thereof, while in outer space or on a celestial body.

23. *See* generally, Virgiliu Pop, 'A Celestial Body Is a Celestial Body Is a Celestial Body ...', International Institute of Space Law, Proceedings of the Forty-Fourth Colloquium on the Law of

and non-commercial activities in outer space.[24] Such activities include the use, the exploration and the scientific investigation in outer space and celestial bodies for civil or military purposes.[25]

International space law is a specific branch of international law[26] and comprises five international treaties adopted in the system of the UN between 1967 and 1979[27] as well as non-binding resolutions that have been adopted by the UN General Assembly from 1982 onwards.[28] In fulfilling their obligations under Article VI of the OST, according to which:

> States Parties to the Treaty shall bear international responsibility for national activities in outer space, including the Moon and other celestial bodies, whether such activities are carried on by governmental agencies or by non-governmental entities [...].

so far, more than twenty-five countries have enacted national space laws.[29]

Outer Space (2000), at 100. Celestial bodies should be distinguished from human-made space objects. *See*, Stephan Hobe, 'Article I Outer Space Treaty', *in* Stephan Hobe, Bernhard Schmidt-Tedd and Kai-Uwe Schrogl (eds), *Cologne Commentary on Space Law*, Volume I (Heymanns, 2009), at 32.

24. Hobe, 'Article I Outer Space Treaty', *in* Hobe, et al., *supra* no. 23, at 35.
25. Outer Space Treaty, *supra* no. 20, Art. I.
26. As such, space law is not a self-contained regime. *See*, on self-contained regimes in international law, Bruno Simma, *Self-Contained Regimes*, Netherlands Yearbook of International Law, Volume 16 (1985), at 111 et seq; Bruno Simma and Dirk Pulkowski, 'Of Planets and the Universe: Self-Contained Regimes in International Law', 17(3) *European Journal of International Law* 483-529 (2006).
27. Outer Space Treaty, *supra* no. 20; the Agreement on the Rescue of Astronauts, the Return of Astronauts and the Return of Objects Launched into Outer Space, 672 UNTS 119, adopted on 22 April 1968, entered into force 3 December 1968 (Rescue Agreement); the Convention on International Liability for Damage Caused by Space Objects, 961 UNTS 187, adopted on 29 March 1972, entered into force 1 September 1972 (Liability Convention); Convention on Registration of Objects Launched into Outer Space, 1023 UNTS 15, adopted on 14 January 1975, entered into force 15 September 1976 (Registration Convention); and the Agreement Governing the Activities of States on the Moon and Other Celestial Bodies, 1363 UNTS 3, adopted on 18 December 1979, entered into force 11 July 1984 (Moon Agreement).
28. UN GA Res. 37/92, Principles Governing the Use by States of Artificial Earth Satellites for International Direct Television Broadcasting, 10 December 1982; UN GA Res. 41/65, Principles relating to Remote Sensing of the Earth from Outer Space, 3 December 1986; UN GA Resolution 47/68, Principles Relevant to the Use of Nuclear Power Sources in Outer Space, 14 December 1992; UN GA Res. 51/122, Declaration on International Cooperation in the Exploration and Use of Outer Space for the Benefit in the Interest of All States, Taking into Particular Account the Needs of Developing Countries, 13 December 1996; UN GA Res. 59/115, Application of the Concept of the 'launching State', 10 December 2004; UN GA Res. 68/74; UNGA Res. 62/217, Space Debris Mitigation Guidelines of the Committee on the Peaceful Uses of Outer Space, 22 December 2007; UN GA Res. 62/101, Recommendations on Enhancing the Practice of States and International Intergovernmental Organizations in Registering Space Objects, 17 December 2008, UN GA Res. 68/74, Recommendations on National Legislation Relevant to the Peaceful Exploration and Use of Outer Space, 11 December 2013.
29. *See*, for a collection of the texts of more than twenty-five national laws, UN Office for Outer Space Affairs, National Space Law Collection, http://www.unoosa.org/oosa/en/ourwork/spacelaw/nationalspacelaw/index.html.

[B] Relevant Principles of Space Law

The guiding principles for human activities in outer space have been laid down in the OST, the chronologically first of the five treaties on space law. These fundamental legal provisions include:

- the principle of non-appropriation of outer space and celestial bodies;[30]
- the principle of the freedom of use, exploration and scientific investigation;[31]
- the principle of partial demilitarisation of outer space and of use of celestial bodies for 'exclusively peaceful purposes';[32]
- the principle of responsibility of States for national space activities;[33]
- the principle of liability for damages caused by space objects;
- the principle of jurisdiction and control over space objects and nationals;[34] and
- the principles of due regard and cooperation.[35]

Thereby, the OST contains the basis for the four subsequent treaties on specific issues, such as the rescue and return of astronauts,[36] the liability for damage caused by space objects in the airspace, on the Earth or in outer space,[37] the registration of space objects[38] as well as the legal regime for the Moon and other celestial bodies.[39] As the OST has been ratified by 110 States as of 2020,[40] it is considered that some of the principles contained in it have acquired the character of CIL. To this extent, it can be argued that, apart from treaty law and national legislation, the *corpus iuris spatialis*

30. Outer Space Treaty, *supra* no. 20, Art. II:

> Outer space, including the moon and other celestial bodies, is not subject to national appropriation by claim of sovereignty, by means of use or occupation, or by any other means.

See, on this so-called non-appropriation principle, Freeland and Jakhu, 'Article II Outer Space Treaty', *in* Hobe, et al., *supra* no. 23, at 50-55.
31. Outer Space Treaty, *supra* no. 20, Art. I.
32. Outer Space Treaty, *supra* no. 20, Art. IV. *See*, on the different military doctrines of States for the use of outer space, Schrogl and Neumann, 'Article IV Outer Space Treaty', *in* Hobe, et al., *supra* no. 23, at 90 et seq.
33. Outer Space Treaty, *supra* no. 20, Art. VI. *See*, for a comparative analysis of the concepts and effects of responsibility and liability in space law, Frans von der Dunk, 'Liability Versus Responsibility in Space Law: Misconception or Misconstruction?', Proceedings of the 34th Colloquium on the Law of Outer Space (1992), at 363-371.
34. Outer Space Treaty, *supra* no. 20, Art. VII and the Liability Convention, *supra* no. 27.
35. *See*, on the discussion on the interpretation of the 'due regard' principle in space law, Marchisio, 'Article IX Outer Space Treaty', *in* Hobe, et al., *supra* no. 23, at 176 et seq.
36. Outer Space Treaty, *supra* no. 20, Art. V and the Rescue Agreement, *supra* no. 27.
37. Outer Space Treaty, *supra* no. 20, Art. VII and specifically, Liability Convention, *supra* no. 27, Arts II and III.
38. Outer Space Treaty, *supra* no. 20, Art. VIII and the Registration Convention, *supra* no. 27.
39. *See*, for the establishment of the framework for a future legal regime for the exploitation of resources on celestial bodies, Moon Agreement, *supra* no. 27, Art. 11.
40. Status of International Agreements Relating to Activities in Outer Space as at 1 January 2020, A/AC.105/C.2/2020/CRP.3.

comprises also norms of CIL as well as non-binding legal documents.[41] So far, however, there have been no cases with specific space law content before international courts. Disputes that have arisen on the grounds of damage caused by space activities have been solved bilaterally, as was the case with the settlement of the claim of Canada against the Soviet Union of 1981,[42] after, in 1978, the Soviet nuclear-powered satellite Cosmos-954 disintegrated over Canada and caused nuclear pollution in Northwest Canadian unpopulated territories.[43]

§5.03 CHALLENGES FOR THE CYBERSECURITY OF SPACE ASSETS

In the context of cybersecurity, it follows to ask which issues are specifically relevant for the use of outer space. First, from a technical point of view, the complexity of satellite infrastructure and the interaction between its multiple links with cyberspace enlarge the inlets for malicious activities. This is probably the biggest challenge for preventing malicious cyber activities aimed against space assets.[44] Second, from a regulatory perspective, it is the legal character of the two intertwined domains outer space and cyberspace that creates a long list of issues concerning the ability to effectively prevent and counteract malicious cyber activities through law. These will be further analysed below.

[A] Factual Challenges

There are numerous challenges for ensuring the stability, integrity and resilience of space assets *vis- à -vis* cyber intrusions. The space domain functions on the basis of a complex technological infrastructure which involves multiple elements and processes ranging from manufacturing and testing to launching, operating and servicing a given space object until the end of its lifetime.[45] Components of this infrastructure are built and delivered from a large, usually international, supply chain consisting of multiple single suppliers. Generally, the supply chain that ensures the functionality of satellite infrastructure includes many components that are external in relation to the satellite system itself. A further factor that adds to the complexity of the space domain is the fact

41. *See*, on the phases of the development of space law from treaty law to non-binding provisions, Stephan Hobe, 'International Space Law in Its First Half Century', *in* Proceedings of the 49th Colloquium of the International Institute of Space Law 373-381 (2006).
42. 'Claim Against the Union of Soviet Socialist Republic for Damage Caused by Soviet Cosmos 954', 18(4) *International Legal Materials* (1979) and Statement of Facts to the Settlement of Claim Between Canada and the Union of Soviet Socialist Republics for Damage Caused by 'Cosmos 954' (Released on 2 April 1981).
43. Alexander F. Cohen, 'Cosmos 954: The International Law of Satellite Accidents', *in* W. Michael Reisman and Andrew R. Willard (eds), *International Incidents: The Law That Counts in World Politics* (Princeton University Press, 1988), at 71 et seq.
44. *See*, for a definition, Chapter 2, section §2.04[K]. *See also*, for details on the multiple entry points of space infrastructure for cyber activities, Chapter 5, section §5.03[A][1].
45. *See*, on the different phases of satellite exploitation, Stephan Hobe, Rada Popova, Hussaine El Bajatti and Julian Scheu, 'The Protection of Satellite Telecommunication Activities under BITs', 5(6) *Journal of World Investment and Trade* 1024-1058 (2018).

that space assets strongly depend on IT, open source software and also on business support systems. As a consequence, the numerous possible vulnerabilities at the junction of space-based or space-derived capability with cybersecurity may cause major national, regional and international security concerns.[46]

The vulnerabilities caused by the multiplicity of space systems elements will be outlined in the following sections.

[1] Elements of Satellite Systems as Entry Points for Cyber Intrusions

Satellite infrastructure consists of multiple interconnected elements on Earth and in outer space (generally encompassed in the terms 'ground segment' and 'space segment', respectively). In the ground segment, such elements are the ground infrastructure, including the hardware and software on the ground station or in a network of ground systems. The space segment includes the space object itself along with the computer system and installed software on board the satellite, as well as other interconnected space objects. The space and the ground segment interact through the uplink and downlink transmission of data and operate with the help of operations support systems.

Vulnerabilities may be exploited to disrupt the command and control systems on satellites or to attack the confidentiality and integrity of data and can result in loss of operational availability and data or even in physical harm or destruction. Data threats can include breaches in system confidentiality, unauthorised access to as well as modification and destruction of information.[47]

Satellite infrastructure is, therefore, a complex collocation of single units, both physical and non-physical, that are located in various places on the Earth and in space orbits. Cyber intrusions can be directed to all segments of these systems – including the hardware, the software and the transmitted data. Examples of inlets prone to malicious cyber activities include satellite links, user terminals and mobile media.

As has been demonstrated above, the inlets for such activities are numerous and involve units from both the ground and the space segment. The hardware of the satellite, the hardware of a ground station, but also the software they are using as well as the uplink and downlink communication can become inlets for and be exploited by malicious cyber activities. Especially problematic are older satellites, as they are technically outdated,[48] and newer ones with a low security level. In any case, every transmission between satellites and ground stations or between two or more satellites opens a way in for intrusion using electromagnetic signals, links and transmission using cyberspace. Thereby, the main aim is usually not to physically gain control over a given satellite but to access its operation and command systems and, in particular, the data that is being transmitted.

46. UK Government, 'National Space Security Policy', *UKSA/13/1292*, April 2014, at 2.
47. Consultative Committee for Space Data Systems, 'Report Concerning Space Data System Standards: Security Threats Against Space Missions', *CCSDS 350.1.-G-2* (December 2015), at 2-1.
48. Jan Kallberg, 'Why Older Satellites Present a Cyber Risk', 28 December 2018, https://www.fifthdomain.com/opinion/2018/12/28/why-older-satellites-present-a-cyber-risk/.

[2] *Remoteness and Interconnectedness of Space Objects as Weakness Factors for Cybersecurity*

Malicious cyber activities against satellite infrastructure can include jamming, spoofing (as long as they are not taking place completely analogously)[49] and hacking attacks on communication networks; targeting control systems or mission packages; and attacks on the ground infrastructure – for example, on satellite control centres. Therefore, the crux of the large 'attack surface' of satellites lies, on the one hand, in the number of interconnected components, and on the other, in the remoteness of the space object that, depending on the system design, might not allow for ensuring comprehensive and timely updates of its malware defence. While new satellites are increasingly being designed to accommodate software updates, this is usually not the case for older ones. Moreover, new small-sized satellites may not be supplied with enough operational capabilities to allow for extensive updates. The fact that after launch not all satellites may be able to accommodate substantial updates, and that such updates are restricted to software only, underlines the advantage vested in persons or organisations targeting the satellite systems as well as the need for a sophisticated and comprehensive risk management approach.[50]

Moreover, further risks for intrusion are created by the fact that components which possibly lack the security level corresponding to the need of protection for high-level satellite data and services are interconnected. To complicate the picture even more, the providers which supply end-users, including the industry and governmental stakeholders, with satellite data may also become a relevant target. Typically, the services and products of such service providers – who constitute a link in the chain of data transmission – do not necessarily concur with the same security standards applied by satellite operators to their space assets. Thus, the levels of resilience to cyber intrusions are strongly mixed not only as far as the single components of satellite infrastructure are concerned, but, in particular, with regard to connected periphery links, including supply chain providers, user terminals and user devices.[51]

[B] Major Types of Security Challenges for Satellite Infrastructure

The known cyber intrusions[52] into the computer systems of satellites and satellite infrastructure include the following exemplary events:

49. *See*, for a definition and examples, Chapter 2, sections §2.04[E] and §2.04[L] and Chapter 6, sections §6.03[B] and §6.03[C].
50. Bloomberg, 'Outer-Space Hacking a Top Concern for NASA's Cybersecurity Chief', 14 April 2017, https://www.datacenterknowledge.com/archives/2017/04/14/outer-space-hacking-top-concern-nasas-cybersecurity-chief.
51. *See*, for a case study analysis of Galileo and Planet's constellations, Technical University of Braunschweig, 'Automated Constellation Management of Space Vehicles (ASIMOV)', Executive Summary Report, *ASIMOV/ IRAS/PR/2019-02/BeG-A* (February 2019), at 8 et seq.
52. *See*, for examples of jamming and spoofing attacks that may include a cyber element, Chapter 6, sections §6.03[B] and §6.03[C].

- In 1998, the Rosat X-Ray satellite was attacked[53] which was believed to have been an intrusion into NASA's computer systems at the Goddard Space Flight Centre causing compromise to command and control codes.
- In 1999, a group of hackers gained control of a UK Ministry of Defense Skynet 4 military satellite, causing security intrusion and disruption of the military communications before re-programming the control system before being discovered.
- In 2007, attacks against NASA satellites took place, which allowed hackers to acquire communication abilities.
- In 2008, the US Terra AM-1 Earth observation satellite was interfered with using cyber means.
- In 2014, the US weather satellites were hacked, probably from the territory of China, in a cyberattack demonstrating that strategic space assets can be an object of cyber intrusion.[54]
- Again in 2014, the satellite data information system of the US National Oceanographic and Atmospheric Administration was hacked and taken offline.[55]
- In 2017, it was reported that NATO officials believed Russia is testing this cyberattacks capability through large-scale exercises, such as Zapad.[56]
- In 2018, according to Norwegian military and NATO officials, Russia jammed civilian Global Positioning System (GPS) signals during NATO's Trident Juncture exercise in Europe's High North region.[57]

The cybersecurity challenges for satellite systems can be divided into three main types:

- physical security of products and devices;
- personal security of the persons involved in operating, maintaining, and using the technology and the provided services; and
- organisational security concerning the procedures to be followed to guarantee and prevent unauthorised access.

53. *See*, Thomas J. Talleur, *Russian Domain Attacks Against NASA Network* Systems (not publicly published. Classified as 'For Official Use Only – No Foreign Dissemination'), NASA Inspector General's office. *See also*, Schneier on Security, 'Cyberattacks Against NASA', https://www.schneier.com/blog/archives/2008/12/cyberattacks_ag.html.
54. Ruben Santamarta, 'A Wake-Up Call for SATCOM Security', https://www.ioactive.com/pdfs/IOActive_SATCOM_Security_WhitePaper.pdf.
55. David Livingstone and Patricia Lewis, 'Space, the Final Frontier for Cybersecurity?', Project: International Security Department, September 2016, https://www.chathamhouse.org/publication/space-final-frontier-cybersecurity.
56. NATO Review, 'ZAPAD 2017 and Euro-Atlantic Security', 14 December 2017, https://www.nato.int/docu/review/2017/also-in-2017/zapad-2017-and-euro-atlantic-security-military-exercise-strategic-russia/EN/index.htm; Brook Tigner, 'Electronic Jamming Between Russia and NATO Is Par for the Course in the Future, But It Has Its Risky Limits', Atlantic Council, 15 November 2018, https://www.atlanticcouncil.org/blogs/new-atlanticist/electronic-jamming-between-russia-and-nato-is-par-for-the-course-in-the-future-but-it-has-its-risky-limits/.
57. Chatham House, Royal Institute of International Affairs, 'Cybersecurity of NATO's Space-Based Strategic Assets' (2019), at 6.

One additional, more recent challenge for cybersecurity of satellite systems is the trend to open up the operation of satellites to users, for example through enabling 'auctioning of satellite data'.[58] This adds new access points to the channels through which satellite data is transmitted and, therefore, contributes to the level of risk of cyber intrusions. Furthermore, satellite networks are getting more complex in terms of the number of connected devices and servicing objects.

A non-exhaustive classification of cyber threats includes the following types of possible intrusions:[59]

- Compromising of data.
- Targeting of single components of the satellite system, including targeting of the uplink and downlink communication.
- Targeting of command and control systems in the ground infrastructure.
- Attacks on the networks of the ground infrastructure, including such in the user segment.[60]

The possible sources of threats from the outside may include, for example, criminals, intelligence services, political activists and commercial competitors. Specific sources of threat from the satellite production and operation supply chain include maintenance and systems personnel, trusted business partners, including their sub-contractors, and staff members.

The effects of such malicious activities may include, but are not restricted to:

- Cracking of encryption codes.
- Stealing of data.
- Corruption of data.
- Modification of data.
- Loss of sensitive data.
- System damage, e.g., shutting down of command and control systems.
- Shutting down of the power source of a satellite, rendering it inactive.
- Loss of access to resources.
- Disruption of communication links.

The scope of these effects may, in the future, reach even to taking physical control over a satellite, altering its orbit, or even so-called cooking or grilling through the exposure of the space object to damaging levels or ionising radiation.[61]

58. European Space Agency, 'Going ... Going ... Gone! Why We Could Soon Be Using Auctions to Download Satellite Data', 24 June 2019, https://www.esa.int/Our_Activities/Preparing_for_the_Future/Discovery_and_Preparation/Going_going_gone!_Why_we_could_soon_be_using_auctions_to_download_satellite_data.
59. *See*, Consultative Committee for Space data Systems (CCSDS), *supra* no. 47, at 5-4.
60. *See*, on jamming and spoofing, which are in the first-place electronic attacks and do not primarily use cyberspace, Chapter 6, section §6.03.
61. Henry B. Garrett, 'Radiation Effects on Satellites: A JPL Perspective', NASA Jet Propulsion Laboratory, 2012, https://www.swpc.noaa.gov/sites/default/files/images/u33/Radiation_Effects_on_Satelliters-A_JPL_Perspective.pdf.

Therefore, the potential outcomes on a large scale may include the following events:[62]

- Compromising of national security and defence capabilities.[63]
- Denial of service of infrastructure.
- Denial of orbits.
- Destruction or serious damage to space objects.

[C] New Activities in Outer Space

One major challenge for cybersecurity in the space domain is posed by activities planned by the so-called small satellite industry.[64] The class of small satellites can be subdivided into mini satellites (500 kg), micro-satellites (10-100 kg), nanosatellites (1-10 kg), pico-satellites (0.1-1 kg) and femto-satellites (10-100 g). There are plans to deploy large constellations (sometimes also referred to as 'mega-constellations') consisting of hundreds or even thousands of low-cost interconnected small satellites to provide services – e.g., Internet broadcasting – on a global scale.[65] With the increasing need for global coverage and global connectivity, companies such as Amazon, Facebook and SpaceX have set a new standard of aspiration, namely to provide global broadband Internet access through the deployment of large constellations in low-Earth orbit.[66] These small satellites, in order to have competitive prices and not exceed a small size, are usually of a shorter lifetime (i.e., up to five years) and might possibly, mostly for cost-related reasons, be equipped only with the most-needed apparatus. This means that such satellites do not have excess to residual fuel and are not necessarily manoeuvrable. These features, combined with a large number of satellites in one large constellation operating predominantly in one orbital region, do not only increase the risk of the creation of space debris, both during normal operations, as well as in case of malfunction or collision. It also multiplies the possible intrusion points.

The interconnectivity of such networks of satellites increases the overall system vulnerability as low-cost satellites are, in general, not highly secured against cyber

62. Livingstone and Lewis, *supra* no. 55.
63. *See* Chapter 6.
64. *See*, for a forecast on the trends in the small satellite industry, Mordor Intelligence, 'Small Satellite Market: Growth, Trends, and Forecast (2019 – 2024)', https://www.mordorintelligence.com/industry-reports/small-satellite-market.
65. As of November 2019, one big constellation had been deployed, of which new satellites are being launched every three to four months. Planet Labs, 'Doves Mission Consisting of Nearly 200 Earth-Imaging Satellites', https://www.planet.com/company/approach/.
66. Jon Porter, 'Amazon Will Launch Thousands of Satellites to Provide Internet Around the World', 4 April 2019, https://www.theverge.com/2019/4/4/18295310/amazon-project-kuiper-satellite-internet-low-earth-orbit-facebook-spacex-starlink; Jonathan Amos, 'SpaceX Puts up 60 Internet Satellites', 24 May 2019, https://www.bbc.com/news/science-environment-48289204; Amy Thompson, 'SpaceX Launches 60 Starlink Satellites for New Megaconstellation, Misses Rocket Landing', 17 February 2020, https://www.space.com/spacex-starlink-4-launch-success-misses-rocket-landing.html; Jackie Wattles, 'Amid Pandemic, SpaceX Launches Another Batch of Starlink Satellites', 18 March 2020, https://www.edition.cnn.com/2020/03/18/tech/spacex-launch-starlink-coronavirus-scn/index.html.

intrusions. The measures that are planned by the operators of such constellations are to counteract potential outdating through ensuring that satellites are deorbited often, and new ones are launched constantly, e.g., every few weeks.[67]

However, it is not only low-cost small satellites and large constellations that trigger concerns for cybersecurity. Even if a given space object is equipped with the latest version of effective software and its data is well encrypted, in a standard case, once launched, the hardware that hosts and enables the satellite software cannot be updated. This means that there is no practicable means to ensure that both the hardware and the software used to protect the satellite and its data are completely as up-to-date and as sufficiently effective to counteract potential cyber intrusions (e.g., malware) originating from Earth.

[D] The Role of Cybersecurity for Space Activities

While it is uncontested that 'classical' space activities, such as the launching and operation of space objects, are governed by general international law, international space law and the relevant national legislation, the increasing role of cyberspace for space activities raises a number of legal problems. These include, for example, the question on which fields of law are applicable to cyber activities in outer space as well as the question on whether, in case they are applicable, the existing instruments of space law are comprehensive and effective enough with regard to the cybersecurity of space operations and space objects.

The main characteristics of outer space that have relevance to cybersecurity can be summarised as follows:

- Outer space, which includes the celestial bodies, asteroids and the space between them, is the natural environment beyond the Earth's atmosphere in which orbital motion, microgravity and vacuum define the natural predispositions for human activities and therefore, set the natural restrictions for using and regulating this domain. As a domain used by humankind, it is also affected by global digitisation and cyber activities can take place in or through and be addressed at outer space.
- Outer space is an area that can be used freely, whereby this freedom is subject to certain limitations. These limitations stem from the fact that outer space as such is free from sovereignty and cannot be appropriated. Sovereign powers of States can be extended only to man-made objects and humans in outer space but must be exercised while observing the freedom of all other States to use, explore and scientifically investigate outer space. Therefore, cyber activities in outer space must be carried out in conformity with the existing legal framework applicable to space activities.

As has been stated recently in a paper by the US Joint Chiefs of Staff:

67. Caleb Henry, 'How OneWeb Plans to Make Sure Its First Satellites Aren't Its Last', 18 March 2019, https://www.nasa.gov/centers/ivv/services/cybersecurity_vulnerability.html.

> While space operations and cyberspace operations (CO) are distinct, operations in space enable many CO and space systems' control segments require use of cyberspace.[68]

Due to the naturally global character of outer space, space activities generally have global effects, the relevance of which is not restricted to certain territories, certain people or certain States only. This underlines the fact that, accordingly, the malicious cyber activities affecting space assets can have widespread and even global side-effects over all domains that are dependent on the use of space applications and on space-based data.

Cyber intrusions are difficult to trace, with anonymity and the difficulties to identify the intruder posing crucial challenges. Apart from the issue of tracing and attributing cyber activities, it must be noted that, after an intrusion has taken place, the consequences become more or less an irreversible fact and can, therefore, only be minimised. As a result, full protection of satellite systems and satellite-transmitted data is generally considered not-feasible, even if the highest standards have been applied prior to the launch of a space object.[69]

In sum, while the main purpose of cybersecurity for space assets should be their protection from malicious cyber activities,[70] it must, as is true for cybersecurity generally, focus on a risk management paradigm.

§5.04 LEGAL CHALLENGES AT THE INTERSECTION BETWEEN OUTER SPACE AND CYBERSPACE

How effective legal regulation can be for implementing cybersecurity in outer space depends on the scope and the reach of challenges that exist for ensuring protection and management of risk. These challenges subsist at the backdrop of the applicable legal regimes for outer space and cyberspace and their correlation.

It can be stated that both terms 'outer space' and 'cyberspace' relate to domains that are not legally defined but are generally perceived in their scope. Common for both is the fact that they are globally used and are not restricted to physical boundaries. As a consequence, their accessibility, per se, is not restricted by geography. The access to both outer space and cyberspace is open in its nature and depends first and foremost on technological (i.e., launch and computer-based) capabilities.[71]

The lack of physical boundaries plays a substantial role in both outer space and cyberspace. It results in a diminished role of sovereignty, in contrast to other international domains for human activities, such as airspace.[72]

68. US Department of Defense, US Joint Chiefs of Staff, 'Joint Publication 3-14, Information Operations', 10 April 2018, https://www.jcs.mil/Portals/36/Documents/Doctrine/pubs/jp3_14.pdf, at I-3.
69. *See*, for example, Rada Popova, 'Cyber Law and Outer Space (Activities): Legal and Regulatory Challenges', *in* Proceedings of the 61st Colloquium of the International Institute of Space Law (Eleven, 2019), at 659-670.
70. *See* Chapter 2, section §2.04[G].
71. *See* Chapter 5, section §5.02[A] and Chapter 2, section §2.02[A].
72. *See* Chapter 2, section §2.01[A] and Chapter 7, section §7.03.

Both cyberspace and outer space are domains beyond national territory, governed by predetermined rules, that are different from the normative framework. In the case of cyberspace, these are the language of protocols and the law of code[73] that is based on the digits '0' and '1'. In outer space, it is the natural laws of physics that determine what types of activities are possible and in what form. The complex of these features is crucial for the legal regulation in both cases as they automatically result in restrictions on the usability of cyberspace and outer space, respectively.

An illustrative example of an attempt concerning outer space to produce regulation at the intersection between natural (or technical) and legal predispositions is the technical and regulatory concept of so-called space traffic management (STM). While being partly comparable with road or air traffic management (ATM) in its objectives, STM as a regulatory set of rules can only function in the frame set by orbital motion, orbital velocity and the other natural factors defining the behaviour of space objects. A look in the architecture of cyberspace as a 'network of networks'[74] reveals that any regulation of cyber activities must take into consideration the defining of technical predispositions and, in particular, the issue of attributability, which is one of the biggest challenges for ensuring cybersecurity.[75]

[A] Regulatory Issues

The regulation of cyberspace through so-called cyber law is not a separated, 'autonomous' legal field, but it is much more integrated into different branches of law insofar as cyberspace has a relevance to the activities governed by the respective legal fields. Therefore, with regard to the cybersecurity of space assets, as much as legal rules exist for cyberspace, they are applicable also to the respective cyber activities pertaining to outer space.

Currently, there is no international 'cyber law' that governs the global cyber infrastructure. Apart from one international agreement – the 2001 Budapest Convention[76] – and some regional[77] and national efforts,[78] States have not yet come up with an international agreement on the regulation of cyberspace. Cyber activities have been extensively discussed in the context of *jus ad bellum* in order to establish whether, and under which circumstances, cyberattacks or attacks in cyberspace may be qualified as

---

73. Lawrence Lessig, *Code: And Other Laws of Cyberspace*, Version 2.0 (Basic Books, 2006).
74. International Electrotechnical Commission, Information Technology – Security Techniques – Guidelines for Cybersecurity ISO/IEC 27032:2012, last reviewed and confirmed in 2018, https://www.iso.org/standard/44375.html. *See* Chapter 2, section §2.02[A].
75. Luke Chircop, 'A Due Diligence Standard of Attribution in Cyberspace', 3(67) *International & Comparative Law Quarterly* 643-668 (2018), at 647; Popova, *supra* no. 69, at 659 and 670.
76. Convention on Cybercrime (opened for signature 23 November 2001, entered into force 1 July 2004), ETS 185. *See* Chapter 3, section §3.02[B].
77. These regional efforts include mainly policy documents of the European Parliament and the Council of the EU, the most recent of which is the so-called cybersecurity package to improve the EU cyber resilience and response. *See*, European Commission, Digital Single Market, 'Cybersecurity', https://www.ec.europa.eu/digital-single-market/en/cyber-security. *See* Chapter 4, section §4.01[B][2].
78. *See* Chapter 9, section §9.06[B].

use, or threat of use, of force as set out in the UN Charter in Article 2(4)[79] and whether the right to self-defence might be applicable in cases of cyber operations which reach the threshold of armed attack.[80] It is not yet clear, however, whether and how far malicious cyber activities fall under the applicability of international law regulating conflicts (e.g., whether a cyberattack can constitute use of force).[81]

It, thus, remains to be seen under which specific conditions international law[82] and space law are applicable to cyber activities in outer space.

[B] Applicability of Space Law to Cyber Activities

It can be argued that cyber operations conducted from or through outer space, or conducted from the Earth but aimed against space objects, are subject of space law if they are predominantly directed at outer space[83] and at assets therein.[84] Following this view, space law is *lex specialis* with regard to cyber activities that are related to space assets.[85] Thereby, the milestone provisions setting the legal framework for human activities in outer space[86] are applicable to cyber operations that are not merely transmitted through but are at least directed at outer space or conducted using space objects. Therefore, cyber activities in outer space, as one possible type of the 'use' of outer space, must not only, as has been demonstrated above, comply with general international law[87] and the prohibition on the use of force[88] but also with the specific provisions of space law.

79. Charter of the United Nations (adopted 26 June 1945, entered into force 24 October 1945), 1 UNTS XVI Annex.
80. *Ibid.*, Art. 51. *See* Chapter 3, section §3.03[B][1].
81. *See* Chapter 3, section §3.03[A].
82. *See*, on the applicability of international law to cyberspace, Nicholas Tsagourias, 'The Legal Status of Cyberspace', *in* Nicholas Tsagourias and Russel Buchan (eds), *Research Handbook on International Law and Cyberspace* (Edward Elgar Publishing, 2015), at 13.
83. Bin Cheng, 'Revisited: International Responsibility, National Activities and the Appropriate State', 27 *Journal of Space Law* (1998), at 19; Henry A. Wassenbergh, 'An International Institutional Framework for Private Space Activities', XXIIII *Annals of Air and Space Law* (1997), at 533. *See*, for a diverging opinion, Martha Mejia-Kaiser, 'Space Law and Unauthorized Cyber Activities', *in* Katharina Tsiolkovsky (ed.), *Peacetime Regime for State Activities in Cyberspace* (NATO Cooperative Cyber Defence Centre of Excellence, 2013), at 360.
84. *See*, for an overview on the different opinions in the literature on which activities shall be considered as taking place 'in outer space', Gerhard, 'Article VI Outer Space Treaty', *in* Hobe, et al., *supra* no. 23, at 107-108.
85. *See*, the chapter titled 'Space Law', *in* Michael N. Schmitt (ed.), *Tallinn Manual 2.0 on International Law Applicable to Cyber Operations* (Cambridge University Press, 2017), at 270 et seq. There, a distinction is undertaken between 'space-enabled cyber operations' and 'cyber-enabled space operations' whereby the latter involve either the operation of space assets or the conduct of space operations by cyber means.
86. *See*, for a definition, Chapter 2, section §2.04[K].
87. Outer Space Treaty, *supra* no. 20, Art. III. *See*. Chapter 5, section §5.02[A].
88. Charter of the UN, *supra* no. 79, Art. 2(4). *See*, for an extensive account, Schmitt (ed.), *supra* no. 85, at 273-277. *See also*, Chapter 3, section §3.03.

In the OST, a common interest "in the progress of the exploration and use of outer space for peaceful purposes" is recognised,[89] and this concurs with the customary interpretation according to which the term 'peaceful' is to be interpreted as 'non-aggressive'.[90] Moreover, cyber operations in outer space must not impede the exercise of jurisdiction and control over space objects.[91] Such an impediment would amount to a violation of sovereignty, as jurisdiction and control are the expressions of sovereignty.[92] Another obligation of States results from Article VI OST, which applies to any activity in outer space[93] and deals with the international responsibility of States for such activities.[94] Article VI requires that any non-governmental activity in outer space is authorised and supervised by the 'appropriate State'.[95] This obligation would, therefore, apply to cyber activities in outer space that are carried out by international intergovernmental organisations and by national non-governmental entities, i.e., if such cyber activities are predominantly and intentionally aimed at outer space.[96] Non-compliance of the State under whose jurisdiction (personal or territorial)[97] non-governmental entities fall within its duty under Article VI OST may thus result in State responsibility.[98] It must, however, be noted that the application of this provision

89. Outer Space Treaty, *supra* no. 20, Recital 2 of the Preamble. *See*, for an extensive account, Schmitt (ed.), *supra* no. 85, at 276.
90. *See*, on the interpretation of the term 'peaceful purposes', Bin Cheng, 'The Legal Status of Outer Space and Relevant Issues: Delimitation of Outer Space and Definition of Peaceful Use', 11 *Journal of Space Law* 89 (1983), at 98 et seq. *See*, with regard to the demilitarisation of celestial bodies, Schrogl and Neumann, 'Article IV Outer Space Treaty', *in* Hobe, et al., *supra* no. 23, at 82-84.
91. As provided for by Art. VIII of the Outer Space Treaty.
92. *See*, on prescriptive, enforcement and adjudicative jurisdiction as an expression of sovereignty, Michael Akehurst, 'Jurisdiction in International Law', 46 *British Yearbook of International Law* 165, 145-208 (1972-1972). *See*, on the concept of jurisdiction of States, Bernhard H. Oxman, 'Jurisdiction of States', *in Max Planck Encyclopedia of International Law* (November 2007). *See*, on jurisdiction over space objects, Gabriel Lafferranderie, 'Jurisdiction and Control of Space Objects and the Case of an International Intergovernmental Organisation (ESA)', 54(2) *German Journal of Air and Space Law* 228-242 (2005).
93. Gerhard, 'Article VI Outer Space Treaty', *in* Hobe, et al., *supra* no. 23, at 109.
94. Outer Space Treaty, *supra* no. 20, Art. VI sentence (1):

> States Parties to the Treaty shall bear international responsibility for national activities in outer space, including the moon and other celestial bodies, whether such activities are carried on by governmental agencies or by non-governmental entities, and for assuring that national activities are carried out in conformity with the provisions set forth in the present Treaty.

95. Outer Space Treaty, *supra* no. 20, Art. VI sentence (3):

> The activities of non-governmental entities in outer space, including the moon and other celestial bodies, shall require authorization and continuing supervision by the appropriate State Party to the Treaty.

On the notion of 'appropriate State', *see* Gerhard, 'Article VI Outer Space Treaty', *in* Hobe, et al., *supra* no. 23, at 117.
96. Cheng, *supra* no. 83, at 19.
97. Horst Bittlinger, 'Private Space Activities: Questions of International Responsibility', Proceedings of the 30th Colloquium on the Law of Outer Space (1987), at 194.
98. As codified in the Articles on Responsibility of States for Internationally Wrongful Acts, International Law Commission, November 2001, adopted by the International Law Commission

on the cyber activities of non-governmental entities is not significant in practice as the duty of a State to authorise and supervise space (cyber) activities can be fulfilled only for activities that the State has been informed about.

Even if this condition is fulfilled, again, clarity is required on the issue of establishing beyond doubt the attributability of the cyber activity which, in most cases, will not be feasible.[99] In general international law, the issue of attribution of malicious cyber activities to States, which would amount to an internationally wrongful act, has not been extensively addressed so far and no agreement has been reached on the issue of whether it suffices for a cyber activity to originate from a State's territory to presume State responsibility.[100] The existing (customary) legal regime on state responsibility as codified in the Articles on the Responsibility of States for Internationally Wrongful Acts[101] makes it clear that the principle of due diligence is applicable in cyberspace and that States should not allow their territory to be used for malicious cyber activities against other States.[102] Of course, for these provisions to apply in practice on specific cyber activities in outer space, it must be established under whose jurisdiction the cyber activity falls.[103]

According to the rather vaguely formulated principles of due regard and non-interference stipulated in Article IX of the OST,[104] cyber activities in outer space may furthermore not cause harmful interference with the space activities of other State Parties.[105] It is questionable whether the liability regime of space law[106] should apply to cases in which the damage caused by a space object[107] results from a cyber

---

at its Fifty-Third session, 2001, http://www.legal.un.org/ilc/texts/instruments/english/commentaries/9_6_2001.pdf; *Military and Paramilitary Activities in and against Nicaragua* (Nicaragua v. US), Merits, Judgment of 27 June 1986, 1986 ICJ Reports 14 and *Application of the Convention on the Prevention and Punishment of the Crime of Genocide* (Bosnia and Herzegovina v. Serbia and Montenegro), Judgment of 26 February 2007, ICJ Reports 2007, at 43.

99. *See* Chapter 5, sections §5.04[C] and §5.04[D] below. *See also*, Tsagourias, 'The Legal Status of Cyberspace', *in* Tsagourias and Buchan (eds), *supra* no. 82, at 28.
100. Mauno Pihelgas, 'Back-Tracing and Anonymity in Cyberspace', *in* Katharina Tsiolkowski (ed.), *Peacetime Regime for State Activities in Cyberspace: International Law, International Relations and Diplomacy* (NATO Cooperative Cyber Defence Centre of Excellence, 2013), at 31 and 33; Antonopoulos, 'State Responsibility in Cyberspace', *in* Tsagourias and Buchan (eds), *supra* no. 82, at 55 and 62.
101. Responsibility of States for Internationally Wrongful Acts, GA Resolution 56/83, UN Doc. A/RES/56/83 (28 January 2002, adopted 12 December 2001), Annex.
102. *Corfu Channel Case* (UK v. Albania), Judgment, International Court of Justice, ICJ Rep. 4, at 22; Report of the Group of Intergovernmental Experts on Developments in the Field of Information and Telecommunications in the Context of International Security, UN Doc. A/70/174 (22 July 2015), at 13(c) and (f).
103. *See*, on the large spectrum of issues for establishing jurisdiction in cyberspace, Kohl, 'Jurisdiction in Cyberspace', *in* Tsagourias and Buchan (eds), *supra* no. 82, at 35 et seq.
104. *See*, on the meaning of the 'due regard' and 'co-operation' principles, Marchisio, 'Article IX Outer Space Treaty', *in* Hobe, et al., *supra* no. 23, at 174 et seq.
105. Outer Space Treaty, *supra* no. 20, Art. IX sentence (3).
106. Outer Space Treaty, *supra* no. 20, Art. VII and the Liability Convention, *supra* no. 27.
107. *See*, for a definition of 'damage', Liability Convention, *supra* no. 27, Art. I(a):

> loss of life, personal injury or other impairment of health; or loss of or damage to property of States or of persons, natural or juridical, or property of international intergovernmental organisations.

activity.[108] For example, if as a result of a cyber activity, a space object causes damage in outer space,[109] fault-based liability could be invoked – provided that fault can be proved,[110] and in cases when the space object causes damage to aircraft in flight or on the surface of the Earth, as a result of a cyber activity – absolute liability could be imposed.[111]

Taking into account that cyber activities could be considered space activities under the conditions set out above, it can be stated that the law of State responsibility[112] is generally applicable to cyber activities in outer space and that the specific liability regime for damage caused by space objects should be applicable as *lex specialis*.[113]

[C] Establishing Jurisdiction, Attributability and State Responsibility for Cyber (Space) Activities: A Feasible Endeavour?

The general applicability of international law and space law on cyber activities in outer space has been affirmed in the previous sections. It follows to identify how, in view of law enforcement in practice, jurisdiction as the lawful power of States to prescribe, adjudicate and enforce legal rules on territory under their jurisdiction and to its national persons[114] can be applied in practice in cyberspace. Notwithstanding the numerous other significant challenges of cyberspace characteristics, such as anonymisation and the rapid pace of technological development which renders legal regulation outdated very quickly,[115] the key challenge for imposing legal consequences for malicious cyber activities through establishing jurisdiction and attribution lies in the

---

See also, Smith and Kerrest, 'Article II Liability Convention', *in* Hobe, et al., *supra* no. 23, at 105 et seq.

108. Applying the criterion of kinetic effects to argue that cyber activities are not to be considered space activities, Mejia-Kaiser brings forward the argument that:

> [The Liability] Convention applies to damage which arises from the kinetic energy and other physical direct damages that unfold following a collision by the space object's body or parts thereof. For that reason, damages directly caused by unauthorised cyber activities to a space object are not covered by the Liability Convention per se. Unauthorised cyber activities against space systems can also not be considered as space activity under Outer Space Treaty Articles III and VI.

See, Mejia-Kaiser, 'Space Law and Unauthorized Cyber Activities', *in* Tsiolkovsky, *supra* no. 83, at 360.

109. *See*, on the notion and scope of the term damage in space law, Marchisio, 'Article IX Outer Space Treaty', *in* Hobe, et al., *supra* no. 23, at176 et seq.
110. Liability Convention, *supra* no. 27, Art. III. *See*, on fault-based liability, Smith and Kerrest, 'Article II Liability Convention', *in* Hobe, et al., *supra* no. 23, at 132 et seq.
111. Outer Space Treaty, *supra* no. 20, Art. II. *See*, on absolute liability, Smith and Kerrest, 'Article II Liability Convention', *in* Hobe, et al., *supra* no. 23, at 125 et seq.
112. *See*, James Crawford, 'State Responsibility', *in Max Planck Encyclopedia of International Law* (Oxford University Press, March 2006).
113. Outer Space Treaty, *supra* no. 20, Art. VIII; *See*, for a different position, Mejia-Kaiser, 'Space Law and Unauthorized Cyber Activities', *in* Tsiolkovsky, *supra* no. 83.
114. Oxman, *supra* no. 92.
115. Tsagourias, 'The Legal Status of Cyberspace', *in* Tsagourias and Buchan (eds), *supra* no. 82, at 29.

lack of physical boundaries and the probable lack of full unambiguity in assessing territorial links in the global cyberspace.[116]

While computer hardware is physically existent and located at a certain geographical place, cyber activities may affect multiple jurisdictions and produce effects anywhere in the world, regardless of the location of the hardware or the person from which the activity originates. Although there is a link between the physical location of the technical infrastructure, e.g., a server, and the information transmitted, attributability of cyber activities as such is refuted by the fact that the location(s) in which the effects of cyber activities are incurred are independent of the geographical location of the physical technical layer. Cyber activities are not located in a single location and territory.[117] They may take place through various online addresses and be completely detached from the original physical source. Moreover, the identification of a computer's address through the Internet Protocol (IP) address can be obscured by modification techniques used to mask an IP address, including methods to simulate a different location.[118]

Therefore, while information and data can be transmitted through cyberspace from and to any physical location, a nexus between jurisdiction and an Internet address does not necessarily exist[119] as often, such cannot be proved beyond doubt. Furthermore, it is rather difficult to determine only one geographical source, or to – conversely – exclude States whose cyber infrastructure has been used or whose nationals may have been involved in malicious cyber activities from claims of other States on the basis of the territoriality principle.[120]

Moreover, not only the allocation of a certain virtual activity to a jurisdiction is problematic.[121] Also, the attribution of a cyber act to a person or entity under the nationality principle[122] may be questionable. First, cyber activities can be 'anonymised' and, second, the technical architecture of cyberspace allows for so-called hackers to log into accounts and to 'simulate' attributability to non-involved actors.[123]

It can thus be stated that because in international law the concept of sovereignty strongly relies on territoriality,[124] and since such is difficult to prove beyond doubt in

116. *See*, Popova, *supra* no. 69, at 660 et seq.
117. Uta Kohl, *Jurisdiction and the Internet: Regulatory Competence over Online Activity* (Cambridge University Press, 2007), at 5.
118. Pirker, 'Territorial Sovereignty and Integrity and the Challenge of Cyberspace', *in* Tsiolkovsky, *supra* no. 83, at 189 and 194.
119. David R. Johnson and David G. Post, 'Law and Borders: The Rise of Law in Cyberspace', 48 *Stanford Law Review* (1996), at 1371; Kohl, 'Jurisdiction in Cyberspace', *in* Tsagourias and Buchan (eds), *supra* no. 82, at 35 et seq.
120. Cedric Ryngaert, 'The Territoriality Principle', *in* Cedric Ryngaert (ed.), *Jurisdiction in International Law* (Oxford University Press, 2015); Oxman, *supra* no. 92.
121. *Nottebohm Case* (Liechtenstein v. Guatemala) [1955] 4 ICJ Reports 23. *See*, Malcolm N. Shaw, *International Law*, Seventh Edition (Cambridge University Press, 2017), at 493-497; Bernard H. Oxman, *supra* no. 92.
122. Antonopoulos, 'State Responsibility in Cyberspace', *in* Tsagourias and Buchan (eds), *supra* no. 82, at 63 et seq.
123. Nicholas Tsagourias, 'Cyber Attacks: Self-Defence and the Problem of Attribution', 17(2) *Journal of Conflict & Security Law* 229-244 (2012).
124. Jens Bartelson, *A Genealogy of Sovereignty* (Cambridge University Press, 1993), at 26.

cyberspace, cyber activities often cannot be attributed reliably to the jurisdiction of persons under the territoriality and the nationality principle.

Next, the issue of attribution to States of malicious cyber activities which would amount to an internationally wrongful act has not been extensively addressed by international law and no agreement has been reached on the issue of whether it suffices for a cyber activity to originate from a State's territory to presume State responsibility.[125]

The existing (customary) legal regime on State responsibility as codified in the Articles on the Responsibility of States for Internationally Wrongful Acts[126] makes it clear that the principle of due diligence[127] is applicable in cyberspace and that States should not allow their territory to be used for malicious cyber activities against other States.[128] This rule undoubtedly applies in all cases where the State knowingly allows its territory to be used for malicious cyber activities and fails to undertake measures to prevent the occurrence of a violation of international law through cyber activities carried out from its territory.[129] Attribution requires that a sufficient nexus is given between the actor – a State organ,[130] a person exercising government authority[131] or a person under the control or direction of the State[132] – and the State in question.

However, as it is difficult to establish attribution due to the technical options to 'mask' and back-trace the origin of a cyber activity, there might not be a nexus between an activity and a State. Additionally, the activities of non-State actors to which the Articles on State Responsibility are not generally applicable, pose an obstacle to establish State responsibility for malicious cyber activities originating from non-State actors. This problem has not yet been regulated through international law. It has so far been addressed through the UN Group of Governmental Experts on Developments in the Field of Information and Telecommunications in the Context of International Security in a series of reports between 2010 and 2015.[133] This was an attempt to derive norms of 'existing international law'[134] which are applicable to and govern State conduct in cyberspace.[135]

125. Pihelgas, 'Back-Tracing and Anonymity in Cyberspace', *in* Tsiolkovsky, *supra* no. 83, at 31 and 33. *See* Chapter 5, section §5.04[B].
126. Responsibility of States for Internationally Wrongful Acts, *supra* no 101.
127. *Corfu Channel Case* (UK v. Albania), *supra* no. 102, at 22.
128. Report of the Group of Intergovernmental Experts on Developments in the Field of Information and Telecommunications in the Context of International Security, *supra* no. 102, at paras 13(c) and (f).
129. Chircop, *supra* no. 75, at 646.
130. Responsibility of States for Internationally Wrongful Acts, *supra* no. 101, Art. 4.
131. *Ibid.*, Art. 5.
132. *Ibid.*, Art. 8.
133. Report of the Group of Intergovernmental Experts on Developments in the Field of Information and Telecommunications in the Context of International Security, UN Doc. A/65/201 (30 July 2010); Report of the Group of Intergovernmental Experts on Developments in the Field of Information and Telecommunications in the Context of International Security, UN Doc. A/68/98 (24 June 2013), at 16; Report of the Group of Intergovernmental Experts on Developments in the Field of Information and Telecommunications in the Context of International Security, *supra* no. 102.
134. *Ibid.*, at 16.
135. *Ibid.*, at 13.

Summarising on establishing jurisdiction and attribution as the main challenge for enforcing the law for cyber activities, the following can be observed: First, while the attribution of a certain act is a matter of evidence,[136] due to the fact that in cyberspace location may be feigned and usually multiple jurisdictions are concerned, the physical location of the infrastructure and of persons may, in practice, not present a sufficiently effective nexus for reliably establishing jurisdiction in cyberspace for intentional malicious cyber activities.[137]

Second, although States are per se the actors that can regulate cyberspace and that possess the technological and economic capabilities needed to enact measures corresponding to the global scope of cyberspace, due to the obstacles to establish attribution therein, both the territoriality and the nationality principle are of restricted effectiveness for the determination of legal consequences for perpetrators. Third, apart from difficulties in establishing attribution and jurisdiction over cyber activities, the open, predominantly non-national character of cyberspace challenges the effectiveness of national enforcement mechanisms over cyber activities. In literature[138] and according to the dedicated UN Group of Experts, the view is held that, while cyberspace is undisputedly subject to international law,[139] any future regulation will need to be elaborated under the involvement of both the public and the private sector.

§5.05 CYBERSECURITY FOR SPACE ASSETS: INTERNATIONAL REGULATION EFFORTS

So far, States have not come to an agreement on an international regulatory framework for cyber activities. Indeed, the ITU has recognised its competence in questions pertaining to the Internet[140] and has elaborated a reference guide for States for developing their national cybersecurity strategy.[141] As a complex intergovernmental organisation, however, the ITU cannot react quickly to the challenges of cyberspace. So far, only one binding international instrument on cybercrime – the 2001 Budapest Convention[142] – has come to existence. Other relevant regulatory international efforts include the OECD Guidelines on the Protection of Privacy and Transborder Flow of Personal Data[143] and the UNCITRAL Model Law on Electronic Commerce.[144]

136. Antonopoulos, 'State Responsibility in Cyberspace', *in* Tsagourias and Buchan (eds), *supra* no. 82, at 63.
137. Uta Kohl, 'Jurisdiction in Cyberspace', *in* Tsagourias and Buchan (eds), *ibid*, at 53-54.
138. *See*, Tsagourias, 'The Legal Status of Cyberspace', *in* Tsagourias and Buchan (eds), *supra* no. 82, at 13.
139. Report of the Group of Intergovernmental Experts on Developments in the Field of Information and Telecommunications in the Context of International Security, *supra* no. 102, at 4.
140. *See*, for more information on the ITU's Role with regard to International Public Policy Issues Pertaining to the Internet and the Management of Internet Resources, including Domain Names and Addresses, ITU Resolution 102 MOD ARB/79A3/2.
141. ITU, 'Guide to Developing a National Cybersecurity Strategy: Strategic Engagement in Cybersecurity (2018)', http://www.handle.itu.int/11.1002/pub/811cf62d-en.
142. Convention on Cybercrime, *supra* no. 76.
143. OECD, 'Guidelines Governing the Protection of Privacy and Transborder Flow of Personal Data', Revised 2013, C(80)58/FINAL, 23 September 1980, as amended on 11 July 2013 by C(2013)79.

A more specific focus on cybersecurity of satellite infrastructure has been put in the work of NATO as the largest peacetime military alliance in the world. It has been stated that "with the exception of anti-terrorism missions, all NATO missions rely on space-based communications."[145] Thus, the NATO strategic military systems depend heavily on space-based assets for:

- navigation and targeting;
- timing and positioning;
- command and control;
- operational monitoring;
- communication;
- intelligence gathering;
- surveillance and reconnaissance;
- space situational awareness;
- environmental monitoring;
- as well as missile defence

among other functions.[146] Taking into consideration the level of cyber threats to the security of NATO and its Member States and the relevance of satellite infrastructure for the NATO defence capabilities, cybersecurity of NATO space-related infrastructure is one highly relevant example of how cybersecurity of space assets and related networks is addressed.

The key points of the Cybersecurity of NATO's space-based strategic assets can be summarised as follows:

- Almost all modern military engagements rely on space-based assets.[147] While NATO does not own satellites, it conducts missions and operations in the air, land, cyber and maritime domains through the provision of data and services using satellites.
- The resilience of space systems for the military domain is key to achieving protection in all other domains.

144. UN, UN Commission on International Trade Law, Model law on Electronic Commerce, with Guide to Enactment (1996) with Additional Article 5 *bis* as adopted in 1998 (1999).
145. Chatham House, *supra* no. 57, at 15.
146. *See*, for a detailed overview on NATO space-dependent capabilities and their role for NATO operations, *ibid.*, at 10-11.
147. *Ibid.*, at 2:

> During the US-led invasion of Iraq in 2003, 68 per cent of US munitions were guided utilizing space-based means (including laser-, infrared- and satellite-guided munitions); up sharply from 10 per cent in 1990-91, during the first Gulf war. In 2001, 60 per cent of the weapons used by the US in Afghanistan were precision-guided munitions, many of which had the capability to use information provided by space-based assets to correct their own positioning to hit a target.

- Cyber vulnerabilities undermine confidence in the performance of strategic systems;[148] uncertainty in information and analysis continues to impact the credibility of deterrence and strategic stability.[149]
- Cyber-related challenges to strategic assets within NATO (e.g., tactical nuclear weapons, short- and medium -range ballistic missiles) and in particular cyber threats to space-based command and control systems must be urgently addressed.[150]
- NATO's space-dependent capabilities have individual functions and are also coupled to each other, with complex cross-dependencies. Thus, the loss of one capability may have a collateral impact on other capabilities.[151]

Moreover, the NATO Member States agreed in the Cyber Defence Pledge of July 2016[152] on a number of steps to enhance the NATO cyber defence and the cyber defence capabilities of the NATO Member States.[153]

The partnerships of NATO with other stakeholders under the NATO Industry Cyber Partnership[154] and with the EU[155] are also of relevance for cybersecurity of space assets of NATO Member States[156] and may, in the future, provide a basis for a more detailed policy and legal framework for the cybersecurity of space assets on the international level.

§5.06 CONCLUSION

Much of the world's critical infrastructure – such as communications, air transport, maritime trade, financial and other business services, weather and environmental monitoring and defence systems – depends on the space infrastructure, including satellites, ground stations and data links at national, regional and international levels. Satellites and other space assets, just like other parts of the digitised critical infrastructure, are vulnerable to cyberattacks.

Outer space has changed from a domain accessible to wealthy states into one that is dominated by market forces. In the 'IoT era', satellites have become a thing in the IoT.[157] Cybersecurity has become an issue and a challenge also for space activities while efforts on guaranteeing the protection of critical infrastructure, to which satellite infrastructure also belongs, had not been focused particularly on satellites. Cyber

148. *See* Chapter 6.
149. Chatham House, *supra* no. 57, at 2.
150. *Ibid.*, at 4.
151. *Ibid.*, at 11.
152. NATO Official Texts, Cyber Defence Pledge, Press Release (2016) 124, 8 July 2016, https://www.nato.int/cps/en/natohq/official_texts_133177.htm.
153. *See* Chapter 3, section §3.05.
154. NATO, 'Industry Cyber Partnership (NICP)', https://www.ncia.nato.int/Industry/Pages/NATO-Industry-Cyber-Partnership.aspx.
155. NATO Official Texts, Joint Declaration on EU-NATO Cooperation, Press Release (2018) 095, 10 July 2018, https://www.nato.int/cps/en/natohq/official_texts_156626.htm.
156. *See*, for an overview of NATO partnerships in cyber defence, Chapter 3, section §3.05.
157. *See*, for a detailed account, Blount, *supra* no. 9.

vulnerabilities in space, therefore, pose serious risks for ground-based critical infrastructure, and insecurities in the space environment will hinder economic development and increase the risks to society.[158]

Possible cyber threats against space-based systems include state-to-state and military actions but may also originate from well-resourced organised criminal elements seeking financial gain or from terrorist groups wishing to promote their causes, even up to the catastrophic level of cascading satellite collisions.

Technology alone cannot provide the basis for policymaking on cybersecurity. The development of a flexible, multilateral cybersecurity regime for space activities is urgently required. As the full protection from cyber threats seems not to be feasible due to the complex issues described in this chapter, any future regulatory paradigm must be based extensively on prevention and risk management rather than on predominantly reactive measures. An international 'community of the willing' – made up of governmental, intergovernmental, private and other critical stakeholders within the international space supply chain and insurance industry – is likely to provide the best opportunity to develop a space cybersecurity regime competent to match the large range of threats.

158. *See*, for example, Richard Parker, 'If Hackers Cripple Your Satellite, Are You Covered? Don't Count on It', 18 September 2019, https://www.spacenews.com/op-ed-an-insurers-perspective-on-defining-cyber-risk-in-space/.

CHAPTER 6

Critical Infrastructure for Aviation and Space Activities: Satellite Communication and Navigation

§6.01 INTRODUCTION

Satellite services are the backbone of modern society and economy. Their dependence on free and unrestricted access to radio spectrum, nevertheless, highlights a vulnerability that has become critical in the past years, and will probably continue to grow in the foreseeable future. Cases of harmful use of radio spectrum by hostile entities are endangering the regular functioning of satellite-based services, thus constituting an indirect threat against civilian as well as military applications.

The present chapter will investigate the role of communication and navigation satellite services and their relationship with the notion of critical infrastructure, putting a particular focus on key features such as interdependency and dual-use. The analysis will continue by illustrating the main radio spectrum-related threats to such services, namely jamming and spoofing, and elaborate on the reasons why they constitute such a dangerous issue. The chapter will then move to the ITU and its role, assessing the suitability of its legal framework – with particular focus on the Radio Regulations – to counter the problem. Lastly, the difference between harmful interference and cyberattack will be explained, in the perspective of both existing legal instruments and possible future ones.

§6.02 SATELLITES AND CRITICAL INFRASTRUCTURES

[A] Critical Infrastructures

Due to the national security dimension of the term, there is no internationally agreed definition of 'critical infrastructure'. The term finds its origin in the late 1990s in the US, when the Marsh Report and the subsequent executive order EO-13010 provided the first definition of infrastructure as "a network of independent, mostly privately-owned, man-made systems that function collaboratively and synergistically to produce and distribute a continuous flow of essential goods and services."[1] According to the same report, an infrastructure is vital whenever "its incapacity or destruction would have a debilitating impact on [...] defense and national security." Following that, the definition has been broadened, and the current description of critical infrastructure corresponds to "systems and assets, whether physical or virtual, so vital to the US that the incapacity or destruction of those systems and assets would have a debilitating impact on security, national economic security, national public health or safety, or any combination of those matters."[2] Despite its domestic origin, such definition can be considered as sufficiently paradigmatic for general considerations. Examples of critical infrastructure sectors – relevant to most of the modern States – include but are not limited to key commercial facilities, power grids, chemical industries, dams, emergency services, telecommunications, government facilities, transportation systems, banking and finance, defence industrial base.[3]

In other words, they are the totality of assets and networks essential to the functioning of the economy and society. In the past two decades, the importance of critical infrastructures and the need to secure them from natural or man-made threats has gained increasing relevance in the eyes of national legislators and policymakers, leading to the elaboration of complex strategies for their protection.[4]

A number of key features shall be highlighted in order to fully appraise the nature and the vulnerability of modern critical infrastructure. The first one is their interdependency.[5] Infrastructures, indeed, do not function in isolation but are dependent on each other, forming a 'system of systems'.[6] Their linkages can be physical, cyber, or related to geographic location.[7] Some sectors, however, are particularly important since they are conditional on the regular operations of the others. The most crucial of

1. Executive Order EO-13010 (1996), Critical Infrastructure Protection, as amended by Executive Order 13077 (1998); Further Amendment to Executive Order 13010, Critical Infrastructure Protection; *see also*, Robert T. Marsch, Report of the President's Commission on Critical Infrastructure Protection (1997).
2. US Patriot Act of 2001 (42 U.S.C. 5195c(e)), section 1016(e).
3. *See*, on the Internet as autonomous critical infrastructure, Georg Kerschischnig, *Cyberthreats and International Law* (Eleven, 2012), at 48-50.
4. *See*, for the US, Presidential Policy Directive/PPD-21 – Critical Infrastructure Security and Resilience, 2013, https://www.obamawhitehouse.archives.gov/the-press-office/2013/02/12/presidential-policy-directive-critical-infrastructure-security-and-resil); *see*, for the EU, Green Paper on a European Programme for Critical Infrastructure Protection Presented by the Commission, COM (2005) 576 Final, 2005, https://www.eur-lex.europa.eu/legal-content/en/TXT/?uri=CELEX:52005DC0576.
5. Interdependency can be defined as 'the bidirectional relationship between two infrastructures through which the state of each infrastructure influences or is correlated to the state of the other'. *See*, Commission Staff Working Document on a New Approach to the European Programme for Critical Infrastructure Protection Making European Critical Infrastructures More Secure, SWD (2013) 318 Final, 2013, at 2, Note 6, https://www.ec.europa.eu/energy/sites/ener/files/documents/20130828_epcip_commission_staff_working_document.pdf.
6. Steven M. Rinaldi, James P. Peerenboom and Terrence K. Kelly, *Identifying, Understanding and Analysing Critical Infrastructure Interdependencies* (IEEE Control Systems Magazine, 2001), at 14.
7. *Ibid.*, at 12.

these 'cross-sectors' are generally considered energy and telecommunications[8] since a disruption of either of the two would have a cascading effect leading – for instance – to the interruption of emergency services such as police, fire, military, medical and transportation on the short term, and to the disruption of financial services and industrial activities on the long term.[9]

A second key feature is the mixed public-private ownership. Most of contemporary, critical infrastructures lie in the hands of private entities, which are often foreign-owned and controlled.[10] As a rule, it is not realistic to expect from private operators to ensure the same level of security that normally can be afforded by governmental entities. This key aspect entails a number of consequences: first, the level of protection of the infrastructures may vary consistently; second, a synergic dialogue between governmental authorities and owners and operators is necessary; third, the allocation of responsibilities for their protection may result unclear; and fourth, foreign ownership and control constitute a challenge for governmental supervision, making international cooperation indispensable.[11]

The third crucial element is their cross-border nature. Critical infrastructures, indeed, increasingly transcend the purely national dimension, and often rely upon – and offer services crucial to – critical infrastructures of third countries, forming an interconnected network. The disruption of a critical infrastructure in a certain State, indeed, would most probably have effects also in third countries due to their cross-border interdependency.[12] An example illustrating such potential for transboundary consequences is the electrical power grid. In November 2006, the effects of a large power disruption in the North-German transmission grid spread over most of the European continent, affecting Austria, Belgium, France, Slovenia and Spain. Fifteen million households were affected and electricity-dependent services, such as rail transport, experienced extensive cancellations and delays.[13]

Notably, due to the interconnected nature of the European services and economy, the cross-boundary dimension of critical infrastructures is particularly relevant in the EU. In 2006, upon request of the European Council, the Commission set out an overall policy approach for critical infrastructure protection in the EU called European

8. US Presidential Policy Directive/PPD-21, *supra* no. 4, at 9; Ted G. Lewis, *Critical Infrastructure Protection in Homeland Security* (A John Wiley & Sons Inc. Publication, 2006), at 56.
9. *See*, for an analysis of cross-sectoral failures of critical infrastructure, Ana Laugé, Josune Hernantes and Jose M Sarriegi, 'Critical Infrastructure Dependencies: A Holistic, Dynamic and Quantitative Approach', 8 *International Journal of Critical Infrastructure Protection* 16-23 (2014).
10. Commission Staff Working Document on a New Approach to the European Programme for Critical Infrastructure Protection Making European Critical Infrastructures More Secure, *supra* no. 5, at 3.
11. Kerschischnig, *supra* no. 3, at 45; Commission Staff Working Document on a New Approach to the European Programme for Critical Infrastructure Protection Making European Critical Infrastructures more secure, *supra* no. 5, at 5.
12. Communication from the Commission on a European Programme for Critical Infrastructure Protection, COM (2006) 786 Final, 4, at 8.
13. Commission Staff Working Document on a new approach to the European Programme for Critical Infrastructure Protection Making European Critical Infrastructures More Secure, *supra* no. 5, Annex III.

Programme for Critical Infrastructure Protection.[14] A cornerstone of the programme is the 2008 Directive on ECI, as amended in 2012, setting out a procedure for the identification of ECI and a common approach for assessing the need to improve their protection. The envisaged hazards cover both technological and man-made threats as well as natural disasters. However, in the Preamble, it is clarified that priority should be given to terrorist attacks.[15] Although its scope is limited to the energy and transport sectors, the Directive was drafted with the view to be expanded to other sectors such as ICT.[16]

In 2019, the European Commission published an external evaluation report on the implementation of the Directive, which confirms its continuing relevance and underlines its added value in paving the way to a European common framework.[17] The report, however, also identifies several criticalities, mainly a limited implementation as well as a considerably heterogeneous interpretation by the Member States, and its inadequacy to keep pace with the evolution of the technological context. A number of potential improvements are proposed, including further defining key terms and provisions; assessing the need to extend the Directive's sectoral scope; strengthening the Directive's monitoring and evaluation framework; and reviewing the roles and responsibilities of the different stakeholders involved in the identification and designation of ECI.[18]

[B] Space Infrastructure

Until a few decades ago, satellites were mainly used by the world super powers – the US and the Soviet Union – for military, intelligence and scientific purposes.[19] The phenomena of commercialisation and privatisation have changed this paradigm, and expanded satellites' role, making them an essential component of the worldwide economy and everyday citizen's life.[20] Space-based systems enable today a wide scope of applications, ranging from broadband Internet and TV broadcasting to financial

14. Communication from the Commission on a European Programme for Critical Infrastructure Protection, *supra* no. 12.
15. Council Directive 2008/114/EC of 8 December 2008 on the Identification and Designation of European Critical Infrastructures and the Assessment of the Need to Improve their Protection, OJ L 345, 23 December 2008, pp. 75-82. The Directive defines a European Critical Infrastructure (ECI) as 'a critical infrastructure located in Member States the disruption or destruction of which would have a significant impact on at least two Member States. The significance of the impact shall be assessed in terms of cross-cutting criteria. This includes effects resulting from cross-sector dependencies on other types of infrastructure'.
16. Council Directive 2008/114/EC, *supra* no. 15, Preamble, at 5.
17. Commission Staff Working Document, Evaluation of Council Directive 2008/114 on the Identification and Designation of European Critical Infrastructures and the Assessment of the Need to Improve Their Protection, Brussels, 23.7.2019 SWD (2019) 308 final.
18. *Ibid.*, at 35.
19. Laura Grego, *A History of Anti-satellite Programs* (Union of Concerned Scientists, 2012), at 5.
20. US, General Accounting Office, Critical Infrastructure Protection: Commercial Satellite Security Should be More Fully Addressed (GAO-02-781) (Washington, DC, US General Accounting Office, 2002), at 1. *See also*, Chapter 2, section §2.04[J].

transactions, transport systems and emergency services.[21] Despite not having the rank of autonomous critical infrastructure in most national security policies, they constitute the backbone for the functioning of most of the others and are a key element of modern society. It is thus common to refer to them as 'space infrastructure'.

The satellite-based components that, together with the ground and user segment, concur to form such space infrastructure are the following:

- communication satellites;
- location, navigation and timing satellites;
- remote sensing satellites; and
- weather forecast satellites.[22]

Due to their major role in economy, society and security, the present chapter will focus on communication and navigation satellites, briefly illustrating their purposes, vulnerabilities and the relevant legal framework.

[C] Satellite Communications

Approximately half of the more than a thousand operational satellites currently in orbit are dedicated to telecommunications, which represent the most prominent component of the satellite service business.[23]

The satellite communication industry, once composed exclusively by governmental and intergovernmental entities, experienced a dramatic process of privatisation and commercialisation that started in the 1980s when the US government decided to allow separate systems to compete with INTELSAT.[24] Currently, several big and small operators around the world provide satellite communication services on a commercial basis.

In terms of critical infrastructures, in the US commercial satellite services are identified as a key component of the Communications Sector,[25] while the EU recognises them as part of the ICT sector.[26] Telecommunications, in turn, constitute the backbone that supports the functioning of several other critical infrastructures, such as energy

21. *See*, for a survey of satellite applications in modern society, Olaf Acker, Florian Potscher and Thierry Lefort, 'Why Satellites Matter: The Relevance of Commercial Satellites in the 21st Century: A Perspective 2012-2020', https://www.esoa.net/Resources/Why-Satellites-Matter-Full-Report.pdf.
22. Linda L. Haller and Melvin S. Sakazaki, *Commercial Space and United States National Security*, prepared for the Commission to Assess US National Security Space Management and Organization, https://www.fas.org/spp/eprint/article06.html.
23. 35% are dedicated to commercial communication, while the remaining 14% to governmental communications. *See*, for a complete overview of the satellite industry, 2017 State of the Satellite Industry Report, Satellite Industry Association, https://www.sia.org/annual-state-of-the-satellite-industry-reports/2017-sia-state-of-satellite-industry-report/.
24. 'Privatisation of Intelsat', 95(4) *The American Journal of International Law* 893-895 (2001).
25. US Communications Sector-Specific Plan 2015, An Annex to the National Infrastructure Protection Plan 2013: Partnering for Critical Infrastructure Security and Resilience, https://www.dhs.gov/sites/default/files/publications/nipp-ssp-communications-2015-508.pdf, at 6.
26. Green Paper on a European Programme for Critical Infrastructure Protection Presented by the Commission, *supra* no. 4, at 24.

grids, emergency and financial services, the IT sector and transportation.[27] Given the multi-layer nature of the telecommunications infrastructure (consisting of landline, wireless, satellite), it could be questioned whether satellites represent a vital component of such infrastructure, or whether other kinds of networks could compensate for their unavailability in case of disruption or even push them out of the market. It is undeniable that terrestrial services are challenging satellites in many respects, especially in the broadband sector, but satellites hold a number of advantages that seem to ensure their long-term indispensability and even integration with the ground networks. An indicative list includes the following benefits:

- satellites are crucial to provide coverage for remote or rough geographic areas where it is more difficult or less profitable to instal land networks;[28]
- they ensure uninterrupted connectivity where no ground-based telecommunication networks are deployable, such as ships at sea or aircraft in flight;[29]
- they provide an excellent means of point-to-multipoint data distribution, indispensable, for instance, in financial transaction services;[30] and
- they are inherently dual-use systems, capable of providing global coverage for intelligence and military communications in parallel to civilian services.[31]

The importance of satellite networks is well exemplified by the outcome of the PANAMSAT's Galaxy 4 satellite technical failure in 1998. As a consequence of such single satellite loss, most of the 45 million pagers across the US were disrupted for several days, leaving 70% of the customers of major oil companies without the possibility to pay for services at the petrol pump.[32] Additionally, a wide range of banking and financial transaction services experienced severe outages, and life-critical services - such as communication with medical staff and emergency workers - were temporarily compromised.[33]

The main characteristics of critical infrastructures analysed above - cross-sector interdependence, mixed public-private ownership and cross-border synergies - are magnified in the case of satellites. Although US-dominated, the satellite industry is a highly globalised sector where private foreign companies and multinational alliances often provide global services to both public and private users.[34] This has raised national security concerns among governments, especially for the provision of critical and defence-related services, and has induced them to stipulate tight agreements with the providers. Such agreements contain clauses which, among others, limit foreign

27. US Communications Sector-Specific Plan 2015, at 9.
28. Haller and Sakazaki, *supra* no. 22, at 13.
29. *Ibid.*
30. *Ibid.*
31. *See* Chapter 6, section §6.01[E].
32. US, General Accounting Office, Critical Infrastructure Protection: Commercial Satellite Security Should be More Fully Addressed, *supra* no. 20, at 14.
33. Perenboom and Kelly, *supra* no. 6, at 11.
34. *See*, for an overview of the privatisation process of the telecommunication satellite industry, Patricia McCormick, Maurie J. Mechanick, *The Transformation of Intergovernmental Satellite Organisations: Policy and Legal Perspectives* (Martinus Nijhoff Publishers, 2013).

access to certain information, impose citizenship requirements, require disclosure of personal data on sensitive personnel and establish reporting duties.[35]

[D] Satellite Navigation

GNSS is considered one of the most critical technological achievements of the 21st century. Such technology consists of a global satellite-based system that provides position, velocity and time of a receiver through the transmission of radio signals with worldwide coverage, and involves three main components: a constellation of satellites transmitting the primary signal; a ground station that elaborates the information and operates the system; the end-user receiver equipment.

GNSS was initially a duopoly dominated by the US and the Soviet Union, which developed respectively GPS and Globalnaya Navigazionnaya Sputnikovaya Sistema (GLONASS) in the later phase of the Cold War for exclusive military uses. Following the shooting down of Korean Air Lines Flight 007 in 1983 by the Soviet air force as a result of trespassing the Soviet airspace due to navigational errors, the Reagan administration decided to share the GPS for civilian uses. In 1994, the US and the Russian Federation formally offered to worldwide civil aviation the availability of their GNSS signals via an exchange of letters with ICAO, making air navigation the first civilian application to benefit from satellite navigation technology.[36]

The main difference between GNSS and the satellite communications market lies in the way that the respective services are provided., While most of the satellite operators have been fully privatised and operate on a commercial basis, in the case of GNSS the service is still directly provided by sovereign States, which detain the full control on the respective systems and have developed the technology originally for military purposes. This is particularly true for the two original constellations, GPS and GLONASS, which were opened to civilian uses only at a later stage,[37] and are today available on a global basis for free and outside any State-to-State agreement or contractual relation with the users.

Currently, there are two other systems under development, the European Galileo and the Chinese Beidou, scheduled for completion in 2020. There will thus soon be a total of four core-constellations with global coverage, flanked by a number of regional navigation systems – such as the Indian Regional Navigation Satellite System – and regional augmentation systems designed to enhance the performance of the core signals mainly for air navigation use, such as the European Geostationary Navigation

35. Haller and Sakazaki, *supra* no. 22, at 19.
36. ICAO, 'Report on the Establishment of a Legal Framework with Regard to CNS/ATM Systems Including GNSS', ICAO Legal Commission A35-WP/75, Annex C. GNSS services for civil aviation have been standardised on a global basis in ICAO Annex 10 on Aeronautical Telecommunications.
37. GPS and GLONASS were initially opened for usage by international civil aviation via an exchange of letters between the ICAO Secretary General and the US FAA Administrator in 1994 and the Russian Minister of Transport in 1996 respectively. *See*, Michael Milde, 'Solutions in Search of a Problem? Legal Aspects of the GNSS', XXII-II *Annals of Air and Space Law* 195-219 (1997).

Overlay Service (EGNOS) or the US Wide Area Augmentation System (WAAS).[38] The current worldwide dominance of GPS in GNSS applications may, therefore, soon be challenged.

The functions served by navigation and timing signals in modern society are countless. Navigation services are an essential component of road, rail, maritime and air transport. In aviation, in particular, they constitute the main support of national air traffic control systems, and ICAO is currently committed to developing dual-frequency, multi-constellation GNSS services as the backbone of international air navigation.[39] They are also indispensable in search-and-rescue, disaster-relief operations and are increasingly employed in precision agriculture and mapping. Such services are also an important component of space activities. On the other hand, the atomic clocks on board of the GNSS satellites provide accurate timing that permit telecommunications companies to synchronise their network, international banking transaction systems to work, and electrical power grids to operate. In conclusion, the very fabric of the modern economy relies on satellite navigation and timing signals.[40]

Despite the numerous recommendations of the National Space-Based Positioning, Navigation, and Timing (PNT) Advisory Board,[41] the US Government has never declared GPS a critical infrastructure per se, defining it as a mere 'enabler'.[42] The EU, on the other hand, appears to be taking a different approach. In 2013, the European Commission identified in a working paper (WP)[43] four critical infrastructures with a European cross-border dimension, including the Galileo satellite system, along with Eurocontrol, the electricity transmission grid and the gas transmission network. Their formal designation as critical infrastructure has to be done under Directive 2008/114/EC which, however, is currently under scrutiny by the European Commission for revision.

38. Satellite-based Augmentation Systems, such as WAAS or EGNOS, improve the accuracy and reliability of GNSS information by correcting signal measurement errors and by providing information about the accuracy, integrity, continuity and availability of its signal. *See*, European GNSS Agency 'What Is SBAS', https://www.gsa.europa.eu/european-gnss/what-gnss/what-sbas.
39. Eurocontrol, 'Moving from one GPS Signal to Eight Signals from Four Constellations', https://www.eurocontrol.int/news/moving-one-gps-signal-eight-signals-four-constellations.
40. The overall impact of GPS just on the US economy is estimated between USD 66 and USD 122 billion per year. *See*, for an analysis of the overall benefits of GPS to the US economy, GPS Innovation Alliance, 'The Economic Benefits of Commercial GPS Use in the U.S. and The Costs of Potential Disruption', http://www.gpsalliance.org/docs/GPS_Report_June_21_2011.pdf.
41. National PNT Advisory Board comments on Jamming the Global Positioning System – A National Security Threat: Recent Events and Potential Cures, National Space-Based Positioning, PNT Advisory Board, 4 November 2010.
42. *See*, for an overview of the debate within the US Government on the issue, Inside GNSS, 'PNT Advisory Board Debates Critical Infrastructure Designation for GPS', 16 June 2015, http://www.insidegnss.com/pnt-advisory-board-debates-critical-infrastructure-designation-for-gps/.
43. Commission Staff Working Document on a new approach to the European Programme for Critical Infrastructure Protection Making European Critical Infrastructures more secure, SWD (2013) 318 Final, *supra* no. 5, at 8.

[E] Dual Use of Commercial Satellites

Communication and navigation satellite networks are inherently dual-use technology, meaning that they are capable of supporting both military and civilian applications. While the previous paragraphs have highlighted the civilian aspects, which can be both of commercial or governmental nature, it is important to recall the military function of such systems.[44] Satellites are deeply integrated into every modern military apparatus, providing passive support functions, such as communications, reconnaissance, early warning of ballistic launches, weather data collection and arms control verification. With technological development, they have increased their relevance by assuming a more active role of force multiplier during wartime: they provide secure and high-volume unsecured communications, targeting and navigation services, as well as command and control links during operations.[45]

Most space-faring nations own and operate dedicated military satellite networks. The large part thereof belong to the US, the Russian Federation and the People's Republic of China, but other countries like France, the UK, Germany, Israel, and Japan have their own military satellites in orbit, although in more modest numbers.[46] Due to secrecy requirements, it is difficult to have a precise assessment of how many military satellites are currently in orbit, but their number is estimated to be more than 300 in total.[47]

The military operational need for bandwidths, however, has increased so sharply that it currently surpasses by far the capacity offered by government-owned satellites.[48] As a consequence, there is a growing trend to lease capacity from commercial operators, both domestic and foreign.[49] For instance, despite the concerns expressed by some officials about the potential risks for national security, it is estimated that 80%-90% of the current US military traffic is transmitted via commercial satellite channels.[50] To point at an exemplary figure, the commercial bandwidth used by the US military has risen by 150 times in just fifteen years, passing from 100 Mbps since the Desert Storm operation in 1990, to 10-15 Gbps today.[51] Not surprisingly, this massive capacity demand has made the military the biggest client of the commercial satellite market.[52]

44. Haller and Sakazaki, *supra* no. 22, at 24.
45. Grego, *supra* no. 19, at 1.
46. UCS Satellite, 'Database', https://www.ucsusa.org/nuclear-weapons/space-weapons/satellite-database#.WyutXFxPLTM.
47. *Ibid.*
48. Ram Jakhu and Karan Singh, 'Space Security and Competition for Radio Frequencies and Geostationary Slots', 58(1) *Zeitschrift Für Luft-und Weltraumrecht* 74-93 (2009), at 82.
49. Haller and Sakazaki, *supra* no. 22, at 25.
50. Loren B. Thompson, 'Lack of Protected Satellite Communications Could Mean Defeat for Joint Force in Future War', http://www.lexingtoninstitute.org/lack-of-protected-satellite-communications-could-mean-defeat-for-joint-force-in-future-war/.
51. SES, 'Satellite, A Critical Infrastructure for Defence and Security', Speech by President and CEO of SES, Karim Michel Sabbagh at the Berlin Security Conference held on Tuesday, 17 November 2015, https://www.ses.com/blog/satellite-critical-infrastructure-defence-and-security.
52. Jakhu and Singh, *supra* no. 48, at 82.

Looking at future trends, commercial systems, rather than replacing military ones, will have an increased complementary role in supporting non-critical transmissions. Certain defence and intelligence functions, indeed, require extra layers of security – such as Telemetry, Tracking and Command (TT&C) signal encryption or hardened satellite components – that are normally not available in commercial systems, and that will need the continuous deployment of secured military satellites.[53] Despite this, due to the increase of capacity demand and budgetary pressure, the parallel tendency to rely on private operators will continue to rise.[54]

§6.03 THE VULNERABILITY OF THE SPACE INFRASTRUCTURE TO ELECTROMAGNETIC INTERFERENCES

[A] Modern Threats to Satellites

As stated above, satellites are a vital component of our society, economy, security and defence systems. However, they also suffer a high degree of vulnerability that makes them a tempting target for State and non-State actors with hostile intentions.

Such threats can be based on different technologies and can target different segments of space systems.[55] In the historical context of the Cold War, in order to disrupt a satellite's functionality, its physical destruction was usually considered necessary.[56] This 'traditional' form of attack could make use of kinetic ASAT, such as interceptor missiles, or non-kinetic means, such as high-altitude nuclear detonations, directed energy weapons or high-powered microwave attacks. Although highly effective, these techniques have significant downsides. First, they require significant financial means and a state-of-the-art anti-satellite technology, meaning that they are thus available only to a restricted number of space-faring nations.[57] Moreover, the physical destruction of a satellite would create a dangerous cloud of space debris, impairing the long-term sustainability of space activities and potentially threatening the space assets of the attacking State itself.[58] Although so far, no such hostile act against satellites has been recorded, three ASAT tests were conducted by the People's

53. US, General Accounting Office, Critical Infrastructure Protection: Commercial Satellite Security Should be More Fully Addressed, *supra* no. 20, at 19.
54. Haller and Sakazaki, *supra* no. 22, at 25. An interesting example in this sense is the creation of public-private joint ventures for the operation of military systems, such as GovSat, a satellite operator and service provider co-owned by the Luxemburg satellite operator SES and the Government of Luxembourg to provide secure satellite communication services for defence and security civilian applications. *See*, Gov Sat, 'Home', https://www.govsat.lu.
55. *See*, for an overview of the potential human threats to space systems, Tom Wilson, 'Threats to United States Space Capabilities', Prepared for the Commission to Assess US National Security Space Management and Organization, https://www.fas.org/spp/eprint/article05.html.
56. Matthew Kleiman and Sonia McNeil, 'Red Lines in Outer Space', *The Space Review*, 2012, http://www.thespacereview.com/article/2038/1.
57. For instance, China and the US have recently tested kinetic ASAT weapons. *See*, Brian Weeden, '2007 Chinese Anti-Satellite Test Fact Sheet', Secure World Foundation, 2010, http://www.swfound.org/media/9550/2007%20chinese%20asat%20test%20factsheet.pdf.
58. The above-mentioned Chinese ASAT test, for instance, has caused the largest ever cloud if space debris ever generated by a single event in orbit. *Ibid.*, at 2.

Republic of China in 1997, the US in 2008 and by India in 2019, respectively, against their own satellites.

Over the last decades, different kinds of non-kinetic threats to space systems have emerged. As analysed in the previous chapter, one of these threats is constituted by cyberattacks and is focusing most of the current debate. The other one, less sophisticated but not less dangerous, is intentional electromagnetic interference with satellite signals. As already mentioned, free access to the radio spectrum is one of the essential pre-conditions for the usability of space, and many actors have started to exploit this vulnerability due to its advantages over kinetic attacks.

An electromagnetic attack could be defined as "any action involving the use of electromagnetic energy and directed energy to control the electromagnetic spectrum or to attack an adversary."[59] The most common forms are jamming and spoofing, which take place in the radio spectrum that is the part of the electromagnetic spectrum used by radio communications. These radio interferences present several benefits over kinetic attacks.

At first, the cost and the skills necessary to carry on such attacks are reduced, as the technology is currently available via the purchase of off-the-shelf components. In 1986, for instance, an insider called 'Captain Midnight' used commercially available equipment to disrupt a cable network uplink feed to a Galaxy I satellite, successfully transmitting a thirty minutes protest message to HBO customers in the eastern US.[60] This makes electromagnetic interference a suitable means for non-space-faring nations or even non-State actors with modest financial means and technical capabilities, and an effective instrument to challenge the technological advantage of an adversary in the case of asymmetric warfare.

Second, the attribution of such acts is problematic, given the technical difficulties in identifying the source of the interference and the responsible entity, especially if the attacker is a non-State actor. Additionally, these attacks can easily be confused for more common unintentional interference or even natural phenomena like solar flares.[61]

Third, unlike kinetic ones, electromagnetic attacks, may be reversible. They do not necessarily result in the physical destruction or harm of the target and may cause only the temporary disruption, denial or deception of radio signals. Once the goal of the attacker is achieved, the interference can be suspended, and the transmission will resume as before, with no material consequence or damage caused to the targeted object. This entails a double benefit: the creation of space debris is avoided, making the act less intolerable by the international space community. Second, the perceived

59. US Department of the Army, 'Cyber Electromagnetic Activities', FN-38, at 4-2. *See also*, Chapter 2, section §2.04[A].
60. David. M. Ewalt, 'The Tale of Captain Midnight, TV Hacker and Folk Hero', Forbes, 2013, https://www.forbes.com/sites/davidewalt/2013/03/18/the-tale-of-captain-midnight-tv-hacker-and-folk-hero/#30a97ad11053.
61. Todd Harrison, Kaitlyn Johnson and Thomas G. Roberts, 'Space Threat Assessment 2018', A Report of the Center for Strategic & International Studies Aerospace Security Project, https://www.aerospace.csis.org/wp-content/uploads/2018/04/Harrison_SpaceThreatAssessment_FULL_WEB.pdf, at 4. On the notion of electromagnetic interference, *see* Chapter 2, section §2.04[B].

gravity of the attack is reduced, thereby decreasing the probabilities – and the potential legal rights – of a strong response by the target State or entity. In conclusion, electromagnetic interference is a highly cost-effective means of attack, especially if compared with more intrusive anti-satellite measures, and is affordable both by entities and individuals.[62]

In recent times, the phenomenon of intentional interference has reached remarkable proportions. Nowadays, operators deal with it on a regular basis, losing millions of dollars per year in terms of lost revenues, extra costs related to specialised personnel and equipment, and company reputation.[63] Although both military and commercial satellites are susceptible to interference, the commercial satellite industry is certainly the most affected. Commercial satellites, indeed, do not afford the same protection as military ones in terms of encrypted transmissions, spread spectrum communication or system redundancy, measures that are generally considered as an unnecessary expense by the private sector.[64] They are also more vulnerable by design, given that they are normally intended to receive users' signals from a large area – and therefore, there will be a large area from which it is possible to interfere with the signal.

The fact that commercial satellites are particularly vulnerable, however, does not mean that only civil applications are under threat. On the contrary, as stated above, communication satellites are inherently dual-use assets, and most military communications pass through commercial satellites, making them susceptible to electromagnetic interference.[65]

Another consequence of the interdependence between the civil and the military sector is that the boundary between targets is blurred, making it difficult to disrupt a civilian service without also interfering with the military signals and vice versa. The interference with a specific signal indeed may not remain confined to its specific frequency, but depending on the technology used, may have effects on neighbouring frequencies, thus disrupting different transmissions carried by the same satellite.[66] Further, this interdependency would facilitate a potential adversary in disrupting both kinds of services by targeting one single satellite. This would allow the causation of extensive cross-sector damage to military communications and civil infrastructures with a relatively minor effort. For instance, in 2007, Libya jammed two satellites belonging to the Abu Dhabi operator, Thuraya Satellite Communications, in an attempt to block a small commercial radio station broadcasting on human rights and freedom of speech. As a collateral effect, not only did the interference knock dozens of TV and radio stations serving Britain and Europe off the air but it also disrupted US diplomatic,

62. Tom Wilson, *Threats to United States Space Capabilities* (Prepared for the Commission to Assess US National Security Space Management and Organization, 2001), at 7.
63. Jakhu and Singh, *supra* no. 48, at 48.
64. US, General Accounting Office, Critical Infrastructure Protection: Commercial Satellite Security Should be More Fully Addressed, *supra* no. 20, at 25.
65. Wilson, *supra* no. 62, at 14.
66. This is the case, for instance, of broadband jamming, normally used when the attacker does not know what is the precise frequency used by the signal to be interfered with and spreads the interference over a larger range of frequencies. David Wright, Laura. Grego and Lisbeth Gronlund, *The Physics of Space Security: A Reference Manual* (American Academy of Arts and Sciences, 2005), at 120.

military and Federal Bureau of Investigation (FBI) communications, causing severe protests by British and US diplomats.[67]

[B] Jamming

The vulnerability of satellite networks to electronic interference lies in the communication links. The uplink refers to the signal sent from the ground up to the satellite, while the downlink is the signal sent back from the satellite to the ground.[68] The TT&C link, also consisting of uplinks and downlinks, is the signal used to control the satellite, check its status and perform corrective manoeuvres if necessary. Since such a link is normally well protected from jamming via encoding and is related to the functionality of the 'bus' rather than of the 'payload', it is usually not targeted unless the objective of the attacker is the destruction of the satellite itself.[69] The communication and navigation service signals, thus, are the typical targets.

Jamming consists of disrupting the communication with a satellite by overpowering the signals being sent to or from it with the use of a signal at the same frequency and at higher power.[70] The receiver, therefore, is no longer able to accurately recover the legitimate signal. Several States are developing military jamming capabilities, but, as mentioned above, the necessary equipment can be easily purchased at affordable prices, making it available to non-State actors such as terrorist groups or single individuals.[71]

There are two main types of jamming: downlink jamming and uplink jamming. A downlink jammer attempts to inject electronic noise into the receivers on the ground, preventing them from receiving a usable signal from the satellite.[72] This technique is used, for example, by authoritarian governments to block access to broadcast transmissions, or by employees to prevent the company from knowing the position of their vehicle via the use of the so-called privacy devices.[73] Such jammers have the advantage of being closer to the receiving station than the space-based emitter, and therefore, they can be much less powerful. Further, they are inexpensive and easy to use.[74] However, they are able to disrupt only the receiving stations within their range. In the case of point-to-multipoint satellite transmission, where receivers are scattered in a large

67. Kleiman and McNeil, *supra* no. 56.
68. Harrison, Johnson and Roberts, *supra* no. 61, at 4.
69. Wright, Grego and Gronlund, *supra* no. 66, at 121.
70. *Ibid.*, at 118.
71. A GNSS jammer can be bought online for less than USD 50, for instance. *See*, David Livingstone and Patricia Lewis, *Space, the Final Frontier for Cybersecurity?* (Chatham House, 2016), at 16.
72. US, General Accounting Office, Critical Infrastructure Protection: Commercial Satellite Security Should be More Fully Addressed, *supra* no. 20, at 13.
73. John Brandon, 'GPS Jammers Illegal, Dangerous, and Very Easy to Buy', Fox News, 2010, http://www.foxnews.com/tech/2010/03/17/gps-jammers-easily-accessible-potentially-dangerous-risk.html.
74. US, General Accounting Office, Critical Infrastructure Protection: Commercial Satellite Security Should be More Fully Addressed, *supra* no. 20, at 13.

geographic area, their effect is, therefore, limited. They are also relatively easy to be located and disabled since they need to be somewhere in the vicinity of the target.[75]

Uplink jamming, on the contrary, interferes directly with the receiver on the satellite in orbit. Communication satellites normally receive a signal from the ground and retransmit it back, routing information from one point to one or several other points on the surface of the Earth. The terrestrial area covered by the satellite signal is called satellite 'footprint'. An important advantage over downlink jamming, thus, is that the affected area of an orbital jammer is not restricted to its physical location but affects all the receiving stations within the satellite footprint.[76] The jammer itself does not need to be near the receiver but can be located anywhere within the broadcast/receive area - the area from which the satellite is designed to receive signals.[77] A transmission originating from one State, therefore, can be disrupted by a jammer located elsewhere, making its localisation and neutralisation more challenging or even impossible. Satellites in geo-synchronous orbit, given their stationary position in relation to a given location on the Earth, are easier to be located and disrupted, while satellites in lower orbits require a more sophisticated tracking technology and can be jammed only when in the line of sight of the jammer.[78]

Orbital jamming has been a rising phenomenon during the recent years, and a particularly perilous one given its potential to disrupt a wide range of services by targeting one single satellite.

[C] Spoofing

Spoofing is in many aspects similar to jamming. It can target the uplink or the downlink, it must originate from the broadcast/receive area of the satellite, and it aims at interfering with the satellite's regular transmissions. Instead of transmitting meaningless noise, however, it replaces the wanted signal with a false one, with the purpose of introducing false or corrupted information into the communication system.[79] Since the counterfeit signal must mimic in detail the characteristics of the true signal,[80] spoofing devices are much more sophisticated than jammers.

Although more complex to carry out, a successful spoofing attack can lead to catastrophic consequence if undetected until it is too late. It could, for instance, paralyse critical infrastructures such as power grids by introducing incorrect timing signals, or cause indirect economic damages by targeting trading systems in the financial sector.[81]

75. During the 2003 Iraqi War, for instance, GPS jammers used by Iraqi forces were promptly located and neutralised by the US military. Wright, Grego and Gronlund, *supra* no. 66, at 120.
76. Livingstone and Lewis, *supra* no. 71, at 17.
77. Commercial communications and broadcast satellites are, thus, particularly vulnerable, as they are designed to receive signals from users spread over large ground areas. *Ibid.*, at 17.
78. Wright, Grego and Gronlund, *supra* no. 66, at 121.
79. Harrison, Johnson and Roberts, *supra* no. 61, at 4.
80. Livingstone and Lewis, *supra* no. 71, at 18.
81. *Ibid.*

An effective defence against spoofing is constituted by signal encryption. As stated above, however, commercial satellite providers rarely find a valid business case to adopt such expensive security measures. Even the GPS military signal, despite being encrypted, has proven vulnerable to spoofing. This particular technique, called 'meaconing', consists of recording the encrypted signal and rebroadcasting it with a slight delay, without the need to decrypt it. Since precise timing is an essential feature of GNSS, this is enough to disrupt the service and give an inaccurate position.[82]

§6.04 ITU LEGAL FRAMEWORK

[A] ITU and Its Role

A fundamental condition to space activities is an interference-free access to the radio spectrum. This requires a coordinated approach to frequency spectrum management at the global level. The UN specialised agency currently in charge of telecommunications and ICT is the ITU.

Deriving from the International Telegraph Union which was created in 1865, it is one of the oldest intergovernmental organisations still in place, as well as one of the most participated, with 193 Member States, and over 800 Sector Members, Associates and Academia Members.[83] Its primary goals are to promote international cooperation for the development and rational use of telecommunication services, to foster the extension of the benefits of communication technologies to all the world's inhabitants, and to harmonise and standardise telecommunications practices around the globe.[84]

It is not the purpose of the present chapter to provide a detailed analysis of such organisation; however, due to its crucial role in the governance of radio spectrum, it is appropriate to briefly recall its structure and competences.[85]

The ITU went through an extensive reform process in the early 1990s, aimed at providing more flexibility to its rigid structure and decision-making mechanisms.[86] The fundamental legal texts stemming out of this reform and still in place today are the ITU Constitution,[87] which defines the ITU structure, the ITU Convention,[88] which is mainly dedicated to its *modus operandi*, and the ITU Radio Regulations.[89] The Radio Regulations constitute an international treaty with binding force on the Member States. They, provide the operational rules for the management of the radio spectrum and can only be amended by the World Radio Conference (WRC) which takes place roughly every

82. Harrison, Johnson and Roberts, *supra* no. 61, at 4.
83. Ram Jakhu and Paul S. Dempsey, *Routledge Handbook of Space Law* (Taylor & Francis, 2016).
84. Constitution of the International Telecommunication Union (22 December 1992), ATS 1994 n. 28, Art. 1.
85. *See*, for a comprehensive history of the ITU, Francis Lyall, *International Communications: The International Telecommunication Union and the Universal Postal Union* (Ashgate Publishing, 2011).
86. Frans von der Dunk and Fabio Tronchetti, *Handbook of Space Law* (Edward Elgar Publishing, 2015), at 4.
87. ITU Constitution, *supra* no. 84.
88. *Ibid.*
89. Radio Regulations Articles, Edition of 2016, https://www.itu.int/pub/R-REG-RR.

four years. While the ITU remains a classical intergovernmental organisation, the reform also changed the membership rules in order to keep pace with the increasing role of the private sector. As of 1994, non-governmental entities were allowed to participate in ITU conferences and institutional settings without voting rights via the Sector, Associate or Academia membership.[90]

With regard to the ITU's structure, the supreme organ is the Plenipotentiary Conference, which convenes approximately every four years - alternating with the WRC - and is composed by delegations representing all the ITU Member States. It decides the general policies of the Union as well as the institutional aspects, retaining the power to amend the ITU Constitution and the ITU Convention.[91] The permanent bodies of the ITU are the Council, which is formed by the Member States elected at the Plenipotentiary Conference and which acts on its behalf by delegated powers, and the General Secretariat.

In 1992, in the context of above-mentioned reforms, the ITU was subdivided into three sectors with differentiated competences:

- the Telecommunication Standardization Sector, entrusted with adopting recommendations to standardise telecommunications on a worldwide basis;
- the Telecommunication Development Sector, which supports the developing States to improve and expand their telecommunication services and networks; and
- the Radio communication Sector, which deals with the management of the radio spectrum and is the most relevant in the light of the present chapter.[92]

The current analysis will focus on the ITU's role in radio spectrum management. Among other purposes, the ITU has been entrusted to coordinate efforts to eliminate harmful cross-border interference between radio communication services by various technical and legal means.[93] In order to achieve this goal, the ITU Radio Regulations - retaining status of an international treaty[94] - set a complex system of *a priori* coordination of radio frequencies made of three steps:

- the allocation of frequency bands to a certain category of services;[95]
- the allotment of radio frequency to individual States;[96] and
- the registration of frequency assignment made by States to radio operators.[97]

Such a process must respect general principles established by the ITU Constitution, such as the rational and equitable use of radio frequency, the commitment of

90. Instrument Amending the Constitution of the International Telecommunication Union of 22 December 1992, as amended 14 October 1994 (9 November 1998), ATS 2000 n. 8.
91. *Ibid.*
92. ITU Constitution, *supra* no. 84, Chapters II-IV.
93. Von der Dunk and Tronchetti, *supra* no. 86, at 464; ITU Constitution, *supra* no. 84, Art. 1(2) 1a.
94. *See* Chapter 3, section §3.01.
95. ITU Radio Regulations, *supra* no. 89, Art. 1(16).
96. *Ibid.*, Art. 1(17).
97. *Ibid.*, Art. 1(18).

States to limit their use to the minimum essential, and their nature of limited natural resources.[98]

The last step of the process, i.e., the inclusion, upon request of the competent State, of the frequency assignment into the Master International Frequency Register (MIFR), grants to such assignment international recognition of interference-free usage rights of those frequencies for the intended purposes.[99]

With specific regard to space services, such technology came into existence later than terrestrial wireless communication and the ITU itself. Following the launch of Sputnik I by the Soviet Union, it became clear that space communications would gain an increased level of importance. The 1963 Extraordinary Administrative Radio Conference, also known as the Space Conference, allocated for the first time radio frequencies to the uplink and downlink space services including them in the ITU frequency coordination system.[100] There are currently twenty-one categories of space services recognised by the ITU Radio Regulations and a special coordination process for orbital positions in the geostationary orbit.[101]

[B] Relevant Provisions for Electromagnetic Interferences

One of the main goals of the ITU is to achieve an interference-free operation of radio communication services.[102] Electromagnetic interference, therefore, is an issue of central importance in the ITU legal framework, and its legal regime is spread over the ITU Constitution, Convention and Radio Regulations.

The ITU regulatory system adopts a two-pronged approach to the problem.[103] The first category of norms is constituted by preventive measures, whose purpose is to avoid *ex ante* the occurrence of interference between radio stations.[104] Such measures consist of:

- the frequency allocation system;[105]
- the coordination and notification procedure;[106] and
- the technical rules for radio stations.[107]

98. ITU Constitution, *supra* no. 84, Art. 44.
99. Frans von der Dunk, 'Maintaining the Master International Frequency Register', *in* Mahulena Hofmann (ed.), *International Regulations of Space Communications* (Larcier, 2013), at 59. ITU Radio Regulations, *supra* no. 89, Art. 11.
100. ITU, 'Radio Conferences', https://www.itu.int/en/history/Pages/RadioConferences.aspx?conf=4.89.
101. ITU Radio Regulations, *supra* no. 89, Arts 5 and 9(1).
102. Mitsushiro Sakamoto, 'Radio Regulations and Procedures in Cases of Harmful Interference', *in* Mahulena Hofmann (ed.), *Regulatory Perspective: Legal Rules for Interference-Free Radio Communication* (Nomos, 2016), at 33.
103. Sakamoto, *supra* no. 102, at 32.
104. ITU Constitution, *supra* no. 84, Art. 1.2(a).
105. ITU Radio Regulations, *supra* no. 89, Art. 5.
106. *Ibid.*, Arts 7, 8, 9, 11.
107. *Ibid.*, Art. 15, sections I, II, III, IV.

The second category comes to relevance when a harmful interference has nonetheless taken place and is constituted by *ex post* measures to remediate the problem.[108]

Focusing now on the second category of measures, it is appropriate to start with some definitions. The ITU legal framework defines interference as "the effect of unwanted energy [...] upon reception in a radiocommunication system, manifested by any performance degradation, misinterpretation, or loss of information [...]."[109] Electromagnetic interferences, thus, are not necessarily harmful. They can also be permissible, when they are contained in certain quantitative and sharing criteria defined in the Radio Regulations or ITU-R Recommendations,[110] and accepted when they surpass such thresholds but have been agreed upon between two or more administrations.[111] Interference becomes harmful – and thus, in principle, prohibited – when it "seriously degrades, obstructs, or repeatedly interrupts a radiocommunication service operating in accordance with Radio Regulations."[112] Only stations operating in conformity with the Radio Regulations and whose frequency assignment are in the MIFR, therefore, afford the right of protection. An assignment not in conformity with such conditions, on the contrary, results unprotected. It is also important to notice that only interferences between stations under the jurisdiction of different States are subject to the ITU legal regime, while domestic interference, instead, is a matter of national competence.

Harmful interference provisions do not address operators directly, but rather bind Member States to the duty of ensuring compliance by operators.[113] In particular, Article 45 of the ITU Constitution obliges the Member States to require the agencies they authorised to "operate in such a manner as not to cause harmful interference."[114] Rather than as a strict prohibition, thus, it is formulated more as a duty of prevention.

According to the ITU Radio Regulations, once interference occurs, the Member States are urged to exercise the utmost goodwill and mutual cooperation.[115] Article 15 of the ITU Radio Regulations sets forth the procedure that national administrations shall follow in order to resolve the interference. The adopted approach is oriented towards the principle of mutual cooperation among States and foresees that the administration having jurisdiction on the station suffering the interference requests the administration having jurisdiction over the originating station to take all the necessary steps to eliminate the interference. Historically, most harmful interference cases have been resolved via bilateral cooperation between administrations.[116] Should this not be sufficient, the Radiocommunication Bureau (RB) may be involved upon request of one of the administrations, with the aim to help in identifying the source of the interference

108. ITU Constitution, *supra* no. 84, Art. 1.2(b).
109. ITU Radio Regulations, *supra* no. 89, Art. 1.166.
110. *Ibid.*, Art. 1.167.
111. *Ibid.*, Art. 1.168.
112. ITU Constitution, *supra* no. 84, Annex 1003; ITU Radio Regulations, *supra* no. 89, Art. 1.169.
113. ITU Constitution, *supra* no. 84, Art. 6.
114. *Ibid.*, Art.45.
115. ITU Radio Regulations, *supra* no. 89, Art. 7.8.
116. Sakamoto, *supra* no. 102, at 37.

and seek the cooperation of the responsible administration. As a further step, the Bureau may send a report to the Radio Regulations Board (RBB), which considers it and formulates recommendations.[117] The RBB has no sanctioning power against a non-cooperative administration, with the exception of the possibility to delete a frequency assignment entry in the MIFR upon certain conditions.[118]

Should the cooperation mechanism established by Article 15 prove to be ineffective, the concerned States may resort to arbitration in accordance with Article 41 of the ITU Convention or seek dispute resolution under Article 56 of the ITU Constitution, upon the condition that all States involved are party to the 'Optional Protocol on the Compulsory Settlement of Disputes Relating to this Constitution, to the Convention, and to the Administrative Regulations' attached to the ITU Constitution.

[C] Effectiveness of the Provisions

The aim of the ITU regime, which is to prevent and eliminate harmful interference, has remained fundamentally unchanged since its conception. The root of the system is based on voluntary compliance by States and mutual cooperation, and, in the historical context of unintentional interference, has proven to work well. Several factors, including the rise in the numbers of public and private operators, the consequent competition for radio frequencies and orbital slots, and the increase of jamming and spoofing episodes, have put it under increasing pressure.[119]

In particular, the ITU regime does not distinguish between accidental and deliberate interference. Notwithstanding, the intentional misuse of the electromagnetic spectrum, such as jamming and spoofing, seems to fall within the general definition of harmful interference provided by the Radio Regulations, and the *ex post* measures to eliminate them are thus applicable. Whether the application of such measures is effective, however, is uncertain. The entire regulatory regime appears indeed tailored to deal with unintentional interference, and its suitability to counter voluntary threats is at least questionable.[120]

If jamming or spoofing occurs, such an episode will constitute a clear violation of Article 45 of the ITU Constitution, and of Article 15 of the ITU Radio Regulations.[121] In case the interfered station recognises them as such, the State having jurisdiction on the interfered station can seek cooperation from the State having jurisdiction on the interfering station according to Article 15 of the ITU Radio Regulations. If the problem is not solved, it can escalate the issue to the RB and to the RBB.

Several issues arise from the application of Article 15 of the ITU Radio Regulations. At first, there is a fundamental problem of attribution. In several instances, the source – in this case, a jamming or spoofing device – remains unknown.[122] As a

117. ITU Radio Regulations, *supra* no. 89, Art. 15 section VI.
118. *Ibid.*, Art. 11.42A.
119. Jakhu and Singh, *supra* no. 48, at 87.
120. Sakamoto, *supra* no. 102, at 32.
121. Jakhu and Singh, *supra* no. 48, at 85.
122. *Ibid.*, at 84.

consequence, it would be difficult to identify the right State to address, and for the addressed State itself to locate the origin of the interference within its territory. It has to be noted, however, that the usage of geo-location by satellite, as well as of non-satellite spectrum monitoring capability has remarkably increased the efficiency of the localisation process of the source of interference in respect to the past. The problem, thus, seems to have been partially overcome by technical means.[123]

Second, if such a State is identified and appropriately addressed, it is its responsibility to ascertain the facts and remediate the problem. In other words, the wilful cooperation of the requested State would be indispensable.[124] Given that in several instances interference has been politically motivated, the State in question might have little or no interest to exercise the 'utmost goodwill' in the spirit of the Radio Regulations,[125] especially when the interference is a State-sponsored operation.[126]

If a State refuses to cooperate, the ITU does not have any enforcement mechanism in order to ensure compliance with the Radio Regulations. The role of the RB and the RBB is limited to provide administrative support upon request of the Member States and excludes any sanctioning power.[127] The only foreseen form of sanction, namely the deletion of a frequency assignment from the MIFR, would work only with legitimate radio communication services, and obviously constitutes no threat against pirate radio signals operating outside the Radio Regulations and the formal control of national administrations. This problem is further aggravated by the absence of any compulsory dispute settlement mechanism under the ITU legal framework since arbitration under the ITU Convention, and the dispute settlement regime under the ITU Constitution are voluntary mechanisms. Significantly, the States have never used them so far.

The effectiveness of the ITU regulatory regime on interference is further limited by two major exceptions. First, Article 48 of the Constitution confers to States' entire freedom with regard to military radio installations, and limits their duty to observe the provisions regarding the prevention of harmful interference 'so far as possible'.[128] The practical result is to exempt military radio communication services from the scope of application of ITU rules and regulations, leaving outside the single largest group of spectrum users. This leads to potential abuses especially with regard to military use of commercial satellites, given the uncertainty on whether such commercial systems should be considered as civilian in nature, and therefore, subject to ITU regulatory regime, or installations for military defence, and therefore, exempted.[129]

123. *See,* in this sense, the role of the International Monitoring System foreseen in Art. 16 of the Radio Regulations and based on the voluntary cooperation of national administrations. ITU, 'Harmful Interference to Satellite Systems', ITU Document WRS18/5-E, 30 October 2018. On general issues of attribution, *see also,* Chapter 5, section §5.04[C].
124. ITU Constitution, *supra* no. 84, Art. 45.
125. ITU Radio Regulations, *supra* no. 89, Art. 7.8.
126. Most of the recorded cases or jamming appear to have been perpetrated, or at least supported by national States. *See,* James G. Savage, *The Politics of International Telecommunications Regulation* (Boulder, 1989).
127. *See,* for further details, ITU, 'Report by the Director of Radiocommunications Bureau to the 48th Meeting of the Radio Regulations Board', ITU Document RRB08-3/3-E (add.1), 14 August 2008.
128. ITU Constitution, *supra* no. 84, Art. 48.
129. Jakhu and Singh, *supra* no. 48, at 88.

The second exception, enshrined in Articles 34 and 35 of the ITU Constitution,[130] entitles States to stop any ingoing or outgoing communication with respect to their own territory, establishing a de facto exception to the principled obligation to prevent interference. This authority derives from the sovereign right of a State to control the flow of information from or to its territory[131] but does not extend beyond its borders, thus leaving untouched the prohibition to interfere with communications in other States.[132] While downlink jamming is likely to fit into such an exception as it targets a specific geographic area, uplink satellite jamming appears more problematic in light of the multiple users and the large service coverage area of a typical communication satellite.[133] For instance, the disruptions operated by Iran and Libya in the early 2000s – although apparently motivated by the will to stop an ongoing transmission into their territory – are to be considered illegal as they affected the regular operations of other States' radio communications.

This does not imply that the ITU ignores the problem, or that it is unwilling to take action. The ITU has indeed acknowledged the increasing problem of harmful interference and the inadequacy of its dispute resolution system.[134] In recent years, improvements have been introduced to cope with unintentional interference. These improvements include *ex ante* measures such as a due diligence procedure for satellite network filings[135] and a mechanism of cost recovery[136] inclusive of the above-mentioned possibility for the RBB to delete a frequency registration from the MIFR.[137] With specific regard to intentional interference, during WRC-12, Article 15.21 of the ITU Radio Regulations was reformulated with a strong majority of votes, establishing the duty of national administrations to 'take the necessary actions' once they have information of an infringement of the ITU legal regime, in particular of Article 45 of the ITU Constitution or Article 15.1 of the ITU Radio Regulations.[138] Such a change, however, although politically significant, is a mere clarification of the types of infringement envisaged, and has proven scarcely effective in increasing the ITU's authority against intentional interferences.

130. ITU Constitution, *supra* no. 84, Arts 34 and 35.
131. Deborah Housen-Couriel, 'Disruption of Satellite Transmissions ad Bellum and in Bello: Launching a New Paradigm of Convergence', 45(3) *Israel Law Review* 445 (2012).
132. ITU Constitution, *supra* no. 84, Art. 38.
133. *See*, George A. Codding, 'Jamming and the Protection of Frequency Assignments', 49(3) *The American Journal of International Law* 384-388 (1955).
134. Julie N. Zoller, 'Satellite Regulations: Improving the International Satellite Regulatory Framework', ITU News, 2012, http://www.itu.int/net/newsroom/wrc/2012/features/satellite_regulations.aspx.
135. Resolution 80, Due Diligence in Applying the Principles Embodied in the Constitution (Rev.WRC-07), in 2012 World Radiocommunication Conference Agenda and References (Resolutions and Recommendations).
136. Decision 482 (Modified 2017) (Adopted at the Tenth Plenary Meeting), Implementation of Cost Recovery for Satellite Network Filings, ITU Document C17/135-E.
137. ITU Radio Regulations, *supra* no. 89, Art. 13.6.
138. *Ibid.*, Art. 15.21.

In the same year, following the disruption suffered by civil aviation operations in South Korea due to repeated interference against GNSS, a further step was undertaken.[139] The ITU signed an MoC with ICAO setting up a framework for the enhanced cooperation between the two agencies to combat harmful interference against GNSS with a potential impact on aviation safety.[140] The stated purpose of the document is to prevent the duplication of efforts and to benefit from potential synergies between the two organisations in order to maximise the effectiveness of their joint effort. To this end, the MoC, which does not have binding force, establishes a cooperation procedure whereby ICAO will share interference reports and its aeronautical expertise with the ITU, and the ITU will keep ICAO informed on the progress of Article 15 procedures of the Radio Regulations for the resolution of harmful interference. Despite the political significance, the practical utility of this document is limited since it formalises a procedure that is already common practice in the relationship between the two agencies. Furthermore, it does not impact the core of the problem, which remains the lack of enforcement powers of the ITU. Further help may come in the future from the Satellite Interference Reporting and Resolution System, an online application developed in response to Resolution 186, aimed at facilitating the communication between the parties concerned in case of harmful interference and at ensuring them assistance in the identification of sources of interference and their prompt elimination in accordance with Articles 15 and No. 13.2 of the Radio Regulations. This system, although constituting a welcome improvement, is still based upon the premise of utmost goodwill, mutual assistance and cooperation among administrations, which is not always a granted condition in case of voluntary interference.[141]

On top of such legal obstacles stands the highly political nature of deliberate satellite interference. States have always refrained from bringing the problem in front of dispute settlement mechanisms and submitting themselves to binding decisions by international bodies, and have favoured bilateral diplomatic channels instead. The ITU, in 2012, for the first time took a strong political stance, expressly condemning Iran for jamming satellite communications, but no concrete actions were undertaken.[142] The absence of enforcement powers and the principle of State sovereignty suggest indeed that the ITU will continue to lack effective sanctioning tools in the foreseeable

139. Between 2011 and 2012 in the Incheon Region 106 airplanes of 18 airlines were affected from 4 March to 13 May 2011, while 1016 aircraft of 33 different airlines and 16 States were disrupted from 28 April to 13 May 2012. Four aircraft, furthermore, made a missed approach due to the Ground Positioning Warning System – GPWS alert activation in response to the interference. *See*, ICAO, 'High-Level Conference on Aviation Security. Working Paper 39 Presented by Republic of Korea – The Impact of GNSS Vulnerabilities and Response Measures', http://www.icao.int/Meetings/avsecconf/Documents/WP%2039/WP.39.Korea.pdf.

140. ICAO and ITU, *Memorandum of Cooperation between the International Civil Aviation Organization and the International Telecommunication Union for Providing a Framework for Enhanced Cooperation Regarding the Protection of the Global Navigation Satellite System from Harmful Interference with a Potential Impact on Aviation Safety*, ACP WG-F/28 IP05.

141. ITU, 'Harmful Interference to Satellite Systems', *supra* no. 123.

142. *See*, ITU, 'ITU Statement on Satellite Jamming Following EBU Press Release of 22 October, 2012', http://www.itu.int/net/pressoffice/press_releases/2012/OS01.aspx#.W09U4VxPLTN.

future, maintaining in its arsenal only soft measures such as political persuasion and naming-and shaming-practices.[143]

§6.05 ELECTRONIC INTERFERENCE VERSUS CYBERATTACKS

The scope of the present book covers two types of hostile acts against satellites, both of non-kinetic nature: cyberattacks *stricto sensu*, which take place via or aim to achieve goals in cyberspace, and electromagnetic interferences such as jamming and spoofing, which make use of the radio spectrum to block or corrupt radio communications via satellite. While part of the literature tends to accommodate the two phenomena in the same category, it is appropriate to notice their different core distinctive elements. Cyberattacks are identified with the content of the data transferred, for instance, malicious code, and technology-neutral as a hacker would not care whether the data is transferred via wire or radio waves or a combination of both. Electromagnetic interferences, conversely, are content-neutral – they are qualified as such not by the content of the signal, which in case of jamming would be just white noise but by the use of radio communication technology. It follows to ask whether they are to be considered distinguished phenomena, though, given that they both fundamentally target information.[144]

The answer, from a regulatory point of view, depends on the terminology and the definitions adopted. It is thus possible to better reformulate the question: do hostile acts that take place in cyberspace fall under the category of harmful interference? Conversely, could cases of intentional electromagnetic interference be treated as cyberattacks?

With regard to the first question, the answer seems quite straightforward. There is an internationally agreed definition of interference, provided by the ITU Radio Regulations, which is bound to the emission of 'unwanted energy' that causes the "degradation, obstruction, or repeated interruption of a radiocommunication service."[145] Interference, thus, is related to the presence of a radio signal in the electromagnetic spectrum which physically interferes with another – legitimate – radio signal. A cyberattack – which takes place in the virtual world of cyberspace and not in the physical world of the electromagnetic spectrum unless as a mere medium – does not satisfy such requirements per se and cannot be considered as harmful interference under the Radio Regulations. Therefore, they are not applicable.

It is possible to envisage a case where malicious software, while being uploaded into a satellite orbiting the Earth via a radio signal, accidentally interferes with a radio communication service operating in conformity with the Radio Regulations, thus resulting in harmful interference. Such a scenario, however, is very unlikely to happen

143. *See*, for a comprehensive overview of the critical aspects of the issue, Mahulena Hofmann (ed.), *Harmful Interference in Regulatory Perspective* (Nomos/Ashgate, 2015).
144. Georg Kerschischnig, *supra* no. 3, at 31. *See also*, for a military doctrine approach to such distinction, US Department of the Army, *Cyber Electromagnetic Activities*, Field Manual No. 3-38, Washington (2014).
145. ITU Radio Regulations, *supra* no. 89, Arts 1.166 and 1.169.

in practice, and even in such a case, the applicability of Radio Regulations would be merely coincidental and would not cover the gravest consequences of the cyberattack.

With regard to the reverse question, i.e., whether cases of intentional electromagnetic interference constitute cyberattacks, the answer is more complex. There is no internationally agreed definition of cyberattacks, and terms such as cyberattacks, cyber operations, and computer network attacks are used in different contexts with different meanings, as highlighted in Chapter 2. The answer, thus, depends on the specific term and definition taken into consideration and on the extent of their scope. The term 'cyber', however, seems to imply that the virtual world of cyberspace has to be involved to some extent, which is not necessarily the case for jamming and spoofing. The fact that both kinds of hostile acts have an intangible nature should not deceive: while cyberattacks *stricto sensu* take place in cyberspace, which is man-made, exists outside the world of nature and is ruled by computer code, radio interferences take place in the electromagnetic spectrum, which has a physical nature, belongs to the world of nature and is ruled by the laws of physics.[146]

Looking at the problem *de iure condendo*, it is possible to wonder whether an agreed terminology and definition will be achieved in the future and whether an international regulatory instrument dedicated to cyber threats should encompass cases of intentional electromagnetic interference. Such questions are outside the scope of the present analysis but are useful to highlight the key importance of the definitional issue in a new-born field like cybersecurity law.

§6.06 CONCLUSION

Communication and navigation satellites serve a fundamental role in the organisation of the contemporary world. They allow aircraft to fly, bank transfers to work, energy grids to be coordinated, military apparatus to operate, and much more. The different networks upon which our society is based, nowadays called critical infrastructures, could not function without their uninterrupted support, and in some cases, satellite systems themselves are qualified as such – like the Galileo GNSS in the EU.

Satellites, however, and consequently, the infrastructures that they support, are affected by an increasing degree of vulnerability to non-kinetic threats, such as cyberattacks and electromagnetic interference. The main danger enshrined in such threats is the structural advantage they have against defensive strategies. While the technology to carry them is increasingly affordable in terms of skills and costs, making them available to State and non-State actors, the techniques to protect satellite systems are very complex and expensive to the point that many commercial operators find it more convenient to live with the risk rather than implement those techniques.

The regulatory responses that the international community has developed so far result inadequate. With particular regard to jamming and spoofing, the ITU legal framework is mainly designed to resolve cases of unintentional interference among

146. *See* Chapter 2, sections §2.02[A], §2.04[C].

legitimate radio services, thus resulting as ill-equipped to prevent or sanction intentional episodes. The most recent amendments to Article 15 of the Radio Regulations have a political value rather than an effective operational relevance, while the high political sensitivity of the issue suggests that it will be unlikely to see a new legal regime under development in the near future. For the moment, thus, the burden of intentional electromagnetic interference is carried almost entirely by satellite operators, which decide whether or not to implement defensive techniques according to purely commercial factors, and by national administrations, which must rely on mutual goodwill and cooperation to effectively combat interference. The dual-use of satellite systems further blurs the boundary between civilian and military targets, contributing to the regulatory complexity of the matter, both from the perspective of the applicability of current legal instruments and from the perspective of the development of new ones.

CHAPTER 7

Public International Civil Aviation Law

§7.01 CONVENTION ON INTERNATIONAL CIVIL AVIATION 1944[1]

The Convention on International Civil Aviation (the 'Chicago Convention 1944'), with its 193 State parties as of March 2020,[2] is the overarching and underpinning legal framework for international civil aviation transport. The Chicago Convention 1944 establishes rules, *inter alia*, on the access and use of the airspace, aircraft registration and safety, as well as the establishment of ICAO, which is a specialised agency of the UN. It is, therefore, of crucial importance to assess whether the Chicago Convention 1944 and the work of ICAO cover cybersecurity.[3]

There are no explicit references to the terms 'cybersecurity' or 'cyberattack', or any other similar terms within the text of the Chicago Convention 1944. As a result, it may be concluded that it does not govern cybersecurity and that ICAO is not competent

1. This chapter has been built on the foundations set in Benjamyn I. Scott, *Aviation Cybersecurity: Regulatory Approach in the European Union* (Eleven, 2019).
2. ICAO, 'Current Lists of Parties to Multilateral Air Law Treaties: Convention on International Civil Aviation Signed at Chicago on 7 December 1944', https://www.icao.int/secretariat/legal/List%20of%20Parties/Chicago_EN.pdf. The predecessors of the Chicago Convention 1944 are the Convention Relating to the Regulation of Aerial Navigation, Paris, France, 13 October 1919 (the 'Paris Convention 1919') as amended by the 1929 Protocol; Ibero-American Air Navigation Convention, Madrid, Spain, 1 November 1926 (the 'Madrid Convention 1926'); and Pan-American Convention on Air Navigation, 129 L.N.T.S. 223, Havana, Cuba, 20 February 1928 (the 'Havana Convention 1928'). Article 80 of the Chicago Convention 1944 provides for denunciation of both the Paris and Havana Conventions. Due to the lack of state interest in the Madrid Convention 1926, it was not necessary to include it in the scope of Art. 80. Convention on International Civil Aviation, 61 Stat. 1180, 15 U.N.T.S. 295, Chicago, US, 7 December 1944.
3. While the Convention has a high number of contracting states, as well as covering a broad scope of topics, it is limited in scope to only international, civil and aviation. Without the fulfilment of these three criteria, of which neither of the three terms are defined within the text of the Convention, including in Art. 96 on definitions, it will not be applicable to cybersecurity. *See*, for a more detailed general introduction to the applicability of the Chicago Convention 1944, Benjamyn I. Scott and Andrea Trimarchi, *Fundamentals of International Aviation Law and Policy* (Routledge, 2019), at Chapter 3.

to deal with this subject matter. However, it may be the case that certain Articles are relevant through:

(1) interpretation;[4]
(2) the creation of complementary bilateral and multilateral treaties; or
(3) activities carried out by ICAO, including the development and application of the 19 Annexes to the Chicago Convention 1944, as well as other aviation stakeholders.

This chapter will explore these areas to assess how international civil aviation cybersecurity is being regulated.

§7.02 INTERPRETATION: CASE STUDY OF ARTICLE 3 *BIS*

Although there is no direct reference to cybersecurity, this does not mean that the Chicago Convention 1944 is silent on the issue; it is possible to interpret certain terms found in the text of the Convention in a way that makes the provisions relevant for cyber.[5] Article 3(a) *bis*, which entered into force on 1 October 1998 and has 156 State parties as of March 2020, will be utilised as a case study.

Article 3(a) *bis* reads as follows:

> The contracting states recognize that every State must refrain from resorting to the use of weapons against civil aircraft in flight and that, in case of interception, the lives of persons on board and the safety of aircraft must not be endangered. This provision shall not be interpreted as modifying in any way the rights and obligations of States set forth in the Charter of the United Nations.[6]

The term 'recognize' refers to an obligation in CIL and the reference to the Charter of the UN affirms the Article's place within the wider scope of public international law. The Article shall only apply when the three criteria are satisfied:

(1) there must be a use of a 'weapon';
(2) the use of a weapon must be 'against a civil aircraft'; and
(3) the aircraft must be 'in flight'.

The first criterion has relevance for cybersecurity as a certain cyberattack may constitute a 'weapon', whereas the other two do not present any new discussions on this topic.[7]

---

4. *See*, for more information on treaty interpretation, Vienna Convention on the Law of Treaties (with Annex) (adopted 23 May 1969, entered into force 27 January 1980), 1155 UNTS 331, Art. 31.
5. *Ibid.*
6. The Article, as an amendment, requires adoption by States and is, therefore, non-binding on those Chicago Convention 1944 contracting state that have yet to adopt Art. 3 *bis*.
7. *See*, Scott, *supra* no. 1, at 139-149. *See also*, Chapter 2, section §2.02[I].

The Chicago Convention 1944 does not define the term 'weapon'.[8] Furthermore, none of the 19 Annexes to the Chicago Convention 1944, nor the treaties concluded under the auspices of ICAO provide a definition:

> The term 'weapons' has not been defined but its interpretation in practice should not cause any difficulties when the ordinary meaning of the word is considered; it would include guns, machine guns, cannons, missiles or targeted drones or any other object or substance that can damage or destroy an aircraft in flight.[9]

While this conclusion may be clear for conventional weapons such as missiles, this is not the case for cyberattack methods. Looking at similar terms in international law is of limited value because they do not look specifically at the term 'weapon'. For example, the focus is either on whether a cyberattack amounts to a 'use of force' or a more specific term is used such as 'cyberweapons'.

A definition of 'weapon' may not be required because, "[n]ot only is software intangible, it is subject to frequent changes; different versions of software can bear little resemblance to each other."[10] A definition could become obsolete with the development of technology. Both the wording and the purpose of Article 3 *bis*[11] should be considered as noted in the Vienna Convention on the Law of Treaties.[12] Article 3 *bis* is neither concerned with the specifics of the attack method nor with how the attack method is implemented. The Article is concerned with the protection of international civil aviation. The classification of 'weapon' should be a de facto one. Therefore, if a cyberattack causes injury, death, damage or destruction, then the cyber means to carry out the cyberattack would amount to a 'weapon'. However, where such a level of interference is missing, then this type of cyberattack would not amount to a 'weapon'.

As a result, it is possible to find references to cybersecurity in the Chicago Convention 1944, as demonstrated by interpreting Article 3 *bis*. This conclusion may also be applicable to the other Articles;[13] however, each Article must be individually assessed.

---

8. This includes Art. 96 which is designated specifically for definitions.
9. Michael Milde, *International Air Law and ICAO*, Third Edition (Eleven, 2016), at 61.
10. Gary Brown and Andrew Metcalf, 'Easier Said than Done: Legal Reviews of Cyber Weapons', 7(1) *Journal of National Security Law and Policy* 115-138 (2014), at 133.
11. Vienna Convention on the Law of Treaties, *supra* no. 4, Art. 31(1).
12. *Ibid.*, Art. 31:

    1. A treaty shall be interpreted in good faith in accordance with the ordinary meaning to be given to the terms of the treaty in their context and in the light of its object and purpose.
    2. The context for the purpose of the interpretation of a treaty shall comprise, in addition to the text, including its preamble and annexes:
       (a) any agreement relating to the treaty which was made between all the parties in connection with the conclusion of the treaty;
       (b) any instrument which was made by one or more parties in connection with the conclusion of the treaty and accepted by the other parties as an instrument related to the treaty.

13. Other references could include:

    (1) Article 89 of the Chicago Convention 1944, which declares that in cases of war or national emergency, whereby in the latter case notification is made to the Council, the provisions

§7.03 CREATION OF COMPLEMENTARY BILATERAL AND MULTILATERAL TREATIES: CASE STUDY OF AIR SERVICE AGREEMENTS

The Chicago Convention 1944 does not exist in a regulatory vacuum, as demonstrated by the reference to the Charter of the UN in Article 3 *bis*. In addition to complementing existing treaties, such as the UN Charter, it also provides a basis for the creation of new international law, which will be discussed in this section. As a result of the complete and exclusive sovereignty of States over their airspace, as recognised in its Article 1, the drafters had to provide a legal mechanism to allow aircraft from one State to enter the airspace of another State, otherwise international civil aviation would not be possible. Therefore, Article 5 - Right of Non-Scheduled Flight,[14] Article 6 - Scheduled Air Services,[15] Article 7 - Cabotage[16] and Article 8 - Pilotless Aircraft[17] provide States with different rights and obligations for different types of international civil aviation activities.[18]

- in whole or in part - of the Chicago Convention shall not apply. No State has yet invoked this Article in the event of a cyberattack, however this may happen in the future if an aviation stakeholder is seriously affected.

(2) Article 35 of the Chicago Convention 1944 is also relevant for 'war' as it prohibits the carriage of 'munitions of war or implements of war' without prior permission from the subjacent State. Each State is free to determine what it constitutes munitions of war or implements of war, so it may wish to team certain technologies that have cyberattack capabilities as such with the aim of prohibiting international civil aviation's interaction with cyberattacks.

See, for more information on Article 89, Jiefang Huang, *Aviation Safety Through the Rule of Law: ICAO's Mechanisms and Practices*, First Edition, (Kluwer, 2009), at 92.

14. ICAO defined a non-scheduled air service as 'a commercial air transport service performed as other than a scheduled air service' ICAO, Tenth Session of the Statistics Division, 'Review of the Classification and Definitions used for Civil Aviation Activities', STA/10-WP/7 (2009), Appendix B.
15. ICAO, 'Definition of Scheduled International Air Service', ICAO Doc. 7278-C/841 (1952):

   A scheduled international air service is a series of flights that possesses all of the following characteristics:

   (a) it passes through the airspace over the territory of more than one state;
   (b) it is performed by aircraft for the transport of passengers, mail or cargo for remuneration, in such a manner that each flight is open to use by members of the public;
   (c) it is operated, so as to serve traffic between the same two or more points; either,
      (i) according to a published time-table, or
      (ii) with flights so regular or frequent that they constitute a recognizable systemic series.

16. Cabotage is, as specified in Art. 7 of the Chicago Convention 1944, where "aircraft of other contracting states [...] take on in its territory passengers, mail and cargo carried for remuneration or hire and [are] destined for another point within its territory."
17. Neither the Chicago Convention 1944, the 19 Annexes nor the specific ICAO unmanned aircraft documents, provide a definition of 'pilotless aircraft'. *See*, ICAO, Manual on Remotely Piloted Aircraft Systems, Doc 100119; and ICAO, Secretary General, Unmanned Aircraft Systems, Circular 328. (*ICAO, Secretary General, UAS, Circular 328*).
18. *See*, for more information on ASA, Scott and Trimarchi, *supra* no. 3, at Chapter 5.

Articles 6–8 require prior permission to be granted by the overflow State, which is usually provided through a bilateral or multilateral Air Service Agreement (ASA), between the concerned States in order to facilitate international air transport. There are currently around 5,000 bilateral ASAs worldwide and some of these may be relevant for cybersecurity.[19] These ASAs regularly contain various provisions, including those on 'safety' and 'security', so these could include cybersecurity rules or could be modified to do so in the future. For example, the dedicated 'security' clause may oblige the States to conform to the aviation security requirements as established by ICAO in its 19 Annexes. Therefore, as Annex 17 makes specific reference to 'cyber threats',[20] such a provision would have direct relevance to cybersecurity.[21] As a result, the relevance of the Chicago Convention 1944 for cybersecurity extends to ICAO and its development of the 19 Annexes.

§7.04 CRIMINAL AIR LAW

The Chicago Convention 1944 does not address criminal activities involving international civil aviation as this was not a priority in the 1940s. However, this changed in the 1950s with an increasing number of terrorist attacks against aviation, as well as growing incidents of unlawful seizure of aircraft.[22] As a result, criminal air law became a core focus for the international community and resulted in the development of treaties under the auspices of ICAO.

(1) Convention on Offences and Certain Other Acts Committed on Board Aircraft 1963 (the 'Tokyo Convention 1963')[23] as amended by the Protocol to Amend the Convention on Offences and Certain Other Acts Committed on Board Aircraft 2014 (the 'Montreal Protocol 2014').[24]
(2) Convention for the Suppression of Unlawful Seizure of Aircraft 1970 (The Hague Convention 1970)[25] as amended by Protocol Supplementary to the Convention for the Suppression of Unlawful Seizure of Aircraft 2010 (the 'Beijing Protocol 2010').[26]

19. *See*, European Parliament, 'Competition in Air Transport Workshop Proceedings', PE 618.984, April 2018.
20. Annex 17 to the Chicago Convention 1944, Security: Safeguarding International Civil Aviation Against Acts of Unlawful Interference, Tenth Edition, April 2017, at 4.9. *See* Chapter 7, section §7.05.
21. *See*, as an example, US-EU Air Transport Agreement, 30 April 2007, Art. 9.
22. ICAO, 'The Postal History of ICAO: Legal Instruments Related to Aviation Security', http://www.icao.int/secretariat/PostalHistory/legal_instruments_related_to_aviation_security.htm.
23. Convention on Offences and Certain other acts Committed on Board Aircraft, 704 UNTS 219; 20 UST 2941; 2 ILM 1042, 14 September 1963.
24. Protocol to Amend the Convention on Offences and Certain Other Acts Committed on Board Aircraft, Montreal, 4 April 2014.
25. Convention for the Suppression of Unlawful Seizure of Aircraft, UN Treaty Series 1973, 16 December 1970.
26. Protocol Supplementary to the Convention for the Suppression of Unlawful Seizure of Aircraft ICAO Doc 9959 (2010).

(3) Convention for the Suppression of Unlawful Acts against the Safety of Civil Aviation 1971 (the 'Montreal Convention 1971')[27] as amended by Protocol for the Suppression of Unlawful Acts of Violence at Airports Serving International Civil Aviation 1988 (the 'Montreal Protocol 1988').[28]
(4) Convention on the Suppression of Unlawful Acts Relating to International Civil Aviation 2010 (the 'Beijing Convention 2010').[29]

These treaties will be analysed below to see how they promote cybersecurity and help combat cyberattacks.[30]

[A] Beijing Convention and Protocol 2010

Motivated by the events of 9/11, the International Conference on Air Law (Diplomatic Conference on Aviation Security) met in Beijing, China, from 30 August to 10 September 2010 where it concluded with the text of the Beijing Convention 2010.[31] This Convention entered into force on 1 July 2018 and has 20 Ratifications as of March 2020. While the Beijing Convention 2010 is a separate legal instrument, i.e., it is not an amending Protocol, it is nevertheless an attempt to modernise and consolidate the

27. Convention for the Suppression of Unlawful Acts against the Safety of Civil Aviation, 974 UNTS 177, 24 UST 564, 10 ILM 1151, 23 September 1971.
28. Protocol for the Suppression of Unlawful Acts of Violence at Airports Serving International Civil Aviation, supplementary to the Convention for the Suppression of Unlawful Acts Against the Safety of Civil Aviation, UN Treaty Series 1990, 24 February 1988.
29. Convention on the Suppression of Unlawful Acts Relating to International Civil Aviation, ICAO Doc. 9960, 10 September 2010.
30. The Conventions listed above have a wider scope than simply listing acts and offences. They also cover, *inter alia*, other aspects:

    (1) Definitions: e.g., 'in flight' or 'in service'.
    (2) Exclusion of military aircraft.
    (3) Limitations of scope to domestic and international flights.
    (4) Custody of alleged offender.
    (5) Prosecution of alleged offender.
    (6) Extradition of alleged offender.
    (7) Location of attack: e.g., on board or to facilities.
    (8) Jurisdiction.
    (9) Exemption of certain motives: e.g., political, racial or religious.

    As these topics are well covered in other legal texts and it is argued that they do not pose any new issue within the context of cybersecurity, it is not necessary to discuss these within the scope of this work. Despite this, they may still be relevant for cyberattacks. For example, a cyberattack can be conducted from a remote location, including in a different State to the target. As a result, issues of jurisdiction and extradition may be very relevant. Further, Article 2 of the Tokyo Convention states that offences of a 'political nature or those based on racial or religious discrimination' do not authorise or require any action from states that have jurisdiction. Past examples of cyberattacks in aviation have been politically motivated, so this could prevent some cyberattacks going unprosecuted.
31. The Beijing Convention 2010 entered into force on 1 July 2018. ICAO, 'Administrative Package for Ratification of or Accession to the Convention on the Suppression of Unlawful Acts Relating to International Civil Aviation', Beijing Convention, 2010, https://www.icao.int/secretariat/legal/Administrative%20Packages/Beijing_Convention_EN.pdf.

Montreal Convention 1971 and the Montreal Protocol 1988: It criminalises "a number of acts constituting new and emerging threats against civil aviation, including certain preparatory acts for the offences," and strengthens "the capacity of States to prevent the commission of these offences, and to prosecute and punish those who commit such offences."[32]

ICAO has acknowledged, in its administrative package for the ratification of the Beijing Convention 2010,[33] as well as in other documents,[34] that "[c]yber attacks on air navigation facilities constitute an offence under this Convention." This is represented in Article 1(d) of the Beijing Convention 2010, which is also found in the Montreal Convention 1971 under the same Article:

> 1. Any person commits an offence if that person unlawfully and intentionally:
>
> [...]
>
> (d) destroys or damages air navigation facilities or interferes with their operation, if any such act is likely to endanger the safety of aircraft in flight.

Therefore, if a cyberattack fulfils these criteria, it shall be deemed as an offence.

Article 1(1)(e) of the Beijing Convention 2010, which is also found in the Montreal Convention 1971, declares it an offence to communicate "information which that person knows to be false, thereby endangering the safety of an aircraft in flight." This can include bomb threats like the ones in February 2016 against Ryanair, which used the Internet to communicate the message.[35] However, it is not clear whether this event will satisfy the criteria as, for example, it has not been established whether it endangered the safety of the aircraft.

Unlike the Beijing Convention 2010, which clarifies that some of the old Articles of the Montreal Convention 1971 apply to cyberattacks, the Beijing Protocol 2010, which entered into force on 1 January 2018 and has 19 Ratifications, appears to address cyber with a new Article. Article II declares that:

> Any person commits an offence if that person unlawfully and intentionally seizes or exercises control of an aircraft in service by force or threat thereof, or by coercion, or by any other form of intimidation, or by any technological means.

The expression 'any technological means' was added in an attempt "to address situations, in which the offenders seek to take control of an aircraft by jamming or otherwise interfering with flight instruments or data transmission systems."[36] The wording is extremely broad and can include all cyberattacks.

---

32. *Ibid.*
33. *Ibid.*
34. *See*, ICAO, High-Level Conference on Aviation Security (HLCAS), Agenda Item 5: Capacity Building and Technical Assistance, Promotion of the Beijing Convention and the Beijing Protocol of 2010, 12 to 14 September 2012, Montreal, Canada, HLCAS-WP/15 20/7/12.
35. Simon Calder, 'Ryanair Wins £220,000 from Twitter User Who Posted Terror Threat', The Independent, 14 July 2017, http://www.independent.co.uk/travel/news-and-advice/ryanair-bomb-threat-terror-twitter-brian-lake-pennsylvania-extortion-a7841446.html.
36. ICAO, Draft Report on the Work of the Legal Committee During its 34th Session, 2-14, LC/34-WP/5-2, 16 September 2009, at. 2.98. *See*, for more information on jamming, Chapter 6.

[B] Interpretation: Case Study of the Hague Convention 1970

It may be possible to apply other articles of the different criminal law conventions, which were not drafted with cybersecurity in mind, to criminalise cyberattacks. For example, Article 1(a) of The Hague Convention 1970 declares that:

> Any person who on board an aircraft in flight:
>
> (a) unlawfully, by force or threat thereof, or by any other form of intimidation, seizes, or exercises control of, that aircraft, or attempts to perform any such act
> (b) [...]
>
> Commits an offence [...].

This Article can be broken down into four constituent elements:

(1) There must be a use of force, threat or other forms of intimidation in the act.
(2) The act must involve seizure, exercise of control of that aircraft or an attempt to do such an act.
(3) The aircraft must be in flight.
(4) It is only applicable to acts committed on board the aircraft.

If an act satisfies all of the above criteria, then it is unlawful and referred to as 'the offence' for the purpose of the Convention, and pursuant to Article 2, each contracting State shall "make the offence punishable by severe penalties." The facts of each cyberattack will have to be assessed to see if it satisfies these criteria. For example, it will not include a remote cyberattack, such as spoofing, because the act did not take place 'on board the aircraft'. It is also questionable if it will include cyberattacks that lack a physical element.[37] However, if there is a physical element, such as forceful control of an IT system, then this could fall under the scope of the Article.

[C] Addressing Cybersecurity Through National Law

Prior to the Tokyo Convention 1963, which entered into force on 4 December 1969 and has 189 contracting States, many offences committed on board aircraft would go unpunished due to a lack of jurisdiction during international flights.[38] Article 1 of the Tokyo Convention 1963 clarifies which offences are covered by the Convention.

> This Convention shall apply in respect of:
>
> (a) offences against penal law;
> (b) acts which, whether or not they are offences, may or do jeopardize the safety of the aircraft or of persons or property therein or which jeopardize good order and discipline on board.

37. ICAO, Report of the Legal Committee, 17th Session, on the Subject of Unlawful Seizure of Aircraft, Minutes and Documents, ICAO Doc. 8877-LC/161, at 28.
38. *See*, US v. Cordova, 89 F. Supp. 298 E.D.N.Y. (1950); and R. v. Martin 2 Q.B. 272 (1956).

Here, it does not specify conduct that is prohibited by the Tokyo Convention 1963. Rather, it is left to domestic 'penal law' (national criminal law) to determine what constitutes an offence. As many States involved in international aviation have penal law prohibiting certain acts, States' cybersecurity law may be covered by Article 1(1)(a).

The Tokyo Convention 1963 does not provide an exhaustive list of definitions, such as for the terms 'jeopardise', 'safety', 'good order' and 'discipline', so the test for assessing its Article 1(1)(b) is unclear with "its definition [having] to be determined by the municipal laws of the contracting states."[39] Therefore, if an attacker commits a cyberattack on board the aircraft in a way that satisfies (b), then the Convention will be applicable. Matters outside of the Convention will then be dealt with under national law. Only if these elements are satisfied shall the Tokyo Convention 1963 be applicable.

§7.05 ANNEXES TO THE CHICAGO CONVENTION 1944

Pursuant to Article 37 of the Chicago Convention 1944:

> Each contracting state undertakes to collaborate in securing the highest practicable degree of uniformity in regulations, standards, procedures, and organization in relation to aircraft, personnel, airways and auxiliary services in all matters in which such uniformity will facilitate and improve air navigation.

In order to achieve this, ICAO[40] "shall adopt and amend from time to time, as may be necessary, international standards and recommended practices and procedures dealing with" the areas specified in the above-mentioned Article.[41] ICAO has developed

---

39. Alona Evans, 'Aircraft Hijacking: Its Cause and Cure', 63(4) *American Journal of International Law* 695-710 (1969), at 708.
40. ICAO is a UN specialised agency, established by the Chicago Convention in 1944 to manage its administration and governance. ICAO works with the Chicago Convention's contracting states and other stakeholders in order to fulfil its aims and objectives set out in the Chicago Convention. Chicago Convention 1944, *supra* no. 2, Art. 44:

    a. Insure the safe and orderly growth of international civil aviation throughout the world;
    b. Encourage the arts of aircraft design and operation for peaceful purposes;
    c. Encourage the development of airways, airports, and air navigation facilities for international civil aviation;
    d. Meet the needs of the peoples of the world for safe, regular, efficient and economical air transport;
    e. Prevent economic waste caused by unreasonable competition;
    f. Insure that the rights of contracting states are fully respected and that every contracting state has a fair opportunity to operate international airlines;
    g. Avoid discrimination between contracting states;
    h. Promote safety of flight in international air navigation;
    i. Promote generally the development of all aspects of international civil aeronautics.

    See, ICAO, 'About ICAO', https://www.icao.int/about-icao/Pages/default.aspx.
41. Chicago Convention 1944, *supra* no. 2, Art. 37:

    (a) Communications systems and air navigation aids, including ground marking; (b) Characteristics of airports and landing areas; (c) Rules of the air and air traffic control

and amended 19 detailed, technical Annexes, which currently contain over 12,000 Standards[42] and Recommended Practices.[43] While Annexes may be relevant for cybersecurity, the practical impact of their SARPs can be limited. First, pursuant to Article 38 of the Chicago Convention 1944, a contracting State may depart from a Standard provided that it follows the notification procedure specified in that Article.[44] States may, therefore, deviate from any cybersecurity SARPs. Second, their status as legally binding is debatable, so states may not feel obliged to adhere to cybersecurity SARPs.[45] Third, SARPs take "approximately two years for an initial proposal for a new or improved Standard, Recommended Practice or procedure to be formally adopted or approved for inclusion in an Annex or a PANS."[46] As a result, even if states adopt the SARPs and strictly adhere to them, it will be some time before they fully cover the existing threat landscape and are likely to become outdated due to the fast-evolving topic. Finally, the majority of SARPs can be divided into either 'safety' or 'security',

---

> practices; (d) Licensing of operating and mechanical personnel; (e) Airworthiness of aircraft; (f) Registration and identification of aircraft; (g) Collection and exchange of meteorological information; (h) Log books; (i) Aeronautical maps and charts; (j) Customs and immigration procedures; (k) Aircraft in distress and investigation of accidents; and such other matters concerned with the safety, regularity, and efficiency of air navigation as may from time to time appear appropriate.

42. Annex 2 to the Chicago Convention 1944, Rules of the Air, Tenth Edition, July (2005), at vi:

> Standards: Any specification for physical characteristics, configuration, matériel, performance, personnel or procedure, the uniform application of which is recognized as necessary for the safety or regularity of international air navigation and to which contracting states will conform in accordance with the Convention; in the event of impossibility of compliance, notification to the Council is compulsory under Article 38.

43. *Ibid.*, at vi:

> Recommended Practices: Any specification for physical characteristics, configuration, matériel, performance, personnel or procedure, the uniform application of which is recognized as desirable in the interests of safety, regularity or efficiency of international air navigation, and to which contracting states will endeavour to conform in accordance with the Convention.

44. The Universal Safety Oversight Audit Programme (USOAP) audits 'determine Member States' safety capabilities and the status of States' implementation of all safety-relevant ICAO Standards and Recommended Practices (found in 17 of the 19 ICAO Annexes), associated procedures, guidance material, and best safety practices.' ICAO, 'Frequently Asked Questions about USOAP', https://www.icao.int/safety/CMAForum/Pages/FAQ.aspx; and ICAO, Universal Safety Oversight Audit Programme Continuous Monitoring Manual, Doc 9735 AN/960 (2011). There is also the Universal Security Audit Programme Continuous Monitoring Approach (USAP-CMA), which focuses on Annex 17 and the security-related provisions of Annex 9 – Facilitation. ICAO, 'The Universal Security Audit Programme Continuous Monitoring Approach (USAP-CMA) and Its Objective', https://www.icao.int/Security/USAP/Pages/default.aspx. *See*, Huang, *supra* no. 13, at 69-72.
45. *See*, Pablo Mendes de Leon, *Introduction to Air Law*, Tenth Edition (Kluwer, 2017), at 25. *See*, Huang, *supra* no. 13, at 58-68.
46. ICAO, 'How ICAO Develops Standards', https://www.icao.int/about-icao/AirNavigationCommission/Pages/how-icao-develops-standards.aspx.

which will affect their desired outcome, and this could produce vulnerabilities. This point will be expanded on below.

As the Annexes contain detailed technical rules on a wide range of areas, it is necessary to examine whether ICAO has developed SARPs that address and impact upon cybersecurity.

[A] 'Cyber Threats'

Annex 17 titled 'Security: Safeguarding International Civil Aviation Against Acts of Unlawful Interference' was adopted by the ICAO Council on 22 March 1974 and "sets out the basis for the ICAO civil aviation security programme and seeks to safeguard civil aviation and its facilities against acts of unlawful interference."[47] It has focused on physical security threats, such as sabotage and hijacking, and is:

> primarily concerned with administrative and co-ordination aspects, as well as with technical measures for the protection of the security of international air transport, requiring each contracting state to establish its own civil aviation security programme with such additional security measures as may be proposed by other appropriate bodies.[48]

Amendment 12, found in the ninth edition of Annex 17 published in March 2011, introduced the first and currently only use of the term 'cyber' into the SARPs.[49] Chapter 4 on Preventive Security Measures, more specifically in title 4.9 on Measures Relating to Cyber Threats, contains two SARPs. The first inclusion is Standard 4.9.1, which was originally a Recommended Practice, and states:

> Each contracting state shall ensure that operators or entities as defined in the national civil aviation security programme or other relevant national documentation identify their critical information and communications technology systems and data used for civil aviation purposes and, in accordance with a risk assessment, develop and implement, as appropriate, measures to protect them from unlawful interference.

This translates into operators and other stakeholders, which have been identified at a national level, must identify both their civil aviation critical information and communications technology systems and data. Then, they must develop and implement measures to protect them from unlawful interference. Therefore, this can have several consequences:

(1) There is a reliance on the States to define the scope of Standard 4.9.1, which can lead to fragmentation among the different States.

47. ICAO, 'The Convention on International Civil Aviation Annexes 1 to 18', https://www.icao.int/safety/airnavigation/NationalityMarks/annexes_booklet_en.pdf.

48. ICAO, 'Annex 17 to the Convention on International Civil Aviation', https://store.icao.int/icao-annex-17.

49. Integral to the amendment of Annex 17 is the Aviation Security Policy Section of the Aviation Security and Facilitation Office as it is tasked with the development of new and amended of existing SARPs within the scope of security of international air transport.

(2) The term 'measures' is vague as no further instructions are given. For example, it could be interpreted to mean, *inter alia*, the creation of new laws, the dissemination of information or even training of personnel. This vagueness could result in, not only in further fragmentation but also potentially minimal steps being taken to satisfy the requirements.
(3) The Standard is limited to the protection of critical ICT systems used for civil aviation. Consequently, it excludes non-critical information and technology systems, so it does not cover all vulnerabilities found in the aviation context.
(4) The measures must only protect against unlawful interference, so it does not cover attack methods that are not prohibited by law.
(5) Its goal is security, so safety aspects are not addressed.
(6) The binding status of SARPs, particularly Recommended Practices, is debatable so States may not be obligated to act. Alternatively, States can register non-compliance with SARPs to ICAO.

As a result of these limitations, the Standard has a limited impact on the promotion of cybersecurity at an international level. However, it must be stated that this is a vast improvement on the original text as it is now broader and clearer, and is a Standard rather than a Recommended Practice.[50]

Recommendation 4.9.2 states:

> Each contracting state should ensure that the measures implemented protect, as appropriate, the confidentiality, integrity and availability of the identified critical systems and/or data. The measures should include, inter alia, security by design, supply chain security, network separation, and the protection and/or limitation of any remote access capabilities, as appropriate and in accordance with the risk assessment carried out by its relevant national authorities.[51]

This Recommendation complements the Standard by providing guidance on how the different implemented measures should protect the identified critical system and or data.

50. The original text included in Annex 17, *supra* no. 20, at 4.9.1:

> Each contracting state should, in accordance with the risk assessment carried out by its relevant national authorities, ensure that measures are developed in order to protect critical information and communications technology systems used for civil aviation purposes from interference that may jeopardize the safety of civil aviation.

The original text of Recommendation 4.9.1, as well as 4.9.2., did not arguably satisfy the ICAO definition of 'Recommendation'. While they are specific in scope, they are vague in which actions are to be taken, so doubt exists as to whether they amount to 'any specification'.

51. Original text contained in Annex 17:

> Each contracting state should encourage entities involved with or responsible for the implementation of various aspects of the national civil aviation security programme to identify their critical information and communications technology systems, including threats and vulnerabilities thereto, and develop protective measures to include, *inter alia*, security by design, supply chain security, network separation, and remote access control, as appropriate.

The Standard and Recommended Practice marks the beginning of ICAO's regulatory work on cybersecurity, rather than the end, where more detailed and targeted SARPs can be expected. This is supported by the fact that they have been amended since their original publication. Further, with the political push coming from the ICAO General Assembly, and the work done at a lower level by the different Study Groups and Task Forces, it can be predicted that more SARPs are to come.

[B] Different Types of Interference

In addition to the direct reference to 'cyber' found in Annex 17, it is possible for other terms to include cyber once their definition is consulted. For example, the term 'unlawful interference' is defined in Annex 17 and may include cyber within its scope:

> These are acts or attempted acts such as to jeopardize the safety of civil aviation, including but not limited to:
>
> - unlawful seizure of aircraft,
> - destruction of an aircraft in service,
> - hostage-taking on board aircraft or on aerodromes,
> - forcible intrusion on board an aircraft, at an airport or on the premises of an aeronautical facility,
> - introduction on board an aircraft or at an airport of a weapon or hazardous device or material intended for criminal purposes,
> - use of an aircraft in service for the purpose of causing death, serious bodily injury, or serious damage to property or the environment,
> - communication of false information such as to jeopardize the safety of an aircraft in flight or on the ground, of passengers, crew, ground personnel or the general public, at an airport or on the premises of a civil aviation facility.

There are certain criteria that must be met in order to fall within the scope of this definition:

(1) The act must be prohibited by a source of law (i.e., unlawful). This could include acts covered by the different international criminal law treaties or under national law.
(2) There must be interference, which is not defined. It may, therefore, be the case that eavesdropping, tapping, keylogging and other non-intrusive passive attack methods do not constitute interference.
(3) The act or attempted act must "jeopardize the safety of civil aviation" so passive attacks will not be included.

The definition then provides a non-exhaustive list of acts that could constitute unlawful interference. If a cyberattack causes "destruction of an aircraft in service," such as through a remote hack that provides control of the aircraft to the hacker, then this would be an act of unlawful interference.

The term 'unlawful inference' is found in different Annexes, including those addressing safety. While these could be interpreted to include cybersecurity, it is important to stress that, although the term 'unlawful interference' is defined, the Annexes take very different approaches to handling this matter.

In some cases, 'unlawful' is omitted or another word is used. For example, part IIIB of Annex 8 on 'Airworthiness of Aircraft' utilises the term 'electromagnetic interference', which is to be understood as lawful, but unwanted interference of an electromagnetic nature.[52] This could include a cyberattack but is limited to those that are not prohibited in law; however, the specifics of each SARP must be individually assessed to determine whether it is relevant to cybersecurity and, if so, to what extent.

[C] Filling the Gaps

While the term 'cyber threats' provides a direct link to cybersecurity, and the two terms 'unlawful interference' and 'electromagnetic interference' show that it is also possible to interpret cybersecurity into SARPs, this conclusion is not limited to these two terms as, for example, Annex 10 on 'Aeronautical Telecommunications' utilises several words with potential relevance,[53] namely 'authorised', 'accuracy',[54] 'integrity',[55] 'availability' and 'functionality'.[56] While these terms were not included with cybersecurity in mind, these terms are well established in cybersecurity vocabulary[57] and could be interpreted to cover cybersecurity. This is not unique to Annex 10 as, for example, Annex 9 utilises the phrase – within the context of security travel documents – "unlawfully altered, replicated or issued."[58] A cyberattack could, for example, be

52. Annex 8 to the Chicago Convention 1944, Airworthiness of Aircraft, Eleventh Edition, July 2010, at IIIB-6-1. *See* Chapter 6.
53. *See*, by way of example of the term 'authorised', Annex 10 to the Chicago Convention 1944, Aeronautical Telecommunications, Volume III – Communication Systems, Second Edition, July 2007.
54. *See*, for example, Annex 15: 'Accuracy. A degree of conformance between the estimated or measured value and the true value.' Annex 15 to the Chicago Convention 1944, Aeronautical Information Services, Fifteenth Edition, July (2016), at 1-1.
55. *See*, for example, Annex 15: 'Integrity (aeronautical data). A degree of assurance that an aeronautical data and its value has not been lost or altered since the data origination or authorized amendment.' Annex 15 to the Chicago Convention 1944, Aeronautical Information Services, Fifteenth Edition, July (2016), at 1-5.
56. *See*, for example, Annex 4: 'Aerodrome Terrain and Obstacle Chart – ICAO (Electronic) – Function, Availability, Identification, Chart coverage, Chart content, Accuracy and resolution, Electronic functionality, Chart data product specifications'.
57. *See*, as way of example, National Initiative for Cybersecurity Careers and Studies, 'Glossary', https://niccs.us-cert.gov/glossary. *See*, for example, Annex 4:

> Area navigation based on performance requirements for aircraft operating along an ATS route, on an instrument approach procedure or in a designated airspace. Note: Performance requirements are expressed in navigation specifications (RNAV specification, RNP specification) in terms of accuracy, integrity, continuity, availability and functionality needed for the proposed operation in the context of a particular airspace concept.

Annex 4 to the Chicago Convention 1944, Aeronautical Charts. Eleventh Edition, July (2009), at 1-7.
58. Annex 9 to the Chicago Convention 1944, Facilitation, Fourteenth Edition, October (2015), at 3.7.

initiated that alters, replicates or issues security travel documents in an unlawful manner.

Consequently, the current reach of the Annexes in terms of cybersecurity is potentially broad. This is because the Annexes have a broad scope, use varied language, and have the overarching goal of promoting safety and security. Furthermore, cybersecurity and cyberattacks are complex and multifaceted so that their unique characteristics may fall under some existing SARPs. As a result, each SARP should be individually assessed to establish whether it applies to cybersecurity within its specific context.

§7.06 ICAO

ICAO is a UN specialised agency which was established by the Chicago Convention 1944 and is headquartered in Montreal, Canada. It manages the administration and governance of the Convention by working with its 193 State parties and other stakeholders in order to fulfil its aims and objectives as set out in Article 44.[59]

[A] Organisational Structure: Safety Versus Security

ICAO, pursuant to Article 43 of the Chicago Convention 1944, is comprises of the Assembly, Council and such other bodies as may be necessary (Secretariat and Air Navigation Commission). The Secretariat requires special mention due to its structure and its involvement in this topic. The Secretariat, which reports directly to the Secretary General,[60] consists of five permanent administrative offices, which are the:

(1) Air Navigation Bureau.

---

59. Chicago Convention 1944, *supra* no. 2, Art. 44:

> The aims and objectives of the Organization are to develop the principles and techniques of international air navigation and to foster the planning and development of international air transport so as to:
>
> a. Insure the safe and orderly growth of international civil aviation throughout the world;
> b. Encourage the arts of aircraft design and operation for peaceful purposes;
> c. Encourage the development of airways, airports, and air navigation facilities for international civil aviation;
> d. Meet the needs of the peoples of the world for safe, regular, efficient and economical air transport;
> e. Prevent economic waste caused by unreasonable competition;
> f. Insure that the rights of contracting states are fully respected and that every contracting state has a fair opportunity to operate international airlines;
> g. Avoid discrimination between contracting states;
> h. Promote safety of flight in international air navigation;
> i. Promote generally the development of all aspects of international civil aeronautics.

See, for more information about ICAO, ICAO, *supra* no. 40.

60. *See*, for the rules on personnel, Chicago Convention 1944, Arts 58-60.

(2) Air Transport Bureau.
(3) Legal Affairs and External Relations Bureau.[61]
(4) Bureau of Administration and Services.[62]
(5) Technical Cooperation Bureau.[63]

The Air Transport Bureau focuses on security and facilitation, economic development of air transport, and environmental protection. As a result, its work is centred around Annex 9 – Facilitation, Annex 16 – Environmental Protection and Annex 17 – Security.[64]

The Air Navigation Bureau[65] has numerous responsibilities, such as aviation safety, air navigation capacity and efficiency, and monitoring and oversight. It, therefore, works on the remaining 16 Annexes.[66] An issue that needs to be resolved by ICAO is where to fit cybersecurity into this structure.

This organisational structure creates an issue of competences within ICAO when it comes to cybersecurity. This is because the scope of responsibilities and work performed within each ICAO Bureau, and, in turn, the resulting panels, workgroups and other elements of ICAO, are driven in support of one or more of the 19 Annexes.

Due to its organisation, ICAO had to place cybersecurity within its existing structure, which translates into managing its cyber activities as either a branch of 'security' or 'safety'. In practical terms, if cybersecurity is treated as a branch of security, it will be dealt with under the Air Transport Bureau, within the scope of Annex 17 and as an act of 'unlawful interference'. This will then result in aviation safety – the responsibility of the Air Navigation Bureau – having little involvement in cybersecurity. Alternatively, if cybersecurity is treated as a branch of safety, it will be dealt with by the Air Navigation Bureau within the scope of the other sixteen safety-based Annexes. This has a profound consequence as it means that the full

61. This Bureau gives legal advice and assistance to the Secretary General, as well as to other ICAO bodies and to States on constitutional, administrative and procedural matters, as well as on international law, air law, commercial law, labour law and other related topics. ICAO, 'Legal Affairs and External Relations Bureau', https://www.icao.int/secretariat/legal/Pages/default.aspx.
62. This Bureau gives administrative support and management through human resources, information management, and linguistic services. ICAO, 'Bureau of Administration and Services', https://www.icao.int/secretariat/Administration/Pages/default.aspx.
63. This Bureau works with States to support their civil aviation development projects, such as facilitating the implementation of the 19 Annexes, assisting civil aviation authorities, and also providing training and infrastructure. ICAO, 'Technical Cooperation Bureau', https://www.icao.int/secretariat/TechnicalCooperation/Pages/default.aspx.
64. ICAO, 'Air Transport Bureau', https://www.icao.int/secretariat/air-transport/Pages/default.aspx.
65. ICAO, 'Air Navigation Bureau', https://www.icao.int/safety/airnavigation/Pages/default.aspx.
66. Annex 1 – Personnel Licensing, Annex 2 – Rules of the Air, Annex 3 – Meteorological Services, Annex 4 – Aeronautical Charts, Annex 5 – Units of Measurement, Annex 6 – Operation of Aircraft, Annex 7 – Aircraft Nationality and Registration Marks, Annex 8 – Airworthiness of Aircraft, Annex 9 – Facilitation, Annex 10 – Aeronautical Telecommunications, Annex 11 – Air Traffic Services, Annex 12 – Search-and-Rescue, Annex 13 – Aircraft Accident and Incident Investigation, Annex 14 – Aerodromes, Annex 15 – Aeronautical Information Services, Annex 16 – Environmental Protection, Annex 17 – Security, Annex 18 – The Safe Transportation of Dangerous Goods by Air and Annex 19 – Safety Management.

aspects of cybersecurity will not be addressed, and the practical applications will not be complete as safety and security SARPs are implemented differently.

This dichotomy is not ideal for a transversal topic like cybersecurity which touches on both safety and security. Currently, cybersecurity is burdened by internal political boundaries and bureaucracy that is preventing ICAO from being fully effective. This is why there are several WPs being presented during the 40th ICAO General Assembly asking for the establishment of either an interdisciplinary entity, thus interacting with both bureaux or a new entity with full cybersecurity competencies that consider both safety and security.[67] It is crucial that ICAO listens to these proposals and creates an entity that deals with cybersecurity as a broad, overarching topic, rather than a subset of either safety or security. However, until things change, the dichotomy is there and is having consequences, which will be assessed below.

[B] Panels and Study Groups

ICAO can create Panels and Study Groups, when required, to support its work. The creation, process and structure of Panel and Study Group are governed by specific ICAO bureaucratic processes. Panels are technical groups of qualified experts (normally state representatives and members from Industry) formed by the Air Navigation Commission. On the other hand, ICAO may decide to assign work to a Study Group. A Study Group functions at the same organisational level as a Panel, but it does not require State-mandated representatives. This means that the entity can be populated with only technical experts, as opposed to political ones, which allows the work to be more technically driven.

[1] AVSEC Panel

In order to address the evolving security threat to civil aviation, ICAO relies on the advice of experts who sit on the AVSEC Panel. The AVSEC Panel was established in the late 1980s and is comprised of mostly members nominated by States, as well as observers from the industry. Its focus, on which it works with the ICAO Secretariat, is to actively develop ICAO's security policy and responses to emerging threats, focusing on the prevention of acts of unlawful interference. This means that the focus is primarily on 'traditional'/'physical' security threats, such as sabotage and hijacking. The key work is on maintaining Annex 17 and related guidance material such as the Aviation Security Manual (Doc 8973 – Restricted) and does include cybersecurity as it is within the scope of Annex 17.

67. *See*, as way of examples, Airport Council International, 'Cybersecurity', A40-WP/243 EX/95, 5 August 2019; Civil Air Navigation Services Organisation, 'Cyber-Resilience', A40-WP/172 EX/70, 1 August 2019; International Coordinating Council of Aerospace Industries Associations, 'Proposal Regarding ICAO Governance Structure for Cybersecurity', A40-WP/219 EX/82, 5 August 2019; and the US, 'Proposal for ICAO Governance of Cybersecurity and Resiliency', A40-WP/427 EX/176, 2 August 2019.

[2] SSGC

During the 39th ICAO General Assembly, ICAO "called for a coordinated approach to achieve an acceptable and commensurate cyber resilience capability on a global scale."[68] This resulted in the establishment of the SSGC. It held its first meeting on 29 August 2017 and falls under the responsibility of the Air Transport Bureau, so the focus of its work is on unlawful interference (i.e., Annex 17), rather than wider safety issues which are the responsibility of the TFSG. The principal outcome of the SSGC was the development of a cybersecurity strategy which the ICAO Council agreed, during its 217th Session, to present at the 40th ICAO General Assembly.[69]

[3] TFSG

ICAO is in the process of establishing a TFSG, which falls under the Air Navigation Bureau. During the 13th Air Navigation Conference, an agreement was reached:

> on the need to develop a global trust framework and to work on governance and policy provisions for a trusted network and now is time for ICAO to work with States and industry to advance developments and raise awareness on cyber threats to the safety and resilience of operations.[70]

Further support was given during the 40th General Assembly by Brazil and the International Coordinating Council of Aerospace Industries Associations (ICCAIA).[71] The TFSG has a main body and three workgroups, which are the Current and Future Operational Needs, Global Resilient Aviation Interoperable Network, and Identity. These groups will be populated by aviation and non-aviation policy, technical and operational experts, and the groups will work on enhancing trust between different stakeholders within the scope of cybersecurity. Trust is important between the providers and users of products or services. This is, *inter alia*, because if a stakeholder cannot trust its supply chain, then it may not want to use a supplier's product, or a customer may not want to buy a product or may want to do its own tests which may be expensive and time-consuming. Thus, the goal is to ensure that the correct level of cybersecurity, which is guaranteed, and which stakeholders can rely on, is in place.

68. ICAO, Recent Developments in Aviation Security, Muscat, Oman, 17 September 2017, DGCA-MID/4-IP/5.
69. *See*, ICAO, 'Assembly Resolutions in Force (as of 4 October 2019)', https://www.icao.int/publications/Documents/10140_en.pdf.
70. ICAO General Assembly Working Paper, 'TRUST Framework for a Digital Environment', A40-WP/197, submitted by Brazil, 1 August 2019, at 3.
71. *Ibid.*; and ICAO General Assembly Working Paper, 'Trust Framework Study Group', A40-WP/369, submitted by the International Coordinating Council of Aerospace Industries Associations, 1 August 2019.

[C] Other Relevant Activities

[1] General Assembly Resolution

The General Assembly is the sovereign body of ICAO and meets at least once every three years to discuss and establish ICAO's worldwide policy for the triennium directly thereafter. The 193 contracting States to the Chicago Convention 1944, as well as a number of international organisations, are invited to participate at the Assembly. During its meetings, known as 'Sessions', "ICAO's complete work programme in the technical, economic, legal and technical cooperation fields is reviewed in detail."[72] During the Assembly, WPs can be presented by States or international organisation on topics specified in the Agenda,[73] and Resolutions are then adopted by the General Assembly.

During the 38th Assembly of 2013, 'Resolution A38-15: Consolidated Statement on Continuing ICAO policies Related to Aviation Security'[74] marked the first time the term 'cyber' was utilised at the General Assembly. Resolution A38-15 simply requests the ICAO Council to direct the Secretary General to "continue to address other threats and risks, including cyber threats to aviation security, [...] in consultation with the Aviation Security Panel."

The 39th Assembly took place at the end of 2016[75] when the Council of ICAO presented 'Working Paper A39-WP/17 EX/5: Addressing Cybersecurity in Civil Aviation', which contains a Draft Assembly Resolution. The draft was adopted as 'Resolution A39-19: Addressing Cybersecurity in Civil Aviation' which was the first Resolution specifically focused on this topic. The Resolution is important as it exposes ICAO's understanding of cybersecurity, and how it plans to work in this area for the next three years and beyond.[76] The Preamble to the Resolution stressed the considerations that ICAO has towards cybersecurity. ICAO:

---

72. ICAO, 'About the Assembly', https://www.icao.int/Meetings/a39/Pages/default.aspx.
73. Each Working Paper should be individually consulted to assess its relevance to cybersecurity. *See*, for example, the Global Aviation Security Plan (GASeP), formally the ICAO Comprehensive Aviation Security Strategy (ICASS), which "provides the foundation for States, industry, stakeholders and ICAO to work together with the shared and common goal of enhancing aviation security worldwide and achieving five key priority outcomes, namely: a) enhance risk awareness and response; b) develop security culture and human capability; c) improve technological resources and innovation; d) improve oversight and quality assurance; and e) increase cooperation and support." ICAO, Global Aviation Security Plan, November 2017, at iii. The overall aim is to raise the level of implementation of Annex 17 through actions at a national, regional and global level. The GASeP contains an extensive Roadmap in Appendix A which contains specific measures and tasks. Specific to cybersecurity are 1.A and 1.B which take a holistic approach to cybersecurity.
74. ICAO, Doc 10022 Assembly Resolutions in Force (as of 4 October 2013).
75. ICAO, Doc 10075 Assembly Resolutions in Force (as of 6 October 2016). The 39th Assembly was attended by over 2,000 delegates that represented 185 Members States, as well as observer delegations from international, regional and other organisations. In total, thirty-eight Resolutions were produced by the Assembly. ICAO, Fourth African-Indian Ocean (AFI) Week Second Security and Facilitation Symposium, Session 3: 39th ICAO Assembly Resolutions Related to Aviation Security and Facilitation, 2nd AFI SECFAL Symposium 2017, 24 May 2017, Gaborone, Botswana, 19 May 2017.
76. ICAO, Journal, Global Aviation Security Plan (GASeP) to be Developed, Volume 71(4), at 16.

(1) clearly sees the need for and benefit of collaborating with stakeholders, in which it makes reference to the IHLG;
(2) is conscious that the factual situation is important to understand, noting the growing reliance on information and communication technology by aviation stakeholders, the multifaceted and multidisciplinary nature of cybersecurity, and the evolving threat landscape;
(3) regards cybersecurity as a high priority as it reaffirms "the importance and urgency of protecting civil aviation's critical infrastructure systems and data against cyber threats"; and
(4) directly references the need to address the safety and security side of cybersecurity.

The Resolution is split into two directions. First, it looks externally and requests the contracting states and industry stakeholders to take certain steps. There is a clear focus on:

(1) cooperation and coordination between different stakeholders, including ICAO;
(2) sharing of information;
(3) identification of risks; and
(4) encouragement of a cybersecurity culture through *inter alia*, designated responsibilities, promotion and development of standards, and the allocation of resources.

Second, it looks internally as it instructs the Secretary General of ICAO to assist and facilitate stakeholders in taking the above actions; and ensure that cybersecurity is fully considered and coordinated across all ICAO's relevant disciplines. As a result, the Resolution covers cooperation between all stakeholders across numerous matters.[77] Whether it covers the full scope of aviation cybersecurity will be revealed in time, such as with amendments resulting from 40th Assembly in 2019.[78]

[2] Dubai Declaration

The 'Declaration on Cybersecurity in Civil Aviation Dubai', more commonly referred to as the Dubai Declaration, was presented during ICAO's inaugural Cyber Summit and

77. In addition, there are numerous references, both directly and indirectly to cybersecurity in other Resolutions resulting from the 39th Assembly, as well as in the many Working Papers presented by aviation stakeholders.
78. Resolution A38-15 should not be considered in isolation as the other Resolutions should be consulted. There is the need for wider consideration as demonstrated by the 13th Air Navigation Conference. The 13th Air Navigation Conference was an 'event for open discussion on issues and proposed solutions relating to flight safety and air navigation capacity, efficiency and other key performance areas of particular interest to the aviation community and which will benefit society in general.' In total, 12 Working Papers were submitted that directly address cybersecurity or, as Agenda Item 5.4 opted for, 'cyber resilience'. ICAO, 'About ICAO Thirteenth Air Navigation Conference', https://www.icao.int/Meetings/anconf13/Pages/default.aspx.

Exhibition in Dubai, United Arab Emirates, from 4 to 6 April 2017. The Dubai Declaration makes six specific declarations:[79]

(1) Declaration 1: States have the ultimate responsibility to mitigate cyber risks, increase cybersecurity and to provide an appropriate legal framework. Other stakeholders, thus, have a secondary role.
(2) Declaration 2: cyber capabilities should only be used for peaceful purposes, with the goal of improving safety, efficiency and security.[80]
(3) Declaration 3: cooperation between relevant stakeholders should be promoted as this is an indispensable element of cybersecurity. This focuses on vertical collaboration and exchange (State - stakeholder) and does not promote horizontal collaboration and exchange (stakeholder - stakeholder).
(4) Declaration 4: cybersecurity matters should be "fully considered and coordinated across all relevant disciplines within State aviation authorities." International civil aviation involves numerous stakeholders, all with different roles, rights, responsibilities, resources and expertise. It is, therefore, prudent to promote cooperation and a multi-stakeholder approach to cybersecurity.
(5) Declaration 5: cyberattacks against a civil aviation stakeholder should "be considered an offence against the principles and arrangement for the safe and orderly development of the international civil aviation."[81]
(6) Declaration 6: both the Beijing Convention 2010 and Beijing Protocol of 2010 should be ratified by States. This is because these instruments "would ensure that a cyberattack on international civil aviation is considered an offence [and] would serve as an important deterrent against activities that compromise aviation safety by exploiting cyber vulnerabilities."[82]

The Dubai Declaration is concluded by a reiteration of the stakeholders' "commitment to the development of a robust, efficient and sustainable civil aviation system." While the Dubai Declaration is a non-binding text and is not the first step taken by the international community toward cybersecurity, it "signifies the commitment and unity of the air transport sector towards achieving effective cyber resilience."[83] It is, therefore, an important attempt in setting and clarifying the international community's policy on aviation cybersecurity.

79. Dubai Declaration. ICAO, 'Declaration on Cybersecurity in Civil Aviation Dubai', Dubai, United Arab Emirates, 4-6 April 2017, https://www.icao.int/meetings/cyber2017/documents/draft%20dubai%20declaration%20on%20cybersecurity%20in%20civil%20aviation_10%20march%202017.pdf.
80. Declaration 2, therefore, identifies within the context of ICAO that both safety and security are relevant for cyberattack.
81. *See* Chicago Convention 1944, *supra* no. 2, Preamble.
82. ICAO, General Assembly Working Pape, 'Cybersecurity', A40-WP/221, submitted by United Arab Emirates, 5 August 2019.
83. ICAO, 'ICAO Summit Formalizes New Dubai Declaration to Ensure Global Aviation Remains United, Proactive on Cybersecurity Preparedness', https://www.icao.int/Newsroom/Pages/ICAO-Summit-formalizes-new-Dubai-Declaration-ensures-global-aviation-remains-united-proactive-on-cybersecurity-preparedness.aspx.

[3] *Cybersecurity Strategy*

Since its inception in August 2017, the SSGC has developed a set of recommendations to address the emerging issue of cybersecurity in aviation, with the main outcome being the development of a comprehensive Cybersecurity Strategy.

The Strategy's framework is built upon seven pillars:

- International Cooperation: aviation is a global industry, where harmonisation is required to ensure adequate levels of safety and security, whereby ICAO is the appropriate forum.
- Governance: States are encouraged to support and build upon the Strategy, as well as develop their own national systems, and to include cybersecurity in their national civil aviation safety and security programmes. To facilitate this, ICAO should include cybersecurity in regional and global plans and work towards a common baseline for cybersecurity SARPs.
- Effective legislation and regulations: international, regional and national law should promote cybersecurity, and States should ensure appropriate legislation and regulations are formulated and applied, including by ratifying ICAO instruments.
- Cybersecurity Policy: States should include cybersecurity in their aviation security and safety oversight systems as part of a comprehensive risk management framework, and risk assessments are required to assess the different levels of risk.
- Information Sharing: information must be shared, but based on a system of trust.
- Incident Management and Emergency Planning: there is a need for pragmatic plans to manage cyber incidents.
- Capacity Building, Training and Cybersecurity Culture: humans are at the centre of cybersecurity, and they must be trained, including supporting the next generation of aviation professionals.

In summary, the Strategy aims for:

a) the protection of civil aviation and the travelling public from cybersecurity threats that might affect the safety, security and trust of the air transport system;
b) maintaining or improving the safety and security of the aviation system in preserving the continuity of air transport services;
c) States to recognize their obligations under the Convention on International Civil Aviation (Chicago Convention) to ensure the safety, security and continuity of civil aviation, taking into account cybersecurity threats; and
d) coordination of cybersecurity measures among State authorities to ensure effective and efficient management of cybersecurity risks.[84]

84. ICAO, General Assembly Working Paper, 'ICAO Cybersecurity Strategy', A40-WP/28, Presented by the ICAO Council, 25 June 19.

In doing so, it aims "to steer the work of States and ICAO with the aim of ensuring the safety, security and continuity of civil aviation through the application of a robust cybersecurity framework."[85]

The ICAO Council, during its 217th Session from 21 May to 21 June 2019, agreed to present the Aviation Cybersecurity Strategy to the 40th Session of the ICAO Assembly. The Council eventually presented it in a WP titled 'ICAO Cybersecurity Strategy'.

[4] Global Aviation Security Plan

The ICAO Comprehensive Aviation Security Strategy (ICASS) was approved by the Council during its 189th Session and endorsed by the 37th Session of the Assembly.[86] WP A39-WP 14 highlights the outcomes and achievements of ICASS's implementation during the 2014-2016 triennium. ICASS has since been replaced by the Global Aviation Security Plan (GASeP). The GASeP:

> provides the foundation for States, industry, stakeholders and ICAO to work together with the shared and common goal of enhancing aviation security worldwide and achieving five key priority outcomes, namely: a) enhance risk awareness and response; b) develop security culture and human capability; c) improve technological resources and innovation; d) improve oversight and quality assurance; and e) increase cooperation and support.[87]

In doing so, the overall aim is to raise the level of implementation of Annex 17 through actions at a national, regional and global level.

The GASeP contains an extensive roadmap in Appendix A, which contains specific measures and tasks specific to cybersecurity, which takes a holistic approach to cybersecurity, are:

> "1.A Identify and address cybersecurity threats to civil aviation's critical infrastructure, data and information and communication technology systems through collaboration using horizontal, cross-cutting and functional approaches to achieve an acceptable and commensurate cyber resilience capability on a global level. It should involve air navigation, communication, surveillance, aircraft operations and airworthiness and other relevant disciplines to ensure the safety and security of civil aviation operations in full alignment with ICAO's Global Air Navigation Plan (GANP) and Global Aviation Safety Plan (GASP)";
>
> "1.B Monitor and address emerging and evolving risks, such as cyber security, remotely piloted aircraft systems (RPAS), and risks arising from conflict zones."

Therefore, the measures imposed here cover identification of current and emerging threats, and the taking of actions to combat cyber threats.

85. *Ibid.*
86. ICAO, General Assembly Working Paper, 'ICAO Comprehensive Aviation Security Strategy (ICASS) Strategic Plan of Action 2011-2016', A37-WP/18, Presented by the ICAO Council, 28 June 2010.
87. ICAO, Global Aviation Security Plan, November 2017, at iii.

The roadmap addresses aviation security, and as a result, other tasks and actions may be applicable, such as 1.Y which proposes to "develop a Manual on Investigating Acts of Unlawful Interference Against Civil Aviation." Therefore, the scope of the roadmap to cybersecurity is potentially wide and must be considered.

[5] European Aviation Security Training Institute

Due to the increased importance that security has developed in international air transport, ICAO and European Civil Aviation Conference (ECAC) have committed to implementing the highest standards in civil aviation security, establishing a training centre in the European region for the enhancement of aviation security. This training centre has been called the 'European Aviation Security Training Institute'.[88] The classroom and e-learning courses cover a wide range of aviation security topics. While none specifically address cybersecurity, this can be expected to change with the growing attention that ICAO and ECAC afford the topic.

[D] IHLG

In addition to regional safety and security cooperation, there is also industry stakeholder cooperation (outside the scope of the European Strategic Coordination Platform (ESCP)). For example, in 2013, five aviation stakeholders established an IHLG. These were Airports Council International,[89] Civil Air Navigation Services Organisation,[90] International Air Transport Association,[91] ICAO and ICCAIA. The IHLG is a mechanism for high-level cooperation on shared important issues in aviation security. Within its scope, it included cybersecurity issues and "the IHLG determined that cybersecurity in civil aviation was a high priority horizontal issue requiring aligned and coordinated actions by all relevant holders."[92] The IHLG's work so far has included:[93]

---

88. EASTI, 'Objectives', https://easti.eu/objectives/.
89. Airport Cooperative Research Program, Guidebook on Best Practices for Airport Cybersecurity, ACRP REPORT 140.
90. CANSO, 'Cyber Security and Risk Assessment Guide', June 2014, https://www.canso.org/sites/default/files/CANSO%20Cyber%20Security%20and%20Risk%20Assessment%20Guide.pdf.
91. *See*, IATA, 'Fact Sheet Cyber Security', https://www.iata.org/pressroom/facts_figures/fact_sheets/Documents/fact-sheet-cyber-security.pdf; IATA, 'Position Paper on Cybersecurity', http://www.iata.org/policy/Documents/cyber-threat-position.pdf; IATA, 'Insider Threat in Civil Aviation, Position Paper for 2015/2016', https://www.iata.org/policy/Documents/insider-threats-position.pdf; and IATA, 'Position Paper on Cybersecurity', http://www.iata.org/policy/Documents/cyber-threat-position.pdf.
92. ICAO, Assembly - 39th Session, Executive Committee, Addressing Cybersecurity in Civil Aviation, Presented by the Council of ICAO, WA39-WP, EX/5, 30 May 2017.
93. ICAO, 'Update on Cybersecurity The Trust Framework', Director of the Air Navigation Bureau and Air Transport Bureau, Presented at GREPECAS/18 Technical Workshop, Punta Cana, Dominican Republic, 11 April 2018, https://www.icao.int/SAM/Documents/2018-GREPECAS18/GRP18_P03.pdf.

(1) An agreement to hand over cybersecurity-related tasks to the ICAO SSGC.[94]
(2) The signing of the 'Civil Aviation Cybersecurity Action Plan' on 5 December 2014.[95]
(3) Preparatory work for ICAO Assembly Resolution A39-19 Addressing Cybersecurity in Civil Aviation.

In addition to the combined efforts, the organisations have also been active individually. Some of these efforts will be described below. While the IHLG comprises of key aviation stakeholders, there are others, such as the International Federation of

94. As a result of the rising threat of cyberattacks, there was a call during the 39th Session of the ICAO Assembly 'for a coordinated approach to achieve an acceptable and commensurate cyber resilience capability on a global scale.' As a result, ICAO established a Secretariat Study Group on Cybersecurity (SSGC). It held its first meeting on 29 August 2017 and 'developed a set of Terms of Reference and established several working groups with a view to addressing all elements and domains of the international aviation framework that may be affected by cyber incidents and attacks.' It is currently a young group and more can be expected from it in the future. ICAO, Recent Developments in Aviation Security, Muscat, Oman, 17 September 2017, DGCA-MID/4-IP/5. The SSGC is:

(1) under the monitoring of the Secretariat Senior Management Group on Common Safety and Security Issues (CSSI);
(2) chaired by Deputy Director, Aviation Security and Facilitation and launched in August 2017;
(3) a response to ICAO Assembly Resolution A39-19, and
(4) leads and seeks to attain a comprehensive cybersecurity work plan and governance structure with all relevant stakeholders.

Ibid.

95. The five organisations declared that they:

- recognize the need to work together, guided by a shared vision, strategy and roadmap to strengthen the aviation system's protection and resilience against cyberattacks;
- will jointly make the necessary effort to prepare civil aviation against future challenges from cyber threats;
- will cooperate on the following commitments:
  - o Develop a common understanding of cyber threats and risks;
  - o Share assessments of risks;
  - o Agree common language and terminology;
  - o Develop joint positions and recommendations;
  - o Present a coherent approach to the public;
  - o Promote cooperation among State-level appropriate authorise and industry to establish coordinated aviation cybersecurity strategies, policies and plans;
  - o Promote a robust cybersecurity culture in all organizations in civil aviation;
  - o Promote the use of existing information security and cyber protection best practices, standards and design principles, and establish new ones, where necessary;
  - o Establish the mechanisms and means to share and communicate information including identification of threats, reporting of incidents and developments in defences;
  - o Communicate threat-related information and assure situational awareness;
  - o Refine best practices, operational principles and defensive systems, as appropriate.
- Support the actions defined in the roadmap attached to this document.

ICAO, Civil Aviation Cybersecurity Action Plan, 5 December 2014, Available, https://www.icao.int/cybersecurity/SiteAssets/ICAO/Civil%20Aviation%20Cybersecurity%20Action%20Plan%20-%20SIGNED.pdf.

Air Line Pilots' Associations (IFALPA)[96] and Eurocontrol,[97] including the latter's work on EATM-CERT,[98] which should not be overlooked.

§7.07 REGIONAL SAFETY AND SECURITY ORGANISATIONS: CASE STUDY OF THE EU

The Chicago Convention 1944 does not regulate every aspect of international civil aviation and, in parts, leaves it to States to fill the gaps with domestic law that is as uniform as possible with those established under the Convention. As a result, there is a vast amount of domestic aviation law regulating domestic and international flights which may contain rules addressing cybersecurity. The aviation cybersecurity efforts of the EU, pursuant to Article 100(2) of the TFEU,[99] will be explored as a case study as the EU has the most developed regional activities and covers twenty-seven different States.

EASA published a report in 2009 that referred to the "security of using standardised data links for controlling [unmanned aircraft],"[100] and the 2014 EASA type certificate datasheet of the Learjet Model 45 makes reference to 'network security',[101]

---

96. *See*, for more information, IFALPA, 'Cyber Threats, Position Paper 16POS08', 6 December 2016, http://www.ifalpa.org/downloads/Level1/IFALPA%20Position%20Papers%20&%20Statements/Security/16POS08%20-%20Cyber%20Threats.pdf. *See also*, IFALPA, 'Cyber Threats, Security Briefing Leaflet 16SECBL01', 6 December 2016, http://www.alpa.co.za/images/16SECBL01_-_Cyber_Threats.pdf.
97. *See*, for more information, Eurocontrol, 'Centralised Service 6-7 Operations and Coordination of Network Security, Ensuring the Resilience of Centralised Services' Cyber-Security and Sharing Cyber Intelligence', February 2017.
98. On 13 March 2017 Eurocontrol and the CERT-EU signed a Service Level Agreement to improve cybersecurity. Under this Agreement, 'CERT-EU will provide services to Eurocontrol in order to support the setting up of the European Air Traffic Management Computer Emergency Response Team (EATM-CERT). CERT-EU will make available some information and cyber-security tools to EATM-CERT as well as sharing experience, expertise, advice and procedures on how to operate a CERT efficiently.' Eurocontrol, 'Agreement with the European Commission's CERT-EU on Cyber-Security', http://www.eurocontrol.int/press-releases/agreement-european-commission-cert-eu-cyber-security. EATM-CERT will provide the following services to ANSPs and Airport Operators of Eurocontrol Member States:

    > Proactive cyber-security services (e.g. penetration testing, vulnerability assessment, infrastructure/best practices review);
    > Collection, generation and distribution of ATM relevant cyber intelligence;
    > Coordination, with National CERTs as appropriate, of the pan-European ATM response to ATM relevant cyber-security alerts/incidents on a voluntary basis.

99. Consolidated Version of the Treaty on the Functioning of the European Union, 2008/C 115/01, 13 December 2007, Art. 100(2):

    > The European Parliament and the Council, acting in accordance with the ordinary legislative procedure, may lay down appropriate provisions for sea and air transport. They shall act after consulting the Economic and Social Committee and the Committee of the Regions.

100. EASA, Final Report of the Preliminary Impact Assessment on the Safety of Communications for Unmanned Aircraft Systems (UAS), Volume 1, 8 December 2009, at 14.
101. EASA, Type Certificate Data Sheet No. TCDS IM.A.020 for Learjet Model 45.

both of which highlight early EASA involvement with cybersecurity. However, two years after the adoption of the EU's Cybersecurity Strategy, the 2nd High-level Conference on the EU Cybersecurity Strategy took place on 28 May 2015 to provide "an overview of the state of play of the implementation of the five main priorities of the Strategy and showcase highlights of its main actions."[102] From this event on, cybersecurity became a central theme in EU aviation policy. Evidence of this lies in the following events:

(1) First Meeting of Member States' Representatives of Cybersecurity in Aviation, 26 May 2016, Brussels, Belgium.
(2) Workshop on the roles and the activities of a European Centre for Cybersecurity in Aviation, 13-14 July 2016, Cologne, Germany.[103]
(3) Cybersecurity in Aviation workshop, 31 May 2017, Brussels, Belgium.[104]

Additional high-level meetings have been held, with more likely to happen as the EU looks deeper into this topic. However, what can be seen is that these three meetings, including other early activities like the Impact Assessment of Cybersecurity Threats project, which was launched on 12 December 2016,[105] all centre around EASA.

[A] Bucharest Declaration

A high-level meeting took place between 8 and 9 November 2016 in Bucharest, Romania, which hosted representatives from the industry, EU Member States, European institutions including the Commission and EASA, academia and cybersecurity institutions. The purpose was to "discuss the aviation cybersecurity risk picture, actions already taken and ways forward"[106] due to the growing threat to aviation

102. Commission, 'Second High-level Conference on the EU Cybersecurity Strategy', 28 May 2015, https://www.ec.europa.eu/digital-single-market/en/news/high-level-cybersecurity-conference-agenda. *See*, for more information on the EU's Cybersecurity Strategy, Chapter 4.
103. During this workshop, four mock cybersecurity crisis scenarios were enacted with the goal of identifying 'the services and functions of a ECCSA during the different events, its added value, possible constraints.' EASA, 'Workshop on the roles and the activities of a European Centre for Cybersecurity in Aviation, Cologne', https://www.easa.europa.eu/newsroom-and-events/news/workshop-roles-and-activities-european-centre-cybersecurity-aviation.
104. EASA and EUROCAE also organised the workshop to 'discuss current activities and future regulatory and standardisation needs with key stakeholders from industry, airspace users, Member States, European Institutions, academia.' EASA, 'Main EASA Activities', https://www.easa.europa.eu/easa-and-you/cyber-security/main-easa-activities.
105. 'The project aims at developing a comprehensive knowledge base for evaluating the safety impact of a number of potential threats to critical aircraft systems, consolidating the methods and techniques used, as well as to enable the EU harmonisation of the associated risk management process.' It is an external project in which the Agency has opened a public tender under Directive 2014/24/EU. Directive 2014/24/EU of the European Parliament and of the Council of 26 February 2014 on Public Procurement and Repealing Directive 2004/18/EC, OJ L 94, 28 March 2014, pp. 65-242.
106. Bucharest Declaration, Bucharest, Romania, Palace of the Parliament, 8-9 November 2016, at 1.

stakeholders from attackers and the changing vulnerabilities. The result of the Conference, which contains the main conclusions of the two-day meeting, was the Bucharest Declaration.[107]

The stakeholders, in appreciating the complexity of cybersecurity in aviation, concluded that a layered approach to increasing cybersecurity and combating cyber-attacks is required to achieve a "comprehensive, seamless and adaptive level of protection of the European aviation system against cyber threats."[108] Seven layers were identified:

(1) Coordination.
(2) Sharing of information and reporting.
(3) Regulations.
(4) Risk assessments.
(5) Cybersecurity promotion, awareness and preparedness.
(6) Knowledge and foresight.
(7) Commitment and resources.

The Bucharest Declaration provides an authoritative policy statement on EU aviation cybersecurity and is, therefore, important for assessing how cybersecurity will be handled within this region.

[B] Krakow Declaration

A High-Level Conference on Cybersecurity in Civil Aviation, known as the Krakow Conference, was organised by the Polish Ministry of Infrastructure and Construction, together with EASA and the Polish CAA, with the goal to discuss the progress of the measures already taken:

> and to establish a ground for the future European strategy for Cybersecurity in Aviation and the Cybersecurity Road Map that will define the future EU actions that have to be undertaken in order to ensure a secure environment for aviation.[109]

The Krakow Conference built upon the discussions held during the Bucharest Conference[110] and resulted in the Twenty-two-point Krakow Declaration.[111] The twenty-two points can be summarised into four categories:

107. *Ibid.*
108. *Ibid.*
109. Krakow Declaration, High Level Conference Cybersecurity in Civil Aviation Krakow Declaration, Krakow, Poland, 8-9 November 2017, at 1.
110. The Krakow Conference also built upon the High Level Conference on Drones held in Warsaw, Poland on 23-24 November 2016. Warsaw Declaration, 'Drones as a Leverage for Jobs and New Business Opportunities', Warsaw, Poland, 24 November 2016.
111. Krakow Declaration, *supra* no. 109.

(1) The role of EASA, both regulatory and non-regulatory.[112]
(2) The role of other stakeholders, such as ENISA, ECAC,[113] Single European Sky ATM Research Joint Undertaking (SESAR).[114]
(3) Non-Regulatory Solutions, such as research through the Research Framework Programme – Research Framework Programme Nine (FP9)[115] and cooperation between stakeholders.
(4) European Strategic Coordination Platform.[116]

The Krakow Declaration, therefore, complements the Bucharest Declaration in spelling out the EU's cybersecurity policy.

[C] Safety

In 2015, the Commission published its 'Aviation Strategy to Enhance the Competitiveness of the EU Aviation Sector'.[117] The strategy stated that the EU wanted to repeal and replace Regulation 216/2008,[118] which regulates aviation safety within the 27 + 4 EU

112. Following the 2nd High-level Conference on the EU Cybersecurity Strategy which took place on 28 May 2015, cybersecurity began to become a central theme in EU aviation policy:

 (1) First Meeting of Member States' Representatives of Cybersecurity in Aviation, 26 May 2016 Brussels, Belgium.
 (2) Workshop on the roles and the activities of a European Centre for Cybersecurity in Aviation, 13-14 July 2016, Cologne, Germany.
 (3) Cybersecurity in Aviation workshop, 31 May 2017, Brussels, Belgium.

 What can be seen from these early meetings is that EASA is the central stakeholder.
113. ECAC Doc. 30 is non-binding so it lacks a legal enforcement mechanism. It is also not publicly available, so further comment on it cannot be made. Jürgen Faust and Christian Leininger, 'Security', *in* Stephan Hobe, Nicolai von Ruckteschell and David Hefferman (eds), *Cologne Compendium on Air Law in Europe*, English Edition (Carl Heymanns Verlag, 2014), at 782. *See also*, Patricia Reverdy, Deputy Executive Secretary ECAC, 'ECAC Priorities for Cyber Security: Building on Our Strengths', ICAO Cyber Summit and Exhibition, Dubai, United Arab Emirates, 5-6 April 2017.
114. SESAR is a European Commission initiative established by Council Regulation (EC) 219/2007 which is a Joint Undertaking with the aim of ensuring the modernisation of the European ATM system. *See*, SESAR, 'Home', http://www.sesarju.eu/.
115. 'The 8th EU Framework Programme for Research and Innovation, Horizon 2020 runs until the end of 2020. In parallel to the Horizon 2020 interim evaluation, which will be finalised in December 2017, the preparations for the future framework programme, FP9, are ongoing.' Kowi, 'EU Research Policy', http://www.kowi.de/en/kowi/research-policy/fp9/fp9.aspx. *See*, for more information on Horizon 2020, Commission, 'Horizon 2020', https://www.ec.europa.eu/programmes/horizon2020/.
116. The ESCP consists of key industry stakeholders, States and EU institutions, which substituted an existing informal group which involved, *inter alia*, manufacturers and airlines. Juan Anton, EASA, 'Cybersecurity; An EASA Perspective on Developments and Challenges', Presentation: IATA Paperless Conference 2017, 13-14 November 2017. *See*, Air Traffic Management Net, 'European Fragmentation Hampering Cyber Effort', 28 March 2017, http://www.airtrafficmanagement.net/2017/03/european-fragmentation-hampering-cyber-effort/.
117. Commission, Commission Presents a New Aviation Strategy for Europe, Brussels, Press Release, IP/15/6144, 7 December 2015.
118. Regulation (EC) 216/2008 of the European Parliament and of the Council of 20 February 2008 on Common Rules in the Field of Civil Aviation and Establishing a European Aviation Safety

Member States.[119] The result was Regulation 2018/1139 of the European Parliament and of the Council of 4 July 2018 on Common Rules in the Field of Civil Aviation and Establishing EASA.[120] Article 1(1) of Regulation 2018/1139 declares that its main objective is to "maintain a high uniform level of civil aviation safety in the Union." In addition to this, Article 1(2)(a)-(k) sets forth an additional eleven objectives which shall be achieved pursuant to Article 1(3). While having a broad scope of competencies, the Regulation – and thus, the Agency – is limited:

(1) It only applies to *civil* activities per Article 2(3)(a)-(c).
(2) The aircraft types contained in Annex I to the Regulation are outside the scope of the Regulation and would instead be regulated at a national level by the Member States.[121]

Many of the fundamentals between Regulation 216/2008 and Regulation 2018/1139 remain the same; however, many changes were brought in by this new Regulation, including a direct reference to the term 'cybersecurity'.

Article 4(1)(c) of Regulation 2018/1139 declares:

> 1. When taking measures under this Regulation the Commission, the Agency and the Member States shall
>
> [...]
>
> (c) allow for immediate reaction to established causes of accidents, serious incidents and intentional security breaches.

The term 'security' includes cybersecurity. This is supported by the inclusion of 'intentional' which requires a level of intent – an attacker. However, it is Article 4(1)(d) which contains the first direct reference to cybersecurity in the substantive Articles:

> take into account interdependencies between the different domains of aviation safety, and between aviation safety, cyber security and other technical domains of aviation regulation.

Agency, and Repealing Council Directive 91/670/EEC, Regulation (EC) 1592/2002 and Directive 2004/36/EC, OJ L 79, 19 March 2008, pp. 1-49. Regulation 216/2008 has been amended four times and an unofficial consolidated version is available at EASA, 'Regulations', https://www.easa.europa.eu/regulations.

119. The +4 States are Iceland, Liechtenstein, Norway and Switzerland. It no longer includes the UK.

120. Regulation (EU) 2018/1139 of the European Parliament and of the Council of 4 July 2018 on Common Rules in the Field of Civil Aviation and Establishing a European Union Aviation Safety Agency, and Amending Regulations (EC) 2111/2005, (EC) 1008/2008, (EU) 996/2010, (EU) 376/2014 and Directives 2014/30/EU and 2014/53/EU of the European Parliament and of the Council, and Repealing Regulations (EC) 552/2004 and (EC) 216/2008 of the European Parliament and of the Council and Council Regulation (EEC) 3922/91, OJ L 212, 22 August 2018, pp. 1-122.

121. The Regulation does not apply to: 'the design, production, maintenance and operation of aircraft the operation of which involves low risk for aviation safety, as listed in Annex I, and to the personnel and organisations involved therein, unless the aircraft has been issued, or has been deemed to have been issued, with a certificate in accordance with Regulation (EC) 216/2008.' *Ibid.*, Art. 2(3)(d).

This, therefore, requires the Commission, the Agency and the Member States to merely *take into account* the relationship between different areas of safety and cybersecurity in the safety-based measures provided in Regulation 2018/1139.

Article 88 on the interdependencies between civil aviation safety and security contains three subsections which are relevant for cybersecurity:

(1) Article 88(1): Cooperation between the Member States, the Commission and the Agency on cybersecurity, where interdependencies between civil aviation safety and security exist.
(2) Article 88(2): The Agency shall, upon request, provide technical assistance to the Commission, where the Agency has the relevant safety expertise, in the implementation of Regulation 300/2008.
(3) Article 88(3): The Agency can react so as to contribute to protecting civil aviation against acts of unlawful interference.

Attached to the substantive Articles of Regulation 2018/1139 are the ten Annexes. The term 'cyber' does not feature in any of the Annexes; however, traces of cybersecurity can be found throughout:

(1) The term 'security' can be found. Due to the link made in Article 88 between security and cybersecurity, it is possible to interpret 'security' to include, where applicable, cybersecurity.
(2) While Article 88 uses the term 'unlawful interference', it is missing from the Annexes.[122] However, five different formulations of interference are used:
    - 'Interference'.
    - 'Intentional and Non-Intentional System Interference'.
    - 'Unauthorised Interference'.
    - 'Harmful Interference'.
    - 'Interference by Electronic Means'.
(3) The Annex also introduces additional terms that can relate to cybersecurity. The term 'information security threats' appears only twice in the Essential Requirements under Annex II 1 and 1.3.5.
(4) In addition to phraseology, there are words used throughout that can have cybersecurity connotations depending upon the context. For example, Annex VIII on the Essential Requirements for ATM/ANS and Air Traffic Controllers hosts the following terms:
    - 'Availability'.
    - 'Integrity'.
    - 'Continuity'.
    - 'Timeliness'.
    - 'Corruption'.
    - 'Reliable'.

122. *See, Ibid.*, Art. 74(8)(f).

(5) Standard aviation safety clauses can also be read to include cybersecurity. For example, the term 'reasonably probable threat' is not defined in the Regulation but could include a cyberattack.

This line of argumentation can also be extended to the Implementing Rules, that fall, *inter alia*, into the following headings:[123]

(1) Initial airworthiness.
(2) Continuing airworthiness.
(3) Aircrew.
(4) Air operations.
(5) ATM, air navigation services and air traffic controllers.
(6) Air traffic controllers.
(7) Airspace usage requirements.
(8) Standardised European rules of the air.
(9) Aerodromes.
(10) Specific aircraft (e.g., unmanned aircraft systems, balloons and sailplanes).[124]

The most notable example is found in Annex III of Regulation 2017/373, which makes a specific reference to the term 'cybersecurity' in the context of security management in ATM.

The Agency has also implemented several rulemaking efforts since 2016, which is an established process that is set out in the Agency's foundational Regulation[125] and

123. Regulation 216/2008 did not mention the word 'cybersecurity' in its Articles or Annexes. However, despite the lack of clearly defined responsibilities for cybersecurity, this did not mean that Regulation 216/2008 was silent nor did it mean that the Agency did not have responsibilities in this area. For example, Annex Vb of Regulation 216/2008 contains the Essential Requirements for ATM/air navigation services and air traffic control, and Implementing Regulation 2017/373 on the same topic covers data. For example, the terms 'data security', 'software integrity and security', and 'cybersecurity' feature in the Regulation. This shows that elements of cybersecurity could be found in Regulation 216/2008 and it should, therefore, not be overlooked and dismissed as irrelevant. Commission Implementing Regulation (EU) 2017/373 of 1 March 2017 Laying Down Common Requirements for Providers of Air Traffic Management/Air Navigation Services and other Air Traffic Management Network Functions and their Oversight, Repealing Regulation (EC) 482/2008, Implementing Regulations (EU) 1034/2011, (EU) 1035/2011 and (EU) 2016/1377 and Amending Regulation (EU) 677/2011, OJ L 62, 8 March 2017, pp. 1-126.

124. *See*, for the full list, EASA, 'Regulations', https://www.easa.europa.eu/regulations. *See*, Mends de Leon, *supra* no. 45, Chapter 7.

125. *See*, for legal basis of cited Rulemaking Programmes, Regulation 2018/1139, *supra* no. 120, Arts 76 and 115.

internal documents.[126] While the current version is Rulemaking Programme 2018-2022, all of the RMTs include:[127]

(1) RMT.0648 – Aircraft Cybersecurity.
(2) RMT.0720 – Cybersecurity Risks.
(3) SPT.071 – Cybersecurity Road Map.
(4) SPT.071 – Strategy for Cybersecurity in Aviation.
(5) SPT.072 – AV-CERT.
(6) RES.012 – Cybersecurity: Common Aeronautical Vulnerabilities Database.[128]

From a regulatory perspective, RMT.0720 is important as it shows there are plans to develop a specific EU aviation cybersecurity regulation within the EU aviation safety regime to govern information safety management systems. In addition, RMT.0648 sets out to amend relevant CS to introduce cybersecurity requirements into the certification process. As a result, it can be expected that there will be an increased number of *lex specialis* regulations and supporting documents for aviation cybersecurity under the EU aviation safety regime.

[D] Security

The EU's Common Rules in the Field of Civil Aviation Security are found in Regulation 300/2008.[129] The objectives of the Regulation are set out in Article 1(1):

1. Establish "common rules to protect civil aviation against acts of unlawful interference that jeopardise the security of civil aviation."
2. Provide "the basis for a common interpretation of Annex 17."

126. EASA Management Board Decision 18-2015, 'Management Board Decision 18-2015 of 15 December 2015 Replacing Decision 01/2012 Concerning the Procedure to be Applied by the Agency for the Issuing of Opinions, Certification Specifications, Acceptable Means of Compliance and Guidance Material ('Rulemaking Procedure')', 15 December 2015.
127. Rulemaking Programme for 2017-2021 makes a fundamental point as it identifies the relationship between safety and security within the context of cybersecurity. This is an important ideological change from the 2016-2020 programme which focused on 'unlawful interference'.
128. The cybersecurity activities cover three standard forms:

(1) SPT: This incorporates 'a set of means, processes and procedures that are used to develop, sustain and improve aviation safety through awareness raising and changing behaviours.'
(2) RES: EASA has the competency to launch and finance research projects within its safety and environment mandate.
(3) RMT: The Agency has the competency to develop different types of regulatory material.

129. Regulation (EC) 300/2008 of the European Parliament and of the Council of 11 March 2008 on Common Rules in the Field of Civil Aviation Security and Repealing Regulation (EC) 2320/2002, OJ L 97, 9 April 2008, pp. 72-84. The origin of European regional security-based measures stems back to ECAC Document 30, which established in 1985 the first uniform standards for security for air transport in Europe. ECAC Policy Statement in the Field of Civil Aviation Facilitation, ECAC Doc. No. 30 (Part I), Eleventh Edition, December 2009.

In pursuance of these objectives, the EU shall, pursuant to Article 1(2), set "common rules and common basic standards on aviation security" and "mechanisms for monitoring compliance." However, this only applies to the stakeholders, as described in Article 2(1):

> 1. This Regulation shall apply to the following:
>   (a) all airports or parts of airports located in the territory of a Member State that are not exclusively used for military purposes;
>   (b) all operators, including air carriers, providing services at airports referred to in point (a);
>   (c) all entities applying aviation security standards that operate from premises located inside or outside airport premises and provide goods and/or services to or through airports referred to in point (a).

Therefore, it only includes those stakeholders with a physical link to the aircraft - both EU and non-EU operators - before and after it is engaged in flight involving an airport in the territory of a Member State. Article 1(2) provides two mechanisms aimed towards protecting civil aviation against unlawful interference:

> The means of achieving the objectives set out in paragraph 1 shall be:
>
> (a) the setting of common rules and common basic standards on aviation security;
> (b) mechanisms for monitoring compliance.

These mechanisms will be at the centre of this subchapter and will be further investigated below to establish their relevance to aviation cybersecurity. Pursuant to Article 4(1), "[t]he common basic standards for safeguarding civil aviation against acts of unlawful interference that jeopardise the security of civil aviation shall be as laid down in Annex I." The content of Annex I then comprises measures designed to protect aviation from unlawful interference. Article 4 divides these common basic standards into two categories. First, Article 4(2) covers general measures, then Article 4(3) covers detailed measures. From a simple reading of the two lists, it is evident that no reference is made to cybersecurity measures.

Article 4(1) allows for the adoption of "[a]dditional common basic standards not foreseen upon the entry into force of this Regulation, which should be added to the Annex in accordance with the procedure referred to in Article 251 of the Treaty."[130] Therefore, the supporting Regulations must also be examined in case relevant measures on cybersecurity can be found.[131]

130. The reference to 'the Treaty' corresponds to the TFEU.

131. One tool to facilitate this is the EU's Stakeholder Advisory Group for Aviation Security (SAGAS), membership of which consists of the Commission (DG-MOVE), Member State security representatives and industry representatives. The SAGAS's is tasked to 'advise the Commission in the preparation of legislative proposals and policy initiatives as well as in relation to the implementation of existing legislation.' Furthermore, there is the Regulatory Committee for Civil Aviation Security, which was created by Art. 19 of Regulation 300/2008 to address the evolving threat to civil aviation. Commission, 'Group Details - Commission Expert Group', http://www.ec.europa.eu/transparency/regexpert/index.cfm?do = groupDetail.groupDetail&groupID = 2883.

Pursuant to Article 6(1), a "Member State may apply more stringent measures than the common basic standards referred to in Article 4." Therefore, Member States are able to develop more stringent measures outside of Annex I, which could provide them with the basis to build on measures aimed towards tackling cybersecurity issues.

Another form of flexibility is provided by Commission Regulation 1254/2009,[132] as amended by Commission Regulation 2016/2096,[133] which sets the criteria to allow the Member States to deviate from the common basic standards on civil aviation security and to adopt alternative security measures. The Member States may then integrate cybersecurity measures via this mechanism.

Direct references to cybersecurity are not made in Regulation 300/2008 and were not included in its Implementing Regulations until September 2019. However, this did not mean that they were not relevant to cybersecurity. This could be through interpretation, development of more stringent measures, flexibility or the future adoption of additional common basic standards. The latter was done in Regulation 2019/1583, which amends Regulation 2015/1998 with regards to cybersecurity measures.[134] When it enters into force on 31 December 2020, this Regulation will bring the EU's aviation security regime, based on Regulation 300/2008, in line with Standard 4.9.1 of Annex 17.[135]

132. Commission Regulation (EU) 1254/2009 of 18 December 2009 Setting Criteria to Allow Member States to Derogate from the Common Basic Standards on Civil Aviation Security and to Adopt Alternative Security Measures, OJ L 338, 19 December 2009, p. 17-17.

133. Commission Regulation (EU) 2016/2096 of 30 November 2016 Amending Regulation (EU) 1254/2009 as Regards Certain Criteria to Allow Member States to Derogate from The Common Basic Standards on Civil Aviation Security and to Adopt Alternative Security Measures, OJ L 326, 1 December 2016, pp. 7-8, Art. 1:

> Article 1: "Member States may derogate from the common basic standards referred to in Article 4(1) of Regulation (EC) 300/2008 and adopt alternative security measures that provide an adequate level of protection on the basis of a risk assessment approved by the appropriate authority at airports or demarcated areas of airports where traffic is limited to one or more of the following categories."

134. Commission Implementing Regulation (EU) 2019/1583 of 25 September 2019 Amending Implementing Regulation (EU) 2015/1998 Laying Down Detailed Measures for the Implementation of the Common Basic Standards on Aviation Security, as Regards Cybersecurity Measures, OJ L 246, 26 September 2019, pp. 15-18.

135. *Ibid.*, Preamble (4):

> By transposing these standards into the implementing EU wide aviation security legislation, it will be ensured that appropriate authorities establish and implement procedures to share, as appropriate and in a practical and timely manner, relevant information to assist other national authorities and agencies, airport operators, air carriers and other entities concerned, to conduct effective security risk assessments relating to their operations and in that way support these entities in conducting effective security risk assessments related to, among other areas, cybersecurity and implement measures addressing cyber threats.

§7.08 CONCLUSION

While the Chicago Convention was not drafted with cybersecurity in mind, this does not prevent it from being relevant. It was shown that certain articles, such as Article 3 *bis*, may be interpreted to apply to cyberattacks. In this case, the use of the term 'weapon' could be understood to include a cyberattack method, such as spoofing an aircraft's communication or navigation links. The Chicago Convention may also be indirectly relevant for cybersecurity. For example, Article 6 has resulted in an extensive network of ASA where these treaties may have certain cyber-based obligations, such as in safety- or security-related articles.

The Chicago Convention also provides for the creation of Annexes. Most explicitly relevant is Annex 17, due to Amendment 12, which includes the term 'cyber threats' in title 4.9. This is the first direct reference to the term 'cyber' in any of the Annexes. However, it should be noted that the applicability of the Annexes to cybersecurity is not limited to title 4.9 as, for example, the Annexes also utilise numerous words that can be linked to cybersecurity. These include, but are not limited to, 'authorised', 'accuracy', 'integrity', 'availability' and 'functionality'. From this, it can be seen that even though they were not drafted to specifically tackle cybersecurity, certain SARPs may nevertheless be relevant for this topic.

Despite all of the above, there are significant gaps in the 19 Annexes, and because of this, more needs to be done by ICAO and its Member States to address all aspects of cybersecurity. ICAO – supported through General Assembly Resolutions, the Cybersecurity Strategy and the Dubai Declaration – is actively engaged in this area as evidenced by the work of the TFSG and SSGC, and cooperation with stakeholders (e.g., IHLG). The effectiveness of this work is, however, undermined by the split in competencies between the Air Navigation Bureau and Air Transportation Bureau, which has resulted in cyber being divided between the two.

In this chapter, it was also shown that the international criminal air law treaties should not be overlooked. For example, if a State criminalises cyberattacks in their national law, then the Tokyo Convention 1969, which leaves it to domestic criminal law to determine what constitutes an offence under that treaty, could include cybersecurity as an offence. Cybersecurity is, however, also more directly addressed in The Hague Convention 1970 as it may criminalise cyberattacks due to its general prohibition on the use of force against aircraft. The Beijing Protocol, which was drafted with cybersecurity in mind, could also directly address cyberattacks as it, *inter alia*, contains a provision that criminalises the unauthorised jamming of aircraft.

The case study of the EU shows that extensive activities are being carried out. For example, EASA is in the process of amending the certification requirements and drafting rules on information safety management systems and is actively engaged in information sharing and safety promotion. Further, the European Commission has also been addressing cybersecurity from a security angle through the Regulation 300/2008 regime. While the EU is in an advanced position, compared with other regions of the world, more needs to be done to regulate cyberattacks taking into account the differences found between aviation safety and security regimes.

CHAPTER 8
Aviation Liability in Cases of Cyberattacks

In the year 2019, the all accident rate in the commercial airline industry was one accident for every 884,000 flights, with a total of 53 accidents, 8 fatal accidents, and 240 fatalities.[1] Although these figures may demonstrate that the commercial airline industry strives to ensure that accidents are completely prevented or, at best, kept to an extreme minimum, the ostensible increase in cyberattacks and cybersecurity risks may cause these figures to grow.

The legal concomitant of accidents, which often entail loss or injury, is liability. For the purposes of this chapter, the notion of liability can be succinctly defined as the duty to indemnify a person, with whom there is a relationship based on the law of obligations or of tort, who has suffered damage in one form or another.[2]

In aviation, liability stems from both a relationship based on the law of obligations and a relationship based on the law of tort: liability stems from the former with regard to air carrier passengers, and liability stems from the latter with regard to third parties. In both cases, passengers and third parties have a right to be indemnified for the damage caused to them.

§8.01 LIABILITY IN THE CASE OF DAMAGE CAUSED TO AIR CARRIER PASSENGERS

Liability in the case of air carrier passengers is governed by two separate - albeit nearly identical - normative frameworks: the so-called Warsaw System[3] and the Convention

1. IATA, 'IATA Releases 2019 Airline Safety Programme', Press Release No. 27, 6 April 2020, https://www.iata.org/en/pressroom/pr/2020-04-06-01/.
2. *See*, for an analysis of the concept of 'liability', Martin Hogg, *Obligations: Law and Language*, 'Chapter 1: Obligation and Liability' (Cambridge University Press, 2017).
3. *See* below, for an explanation of the composition of the Warsaw System.

for the Unification of Certain Rules for International Carriage by Air[4] (Montreal Convention) of 1999.[5]

The Warsaw System is composed of several legal instruments,[6] the first of which was the Convention for the Unification of Certain Rules Relating to International Air Carriage (Warsaw Convention) of 1929.[7] In essence, this convention was envisaged to protect the then-fragile aviation industry[8] and to regulate, *inter alia*, the liability of international air carriers.[9]

Rather than regulating carriage by air in each and every possible manner, the Warsaw Convention, as suggested by its complete title, regulates certain facets thereof. To this end, the Warsaw Convention establishes a liability regime for air carriers in the event of damage caused to passengers, baggage, and goods in their international carriage by air, and in the event of damage caused by delay.[10]

Following the adoption of the Warsaw Convention in 1929, the international community proceeded to amend and supplement it on various occasions throughout the years by means of several other instruments which, altogether, compose the Warsaw System. The legal instruments which amend and supplement the Warsaw Convention are:

- the Protocol to Amend the Warsaw Convention of 1955;[11]
- the Convention, Supplementary to the Warsaw Convention, for the Unification of Certain Rules Relating to International Carriage by Air Performed by a Person Other than the Contracting Carrier of 1961;[12]

4. Montreal Convention for the Unification of Certain Rules for International Carriage by Air, 28 May 1999, 2242 U.N.T.S. 309. Currently 136 ratifications; ICAO, 'Convention for the Unification of Certain Rules for International Carriage by Air done at Montreal on 28 May 1999', https://www.icao.int/secretariat/legal/List%20of%20Parties/Mtl99_EN.pdf. Although the Warsaw System and the Montreal Convention are separate, Art. 55 of the latter provides that the Montreal Convention shall prevail over the Warsaw System.
5. George Leloudas, *Risk and Liability in Air Law* (Informa Law, 2009), at Chapter 4.
6. Benjamyn I. Scott and Andrea Trimarchi, *Fundamentals of International Aviation Law and Policy* (Routledge, 2019), at Chapter 7.
7. Convention for the Unification of Certain Rules Relating to International Carriage by Air, 12 October 1929, 49 Stat. 3000 (1934), 137 L.N.T.S. 11. Currently 152 ratifications; ICAO, 'Contracting Parties to the Convention for the Unification of Certain Rules Relating to International Carriage by Air signed at Warsaw on 12 October 1929 and the Protocol Modifying the said Convention signed at The Hague on 28 September 1955', http://www.icao.int/secretariat/legal/List%20of%20Parties/WC-HP_EN.pdf.
8. Morris v. KLM Dutch Airlines, [2002] 2 AC 628.
9. Avero Belgium Ins. v. American Airlines, Inc., [2005], US CA (Second Circuit), at footnote 2.
10. Pablo Mendes de Leon, *Introduction to Air Law*, Tenth Edition (Kluwer, 2017), at 149.
11. Currently 137 ratifications; ICAO, 'Contracting Parties to the Convention for the Unification of Certain Rules Relating to International Carriage by Air signed at Warsaw on 12 October 1929 and the Protocol Modifying the said Convention signed at The Hague on 28 September 1955', http://www.icao.int/secretariat/legal/List%20of%20Parties/WC-HP_EN.pdf.
12. Currently 86 ratifications; ICAO, 'Convention, Supplementary to the Warsaw Convention, for the Unification of Certain Rules Relating to International Carriage by Air Performed by a Person Other than the Contracting Carrier signed at Guadalajara on 18 September 1961', https://www.icao.int/secretariat/legal/List%20of%20Parties/Guadalajara_EN.pdf.

- the Protocol to Amend the Warsaw Convention as Amended by the Hague Protocol of 1971;[13] and
- the Montreal Additional Protocols No. 1,[14] No. 2,[15] No. 3,[16] and No. 4[17] of 1975.

Notwithstanding the protection afforded to passengers by the Warsaw System, with the passage of time and the evolution of the air transport industry, the satisfaction derived therefrom inevitably diminished. As a result, the adoption of a new legal instrument to modernise the then-existing liability system became a necessity.[18]

The Montreal Convention was consequently born, and although it was intended to harmonise the hodgepodge of amendments and supplements to the Warsaw System,[19] its scope was similar to that of this System as it sought to establish liability of air carriers in various cases of carriage by air.

The difference between the Warsaw System and the Montreal Convention, however, is that the Montreal Convention represents a significant shift away from a regime - created by the Warsaw System - which primarily favoured air carriers to a system that protects air carriers from crippling liability while showing an increased concern for the rights of passengers and shippers.[20]

Indeed, almost as if deliberately acknowledging the imbalance of interests found within the Warsaw System, the Montreal Convention makes explicit the importance of ensuring the protection of the interests of consumers in international carriage by air,[21]

13. Currently 7 ratifications and not in force; ICAO, 'Protocol to Amend the Convention for the Unification of Certain Rules Relating to International Carriage by Air signed at Warsaw on 12 October 1929 as amended by the Protocol done at The Hague on 28 September 1955 signed at Guatemala City on 8 March 1971', https://www.icao.int/secretariat/legal/List%20of%20Parties/Guatemala_EN.pdf.
14. Currently 51 ratifications; ICAO, 'Additional Protocol No. 1 to Amend the Warsaw Convention, signed at Warsaw On 12 October 1929, signed At Montreal on 25 September 1975', https://www.icao.int/secretariat/legal/List%20of%20Parties/AP1_EN.pdf.
15. Currently 52 ratifications; ICAO, 'Additional Protocol No. 2 to Amend the Warsaw Convention, signed at Warsaw On 12 October 1929 as Amended by the Hague Protocol done at The Hague On 28 September 1955, Signed At Montreal on 25 September 1975', https://www.icao.int/secretariat/legal/List%20of%20Parties/AP2_EN.pdf.
16. Currently 21 ratifications; ICAO, 'Additional Protocol No. 3 to Amend the Warsaw Convention, signed at Warsaw On 12 October 1929 as Amended by the Hague Protocol done at The Hague On 28 September 1955 and the Guatemala City Protocol done at Guatemala City on 8 March 1971, Signed At Montreal on 25 September 1975', https://www.icao.int/secretariat/legal/List%20of%20Parties/AP3_EN.pdf.
17. Currently 60 ratifications; ICAO, 'Additional Protocol No. 4 to Amend the Warsaw Convention, signed at Warsaw On 12 October 1929 as Amended by the Hague Protocol done at The Hague On 28 September 1955, Signed At Montreal on 25 September 1975', https://www.icao.int/secretariat/legal/List%20of%20Parties/MP4_EN.pdf.
18. Mendes de Leon, *supra* no. 10, at 152.
19. Ehrlich v. American Airlines, Inc., [2004] US CA (Second Circuit), at fn 4.
20. Weiss v. El Al Israel Airlines, Ltd., [2006] District Court, SD New York, at para. 11.
21. Montreal Convention 1999, *supra* no. 4, at Preamble, para. 3; Bin Cheng, 'A New Era in the Law of International Carriage by Air: From Warsaw (1929) to Montreal (1999)' 53 *International and Comparative Law Quarterly* 833 (2004), at 844-846.

and more specifically, the need for equitable compensation based on the principle of restitution.[22]

In order to achieve this objective, the Montreal Convention, which applies to all international carriage of persons, baggage, or cargo performed by aircraft for reward, and to gratuitous carriage by aircraft performed by an air transport undertaking,[23] provides different criteria for an air carrier to be held liable in cases of death and injury of passengers and damage to baggage,[24] damage to cargo,[25] and delay of passengers, baggage, or cargo.[26]

In the specific event of death and injury of passengers, the Montreal Convention – similar to the Warsaw Convention[27] – establishes a two-tier liability system of compensation, with the first tier being one of limited liability, and the second tier being one of unlimited liability.[28] More specifically, the first tier imposes strict liability on an air carrier which is limited at Special Drawing Right ('SDR', now also known as 'XDR') 128,821,[29] while the second tier imposes fault-based liability which starts at SDR 128,822 but does not have any upper limit.[30]

With regard to fault-based liability (imposed by the latter tier), an air carrier may avoid liability in excess of SDR 128,821 by invoking one of two defences: either that the damage was not due to its negligence or other wrongful act or omission, or that the damage was solely due to the negligence or other wrongful act or omission of a third party.[31]

The first defence can be effectively met if the air carrier proves force majeure which, however, is generally quite difficult to do in practice.[32] The second defence, although seemingly easier to meet, is less likely to be invoked by the air carrier since it will have to prove that the damage was caused by the negligence or other wrongful act or omission of a third party alone.[33]

22. Montreal Convention 1999, *supra* no. 4, at Preamble, para. 3.
23. *Ibid.*, Art. 1(1).
24. *Ibid.*, Art. 17.
25. *Ibid.*, Art. 18.
26. *Ibid.*, Art. 19.
27. Warsaw Convention 1929, *supra* no. 7, Art. 22. The Warsaw Convention does not impose a two-tier system of compensation; rather, it only imposes a singular form of liability which is limited at XFO 125,000 (i.e., Poincaré gold francs) per passenger, which amount was doubled under the Hague Protocol of 1971 to XFO 250,000 (i.e., Poincaré gold francs). *See*, Mendes de Leon, *supra* no. 10, at 183.
28. Montreal Convention 1999, *supra* no. 4, at Art. 21.
29. *Ibid.*, Art. 21(1). Formerly, the first tier had a limit of SDR 100,000, yet this was raised to SDR 113,000 as of 30 December 2009, and was further raised to SDR 128,821 as of 28 December 2019. ICAO, '2019 Revised Limits of Liability under the Montreal Convention of 1999', https://www.icao.int/secretariat/legal/Pages/2019_Revised_Limits_of_Liability_Under_the_Montreal_Convention_1999.aspx. *See*, for a concise summary of these increases, John Balfour and Pablo Mendes de Leon, 'Increase of the Limits Laid Down in the Convention for the Unification of Certain Rules for International Carriage by Air, Done at Montreal, 1999 (Montreal Convention, 1999)', 45(2) *Air and Space Law* 227-228 (2020), at 227.
30. Montreal Convention 1999, *supra* no. 4, at Art. 21(2).
31. *Ibid.*
32. Mendes de Leon, *supra* no. 10, at 182.
33. *Ibid.*

[A] Death or Injury of Passengers Resulting from a Cyberattack

In light of the above, it is possible to seek to determine whether air carriers could be held liable under the Montreal Convention for death or injury of passengers resulting from a cyberattack during international carriage by air.

In order to conduct such a determination, it is pertinent to scrutinise the notion of 'accident', not least because the Montreal Convention specifies that, in cases of death and injury, the air carrier is liable "upon condition only that the accident which caused the death or injury took place on board the aircraft or in the course of any of the operations of embarking or disembarking."[34]

Prior to delving into this terminological analysis, it must be clarified that a claim under the Montreal Convention will be brought before a national court of a State. Should an air carrier be subject to a cyberattack, and should passengers proceed to sue said carrier, it will, therefore, be up to the court seised of the matter to determine whether the cyberattack constitutes an accident in terms of the Montreal Convention or not.

At the outset, it must be made clear that the term 'accident' goes undefined under the Montreal Convention[35] as well as under the Warsaw Convention and the other legal instruments constituting the Warsaw System.[36]

This shortcoming was first rectified by the US Supreme Court in Air France v. Saks.[37] In this case, rather than defining what an accident is, the Supreme Court defined when an accident happens. According to the Supreme Court, an accident arises only if "a passenger's injury is caused by an unexpected or unusual event or happening that is external to the passenger."[38]

The US Supreme Court, while clarifying that this definition should be flexibly applied after an assessment of all the circumstances surrounding the injuries of a passenger,[39] added that an injured passenger is "only required to prove that some link in the chain of causes was an unusual or unexpected event external to the passenger,"[40] even though the said link in the causal chain must be attributable to the cause of the accident, and not merely the occurrence itself.[41]

The US Supreme Court elaborated further upon the notion of 'accident' in the subsequent case of Olympic Airways v. Husain.[42] In this case, the US Supreme Court stated that, according to *Saks*, the term 'accident' had two definitions, that is, either an

34. Montreal Convention 1999, *supra* no. 4, at, Art. 17(1).
35. Buckwalter v. US Airways, Inc., [2014] No. 12-2586, 2014 WL 116264 E.D. Pa.
36. Reference may be made to jurisprudence which interprets the term 'accident' under the Warsaw Convention. This is because cases which interpret a provision of the Warsaw Convention where the language employed in the Montreal Convention is substantively equivalent may be relied upon, as confirmed in the case of Baah v. Virgin Atlantic Airways Ltd. [2007] 473 F. Supp. 2d 591.
37. Air France v. Saks, [1985] 470 U.S. 392.
38. *Ibid.*
39. *Ibid.*
40. *Ibid.*
41. Mendes de Leon, *supra* no. 10, at 192.
42. Olympic Airways v. Husain, [2004] 541 U.S. 1007.

unintended event or an event that is unusual or unexpected whether it is the result of intentional action or not.[43]

Prior to proceeding further, reference must be made to GN v. ZU, decided by the Court of Justice of the European Union (CJEU) on the 19 December 2019.[44] In this case, a girl was sitting on board an aircraft next to her father, and when her father was served coffee during the flight, the cup, which was placed on the tray table in front of him, tipped over onto his thighs and onto the chest of his daughter.[45] As a result, the daughter suffered second-degree scalding.[46]

The CJEU was asked whether Article 17(1) of the Montreal Convention must be interpreted as meaning that the concept of 'accident' covers a situation in which an object used when serving passengers has caused bodily injury to a passenger, without it being necessary to examine whether that accident stems from a hazard typically associated with aviation.[47]

The CJEU held that:

> The ordinary meaning given to the concept of 'accident' is that of an unforeseen, harmful and involuntary event.
>
> [...]
>
> It follows that [...] making the carrier's liability subject to the condition that the damage is due to the materialisation of a hazard typically associated with aviation or to there being a connection between the 'accident' and the operation or movement of the aircraft is not consistent with the ordinary meaning of the concept of 'accident' referred to in Article 17(1) of the Montreal Convention or the objectives pursued by that convention.
>
> Furthermore, limiting the obligation on air carriers to pay compensation solely to accidents related to a hazard typically associated with aviation is not necessary in order to avoid imposing an excessive compensation burden on air carriers. As noted in paragraph 39 of the present judgment, those carriers may exclude or limit their liability.
>
> In those circumstances, the answer to the question referred is that Article 17(1) of the Montreal Convention must be interpreted as meaning that the concept of 'accident' within the meaning of that provision covers all situations occurring on board an aircraft in which an object used when serving passengers has caused bodily injury to a passenger, without it being necessary to examine whether those situations stem from a hazard typically associated with aviation.[48]

Consideration of this judgment is of particular relevance in the context at hand because this judgment can be distinguished from those common law judgments – such

43. *Ibid.*
44. GN v. ZU C-532/18 [2019].
45. *Ibid.*, at paras 13-14.
46. *Ibid.*, at para. 14. It could not be established whether the cup of coffee tipped over due to a defect in the folding tray table on which it was placed or due to vibration of the aircraft. *Ibid.*, at para. 15.
47. *Ibid.*, at para. 26. The Montreal Convention entered into force, so far as the EU is concerned, on the 28th of June 2004, and has, as from that date, been an integral part of the EU legal order. Accordingly, the CJEU has jurisdiction to give a preliminary ruling concerning its interpretation. *Ibid.*, at para. 30.
48. *Ibid.*, at paras 35-43.

as the above-mentioned *Saks* and *Husain* – which define the notion of 'accident'.[49] As a matter of fact, by defining 'accident' as "an unforeseen, harmful and involuntary event," and without requiring this to stem from an aviation hazard, the CJEU has effectively broadened the definition of 'accident'.[50]

Consequently, by following the reasoning of the CJEU in GN v. ZU, a cyberattack which causes physical injury to a passenger on board an aircraft is very much likely to lead to an accident since, in all probability, the cyberattack will bring about "an unforeseen, harmful and involuntary event" which, in turn, will cause physical injury to a passenger.

The analysis of 'accident' in *Saks* and *Husain*, which is not as broad as the analysis offered by the CJEU, has been both accepted and criticised – the latter, particularly, in the UK, Australia, and Canada[51] – by different courts around the world. In any event, it appears that there is unanimous agreement among the different courts on the fact that the notion of 'accident' – per *Saks* and *Husain* – encompasses torts committed by "terrorists or fellow passengers."[52]

This agreement among the different courts is of particular relevance in cases of cyberattacks on air carriers in two respects: first, it is relevant in terms of torts committed by terrorists; second, it is relevant in terms of torts committed by fellow passengers.

Reference to the possibility of torts being committed by terrorists is relevant in the context of the discussion at hand because cyberattacks[53] have a demonstrable element of terrorism to them. Indeed, and as exemplified in Chapter 1, the majority of cyberattacks to date, similar to terrorist attacks, appear to be conducted against States.[54]

In light of the fact that an aircraft does not offer much potential to be attacked for purely monetary reasons (unless, for example, it is used as ransom against the air carrier), it may be reasoned that most attacks against aircraft would be, in effect, attacks conducted against States. This thus qualifies any resultant damage as damage ensuing from torts conducted by terrorists, *ergo* as damage ensuing from accidents under the Montreal Convention.

In terms of torts committed by fellow passengers, this is also relevant because instances have already occurred where passengers committed cybersecurity breaches

---

49. Mark Welbourn and Sam Mason, 'CJEU Renders Decision on Meaning of "Accident" under Article 17 of the Montreal Convention', Kennedys, 6 January 2020, https://www.kennedyslaw.com/thought-leadership/case-review/cjeu-renders-decision-on-meaning-of-accident-under-article-17-of-the-montreal-convention.
50. *Ibid.*
51. Paul Stephen Dempsey, 'Accidents & Injuries in International Air Law: The Clash of the Titans', 24(2) *Korean Journal of Air & Space Law and Policy* 235 (2009), at 249. The courts of the UK, Australia and Canada disagree with the US Supreme Court because, unlike it, they hold that inaction cannot constitute an 'accident'. *See*, for an extensive analysis of this point, *Ibid.*, at 241.
52. Air France v. Saks, *supra* no. 37; Husain; Povey v. Qantas Airways Limited, [2005] HCA 33, McHugh J, at para. 74 and Kirby J, at para. 153; *Deep Vein Thrombosis and Air Travel Group Litigation*, [2005] UKHL 72, Lord Mance, at para. 66.
53. *See* Chapter 2, section §2.02[G].
54. Marco Roscini, *Cyber Operations and the Use of Force in International Law* (Oxford University Press, 2014), at 80.

while on board an aircraft. Case in point, between 2011 and 2014, a cybersecurity consultant allegedly hacked the in-flight entertainment systems, on several occasions, on various aircraft in which he was travelling, at one time even causing the aircraft to move laterally.[55]

Had this activity resulted in injury or death of another passenger or passengers, one may infer that, on the basis of the fact that *Saks* and *Husain* – as well as the courts critical thereof – agree that accident encompasses torts committed by fellow passengers, such injury or death would have been qualifiable as an accident under the Montreal Convention.

On this note, it must be pointed out that the person conducting such a cyberattack would not be necessarily able to claim compensation from the air carrier. If the air carrier proves that the damage or death was caused or contributed to by the negligence or other wrongful act or omission of the person claiming compensation, it shall be wholly or partly exonerated from its liability to the claimant to the extent that such negligence or wrongful act or omission caused or contributed to the damage.[56]

Ultimately, should a court deem a cyberattack to constitute an accident in terms of the Montreal Convention, Article 37 of this Convention provides air carriers with a right of recourse against third parties, meaning that air carriers may seek to take legal action against those – if identified – responsible for the cyberattack.

[B] Damage to Passengers Resulting from a Cyberattack Within the EU

Although the focus of this chapter is on liability of air carriers stemming from accidents, reference shall also be made to liability of air carriers stemming from delays.

This reference shall be specifically made within the context of the EU whereby such liability is regulated by Regulation 261/2004 of the European Parliament and of the Council of 11 February 2004 establishing common rules on compensation and assistance to passengers in the event of denied boarding and of cancellation or long delay of flights and repealing Regulation (EEC) 295/91.[57]

As stated in the third recital of Regulation 261/2004, the number of passengers denied boarding against their will and the number of passengers affected by cancellations without prior warning and long delays was too high notwithstanding that there already existed an EU regulation[58] which sought to address such a situation.[59]

---

55. Affidavit of FBI Agent Mark Hurley, at 12, para. 19(E), Application for a Search Warrant [2015] NDNY Case No. 5:15-MJ-00154 (ATB).
56. Montreal Convention 1999, *supra* no. 4, at Art. 20.
57. Regulation (EC) No 261/2004 of the European Parliament and of the Council of 11 February 2004 Establishing Common Rules on Compensation and Assistance to Passengers in the Event of Denied Boarding and of Cancellation or Long Delay of Flights, and Repealing Regulation (EEC) No 295/91, OJ L 46, 17 February 2004, pp. 1-8.
58. Council Regulation (EEC) No 295/91 of 4 February 1991 Establishing Common Rules for a Denied Boarding Compensation System in Scheduled Air Transport, OJ L 36, 8 February 1991, pp. 5-7.
59. Regulation 261/2004, *supra* no. 57, at Preamble para. 3.

Under the mantle of Regulation 261/2004, passengers are offered protection akin to that offered by the Warsaw System and the Montreal Convention.[60] The protection is 'akin' - rather than 'identical' - to that offered by the Warsaw System and the Montreal Convention for two reasons.

The first reason is that Regulation 261/2004 seeks to redress damage suffered by air passengers during air travel[61] only in cases of denied boarding, cancellation, and delay.[62] The second is that according to the CJEU in IATA and ELFAA v. Department for Transport,[63] the protection offered by Regulation 261/2004 relates to damage which is almost identical for every passenger and which can thus be compensated immediately and in a standardised manner.[64] This damage, the CJEU held, is different from that contemplated in the Warsaw System and Montreal Convention as the latter is unique for every passenger and can only be compensated upon a case-by-case assessment.[65]

Thus, by virtue of Regulation 261/2004, passengers are generally to be compensated in cases of denied boarding and cancellations.[66] Further, according to the jurisprudence of the CJEU and despite no express provision in Regulation 261/2004 to this specific end, passengers are also to be compensated for delays above three hours, which delays equate to cancellations.[67]

As held in Emeka Nelson and Others v. Deutsche Lufthansa AG, and TUI Travel plc and Others v. Civil Aviation Authority:

> Articles 5 to 7 of Regulation No 261/2004 must be interpreted as meaning that passengers whose flights are delayed are entitled to compensation under that regulation where they suffer, on account of such flights, a loss of time equal to or in excess of three hours, that is, where they reach their final destination three hours or more after the arrival time originally scheduled by the air carrier.[68]

In cases of cancellations, including delays longer than three hours, air carriers are exonerated from compensating passengers only if they can prove that the cancellation or delay was caused by "extraordinary circumstances which could not have been avoided even if all reasonable measures had been taken."[69]

60. The provisions of the Montreal Convention are applicable within the EU, as well as within a single Member State. Regulation (EC) No 889/2002 of the European Parliament and of the Council of 13 May 2002 amending Council Regulation (EC) No 2027/97 on Air Carrier Liability in the Event of Accidents, OJ L 140, 30 May 2002, pp. 2-5, Art. 1(2).
61. Sturgeon and Others v. Condor Flugdienst GmbH and Stefan Böck and Others v. Air France SA, Joined Cases C-402/07 and C-432/07 [2009], at para. 49.
62. Regulation 261/2004, *supra* no. 57, at Art. 1(1).
63. IATA and ELFAA v. Department for Transport, C-344/04 [2006].
64. *Ibid.*, at para. 43.
65. *Ibid.*
66. Regulation 261/2004, *supra* no. 57, at Arts 4, 5 and 7.
67. Martine de Serres, 'Consumer Protection', *in* Paul Stephen Dempsey and Ram S. Jakhu (eds), *Routledge Handbook of Public Aviation Law* (Routledge, 2017), at 330 and 334.
68. Joined Cases C-581/10 and C-629/10 [2010] ECLI:EU:C:2012:657, at para. 40. *See*, Sturgeon and Others v. Condor Flugdienst GmbH and Stefan Böck and Others v. Air France SA, *supra* no. 61, at para. 69.
69. Regulation 261/2004, *supra* no. 57, at Art. 5(3).

At this juncture, it is fitting to ask what 'extraordinary circumstances' are. This question was addressed by the CJEU in Wallentin-Hermann v. Alitalia[70] where a flight was cancelled as a result of a complex engine defect in the turbine which was discovered during a check the day before the flight.

The CJEU commenced by stating that, according to the preamble of Regulation 261, extraordinary circumstances may "occur in cases of political instability, meteorological conditions incompatible with the operation of the flight concerned, security risks, unexpected flight safety shortcomings and strikes that affect the operation of an air carrier."[71] Nevertheless, the CJEU clarified that these events in this indicative list in the preamble did not themselves constitute extraordinary circumstances, but could produce such circumstances.[72]

The CJEU acknowledged that this indicative list included unexpected flight safety shortcomings and that a technical problem in an aircraft may be amongst them. Yet, the CJEU held that the circumstances surrounding such an event can be characterised as extraordinary only if they relate to an event which is "not inherent in the normal exercise" of the activity of the air carrier concerned, and is "beyond the actual control" of that carrier on account of its nature or origin.[73]

The CJEU concluded that a technical problem in an aircraft which leads to the cancellation of a flight is not covered by the concept of 'extraordinary circumstances' within the meaning of Regulation 261/2004, unless that problem stems from events which, by their nature or origin, are not inherent in the normal exercise of the activity of the air carrier concerned, and are beyond its actual control.[74]

The logic behind this conclusion of the CJEU was that, as a matter of course in the exercise of their activity, air carriers are confronted with various technical problems to which aircraft operation inevitably gives rise, and it is precisely to avoid such problems and to take precautions against incidents compromising flight safety that those aircraft are subject to regular checks.[75]

The CJEU thus reasoned that the resolution of a technical problem caused by failure to maintain an aircraft must be regarded as inherent in the normal exercise of an air carrier's activity, and on that basis, technical problems which come to light during aircraft maintenance or on account of failure to carry out such maintenance cannot, in themselves, constitute extraordinary circumstances.[76]

Nevertheless, the CJEU added, it cannot be ruled out that technical problems are covered by those exceptional circumstances to the extent that they stem from events which are not inherent in the normal exercise of the activity of the air carrier concerned and are beyond its actual control, as would be damage to aircraft caused by acts of sabotage or terrorism.[77]

70. Wallentin-Hermann v. Alitalia, Case C-349/07 [2008].
71. Regulation 261/2004, *supra* no. 57, at Preamble para. 14.
72. Wallentin-Hermann v. Alitalia, *supra* no. 70, at para. 22.
73. *Ibid.*, at para. 23.
74. *Ibid.*, at para. 34.
75. *Ibid.*, at para. 24.
76. *Ibid.*, at para. 24-25.
77. *Ibid.*, at para. 26.

This caveat, that is, that certain technical problems may constitute extraordinary circumstances and that this would hold for damage to aircraft caused by acts of sabotage or terrorism, was reaffirmed by the CJEU in two subsequent cases, namely Siewert and Others v. Condor Flugdienst GmbH[78] and van der Lans v. Koninklijke Luchtvaart Maatschappij NV,[79] and it is very much relevant in cases of cyberattacks.[80]

Having already seen that cyberattacks are drawing closer to terrorist attacks, this caveat is relevant because, according to it, cyberattacks would therefore qualify as extraordinary circumstances under Regulation 261, thereby exonerating air carriers from compensating passengers in terms of that same Regulation.

Upon closer inspection, however, this conclusion is not particularly convincing. It is hereby contended that, although cyberattacks are indeed drawing constantly closer to acts of sabotage or terrorism, their classification as extraordinary circumstances on this basis is not altogether watertight.

This is particularly because:

> The European Commission currently regards cyber security as the number one challenge for the air transport industry. This reflects both the growing number of cyber attacks on airlines, airports and other industry players and the convergence of information technology with operational technology, which is creating new and critical areas of vulnerability across the industry.[81]

Considering that an extraordinary circumstance relates, *inter alia*, to an event which is *not inherent in the normal exercise* of the activity of air carriers, it would therefore be rather contradictory to classify cyberattacks as not inherent in the normal exercise of the activity of air carriers when, at present, they have virtually become part and parcel of the day-to-day concerns of the air transport industry, as noted by the European Commission itself.

In essence, it transpires that, although cyberattacks have been drawing closer to acts of sabotage or terrorism, they have contemporaneously become inherent in the normal exercise of the activity of air carriers so that classification thereof as extraordinary circumstances or otherwise is not as straightforward as it may seemingly be.

Cyberattacks consequently purport to hold a sui generis position in relation to extraordinary circumstances since, while upon prima facie inspection they correspond with acts of sabotage or terrorism, upon closer inspection they conversely correspond with events which are inherent in the normal exercise of the activity of the air carrier.

78. Siewert and Others v. Condor Flugdienst GmbH, Case C-394/14 [2014], at para. 19.
79. Lans v. Koninklijke Luchtvaart Maatschappij NV, Case C-257/14 [2015], at para. 38.
80. *See*, Benjamyn I Scott and Andrea Trimarchi, 'The Digital Aviation Industry: A Balancing Act Between Cybersecurity and European Consumer Protection', 42(4/5) *Air and Space Law* 443-462 (2017), at 447.
81. IATA, *Guidance Document: Crisis Communication and Reputation Management in the Digital Age – A Guide to Best Practice for the Aviation Industry*, 31 May 2019, at 31. Although the date of publication is not included in the document, the date of publication was extrapolated from IATA, 'IATA Publishes Latest Crisis Communication Best Practice Guidelines', https://www.airlines.iata.org/news/iata-publishes-latest-crisis-communications-best-practice-guidelines.

§8.02 LIABILITY IN THE CASE OF DAMAGE TO THIRD PARTIES

Liability in the case of damage to third parties stems from the Convention on Damage Caused by Foreign Aircraft to Third Parties on the Surface of 1952[82] (the 'Rome Convention') as amended in 1978,[83] which replaced the International Convention for the Unification of Certain Rules Relating to Damage Caused by Aircraft to Third Parties on the Surface of 1933 and its Additional Protocol for the Unification of Certain Rules Relating to Damage Caused by Aircraft to Third Parties on the Surface of 1938.

Although the Rome Convention is currently in force, States of geographical extensiveness and aviation importance such as Canada, France, Germany, the UK, and the US have not become parties thereto.[84] The absence of these types of States affects the effectiveness of the Rome Convention because, under it, "any person who suffers damage on the surface shall, upon proof only that the damage was caused by an aircraft in flight or by any person or thing falling therefrom, be entitled to compensation."[85]

In the various States where the Rome Convention does not apply, the applicable law to damage caused by aircraft on the surface is the national law of the State where the damage is caused.[86] In addition, national law always applies when the damage on the surface of a State is caused by an aircraft registered in the territory of that same State, the reason being that the Rome Convention only applies to damage on the surface of a State caused by an aircraft registered in the territory of another State.[87]

The Rome Convention further provides that liability for compensation attaches to the operator of the aircraft,[88] that is, the person who was making use of the aircraft at the time the damage was caused.[89] To this end, if control of the navigation of the aircraft was retained by the person from whom the right to make use of the aircraft was derived, whether directly or indirectly, that person shall also be considered the operator.[90]

---

82. Convention on Damage Caused by Foreign Aircraft to Third Parties on the Surface of 1952 (Rome Convention 1952), ICAO Doc. 7364/310 UNTS 182. Currently 51 ratifications; ICAO, 'Convention on Damage Caused by Foreign Aircraft to Third Parties on the Surface Signed at Rome on 7 October 1952', http://www.icao.int/secretariat/legal/List%20of%20Parties/Rome1952_EN.pdf.
83. Protocol to Amend the Convention on Damage Caused by Foreign Aircraft to Third Parties on the Surface of 1978, ICAO Doc. 9357. Currently 12 ratifications; ICAO, 'Protocol to Amend the Convention on Damage Caused by Foreign Aircraft to Third Parties on the Surface signed at Rome on 7 October 1952 Signed at Montreal on 23 September 1978', https://www.icao.int/secretariat/legal/List%20of%20Parties/Mtlpr78_EN.pdf.
84. Peter P.C. Haanappel, *The Law and Policy of Air Space and Outer Space: A Comparative Approach* (Kluwer, 2003), at 86.
85. Rome Convention 1952, *supra* no. 82, Art. 1(1).
86. Haanappel, *supra* no. 84, at 86.
87. Rome Convention 1952, *supra* no. 82, Art. 23.
88. *Ibid.*, Art. 2(1).
89. *Ibid.*, Art. 2(2)(a).
90. *Ibid.*, Art. 2(2)(a). In this respect, the Rome Convention further provides that the registered owner of the aircraft shall be presumed to be the operator and shall be liable as such unless, in the proceedings for the determination of his liability, he proves that some other person was the operator and, in so far as legal procedures permit, takes appropriate measures to make that other person a party in the proceedings. *See*, *Ibid.*, Art. 2(3).

The Rome Convention proceeds to provide two types of liability: limited liability and unlimited liability. Liability is limited in cases of both damage – to persons and property – and death. In cases of damage, compensation is limited according to the weight of the aircraft,[91] whereas, in cases of death, compensation is limited to XFO 500,000 (i.e., Poincaré gold francs) per person.[92]

Liability is to the contrary unlimited if the person who suffered the damage proves that it was caused by a deliberate act or omission of the operator, his servants, or agents acting in the course of their employment and within the scope of their authority, done with intent to cause damage.[93]

The Rome Convention provides that the operator of the aircraft can exonerate itself from liability if:

- the damage is a direct consequence of armed conflict or civil disturbance;[94] or
- the operator had been deprived of the use of the aircraft by an act of public authority;[95] or
- the operator proves that the damage was caused solely through the negligence or other wrongful act or omission of the person who suffers the damage, or of the servants or agents of this person.[96]

Of particular relevance in the context of cyberattacks is the possibility of the operator to exonerate itself from liability if the damage is a direct consequence of an armed conflict or civil disturbance. In this respect, it must be noted that (international) armed conflict "exists whenever there is a resort to armed force between States."[97]

While the possibility of classifying cyberattacks as 'armed force' has already been discussed in considerable depth, it is reiterated that a cyberattack may qualify as 'force' if it causes the damage normally produced by kinetic weapons.[98]

In the context of the Rome Convention, this threshold is likely to be met if damage is caused on the ground by an aircraft due to a cyberattack, meaning that, in such cases, in all likelihood, an operator would thus be able to exonerate itself from liability.

At this stage, concise reference can be made to the Convention on Compensation for Damage to Third Parties, Resulting from Acts of Unlawful Interference Involving

91. Rome Convention 1952, *supra* no. 82, Art. 11(1).
92. *Ibid.*, Art. 11(2).
93. *Ibid.*, Art. 12.
94. *Ibid.*, Art. 5.
95. *Ibid.*, Art. 5.
96. *Ibid.*, Art. 6(1).
97. Where violence between a State and a non-State armed group or between such groups has reached a threshold of intensity and the armed group or groups are operating with a certain level of organisation, the situation may be classified as a non-international armed conflict. *See*, Prosecutor v. Tadić et, ICTY, IT-94-1-T, 7 May 1997, at paras 561-568; and Prosecutor v. Limaj, Judgment, ICTY, IT-03-66-T, 30 November 2005, at para. 84; Daragh Murray, *Practitioners' Guide to Human Rights Law in Armed Conflict* (Oxford University Press, 2016), at 43.
98. Roscini, *supra* no. 54, at 47. *See* Chapter 3, section §3.03[A].

Aircraft (Unlawful Interference Compensation Convention)[99] which, although currently not in force, would prevail over the Rome Convention if it were to do so.

The Unlawful Interference Compensation Convention provides that it applies to damage caused to third parties, in the territory of a State Party, by an aircraft in flight on an international flight as a result of an act of unlawful interference.[100]

Of relevance in the context of cyberattacks is the definition of 'act of unlawful interference'. The Unlawful Interference Compensation Convention defines an 'act of unlawful interference' as an act which is defined as an 'offence' in the Convention for the Suppression of Unlawful Seizure of Aircraft[101] of 1970, or the Convention for the Suppression of Unlawful Acts Against the Safety of Civil Aviation[102] of 1971.[103]

According to the Convention for the Suppression of Unlawful Seizure of Aircraft of 1970, an offence is committed by any person who, on board an aircraft in flight:

(1) unlawfully, by force or threat thereof, or by any other form of intimidation, seizes, or exercises control of, that aircraft, or attempts to perform any such act, or
(2) is an accomplice of a person who performs or attempts to perform any such act.[104]

According to the Convention for the Suppression of Unlawful Acts Against the Safety of Civil Aviation of 1971, an offence is committed or attempted to be committed by any person – be such person the perpetrator or an accomplice – who unlawfully and intentionally:

(1) performs an act of violence against a person on board an aircraft in flight if that act is likely to endanger the safety of that aircraft; or
(2) destroys an aircraft in service or causes damage to such an aircraft which renders it incapable of flight or which is likely to endanger its safety in flight; or
(3) places or causes to be placed on an aircraft in service, by any means whatsoever, a device or substance which is likely to destroy that aircraft, or to

99. Convention on Compensation for Damage to Third Parties, Resulting from Acts of Unlawful Interference Involving Aircraft of 2009, ICAO Doc. 9920. Currently 9 ratifications/accessions; ICAO, 'Convention on Compensation for Damage to Third Parties, Resulting From Acts of Unlawful Interference Involving Aircraft of Done at Montreal on 2 May 2009', https://www.icao.int/secretariat/legal/List%20of%20Parties/2009_UICC_EN.pdf.
100. *Ibid.*, Art. 2(1).
101. Convention for the Suppression of Unlawful Seizure of Aircraft of 1970, ICAO Doc. 8920, Art. 1. Currently 185 ratifications; ICAO, 'Convention for the Suppression of Unlawful Seizure of Aircraft signed at the Hague on 16 December 1970', https://www.icao.int/secretariat/legal/List%20of%20Parties/Hague_EN.pdf.
102. Currently 188 ratifications. ICAO, 'Convention for the Suppression of Unlawful Acts Against the Safety of Civil Aviation Signed at Montreal on 23 September 1971', https://www.icao.int/secretariat/legal/List%20of%20Parties/Mtl71_EN.pdf.
103. Unlawful Interference Compensation Convention, *supra* no. 99, Art. 1(a).
104. Convention for the Suppression of Unlawful Seizure of Aircraft of 1970, Art. 1.

cause damage to it which renders it incapable of flight, or to cause damage to it which is likely to endanger its safety in flight;
(4) destroys or damages air navigation facilities or interferes with their operation, if any such act is likely to endanger the safety of aircraft in flight; or
(5) communicates information which he knows to be false, thereby endangering the safety of an aircraft in flight.[105]

In the event that an aircraft in flight causes damage to third parties in the territory of a State Party as a result of an act of unlawful interference as defined above, the Unlawful Interference Compensation Convention stipulates that the operator shall be liable to compensate the damage so caused.[106]

Notwithstanding that various acts are defined as offences in the Convention for the Suppression of Unlawful Seizure of Aircraft of 1970 and the Convention for the Suppression of Unlawful Acts Against the Safety of Civil Aviation of 1971, it is evident that not all such acts would be committed by cyberattacks.

In terms of the Convention for the Suppression of Unlawful Seizure of Aircraft of 1970, an act which would be potentially committed by a cyberattack is that of a person exercising control of an aircraft. Indeed, this happened when the cybersecurity consultant allegedly hacked the in-flight entertainment systems on various aircraft and at one time caused the aircraft to move laterally.[107]

In terms of the Convention for the Suppression of Unlawful Acts Against the Safety of Civil Aviation of 1971, three types of acts would be potentially committed by cyberattacks:

(1) the destruction of an aircraft in service or the causing of damage to it which renders the aircraft incapable of flight or which is likely to endanger its safety in flight;
(2) the destruction or damage to air navigation facilities or interference with their operation, if any such act is likely to endanger the safety of aircraft in flight; and
(3) the communication of information which a person knows to be false, thereby endangering the safety of an aircraft in flight.

Apart from these instances, it is hard to conceive how a cyberattack could qualify as an offence in terms of the Convention for the Suppression of Unlawful Seizure of Aircraft of 1970 and the Convention for the Suppression of Unlawful Acts Against the Safety of Civil Aviation of 1971, and consequently, as an act of unlawful interference in terms of the Unlawful Interference Compensation Convention.

105. Convention for the Suppression of Unlawful Acts Against the Safety of Civil Aviation of 1971, Art. 1.
106. Unlawful Interference Compensation Convention, *supra* no. 99, Art. 3(1).
107. *See* Chapter 8, section §8.01[A].

§8.03 OTHER CASES OF LIABILITY

In the present context of aviation liability, reference shall also be made to the Convention on the Suppression of Unlawful Acts Relating to International Civil Aviation[108] of 2010 (the 'Beijing Convention').

The Beijing Convention improves the provisions of the Convention for the Suppression of Unlawful Acts against the Safety of Civil Aviation[109] of 1971, as supplemented by the Protocol for the Suppression of Unlawful Acts of Violence at Airports Serving International Civil Aviation[110] of 1988, which criminalised the intentional engagement in an act of violence which is likely to endanger the safety of flight and air navigation facilities.[111]

To this end, the salient features of the Beijing Convention include the criminalisation of "an act of using civil aircraft in service as a weapon, an act of using certain dangerous substances to attack aircraft or other targets, an act for the unlawful air transport of biological, chemical and nuclear weapons, and an act of cyber attack on air navigation facilities."[112]

For the first time in an aviation treaty, the Beijing Convention explicitly states that an offence is committed when a person unlawfully and intentionally destroys or damages air navigation facilities – which "include signals, data, information or systems necessary for the navigation of the aircraft"[113] – or interferes with their operation if any such act is likely to endanger the safety of aircraft in flight.[114]

The Beijing Convention proceeds to state that each State Party may take the necessary measures to enable a legal entity located in its territory or organised under its laws to be held liable when a person responsible for management or control of that legal entity has, in that capacity, committed an offence set forth in Article 1.[115]

What is essential in this respect is that the Beijing Convention stipulates that such liability – that is, liability of a legal entity when a person responsible for its management or control has committed an offence – may be criminal, civil or administrative.[116]

108. Currently 31 ratifications/accessions; ICAO, 'Convention on the Suppression of Unlawful Acts Relating to International Civil Aviation Done at Beijing on 10 September 2010', https://www.icao.int/secretariat/legal/List%20of%20Parties/Beijing_Conv_EN.pdf.
109. Currently 188 ratifications. ICAO, 'Convention for the Suppression of Unlawful Acts Against the Safety of Civil Aviation Signed at Montreal on 23 September 1971', https://www.icao.int/secretariat/legal/List%20of%20Parties/Mtl71_EN.pdf.
110. Currently 176 ratifications. ICAO, 'Protocol for the Suppression of Unlawful Acts of Violence at Airports Serving International Civil Aviation, Supplementary to the Convention for the Suppression of Unlawful Acts Against the Safety of Civil Aviation, done at Montreal on 23 September 1971 Signed at Montreal On 24 February 1988', https://www.icao.int/secretariat/legal/List%20of%20Parties/VIA_EN.pdf.
111. Mendes de Leon, *supra* no. 10, at 503.
112. Jiefang Huang, 'Security Regulations: International Requirements', *in* Paul Stephen Dempsey and Ram S. Jakhu (eds), *Routledge Handbook of Public Aviation Law* (Routledge, 2017), at 149.
113. Convention on the Suppression of Unlawful Acts Relating to International Civil Aviation, ICAO Doc. 9960, 10 September 2010, Art. 1(1)(d).
114. *Ibid.*, Art. 2(c).
115. *Ibid.*, Art. 4(1).
116. *Ibid.*, Art. 4(1).

In the context of cyberattacks, the Beijing Convention thus allows States to take measures to enable a legal entity, located in its territory or organised under its laws, to be held civilly liable if a person responsible for its management or control unlawfully and intentionally destroys or damages air navigation facilities or interferes with their operation, if any such act is likely to endanger the safety of aircraft in flight.

Scrutiny of this conclusion of the Beijing Convention leads to the observation that the Beijing Convention only provides for the possibility of States taking measures to enable a legal entity to be held civilly liable, but not also a natural person or group of persons acting in a personal capacity.

Regardless of whether a State takes such measures or not, persons who commit a cyberattack in their personal capacity, that is, persons who commit a cyberattack and are not responsible for the management or control of a legal entity, are certainly still subject to civil liability under both national and international law.

§8.04 INSURANCE

In the introductory section of this chapter, it was determined that the legal concomitant of accidents is liability. In turn, it is contended, the by-product of the risk of being held liable for, among other things, an accident, is insurance and reinsurance.

Risk, in aviation, varies drastically not least because, as already seen, air carriers are potentially subject to liability from various angles such as injury and death of passengers and cargo, delays, and damage to third parties on the ground. To this end, insurance and reinsurance play a critical role in providing financial protection to air carriers against such risk.

While under international law, there is no universally recognised definition of what a contract of insurance is, for the purposes of this chapter, the definition provided under English law is deemed to suffice, that is:

> a contract for the payment of a sum of money, or for some corresponding benefit such as the rebuilding of a house or the repairing of a ship, to become due on the happening of an event, which event must have some amount of uncertainty about it, and must be of a character more or less adverse to the interest of the person effecting the insurance.[117]

From this definition, it follows that the role of insurers is not to remove or mitigate risk in itself, but to give security to the insured, in consideration of a price adequate to the risk, that the insured shall not suffer loss, damage, or prejudice by the happening of the perils specified to certain things which may be exposed to them.[118]

With the increased number of cyberattacks on air carriers, and with cybersecurity being the primary challenge for the air transport industry,[119] it is foreseeable that insurers and reinsurers will have to provide much more detailed coverage for cyber

117. Prudential Insurance Co v. Inland Revenue Commissioners, [1904] 2 KB 658, Per Channell J.
118. Lucena v. Craufurd, [1806] Bosauquet and Puller's New Report (1804-1807) 269, at 302.
119. IATA, *Guidance Document: Crisis Communication and Reputation Management in the Digital Age – A Guide to Best Practice for the Aviation Industry* (n 66).

risk[120] related thereto. Indeed, Munich Re, for instance, maintains that the (general) cyber insurance market could be writing USD 8 billion–USD 9 billion by the year 2020.[121]

[A] Applicable Insurance Law in Aviation

Compulsory insurance is a common requirement in the international liability treaties related to aviation. Starting with the Montreal Convention, its Article 50 requires air carriers to "maintain adequate insurance covering their liability under this Convention."[122] Conversely, however, the Warsaw Convention does not contain a compulsory insurance clause.[123]

Turning to the Rome Convention, its Article 15(1) stipulates that:

> Any Contracting State may require that the operator of an aircraft registered in another Contracting State shall be insured in respect of his liability for damage sustained in its territory for which a right to compensation exists under Article 1 by means of insurance up to the limits applicable according to the provisions of Article 11.

Within the EU, Regulation (EC) 785/2004 of the European Parliament and of the Council of 21 April 2004 on Insurance Requirements for Air Carriers and Aircraft Operators[124] regulates insurance requirements for air carriers and aircraft operators, and its objective is to establish minimum insurance requirements for air carriers and aircraft operators in respect of passengers, baggage, cargo and third parties.[125]

---

120. According to the European Insurance and Occupation Pensions Authority, which in turn cites the International Association of Insurance Supervisors, 'cyber risk' is 'any type of risk emanating from the use of electronic data and its transmission, including technology tools such as the internet and telecommunications networks. It also encompasses physical damage that can be caused by cybersecurity incidents, fraud committed by misuse of data, any liability arising from data storage, and the availability, integrity and confidentiality of electronic information – be it related to individuals, companies, or governments'. EIOPA, 'Understanding Cyber Insurance – A Structured Dialogue with Insurance Companies' (EIOPA, 2018), at 3; IAIS, 'Issues Paper on Cyber Risk to the Insurance Sector' (IAIS, 2016), at 4.
121. The Economist, 'Black Swans and Fat Tails: The Market for Cyber-Insurance is Growing', 26 January 2019, https://www.economist.com/finance-and-economics/2019/01/26/the-market-for-cyber-insurance-is-growing.
122. Montreal Convention 1999, *supra* no. 4, at Art. 50:

    > Insurance States Parties shall require their carriers to maintain adequate insurance covering their liability under this Convention. A carrier may be required by the State Party into which it operates to furnish evidence that it maintains adequate insurance covering its liability under this Convention.

123. Mendes de Leon, *supra* no. 10, at 183.
124. Certain liability limits have been updated by Commission Regulation (EU) No 285/2010 of 6 April 2010 Amending Regulation (EC) No 785/2004 of the European Parliament and of the Council on Insurance Requirements for Air Carriers and Aircraft Operators In Line with the Revised Limits Applicable under the Montreal Convention, OJ L 87, 7 April 2010, pp. 19-20.
125. Regulation (EC) No 785/2004 of the European Parliament and of the Council of 21 April 2004 on Insurance Requirements for Air Carriers and Aircraft Operators, OJ L 138, 30 April 2004, pp. 1-6, Art. 1(1).

Although aviation insurance has demonstrably been addressed on the international plateau, generally, aviation insurance is "governed by national law and the terms and conditions of insurance policies are defined and interpreted by national law."[126]

[B] Underwriting Considerations

An underwriter helps insurance companies determine whether the risk should be accepted, and insurance offered, and if so, what the necessary acceptance conditions to those risks should be.[127]

During this process, the underwriter must consider many aspects, such as the experience of the air carrier, the destinations and routes of flights, the age of the aircraft, the number of annual flight cycles, and the past safety record of the aircraft type. However, within the context of cyber risk, there are special considerations which must be given thereto.

First, insurers must contend with a constantly developing regulatory environment. The regulation of cybersecurity is currently very limited and fragmented as, while focus is mostly given to the criminalisation of certain acts under – virtually only – national law, regulation is fairly silent on ensuring the safe operation of a flight, over and above general safety, from cyberattacks.

This current regulatory deficiency is, however, likely to change with the growing mandate of EASA to explicitly address cybersecurity. Thus, as the relevant EU regulations on airworthiness, air operations, aircrew, and navigation get amended to cover cybersecurity, the regulatory landscape will inevitably change, thereby aiding underwriters in their considerations.

Second, on the one hand, attack methods are constantly evolving to either become more sophisticated or exploit vulnerabilities which would have been unthought of up until the attack. On the other hand, cybersecurity methods are adapting to such evolving attack methods. Therefore, considering that the cyberattack-defence dynamic is not static, underwriters must also take into consideration potential future risk that could manifest during the life of the policy.

Third, the specifics of the aviation industry should also be taken into account, particularly since aviation technology is constantly advancing so as to become more reliant on systems and networks. For instance, this could be particularly relevant if the aviation industry were to embrace and apply distributed ledger technology such as blockchain, which is an open, distributed ledger that can record transactions between two parties efficiently and in a verifiable and permanent way.[128]

126. Wolf Müller-Rostin, 'Part 9 insurance', *in* Stephan Hobe, Nicolai von Ruckteschell and David Hefferman (eds), *Cologne Compendium on Air Law in Europe* (Carl Heymanns Verlag, 2014), at 1095. *Note* that it is beyond the scope of this chapter to explore individual national laws.
127. Lionel Macedo, 'The Role of the Underwriter in Insurance', 1(8) *Primer Series on Insurance* (2009), at 1-2.
128. Marco Iansiti and Karim R. Lakhani, 'The Truth about Blockchain', HARV. BUS. REV., January-February 2017, https://hbr.org/2017/01/the-truth-about-blockchain. *See*, for more on the potential applications of distributed ledger technology, Roberto Cassar, 'Distributed Ledger

Last, a significant body of key statistics is collated throughout the life of aviation technology. Prior to being released to the public, an aircraft produces significant amounts of data and information through the airworthiness and type certification process, as do various aviation products in order to comply with product safety rules.

Following the release to the public, the aviation safety system provides for accident reporting. Nevertheless, not all aviation products – especially the older ones – are designed with cybersecurity in mind, and accident and incident reporting is currently not sufficient to fully encompass cybersecurity.

[C] Insurance Contract

Although aviation insurance contracts are tailor-made, insurers do however make extensive use of standard form policies. One such example is the AVN 1C General Form,[129] provided by the Aviation Insurance Clauses Group, which "contains standard policy and proposal forms as well as standard wording for clauses and endorsements that are frequently inserted into standard policy wordings in addition to or in place of existing policy provisions."[130]

The insurance contract provides financial cover against the fortuity of certain risk affecting persons or property. Although insurance is a specific type of contract, many jurisdictions have nevertheless constructed specific rules.[131] The specifics of each insurance contract, however, are found in the individual wording of the contract between the insurer and insured.

As each contract differs from one another, the standard template AVN 1C, which provides the aviation industry with a number of standard clauses that can be incorporated into a policy, will be analysed. AVN 1C is an all-risk insurance, meaning that "the insuring clause provides that loss or damage is covered but without qualification as to the cause of the loss."[132] It is the obligation of the insured to show that one of the covered perils has occurred and then, the burden of proof rests with the insurer to show that an exclusion applies.

It is common for an insurance contract to provide exclusions, which serve "to limit the scope of the policy by removing types of loss from the ambit of the insuring clause such that a claim may be denied without affecting the validity of the policy."[133]

Relevant to cybersecurity is exclusion clause 10, in section 4(A) of AVN 1C, which excludes cover for war, hijacking, and allied perils:

Technology in the Airline Industry: Potential Applications and Potential Implications', 83(3) *Journal of Air Law and Commerce* 455 (2018).

129. A variant thereof was produced in 2014, this being 'AVN 1D', which provides similar cover. *See*, Mendes de Leon, *supra* no. 10, at 418.

130. Müller-Rostin, *supra* no. 126, at 1099.

131. *See*, John Birds, et al., *McGillivray on Insurance Law*, Twelfth Edition (Sweet & Maxwell, 2012), at Chapter 11.

132. Nicholas Medniuk, 'Aspects of Insurance for Unmanned Aircraft Systems', *in* Benjamyn Scott (ed.), *The Law of Unmanned Aircraft Systems: An Introduction to the Current and Future Regulation of UAS under National, Regional and International Law* (Kluwer, 2016), at 97.

133. *Ibid.*, at 100.

This policy does not apply to claims caused by:

(a) War, invasion, acts of foreign enemies, hostilities (whether war be declared or not), civil war, rebellion, revolution, insurrection, martial law, military or usurped power or attempts at usurpation of power.
(b) Any hostile detonation of any weapon of war employing atomic or nuclear fission and/or fusion or other like reaction or radioactive force or matter.
(c) Strikes, riots, civil commotions or labour disturbances.
(d) Any act of one or more persons, whether or not agents of a sovereign Power, for political or terrorist purposes and whether the loss or damage resulting therefrom is accidental or intentional.
(e) Any malicious act or act of sabotage.
(f) Confiscation, nationalisation, seizure, restraint, detention, appropriation, requisition for title or use by or under the order of any Government (whether civil military or de facto) or public or local authority.
(g) Hi-jacking or any unlawful seizure or wrongful exercise of control of the Aircraft or crew in Flight (including any attempt at such seizure or control) made by any person or persons on board the Aircraft acting without the consent of the Insured.

While the wording of this clause does not explicitly cover cyberattacks, it is hereby argued that the inclusion of terms such as "any act for political or terrorist purposes," "any malicious act or act of sabotage," "hijacking," and "wrongful exercise of control" may nevertheless include cyberattacks within their remit.

For instance, in the event that a cyberattack causes the aircraft to become inoperable, one may argue that that aircraft was sabotaged. Further, the "hi-jacking or any unlawful seizure or wrongful exercise of control of the aircraft" could be likewise interpreted to include cyberattacks such as spoofing or cyberattacks which allow the attacker to control the aircraft.[134]

In addition, it is for the national courts which have jurisdiction over the contract to interpret either whether cyber risk falls under the scope of AVN 1C and is, therefore, covered by the general policy, or whether it is excluded due to the broad wording of the above-mention exclusion clause. To this end, one should not overlook the fact that:

> Well-established principles of contract interpretation require that an insurance policy be construed according to the entirety of the terms and conditions as set forth in the policy and as amplified in any attached documentation. In interpreting the meaning of an insurance policy, courts apply the plain meaning of the words and phrases used in the contract to the facts before it. Any ambiguity in insurance policies are construed against the insurer and in favour of coverage.[135]

In this respect, it would be thus ideal for the inclusion or exclusion of cyber risk to be expressly addressed by the wording of the insurance contract, whether such wording be to include cyber risk from the general coverage or to exclude it therefrom. Moreover, in order to address cyber risk as broadly as possible, the inclusion or exclusion of liability relating to privacy breaches, data breaches, and trespass could also be expressly addressed by the wording of the insurance contract.

134. *Ibid.*, at 101.
135. Müller-Rostin, *supra* no. 126, at 1098.

Still further, it may be the explicit desire of the parties to the insurance contract to refrain from including the content of the above-mentioned exclusion clause in whole or in part. Nevertheless, a write-back clause may be included in the insurance contract, thereby causing the reintroduction of coverage for certain items which would have been originally excluded. Alternatively, a specialised war risk policy can be taken out.

While this exposes a potential issue for insurance, it demonstrates a wider issue that the exclusions found in the above-mentioned clause are linked to more classical aviation risks, such as the use of weapons and in situ hijacking. Thus, there could be a tendency by the aviation insurance market to view cybersecurity along the same classical lines, which would inadvertently fail to take into account the complexities of the novel implications of cybersecurity.

§8.05 CONCLUSION

Liability features strongly in the aviation industry. Legislation thereof is abundant, as is the ensuing litigation thereon which, more likely than not, will persist for the foreseeable future. With cyberattacks on constant growth, legislation and litigation related to liability can be expected to evolve.

Liability, in the context of aviation, can be divided into liability in the case of damage to passengers and liability in the case of damage to third parties. In terms of the former, it is yet to be seen whether cyberattacks leading to physical injury to a passenger on board an aircraft shall be classified as ‘accidents’ in accordance with the Montreal Convention. Likewise, it is yet to be seen whether the CJEU would classify a cyberattack leading to a delay as an ‘extraordinary circumstance’, thereby exonerating airlines from paying compensation.

In terms of liability in the case of damage to third parties, it seems more probable that, in the case of a cyberattack leading to such damage, airlines would still be liable for damages. One possible method of exoneration from liability, however, is if the damage is a direct consequence of armed conflict or civil disturbance.

Finally, turning to insurance, it is possible to see that cyberattacks may provide difficulties to the parties to insurance policies. Problems may, for instance, arise in terms of policy cover (or lack thereof), not least because many policies tend to provide that they do not cover claims caused by, *inter alia*, war, hostilities, and rebellion. Should cyberattacks be considered as means of warfare, or even as means of political or civil rebellion, any damages ensuing therefrom may prove to be unclaimable.

Cyberattacks shall certainly lead to interesting legal questions in the context of liability and aviation, and the courts or bodies seized with answering them shall have to tread cautiously, keeping in mind that cyberattacks are no longer exceptional means used by the few, but more common means which are consistently growing in terms of frequency and breadth.

CHAPTER 9

Lessons Learned

§9.01 INTRODUCTION

It is widely recognised that all IT systems have intrinsic vulnerabilities that can be potentially exploited by actors with malicious intent, and that there is no panacea known today against these kinds of dangers and their shifting nature. Furthermore, the conflict between cyberattacks and defence activities seems to have an inherent asymmetrical nature, as the former are in constant development, whereas it is difficult for the latter to keep pace and identify vulnerabilities, anticipate attacks and implement the necessary defences.

The recognition of this asymmetry does not imply, though, that stakeholders should refrain from developing defence mechanisms with the purpose to mitigate threats and manage their consequences. The key element in implementing an effective defence strategy is to adopt a multidisciplinary approach based on technological solutions, organisational elements, procedures and human skills. This chapter will navigate through the main cybersecurity principles and strategies on the basis of international standards and industry practice, connecting them with the other chapters of this book. Although space activities and air transport have their own peculiarities and may require additional tailored measures, the cyber defence strategies described in this chapter are transversal across sectors and need to be applied by all stakeholders relying on cyberspace independently of the specific field of activity.

§9.02 INCREASING NUMBER OF CYBERATTACKS

As it clearly emerges from the previous chapters, and even more from daily experience, the advent of cyberspace has changed the world at multiple levels. The nature of cyberspace has changed over the years, mutating from an environment made of isolated, self-reliant systems to a network of interdependent systems fundamentally interconnected via digital means such as the Internet and its protocols. What happens in the digital world, furthermore, not only matters due to its predominant role in the collection, management and transmission of information but also due to the increasing impact that it has on the material world.[1] This becomes even more relevant when one thinks about the increasing interaction between the two worlds via the technological revolutions carried out by the IoT, and the automation of industrial and commercial processes. These changes come together with an evolution of related security threats which have similarly evolved in their nature and in the harmful consequences that they can inflict. A cyber threat against a certain target nowadays constitutes a potential danger against all subjects connected to the target via the Internet or other digital means, whether the subject is an individual user, a private entity or a governmental organisation, and this threat might have consequences far beyond the original intent.

§9.03 GENERAL CHARACTERISTICS OF A CYBERATTACK

[A] Attackers

The landscape of cyber threats is becoming increasingly complex, showing a great diversification in terms of employed techniques, motivations, identity of attackers and types of damage inflicted. The actors with a malicious intent range from amateurs, employing simple software solutions to probe the web, to States with massive amounts of resources and technical sophistication aiming at geopolitical objectives. Given the evolving nature of the field, a non-exhaustive list of such actors is hereby presented.

[1] White Hat v. Black Hat hackers

Originally, the term 'hacker' had a neutral connotation, and just indicated "a person who enjoys exploring the details of programmable systems and how to stretch their capabilities, as opposed to most users, who prefer to learn only the minimum necessary."[2] With time, however, the term has gained an intrinsically negative connotation and has been used by mainstream media to indicate individuals that use their skills to sneak into other people's computers or networks. Whereas the term 'hacking' encompasses different activities and has multiple illegal profiles, it is necessary to distinguish 'White Hat' hackers from 'Black Hat' hackers. While the former often work as security consultants in the software industry and contribute to security by identifying and fixing vulnerabilities, the latter ones illegally break into systems and exploit their flaws, not necessarily for profit, but also to show off or to practice their skills. The community of Black Hat hackers has developed a form of

1. For instance, in the framework of the 'Operation Olympic Games' allegedly launched by the US Government against Iran starting from 2006, the malicious computer worm called 'Stuxnet' eventually resulted in the physical damage of several Iranian nuclear centrifuges. *See*, for more information, Kim Zetter, *Countdown to Zero Day* (Crown Publishers, 2014). For a definition of the terms cyberspace and cyberattack *see* Chapter 2, sections §2.02[A], §2.02[G].
2. Ben Yagoda, 'A Short History of Hack', https://www.newyorker.com/tech/annals-of-technology/a-short-history-of-hack.

subculture and proclaimed its own ethical principles, which distinguishes them from cybercriminals. If a hacker engages in activities considered as unethical by the community, they could be 'excommunicated'.

[2] States

State actors have quickly integrated cyber into their espionage and warfare strategies, and are increasingly investing to build up and improve their offensive and defensive capabilities in this domain. Even if attackers do not need to be of significant size or sophistication to inflict considerable damage, the major disposability of resources and technologies allows States to more profoundly infiltrate and leverage critical information or infrastructure of other States. Several goals and strategies can be pursued with different levels of disruptiveness: the 'passive' gathering of intelligence for cautionary reasons; the theft of intellectual property and sensitive information for domestic financial or political gains; or the exercise of active control over other States' networks, for instance, to remotely disable critical enemy technologies and services. State capabilities can be directed not only against other States but also against non-State actors, such as multinational tech companies, humanitarian organisations and financial institutions.

[3] State-Sponsored Entities

Although not formed by personnel under the direct control of States, these groups are supported by the latter to pursue geopolitical goals such as the theft of sensitive data from sensitive targets or the cyber aggression against foreign critical infrastructure providers.

[4] Cyber-Terrorists

This category engages in cyber activities to serve a broader long-term objective, which is normally political in nature but characterised by anti-society crimes. The short-term purpose of such actors is mainly to raise funds to finance their activities, but also to gain visibility or directly harm the targeted individuals or entities.

[5] Hacktivists

Hacktivists are hackers that use their abilities – individually or in a group – to pursue a political or social agenda that they consider of broader interest. They may be engaged in illegal activities, such as breaking into computer networks without permission and possibly causing damage. Like terrorists, they are motivated by a broader goal. Certain elements, however, distinguish them from the latter: they do not seek to raise financial resources for their activities and do not wilfully engage in crimes that will harm people's lives or finances. The distinction, however, is blurry.

[6] Cybercriminals

The normal purpose of criminals is financial gain, whether direct or indirect. In order to raise money, they engage in direct methods like the theft of credit card information or breaking into banking systems to illicitly move funds. Examples of indirect methods, on the other hand, are stealing sensitive information for blackmailing or for other forms of extortion. Organised criminal groups may have the structure, funding and sophistication to set up larger and more effective attacks, and make better use of the stolen financial information.

[7] Insiders

People inside an entity or inside a supply chain can use their access privileges to get past the cybersecurity defences in place and cause harm. Normally, they belong to two categories: disaffected employees, who act out of resentment and aim to cause damage to the begrudged organisation or person; and opportunists, who act to achieve financial gain with the expectation not to be detected. These should be distinguished from persons, such as employees, who are unknowingly or unwillingly exploited in an attack.[3]

[B] Attack Methods

There are several cyber tools used by malicious actors to achieve their goals and interfere with the targeted systems. These tools can be specific malicious software, also called malware or just techniques that, despite not identifying with the use of particular malicious software, still involve the use of cyberspace. Furthermore, there are techniques that, despite not taking place in cyberspace, still affect IT systems.

Some of the most common types of malware include:

- Viruses and Worms: These are programs that infect other programs or files and carry on their harmful effects like corrupting or deleting information. They are designed to replicate themselves.
- Trojans: They are designed to provide to the attacker a backdoor to access and capture protected information.
- Ransomware: Their function is to encrypt files in a system or network, rendering them inaccessible and possibly destroying them. The files will be made accessible again upon payment of a ransom.
- Botnets: Secretly taking control of the targeted system, they submit it to the instructions of a master server. They spread creating a network of entangled

3. *See,* for a comprehensive overview of the main categories of malicious cyber actors, Georg Kerschischnig, *Cyberthreats and International Law* (Eleven, 2012), at 23-31; Rauf Meeuwisse, *Cybersecurity for Beginners* (Lulu Publishing Services, 2015), at 210-229. *See,* for a detailed description of the most impactful existing groups of attackers, Thales and Verint, *The Cyberthreat Handbook* (2019).

computers, and as a result, the originator of the attack is extremely difficult to locate.

The most common types of techniques include:

- Denial of Service: In this technique, the attacker overloads a server with a number of rapid and continuous requests that it cannot handle, causing networks to crash or at least slowdown.
- Infiltration: It can be digital or physical. In the former case, the attacker acts remotely and breaches into the system via cyberspace. In the latter, the premises where the target system is located are materially infiltrated, and the system is accessed – for instance, via a USB pen.
- Probing, Sniffing and Mapping: They account for preparatory activities to the main cyber operation. In this phase, the attacker searches for backdoors and vulnerabilities of the target system, and it can take a long period of time.
- Anonymisation: The attacker affects and 'hops over' several intermediate systems before aiming for the targeted one. As a result, the original source is very difficult to locate. The use of anonymisation techniques and the resulting challenge in the identification of malicious actors is one of the main challenges in modern cybersecurity.
- Eavesdropping: The act of secretly intercepting the private digital communications between two points in a network, normally via the use of specialised programs.
- Phishing: The attacker sends an electronic message – for instance, an email – to the designated victims, pretending to be a legitimate sender. By opening an attachment or clicking on a link to a webpage, the recipient allows the malware to take control of the device.
- Tampering: It consists of accessing and modifying data in rest or in transit by destroying, manipulating, or editing it.

Techniques that instead do not take place in the cyberspace, but still affect IT systems are:

- Jamming and Spoofing: These techniques do not effectively take place via cyberspace, but rather via the radio spectrum in the form of an electromagnetic signal that disturbs or replaces the legitimate one and affects the functioning of a radio-communication apparatus.[4]

4. *See*, for a deeper overview of malicious cyber tools and techniques, Kerschischnig, *supra* no. 3, at 31-39; Scott E. Donaldson, et al., *Enterprise Cybersecurity: How to Build a Successful Cyberdefense Program Against Advanced Threats* (Apress, 2015), at Appendix A. For further explanation of certain terms, *see also*, Chapter 2, sections §2.02[G], §2.02[I], §2.04[E], §2.04[L], §2.05[B], §2.05[E].

[C] Victims

As illustrated by the various examples analysed throughout the previous chapters, virtually any physical person or organisation, whether governmental or non-governmental, can be subject to cyberattacks. The aerospace sector makes no exception and needs to take cybersecurity into primary consideration during all its activities – including the design, development and operation of aircraft and spacecraft. This requires all involved stakeholders to implement adequate cybersecurity measures and coordinate with each other. Space and aviation, however, are characterised by certain peculiarities that increase their vulnerability when compared to other sectors. They both rely on complex and highly integrated supply chains involving different entities with dissimilar cyber defence capabilities. Moreover, all actors involved in the aerospace industry are increasingly dependent on each other directly or indirectly. Also, they are involved in activities with a strong relation with a safety-of-life element, such as the provision of navigation and positioning signals to aircraft in flight.

All these factors make the necessity for increased attention to cybersecurity even more pressing. An illustrative list of potentially targeted entities includes:

- States and Public Agencies: These encompass governments and public entities in charge of regulatory and monitoring functions, such as ministries and national aviation authorities, but also operational entities such as space agencies.
- International Organisations and EU Agencies: On the international level, the same can be said of international organisations, which can have coordination and regulatory functions, such as ICAO, or an operational mandate such as EUROCONTROL or ESA; at the EU level, particular attention should be given to EASA and the European GNSS Agency.
- Manufacturers: the aviation and space industries heavily rely on the manufacturing of ground, air or space components by large multinational companies, such as Airbus or Boeing, and on the connected supply chains of small and medium enterprises, as well as on the design of sophisticated software.
- Operators: This category comprises mainly airlines, air navigation service providers and satellite services providers, including governmental-controlled GNSS systems, in a situation where the former are increasingly dependent on the latter for the provision of safety and non-safety communication and navigation services.
- Airports and Launch Sites: An attack against the ground infrastructure would also have a great impact as it would paralyse civilian flights or the launch of spacecraft from a certain location for an unforeseeable amount of time.
- Users: final users might be targeted as well. The victims in this category could be members of the general public making use of satellite-based services and apps on their devices, or passengers using onboard Wi-Fi during flight.

Thus, it is necessary to ensure close cooperation among all actors and possibly to consider the development of a shared cybersecurity strategy.[5] A paradigmatic example of effective cooperation is represented by the action of 'IOActive', a White Hat cybersecurity company that found vulnerabilities in the passenger Wi-Fi on-board of aircraft provided through satellites. IOActive made EASA aware of this through 'responsible disclosure'. Once EASA was made aware, it coordinated with involved operators and authorities, then performed independent verifications. As IOActive was only able to access passengers' phones, laptops and tablets, there was no risk from aviation safety and security perspective as access to the aircraft could not be gained. The vulnerability was then closed. This example shows the clear benefit of the cross-sector exchange of information, as well as the need for close collaboration among different aviation stakeholders. Additionally, it demonstrates the utility of White Hats in improving cybersecurity and the need for continuous monitoring of old and new technologies.[6]

[D] Life Cycle

A malicious cyber operation does not normally consist of one single malicious act, but rather of different activities distinguished in time and type, the understanding of which is essential to establish adequate defensive measures. Such activities can be distinguished, generally, between cyberattacks, aimed at causing harm to the victim, and cyber exploitation, aimed at stealing sensitive data from the target system.[7] Each of these activities is rather unique, but there are certain steps that are mostly common as briefly illustrated hereunder:

- Initial Reconnaissance: This step has the purpose of providing the attacker with the essential information to identify the target and its vulnerabilities. It can consist of passive activities, such as analysing traffic, monitoring communications, and intercepting authentication information and credentials. It can also refer to more intrusive measures, such as standing outside of the victim's premises, following employees or stealing equipment.
- Penetration and Gaining a Foothold: Penetration is the activity by which the attacker compromises the target system, and this can take place by several means, for instance, phishing malware. Once access has been gained, it is necessary to ensure continuous access and control, for instance, by creating a hidden backdoor in the software, or by appropriating login credentials.

5. In case of aviation, for instance, there is a comprehensive European Aviation Strategy developed by EASA. *See*, EASA, 'ESCP: Strategy for Cybersecurity in Aviation', https://www.easa.europa.eu/sites/default/files/dfu/Cybersecurity%20Strategy%20-%20First%20Issue%20-%2010%20September%202019.pdf. *See* Chapter 7.
6. EASA, 'Engaged in a "Responsible Disclosure" of Cybersecurity Issues in Coordination with Operators and Authorities', August 2018, https://www.easa.europa.eu/newsroom-and-events/news/easa-engaged-"responsible-disclosure"-cybersecurity-issues-coordination.
7. Infosec, 'Cyber-exploitation', February 2013, https://www.resources.infosecinstitute.com/cyber-exploitation/.

- Following Access: In this step, the attacker can proceed with the internal exploration of the target system, in order to achieve a better understanding of it and locate further sensitive files and information. Once inside, the attack can be extended to other computers within the same network in a technique called 'lateral movement'.
- Exfiltration: Proper to cyber exploitation activities, it consists of transferring data from the compromised system to the attacker or to third parties. Exploitation activities are normally clandestine in nature and do not have the immediate purpose of causing harm to the victim. A negative effect can, however, manifest itself at a later moment when the stolen data is used.
- Malware Insertion and Clean Up: Cyberattacks, on the contrary, usually aim at harming the victim. This takes place by implanting malicious software that carries on whatever task it has been designed for, and a subsequent clean up whose purpose is to erase the evidence and traces of the attack.[8]

§9.04 PURPOSE OF CYBERSECURITY MEASURES

As has been clarified in the previous chapters, the usual target of a cyberattack is information and data. It is important, however, to recall that the concept of cybersecurity is distinguished from information security, although they are often used interchangeably. Whereas the former is associated with protecting and securing anything in cyberspace, the latter pertains to the protection of information, whether in digital form or otherwise.[9] More specifically, information security refers to the protection of information and information systems from unauthorised access, use, disclosure, disruption, modification, recording or destruction in order to provide confidentiality, integrity, and availability.[10] The concept of information security, therefore, despite being autonomous, is a key element of cybersecurity and related strategies.

This concept is summarised in the so-called CIA Triad. Such term, elaborated in 1995 by the (US) National Institute of Standard and Technology (NIST),[11] stands for 'Confidentiality, Integrity and Availability', and identifies the essential properties of information security. In particular, according to the International Standard ISO/IEC 27000 definitions:

- 'confidentiality' is concerned with the protection of sensitive data from unauthorised disclosure. It ensures that computer-related assets are only accessed by authorised parties. Being authorised to 'access' a particular asset means viewing, printing or simply knowing about the existence of the asset.

8. Infosec, 'The Cyber Exploitation Life Cycle', March 2013, https://resources.infosecinstitute.com/the-cyber-exploitation-life-cycle/#gref.
9. RM Studio, 'Information Security-vs-Cybersecurity', https://www.riskmanagementstudio.com/information-security-vs-cybersecurity/.
10. NIST Special Publication 800-53, Revision 2.
11. NIST, 'Home', https://www.nist.gov.

- 'integrity' is concerned with the correctness or accuracy, preventing data modifications by unauthorised users. It means that only authorised parties can modify, create, delete, change status etc. on computer-related assets.
- 'availability' concerns having the right access to computer-related assets at the right time. It assures that a system's authorised users have timely and uninterrupted access to the data.[12]

Although elaborated more than twenty years ago, this conceptual framework is still relevant today and constitutes the theoretical basis for defining security goals are defined and upon which the need for a specific application and software security is assessed.

§9.05 CONTROL TYPES

Any sound cybersecurity approach needs to be of a multidisciplinary nature in order to cover all possible threat vectors.[13] Four different types of controls can be identified: 'physical', 'technical', 'procedural' and 'legal'.[14]

Physical controls refer to "measures designed to deter, prevent, detect or alert unauthorised real-world access to a site or material item."[15] These are security measures designed to protect IT assets against unauthorised access and intentional theft or destruction and can take the shape of traditional controls such as perimeter security around office buildings, or controls that are more specific focusing on the computers, peripherals and storage media.[16] Physical security is often overlooked in the context of cybersecurity, but without such controls, sophisticated cyberattacks become unnecessary as the attacker could simply access a building and walk out with sensitive data with little investment in time, money and other resources. This would circumvent any technical controls put in place by the target entity and turn it into a wasted investment.

Technical controls are the core element of cybersecurity strategies. They constitute "the use of an electronic or digital method to influence or command how something is or is not able to be used,"[17] and they include, *inter alia*, anti-malware software, firewalls and encryption. Due to their key importance, it is appropriate to briefly describe these tools.

Anti-malware software is a "security technology that catches malware by identifying its malicious behaviours, such as unusual network connections or attempts to change the operating system. Anti-virus vendors frequently label their products anti-malware when they have advanced features."[18]

12. ISO/IEC 27000. *See*, Jason Andress, *The Basics of Information Security*, Second Edition (Syngress, 2014), at 5.
13. Donaldson, et al., *supra* no. 4, at 39.
14. Meeuwisse, *supra* no. 3, at 48-50. *See also*, Andress, *supra* no. 12, at 15.
15. *Ibid.*, at 49.
16. Steven Chabinsky, 'Securing the Physical Side of Cybersecurity', https://www.securitymagazine.com/articles/86472-securing-the-physical-side-of-cybersecurity.
17. Meeuwisse, *supra* no. 3, at 50.
18. Donaldson, et al., *supra* no. 4, at 467.

Firewall is a "security capability that connects to a network and applies a security policy to determine what network traffic is allowed to pass and what network traffic is blocked. It can also alert on certain types of network traffic that might indicate an attack."[19]

Encryption, on the other hand, is a "cryptographic technique for protecting data so it can only be read by holders of the legitimate key. The effectiveness of encryption is dependent on the strength of the algorithms used, computation of strong pseudo-random number sequences, the length of the encryption key used, the distribution of the encryption key over its life cycle, and numerous other technical factors."[20]

The procedural controls consist of "the use of a sequence of steps to influence or command how something is or is not able to be used."[21] It normally consists of either the establishment of rules, working methods or steps in which authorised users should operate, or means to set controls in the technology so as to ensure it is used in an authorised way. This can include, for instance, the prohibition of the use of external USB sticks as these can carry malware from less secure computers.

The fourth kind of control is the legal one. Such measures are of a legislative and contractual nature. The former are aimed at "promoting and investing in positive security methods and also to deter and correct infringements,"[22] while the latter are implemented by companies on a private foot in their relations with customers and suppliers. They concern aspects like the implementation of technical measures, caps on liability and audit.

In order to have effective cybersecurity, all four types of control need to be implemented. For example, if there are insufficient technical controls, then a victim may never know that it has been attacked or the lack of tools may not allow the attacker to be identified. In a similar case, the need for reactive legal controls is null as legal sanctions cannot be placed on an attacker when identification is impossible.

§9.06 MEASURES TO INCREASE CYBERSECURITY

[A] Law and Regulations

Defending oneself or one's property from cyberattacks is a complex issue that does not involve only technology-based measures. It requires a complex, multidisciplinary approach and knowledge, and needs to be based on a comprehensive, risk management strategy able to take into account all possible vulnerabilities. At first, any operator needs to be aware of the applicable national and supra-national legal framework and implement all the measures and policies there established.[23]

19. *Ibid.*, at 471.
20. *Ibid.*
21. Meeuwisse, *supra* no. 3, at 122.
22. *Ibid.*
23. *See* Chapters 3, 4.

In an attempt to address pressing questions of cybersecurity and to create national cyber regulation, States are establishing defence centres and issuing cybersecurity strategies against cyberattacks in close cooperation with police and national secret services, but also with the help of non-governmental entities and the private industry, in order to enhance knowledge and to develop capacities for a timely and adequate reaction against malicious cyber activities. These instruments mainly address the content regulation, including data privacy, data protection, protection of intellectual property rights, economic transactions, illegal content and conduct.[24] National policies, laws and procedures also establish specific measures which can be proactive, compelling entities to reach a certain maturity level with regard to cybersecurity, rather than allowing market forces to dictate this alone.[25] Legislative measures can also be reactive; for instance, the enactment of laws that criminalise cyberattacks and allow authorities to prosecute perpetrators.[26] Reactive measures of this kind, such as hefty fines and imprisonment, would also act as a deterrent to potential future attackers via the threat of serious criminal repercussions, such as heavy fines and imprisonment.

A further key function of public regulation is to guarantee privacy and data protection. These have indeed a strong connection with cybersecurity, and an organisation's cybersecurity activities can create risks to civil liberties by using, collecting, maintaining or disclosing personal information.[27] This, for instance, can result in the over-collection or over-retention of personal information; in the disclosure or use of personal information unrelated to cybersecurity activities; and in the denial of service or other similar potentially adverse impacts that can indirectly result in the inhibition of freedom of expression or association.[28] Public regulations have, therefore, the responsibility to achieve a balance between these potentially conflicting priorities, and governments must establish appropriate agencies and entities to ensure appropriate compliance.[29]

Below, a short, non-exhaustive overview of some of the existing national laws and regulations related to cybersecurity will be given in alphabetical order of the respective States.

24. Stephan Hobe and Rada Popova, 'Law in Cyberspace?', 67(2) *German Journal for Air and Space Law* 254-278 (2018), at 268.
25. *See*, for instance, French Military Programming Act of 18 December 2013 (Arts L, 1332-6-1-L, 1332-6-6 of the French Defence Code).
26. *See*, for instance, Computer Fraud and Abuse Act, 18 U.S.C. § 1030 1986. It prohibits unauthorised access or damage of 'protected computers' as defined in 18 U.S.C. § 1030(e)(2).
27. ENISA, *NCSS Good Practice Guide: Designing and Implementing National Cyber Security Strategies* (ENISA, 2016), at 36.
28. *Ibid*. For a focus on the EU legal framework in this regard *see* Chapter 4, section §4.02[D].
29. The Finnish Data Protection Ombudsman, for instance, guides and controls the processing of personal data and provides related consultation. exerting power in issues related to the implementation of the right of verification and the correction of personal data. Office of Data Protection Ombudsman, 'Home', https://www.tietosuoja.fi/en/home.

[1] Canada

A State which has introduced a cybersecurity strategy is Canada. Its national strategy aims at encouraging cooperation between the private and public sector for strengthening awareness about cybersecurity and enhancing the protection and elimination of gaps in the security of cyber systems.[30] Cyber incidents of national significance are addressed by the Canadian Centre for Cyber Security.[31]

[2] China

China is considered to be one of the countries with well-developed cyber capabilities which can also be used in hostile activities against other States.[32] A Chinese national cybersecurity strategy was made public in 2016[33] which is governed by a national Cyberspace Administration.[34]

[3] Israel

Israel is one of the most active States in terms of cybersecurity. A National Cyber Directorate has been established on the governmental level with a responsibility "for all aspects of cyber defense in the civilian sphere, from formulating policy and building technological power to operational defense in cyberspace."[35] The Directorate provides services to entities and critical infrastructures for increasing the resilience of the civilian cyberspace[36] and provides publications on current cyber threats and cyberattacks.[37] The Israeli cybersecurity industry is growing, currently with an annual growth factor of 22%.[38]

---

30. Government of Canada, 'National Cyber Security Strategy: Canada's Vision for Security and Prosperity in the Digital Age (2018)', https://www.publicsafety.gc.ca/cnt/rsrcs/pblctns/ntnl-cbr-scrt-strtg/ntnl-cbr-scrt-strtg-en.pdf.
31. Canadian Centre for Cyber Security, 'An Introduction to the Cyber Threat Environment', https://www.cyber.gc.ca/en/.
32. Marc Pomerlau, 'Breaking Down China's Electronic Warfare Tactics', 22 March 2017, https://www.c4isrnet.com/c2-comms/2017/03/22/breaking-down-chinas-electronic-warfare-tactics/.
33. Office of the Central Cyberspace Affairs, 'China Publishes First National Cybersecurity Strategy', 2016, http://www.usito.org/news/china-publishes-first-national-cybersecurity-strategy.
34. Mikk Raud, 'China and Cyber: Attitudes, Strategies, Organisation', NATO Cooperative Cyber Defence Centre of Excellence, 2016, https://www.ccdcoe.org/uploads/2018/10/CS_organisation_CHINA_092016_FINAL.pdf.
35. Israel National Cyber Directorate 'About the Directorate', https://www.gov.il/en/departments/israel_national_cyber_directorate.
36. *Ibid.*
37. *See,* for a register with a publicly available search engine, Israel National Cyber Directorate, 'Publications', https://www.gov.il/en/departments/publications/?OfficeId=4bcc13f5-fed6-4b8c-b8ee-7bf4a6bc81c8&skip=0&limit=10.
38. Yoav Leitersdorf and Ofer Schreiber, 'A Look Back at the Israeli Cyber Security Industry in 2018', 6 January 2019, https://www.techcrunch.com/2019/01/06/a-look-back-at-the-israeli-cyber-security-industry-in/. *See also,* Israel National Cyber Directorate, 'Israeli Cyber Industry Report (2013-2018)', 14 July 2019, https://www.gov.il/en/departments/news/cyber_industry.

In 2018, a draft Cyber Security and National Cyber Directorate Bill was proposed. It sets "the framework for the national regulation of cyber security to further the resilience and response of organisations in the various sectors of Israeli economy to cyberattacks."[39]

[4] Japan

The national cybersecurity strategy of Japan confirms that cybercrimes should be handled as crimes in physical space and makes cyberspace subject to domestic legislation. These efforts are enhanced by the Cyber Security Basic Act of 2014 and the cybersecurity Strategy and through the established National Center of Incident Readiness and Strategy for Cyber Security.

[5] Russian Federation

Also, the Russian Federation, which along with China and the US is considered to dispose of vast cyber capacities, has enacted a national strategy originally incorporated in the 2000 Information Security Doctrine of the Russian Federation which was updated in 2016.[40]

[6] Singapore

Another State that has adopted a law on cybersecurity is Singapore.[41] The 2018 Cybersecurity Act sets the legal basis for requiring or authorising "the taking of measures to prevent, manage and respond to cybersecurity threats and incidents, to regulate owners of critical information infrastructure, to regulate cybersecurity service providers, and for matters related thereto" and for designating computers or computer systems as critical information infrastructure,[42] under the criteria listed in the Act.[43] It also regulates the powers for the investigation and prevention of cybersecurity incidents.[44]

39. Amir Cahane and The Federmann Cyber Security Center, 'The New Israeli Cyber Draft Bill: A Preliminary Overview', https://www.csrcl.huji.ac.il/news/new-israeli-cyber-law-draft-bill.
40. The Ministry of Foreign Affairs of the Russian Federation, 'Doctrine of Information Security of the Russian Federation, approved by Decree of the President of the Russian Federation No. 646 of December 5, 2016', 5 December 2016, http://www.mid.ru/en/foreign_policy/official_documents/-/asset_publisher/CptICkB6BZ29/content/id/2563163.
41. Cybersecurity Act 2018 (No. 9 of 2018), passed by Parliament on 5 February 2018 and assented to by the President on 2 March 2018. Full text available at, https://www.sso.agc.gov.sg/Acts-Supp/9-2018/.
42. *Ibid.*, at Part 3.
43. *Ibid.*, Art. 7.
44. *Ibid.*, at Part 4.

[7] The US

In the US, laws criminalising the unauthorised access and transmission of malware into computers, computer espionage, committing fraud with a computer at accessing, among others, private information without authorisation, have been introduced already in the 1980s.

In 2002, a special division in the FBI was established to investigate cybercrimes, and a Cybersecurity National Action Plan was established under President Obama in 2016.

Again in 2016, The New York Department of Financial Services made a proposal for a Cybersecurity Regulation to protect consumers and financial institutions from cyberattacks which requires that financial services companies put risk assessments and processes in place for employees to use and follow and that firms report on the attempted data breach.

Specifically, cyber defence has been declared the highest priority for the US military. For NASA missions and operations, a 'Vulnerability Assessment Program', as well as an 'Independent Verification and Validation Program Cybersecurity' have been set up to ascertain the cybersecurity of the critical network of systems and infrastructure components.

[B] Challenges for National Regulatory Frameworks

At this current stage, while recognising critical infrastructures as the main target of malicious cyber activities, national cybersecurity regulatory and policy frameworks do not specifically address the fields of aviation and outer space. Nevertheless, States play a significant role in establishing regulatory frameworks to ensure better cybersecurity that are generally applicable to these sectors. They are also responsible for private persons and their exposure to cyber threats. While every user should be aware that Internet activity also means personal responsibility regarding the sharing and uploading of data, the average person cannot be considered prepared for sophisticated malicious cyber activities. This is even more so since personal computers are an easy target. According to FBI officials, it takes thirty minutes for an unprotected computer on the Internet to be compromised while according to studies, 80 % of home computers lack "at least one of the three critical protections: updated anti-virus software, spyware protection, or a working firewall."[45] Therefore, it is part of the role of States as sovereigns to protect the interests of their nationals and enhance domestic mechanisms and develop defensive strategies.

45. Scott J. Schackelford, *Managing Cyber Attacks in International Law, Business, and Relations: In Search of Cyber Peace* (Cambridge University Press, 2014), at 13.

Obviously, the traditional basis for sovereignty based on territory[46] would fail to provide sufficient control possibilities to States over cyber activities.[47] Moreover, the anonymity of cyber activities[48] will remain an obstacle for any attribution. While existing regulatory and governance efforts are still not comprehensive and detailed as needed to effectively counteract malicious cyber activities, it can be expected that national efforts will be increasingly concentrated to develop them and may become the basis for a future more encompassing cyber regulation.

The legislative process, however, is inherently slower than the technical development, and it is hardly able to keep pace with the evolution of security threats, particularly in the IT field.

[C] Industry Standards

In addition to binding legal requirements, a number of more flexible guidelines and sets of standards has been published by national administrations and international standardisation bodies to help private and public entities to set up an effective cybersecurity strategy. These documents, which are not binding and include potential means of compliance with detailed industry best practices, are normally updated on a regular basis and provide for additional measures to be implemented on a voluntary basis. In this way, additionally, a common language framework is established across sectors and can be applied by all entities independently of their sector of activity, size or nationality.[49]

The most popular standards include:

- The ISO/IEC 27000 standard family:[50] The International Standard Organization has created the ISO 27000 series of standards which covers all types of organisations and all kinds of industries and markets. ISO/IEC 27001 specifies the requirements for an enterprise Information Security Management System (ISMS), while ISO/IEC 27002 provides guidelines for the ISMS implementation. Enterprises can obtain a certificate of compliance with ISO/IEC 27001 by a number of accredited Registrars worldwide.

46. *See*, on the application of territoriality in non-territorial cyberspace, Uta Kohl, 'Jurisdiction in Cyberspace', *in* Nicholas Tsagourias (ed.), 'The Legal Status of Cyberspace', *Research Handbook on International Law and Cyberspace* (Edward Elgar Publishing, 2015), at 37 et seq.
47. Rada Popova, 'Cyber Law and Outer Space (Activities): Legal and Regulatory Challenges', *in Proceedings of the 61st Colloquium of the International Institute of Space Law* (Eleven, 2019), at 669. *See*, Stephan Hobe and Rada Popova, 'Law in Cyberspace?', 67(2) *German Journal for Air and Space Law* 254-278 (2018), at 276.
48. Kerschischnig, *supra* no. 3, at 9.
49. Framework for Improving Critical Infrastructure Cybersecurity, Version 1.1, NIST, April 2018, https://www.nist.gov/publications/framework-improving-critical-infrastructure-cybersecurity-version-11, at v.
50. International Organization for Standardization/International Electrotechnical Commission – Information Security Management Systems, ISO/IEC 27000:2018, 2018. ISO, 'ISO/IEC 27001 Information Security Management', https://www.iso.org/isoiec-27001-information-security.html.

- The NIST Cybersecurity Framework:[51] The NIST elaborated this framework to provide guidance in identifying and developing cybersecurity risk frameworks for voluntary use by critical infrastructure owners and operators. It was created in response to Executive Order 13636 which requested a "prioritized, flexible, repeatable, performance-based, and cost-effective approach" for enterprise cybersecurity, and focuses on using business drivers to guide cybersecurity activities and considering cybersecurity risks as part of the organisation's risk management processes.
- The ENISA guidelines.[52] In 2012 ENISA published National Cyber Security Strategy Good Practice Guide. It does not target enterprises directly, but rather, it is a document aimed at supporting the EU Member States in the development and updating of their national cybersecurity strategies. Its audience, thus, is rather constituted by public officials and policymakers.[53]

An effective cybersecurity strategy aims at identifying, assessing and managing cybersecurity risks in an efficient way. In order to do so, the above-mentioned guidelines refrain from establishing a single standard or procedure and instead help organisations to establish a clear approach to cyber resilience that can be adapted on the basis of their particular business needs. Such needs are not the same and vary according to the sector, the nature of the entity and its drivers, and take into account its risk tolerance margins and available human, technical and financial resources.[54]

[D] Private Self-Regulation

In addition to such institutional guidelines, further efforts undertaken by private organisations have resulted in private self-regulation of cyberspace.[55] Examples for non-governmental entities that have provided relevant private regulatory models for the technical cyber infrastructure include Internet Corporation for Assigned Names and Numbers (ICANN), Internet Assigned Numbers Authority (IANA), the Internet Engineering Task Force (IETF) and the World Wide Web Consortium (W3C). ICANN is a private, non-governmental organisation which acts 'on behalf of the global Internet community' and coordinates the Domain Name System (DNS) of the Internet. DNS is vital for identifying and locating computer systems and services as well as devices linked with the IPs that build up the universal language of a major part of cyberspace.

51. Framework for Improving Critical Infrastructure Cybersecurity, *supra* no. 49.
52. ENISA, NCSS Good Practice Guide: Designing and Implementing National Cyber Security Strategies, European Union Agency for Network and Information Security, November 2016. NIST, 'Framework for Improving Critical Infrastructure Cybersecurity Version 1.1', https://www.enisa.europa.eu/publications/ncss-good-practice-guide. *See also*, Chapter 4, section §4.03[A].
53. *See*, for further references, Donaldson, et al., *supra* no. 4, at Appendix B. For aviation-specific EUROCAE standards *see* Chapter 4, section §4.02[C][2].
54. Framework for Improving Critical Infrastructure Cybersecurity, *supra* no. 49, at 7.
55. Hobe and Popova, *supra* no. 47, at 267-268.

IANA is another non-profit private corporation and part of ICANN that is responsible for IP address allocation and the regulation of domain names.[56] IETF is a non-profit organisation which promotes and develops Internet standards through best practices, i.e., standardised specifications. Also, W3C – a standards organisation functioning as a consortium of more than 470 organisations – proposes guidelines and standards for the technologies used in the world wide web with the aim to ensure its long-term global and equal accessibility, functionality and growth.[57]

Once it has identified its cybersecurity requirements, on the basis of the aforementioned guidelines and standards, an entity will then align related measures and activities, integrating cybersecurity in the general risk management processes.[58]

For instance, the NIST framework provides entities with a common taxonomy and mechanism to achieve the following security:

- Describe their current cybersecurity posture;
- Describe their target state for cybersecurity;
- Identify and prioritise opportunities for improvement within the context of a continuous and repeatable process;
- Assess progress toward the target state;
- Communicate among internal and external stakeholders about cybersecurity risk.[59]

It has to be noted that some key core elements are common to cybersecurity strategies of most organisations, and will be briefly described in the next paragraphs.

In order to reach the aforementioned security goals, it is necessary for an entity to establish a comprehensive approach in the form of an 'ISMS', which, as specified in ISO/IEC 27001, is "a systematic approach to managing sensitive company information so that it remains secure. It includes people, processes and IT systems by applying a security risk management process."[60] The adoption of a fragmented and uncoordinated number of information security measures, tailored at resolving specific issues, may leave vulnerabilities in the information security system. This might happen, for instance, with regard to the non-IT related aspects such as physical access to premises, non-IT personnel training, or organisational features. By defining and implementing an ISMS, entities ensure to have in place a coordinated set of policies and procedures which expand beyond software-related measures and grant a more comprehensive defence strategy.

56. Internet Engineering Task Force, 'The Internet Standards Process – Revision 3', Network Working Group, October 1996, https://www.tools.ietf.org/html/rfc2026.
57. World Wide Consortium, 'W3C Mission', https://www.w3.org/Consortium/mission.
58. Framework for Improving Critical Infrastructure Cybersecurity, *supra* no. 49, at v.
59. *Ibid.*, at 2.
60. ISO, 'ISO/IEC 27001 Information Security Management', https://www.iso.org/isoiec-27001-information-security.html.

[E] Information Sharing and Reporting

The reporting of cybersecurity incidents is of fundamental importance to improve the cybersecurity capabilities of an entity. It allows an entity to identify potential vulnerabilities, as well as to adjust and tailor the security measures to the changing threat landscape.[61] the goals of reporting are, in particular, the following:

- To gain knowledge on the overall threat environment.
- To allow for the assessment of the impact of incidents (e.g., security breaches, network failures, service interruptions).
- To provide knowledge on existing and new vulnerabilities and types of attacks.
- To update security measures accordingly.[62]

Information reporting can be mandatory or voluntary, often depending on the gravity of the incident. In this sense, it is necessary to establish appropriate reporting mechanisms and structures, as well as to create the appropriate culture within the entity to foster the practice of identifying and sharing cybersecurity breaches by the personnel.[63]

It is also necessary to establish information-sharing mechanisms among the different stakeholders, and in particular to bridge the distance between the private and public sector. While the former could share their inputs with public authorities on existing threats, vulnerabilities and risk mitigation techniques, the latter could share on a 'need-to-know basis' information gathered by intelligence and cybercrime units. This would allow for a better understanding of the continuously changing threat landscape and for creating virtuous cyber defence synergies between public and private stakeholders.[64]

[F] Risk Assessment

Another paramount element of a sound cybersecurity strategy is the activity of risk assessment, which consists in identifying and understanding the cybersecurity risk to organisational operations (including mission, functions, image, or reputation), assets, and individuals.[65] In order to do so, an entity must first have a clear understanding of its organisational objectives and then take into account the cost and benefits of the measures taken in order to reduce risks to acceptable levels. In this way, it is possible to adopt a more rational and effective cybersecurity approach, as well as to ensure adequate effectiveness of the related investments. Such an assessment has a dynamic nature, given the necessity to continuously revise and update the risk measurement

61. ENISA, *supra* no. 52, at, at 28.
62. *Ibid.*, at 28.
63. Meeuwisse, *supra* no. 3, at 133.
64. ENISA, *supra* no. 52, at 20.
65. Framework for Improving Critical Infrastructure Cybersecurity, *supra* no. 49, at 26.

metric to the changing threat landscape, and can be accomplished either internally or via a third party.[66]

[G] Training

The human factor is a central vulnerability in any cybersecurity defence system. It can be identified as the cause root or the single main contributing factor to most successful cybersecurity breaches.[67] In order to mitigate it, any organisation has to devote substantial attention to cybersecurity training. This includes both individuals with specialised cybersecurity responsibilities and the general staff.[68]

The first category can include system administrators, application developers and incident responders. In this sense, it is essential to require that such personnel hold specific skills in the matter by maintaining current certification from a recognised authority.[69]

The education of the second category, i.e., the employees at any level without specific cybersecurity responsibilities, is equally important and aims at raising the general level of cybersecurity awareness.[70] Although it is unfeasible to maintain the general staff fully updated in detail on all potential threats and attack vectors, as these change at a very fast pace, training should include the entity's policies and processes, the main cybersecurity threats, and how to avoid them.[71] Training is also essential to create the above-mentioned sharing and reporting culture across the whole organisation, as well as to avoid the so-called silo thinking where an employee does not report a detected threat or vulnerability because it does not impact the person's own department, budget or location directly.[72]

[H] Incident Response

The last element of a cybersecurity strategy is the reactive one, and it refers to the measures designed for the containment of the harmful consequences of the cyberattack and for the restoration of the capabilities or services that were impaired. They can include a pre-defined response procedure, such as the resort to a CERT,[73] which is initiated once an attack has been discovered. In such an instance, time is a critical factor to counter the attack before it reaches its goals or spreads into the system.

66. *Ibid.*, at 20.
67. Meeuwisse, *supra* no. 3, at 128.
68. Donaldson, et al., *supra* no. 4, at 334.
69. Meeuwisse, *supra* no. 3, at 132.
70. Framework for Improving Critical Infrastructure Cybersecurity, *supra* no. 49, at 31.
71. Donaldson, et al., *supra* no. 4, at 334.
72. Meeuwisse, *supra* no. 3, at 133.
73. *See*, for instance, Cybersecurity and Infrastructure Security Agency, 'Home', https://www.us-cert.gov/; First, 'Home', https://www.first.org. For further information on CERT-EU *see also*, Chapter 4, section §4.03[B].

[I] A Focus on Contractual Practice

The key importance of cybersecurity has been rapidly understood by the private sector, which, in addition to the implementation of security measures in obedience to State regulations, has developed its own contractual customs. Industry contractual practices tackle cybersecurity with the aim to ensure the due management of the risks between different stakeholders in their commercial relations.

There are three main cybersecurity-related aspects that are usually dealt with in contracts: the implementation of cybersecurity measures, the limitation of liability, and the auditing.[74]

The implementation of cybersecurity measures is a key feature in IT-related contracts, often qualifying as an essential obligation. The parties – the provider in particular – commit to put in place a certain number of security measures and to deliver a product or service that meets the state-of-the-art cybersecurity standards at the date of the signature of the agreement. Such clause may qualify either as an 'obligation of result', where the provider will be presumed liable unless it can show that the failure was due to an occurrence of force majeure or a wrongful act on the part of the operator or as a 'best effort obligation', depending on the level of provider's commitment that the parties agree upon. These provisions may bind the provider also with regard to its staff and any subcontractors and may include the duty to immediately inform the client of any actual or potential breach.[75]

In the event of a security breach, loss of data and/or non-compliance with cybersecurity provisions, clauses on the limitation of liability of the provider may be included. The cost for the recovery of lost data may be pre-qualified as direct damage in order to include it in the compensation duties of the provider.[76]

Furthermore, the customer may retain the right to carry audits on the provider, also specifying the rules and penalties applicable to the audit procedure with the aim to verify that the service provider meets all the requirements to comply with the obligations under the contract. The audits may be carried out by the customer itself, using its own internal audit team, or, more likely, by an external independent audit firm. Sometimes, the contract may give the customer the ability to require the provider to perform audits on its subcontractors and to provide it – the customer – with the resulting audit reports.[77]

It is evident that the way in which the clauses are drafted would shift the risk either on the side of the customer or on the side of the provider. The balance of all such elements depends on various factors, such as the nature and object of the contract, the relative bargaining power of the parties, the short- or long-term nature of the parties' commercial relations, and the regulatory requirements flowing down form applicable laws.

---

74. Francesco Amicucci (Thales Alenia Space Italia SpA), *Contractual Guidelines and Other Recommendations to Maximise the Legal Security of the Space Activities*, Presentation at EUspace Summer School, Genova, 2018, at 17-20.
75. *Ibid.*, at 22 and 25-27.
76. *Ibid.*, at 23 and 27-28.
77. *Ibid.*, at 24 and 29-31.

§9.07 FINAL CONCLUSIONS

Cyber threats and cyberattacks are evolving fast and will continue to increasingly menace the operations of businesses and services. Sectors such as aviation, telecommunications and space are no exception in this respect. On the contrary, their heavy reliance on digital and cyber systems as well as their integrated nature make them particularly vulnerable and exposed. As seen throughout the book, a cyberattack against one or more stakeholders from the aviation or space segments can have repercussions on numerous other industries or sectors, leading to substantial economic loss and, not least, to the interruption of critical services. Key functions of the global society, such as international civil aviation and satellite services might be disturbed or interrupted with dramatic consequences for operators and end-users. Facing this growing concern, it is of paramount importance that all relevant stakeholders make cybersecurity one of their top priorities, comply with applicable regulations, and set up appropriate cybersecurity measures. Additionally, of equal importance is the sharing of information among all involved entities, both private companies and public actors, in order to have a constantly updated threat landscape and common best cybersecurity practices.

Index

AEROSPACE LAW AND POLICY SERIES

1. Erwin von den Steinen, *National Interest and International Aviation* (ISBN 90-411-2455-1).
2. Ludwig Weber, *International Civil Aviation Organisation: An Introduction* (ISBN 978-90-411-2622-1).
3. Niels van Antwerpen, *Cross-Border Provision of Air Navigation Services with Specific Reference to Europe: Safeguarding Transparent Lines of Responsibility and Liability* (ISBN 978-90-411-2688-7).
4. Brian F. Havel, *Beyond Open Skies: A New Regime for International Aviation* (ISBN 978-90-411-2389-3).
5. Jiefang Huang, *Aviation Safety through the Rule of Law: ICAO's Mechanisms and Practices* (ISBN 978-90-411-3115-7).
6. Marian Hoeks, *Multimodal Transport Law: The Law Applicable to the Multimodal Contract for the Carriage of Goods* (ISBN 978-90-411-3246-8).
7. George N. Tompkins, Jr., *Liability Rules Applicable to International Air Transportation as Developed by the Courts in the United States: From Warsaw 1929 to Montreal 1999* (ISBN 978-90-411-2646-7).
8. Daniel Calleja Crespo and Pablo Mendes de Leon (eds), *Achieving the Single European Sky: Goals and Challenges* (ISBN 978-90-411-3730-2).
9. Donal Patrick Hanley, *Aircraft Operating Leasing: A Legal and Practical Analysis in the Context of Public and Private International Air Law*, Second Edition, (ISBN 978-90-411-6050-8).
10. Mikołaj Ratajczyk, *Regional Aviation Safety Organisations: Enhancing Air Transport Safety through Regional Cooperation* (ISBN 978-90-411-5861-1).
11. Benjamyn I. Scott (ed.), *The Law of Unmanned Aircraft Systems: An Introduction to the Current and Future Regulation under National, Regional and International Law* (ISBN 978-90-411-6126-0).
12. Stamatis Varsamos, *Airport Competition Regulation in Europe* (ISBN 978-90-411-6831-3).
13. Katarzyna Malinowska, *Space Insurance: International Legal Aspects* (ISBN 978-90-411-6784-2).
14. John Milligan, *European Union Competition Law in the Airline Industry* (ISBN 978-90-411-6618-0).

15. Dejian Kong, *Civil Liability for Damage Caused by Global Navigation Satellite System* (ISBN 978-94-035-1171-9).
16. Pablo Mendes de Leon and Niall Buissing (eds), *Behind and Beyond the Chicago Convention: The Evolution of Aerial Sovereignty* (ISBN 978-94-035-1131-3).
17. Neta Palkovitz, *Regulating a Revolution: Small Satellites and the Law of Outer Space* (ISBN 978-94-035-1762-9).
18. Federico Bergamasco, Roberto Cassar, Rada Popova & Benjamyn I. Scott, *Cybersecurity: Key Legal Considerations for the Aviation and Space Sectors* (ISBN 978-94-035-0110-9).

www.ingramcontent.com/pod-product-compliance
Lightning Source LLC
Chambersburg PA
CBHW071242230926
51849CB00001B/199
9789403501109